Politics and Literature
in the Reigns
of Henry VII and Henry VIII

For Kirsten, Bridget, and Jeremy

Politics and Literature
in the Reigns
of Henry VII and Henry VIII

Alistair Fox

Basil Blackwell

Copyright © Alistair Fox 1989

First Published in 1989

Basil Blackwell Ltd
108 Cowley Road, Oxford, OX4 1JF, UK

Basil Blackwell Inc.
432 Park Avenue South, Suite 1503
New York, NY 10016, USA

British Library Cataloguing in Publication Data
Fox, Alistair
Politics and literature in the reigns of Henry VII and Henry VIII.
1. English literature, 1400–1625 – critical studies
I. Title
820.9'002

ISBN 0–631–13566–9
Library of Congress Cataloging in Publication Data
Fox, Alistair.
Politics and literature in the reigns of Henry VII and Henry VIII Alistair Fox.
p. cm.

Bibliography: p.
Includes index.
ISBN 0–631–13566–9
1. English literature – Early modern. 1500–1700 – History and criticism. 2. English literature – Middle English, 1100–1500– History and criticism. 3. Henry VIII, King of England, 1491–1547 – Art patronage. 4. Henry VII, King of England, 1457–1509 – Art patronage. 5. Great Britain – Politics and government – 1485–1603. 6. Politics and literature – Great Britain – History. 7. Literature and state – Great Britain – History. 8. Authors and patrons – Great Britain – History. I. Title.
PR418.P65F6 1989
820'.9'358 – dc19   88–31897
                                                                    CIP

Printed and bound in Great Britain at
The Camelot Press Ltd, Southampton

Contents

Preface

In the course of writing this book I have incurred many debts of gratitude. It was written during a very happy year spent by the author as a Visiting Fellow at All Souls College, Oxford, and my chief thanks, therefore, go equally to the Fellows of All Souls and to the University of Otago for making this year possible. At All Souls I found generally not only the intellectual stimulation and resources of which all scholars dream, but also an abundance of friendly support and professional advice offered by its individual Fellows. While it is invidious to single out names, I must thank, in particular, Mr John Simmons, Professor Rodney Needham, Dr Alan Tyson, and Professor Karl Leyser for freely making available their expertise (although they are in no way responsible for any errors or views that may be deemed to be foolish in this book). Many others offered the kind of friendship and encouragement that made the task of writing a pleasure, rather than a burden. I am especially indebted to Dr Mark Franklin for making available to me his computerized Index Builder.

The University of Otago has been, as always, equally supportive. I should like to acknowledge my debt to the University for the research and travel grants I have received over the past few years, and for granting me the privilege of sabbatical leave. I am indebted, too, to my colleagues in the English Department whose willingness to shoulder my teaching burden made my leave possible.

Many others both at home and abroad have assisted me in ways too various to enumerate fully, but I should like to thank, in particular, the following scholars who allowed me to read their books either in typescript or proof-copy: Dr John Guy for his *Tudor England*, Dr Greg Walker for his *John Skelton and the Politics of the 1520s*, and Dr Thomas Mayer for his *Thomas Starkey and the Commonweal*. My thanks go also to Professor Sir Geoffrey Elton, Professor Douglas Gray, Dr John Guy, and Dr Janet Wilson for reading the final draft of the present book and for offering helpful advice, to Professor Emrys Jones for the gift of a copy of his edition of the poems of the Earl of Surrey, which has long been out of print, and to Mrs. Mary Sullivan for assisting me to check the proofs. These scholars are not responsible, however, for any oversights, errors, or misjudgements that may remain in my text.

Like all other authors, I am indebted to the staff of the various libraries I have used: Miss Isobel Andrews of the Central Library at the University of Otago for assiduously procuring research materials on my behalf; Miss Norma Aubertin-Potter and Miss Alyx Bennett of the Codrington Library, All Souls College, for scaling the terrifying heights of the Gallery on occasions, and for their expertise in tracking my quarries through the labyrinthine Bookstack; and the respective staffs of the Bodleian and English Faculty Libraries in Oxford.

Finally, I should like to express deep gratitude to my wife, Ana Fox, who assisted me at every stage, both professionally and personally, and to my children – to whom this book is affectionately dedicated – for their forebearance and support.

Alistair Fox
Dunedin

Acknowledgements

The Author wishes to acknowledge permission granted by the editor of *English Literary Renaissance* to reproduce material in Chapter 4 that first appeared in an article titled 'Stephen Hawes and the Political Allegory of *The Comfort of Lovers*', *English Literary Renaissance*, 17:1 (1987), pp. 3–21.

Introduction

For nearly four hundred years early Tudor literature has had a very poor reputation. It started to acquire a bad press as early as the sixteenth century itself, when poets and theorists in the later half of Elizabeth's reign began to take a disparaging view of it. Having been taught the desirability of order, coherence, and copiousness in writing by several generations of humanist educators, and having discovered the secrets of how to reproduce in English the effects of the mellifluous Italianate manner, the Elizabethans looked back on their predecessors and decided that they had been 'barbarous'. Puttenham, for example, regarded Wyatt and Surrey as mere 'nouices newly crept out of the schools of *Dante Arioste* and *Petrarch*', and refused to believe that Skelton had any claim to the title of 'Poet *Laureat*' at all.[1]

In the twentieth century the adverse judgements of the early commentators have been reiterated even more harshly by the few critics who have bothered to encompass early Tudor writing in historical accounts of sixteenth century literature. Berdan dutifully surveyed the major poets in his 1920 volume, but warned against trying to find aesthetic beauties where none existed.[2] The most damaging condemnation of writing from the earlier sixteenth century was voiced by C. S. Lewis in his volume for *The Oxford History of English Literature*. Classifying the literature written up to Edward VI's reign as 'Late Medieval', he judged it to be 'dull, feeble, and incompetent – even worse, in fact, than that of the 'Drab Age' which followed it, in which the metrical disorder of previous poetry was replaced by 'a lifeless and laboured regularity' in verse, accompanied by a prose that was flat and monotonous. It was only in the 1580s and 1590s, so Lewis claims, that this dismal state of affairs was superseded and redeemed by a 'Golden Age', in which 'good is as visible as green', and in which fantasy, conceit, paradox,

---

[1] George Puttenham, *The Arte of English Poesie*, ed. Edward Arber, English Reprints (London, 1869), p. 74.

[2] John M. Berdan, *Early Tudor Poetry, 1485–1547* (New York, 1920), p. viii. Berdan concluded that 'the interest is not in the literature of the age so much as in the succeeding literature of the time of Elizabeth, which it conditioned' (p. vii).

colour, incantation return'.[3] Lewis's disparaging assessment has been reproduced without demur or essential qualification by the latest literary historian of the sixteenth century.[4]

Developments in literary theory during the past two decades have rendered suspect the foundations of this conventional view. 'Marxist' and feminist critics have effortlessly demonstrated that the 'canon' of works approved and taught in the academies has been determined by cultural taste as much as objective judgement.[5] That taste was first formulated by the very people who found early Tudor literature unsatisfactory. They looked back at it, found that, for the most part, it did not embody the intellectual and aesthetic values they had come to espouse, and understandably rejected it. Since the Second World War, however, a general revolution of consciousness and sensibility has taken place that makes early Tudor literature seem much closer to contemporary interests. Whereas the culture of the previous four hundred years was 'homocentric', in that it placed man at the centre of the universe and invested him with an essential nature, 'logocentric', in that it assumed the existence of transcendent meaning, 'idealist', in that it supposed the existence of timeless universals, and 'providentialist', in that it supposed that there was an underlying purpose in the nature of things, late twentieth century culture appears to be swinging towards the view that all meaning, and hence all values, are relative and historically determined.[6]

Early Tudor literature, when viewed in the light of some of the newer critical assumptions, starts to look very different from the way it has traditionally been depicted. The period constituting the reigns of the first two Tudors was comparable to the late twentieth century in that it, too, witnessed a major shift of consciousness into a new cultural mentality, the birth of which involved considerable pains. Almost all the literature written between 1485 and 1550 was produced in response to extremely disturbed and disturbing circumstances, in a world that was undergoing a major historical transformation. Literature played a vital role in the process by which that revolution was brought about, both in the form of propaganda and polemic designed to influence the nature of change, and also in imaginative fiction that served to represent symbolically, and thus helped to clarify, the experience of those who had to live through these times. Whereas

[3] C. S. Lewis, *English Literature in the Sixteenth Century Excluding Drama* (Oxford, 1954), pp. 1–2; cf. pp. 64–5.

[4] See Gary Waller, *English Poetry of the Sixteenth Century* (London, 1986), esp. pp. x, 27–8. Lewis's account of the century has, nevertheless, been substantially modified by John N. King, *English Reformation Literature: The Tudor Origins of the Protestant Tradition* (Princeton, 1982), who draws attention to a large body of mid-Tudor literature virtually ignored by Lewis.

[5] See, for example, Jonathan Dollimore, *Radical Tragedy: Ideology and Power in the Drama of Shakespeare and His Contemporaries* (Chicago, 1984).

[6] See Jean E. Howard, 'The New Historicism in Renaissance Studies', *English Literary Renaissance*, 16 (1986), pp. 13–43.

the older critics assessed early Tudor literature almost exclusively in terms of its aesthetic quality according to their own criteria, it now seems more profitable to assess it in terms of its purpose and function. Viewed in these terms, apart from seeming much more accomplished than the older critics allowed, such literature also becomes a major source of untapped historical evidence. In order to make use of it, however, one must appreciate the complex relationship existing between the works themselves and the historical circumstances to which they are a response.[7]

One striking phenomenon about early Tudor literature is that it was almost invariably concerned with politics, either directly or indirectly, and that this political bearing had a major impact on the nature of its literary forms.[8] Nearly all the writers of this period were courtiers and servants of the crown (or desired to be so), or else were directly affected by decisions taken at the court. This meant, of necessity, that much literary expression had to be indirect. Social codes and political discretion determined that many of the things most writers desired to say could not be said openly, and as a result early Tudor literature is, above all, dramatized and indirect.

The weakness of judgements that find this literature 'feeble' or inadequate springs from lack of awareness of the function it was designed to serve for those who wrote it. Early Tudor writers were moved to create fictive literary representations most frequently when they suffered setbacks, frustrations, or doubts that a desire for self-preservation or a sense of propriety prevented them from expressing in any other way. Imaginative fiction provided a form of displaced expression that enabled individuals and groups to relieve their minds without suffering punitive or humiliating consequences. It is not coincidental that this is the period that saw the rise of secular drama, or that it witnessed the development of the dramatized dialogue and the art of creative translation, in which the work being translated became a displaced and objectified statement of the translator's personal attitudes or predicament. Even in their correspondence, English men and women chose to represent their perceptions in the form of dramatized scene and dialogue. A cursory glance through any of the political correspondence of the time will show how ingrained this habit was as an indirect means of communi-

---

[7] For some invaluable theoretical speculations on this issue, see Lauro Martines, *Society and History in English Renaissance Verse* (Oxford, 1985).

[8] There is very little literature of the period that I have been unable to include under the umbrella of the stated topic of this book. I regret not being able to include Skelton's *Phyllyp Sparowe*, his lyrics, and his *Elynour Rummynge*, More's early verses in English, and the various collections of *facetiae*, but almost all other literature that seems to me of worth has fallen under its purview – allowing for the author's inevitable subjectivity.

cating things that were dangerous or indiscreet to state otherwise, or else needed to be reported with exactitude.[9]

Another salient feature of this literature is what it reveals about the inner lives of the people who had to live through these times. The most sensitive minds of the period found the early Tudor world problematical. It was full of tensions, ambiguities, and paradoxes, and these are precisely the aspects of life that their literature dramatizes. Just as vividly as the writings of the later Elizabethans and Jacobeans, the literary works of the early to mid 1500s depict the inner drama of those who found themselves in a world where all stable values were threatened with subversion. The strategies early Tudor writers adopted to deal with this experience impart to Henrician literature a distinctive character that makes it most congenial to the late-twentieth century sensibility.

Any viable reassessment of this literature, therefore, must trace the lines of connection between the works and their socio-political context. In order to do this, one must identify the nature of the displacement that tends to take place, and any other strategies the author has adopted to find a means of indirect expression.

There are, of course, problems of method with such an enterprise. If a modern theory is applied deductively, the result tends to be that the literature under discussion is merely turned into an allegory exemplifying the theory. On the other hand, a purely inductive approach can fill the prospect with so many specific details that one cannot see the wood for the trees. My own approach has been to match the circumstances of the author that motivate him to construct his imaginative fiction, with the nature of the fiction itself. This allows one, in most cases, to make reasonable inferences about the desired function of the work for the author.

The method inevitably requires some degree of psychological speculation. Earlier this century, critical practice in some quarters frowned upon the notion that the author had any important connection with the literary artefact, or even existed as a valid focus of study as far as the critic is concerned, but recent demonstrations of the subjectivity and historicity of all literary writing (whether fictive or critical) have shown this attitude to be far too restrictive to be capable of serving as a general critical imperative. Consequently, I have not hesitated to

---

[9] See, for example, the letter written by John Flamank to Henry VII in 1503, informing him of a discussion he overheard on matters relating to the succession (*Letters and Papers Illustrative of the Reigns of Richard III and Henry VII*, 2 vols, ed. James Gairdner (London, 1861), I, no. 26, pp. 231–40); or Margaret Roper's Letter to Alice Alington of August 1534, reporting her conversation with Thomas More in the Tower (*The Correspondence of Sir Thomas More*, ed. Elizabeth Frances Rogers (Princeton, 1947), no. 206, pp. 514–32); or Bonner's letter to Cromwell of 2 September 1538, informing on Wyatt's misdeeds (Kenneth Muir, *Life and Letters of Sir Thomas Wyatt* (Liverpool, 1963), pp. 63–9, items v and vii).

speculate on the psychological motives of authors when the relationship between their circumstances and the literary work they produced seems to warrant it. Cumulatively, the evidence overwhelmingly supports the conclusion that early Tudor writers used fiction, consciously and unconsciously, to serve much the same purposes as dreams serve for the majority of human beings. One can trace in these works many of the strategies of repression, denial, rationalization, and self-projection and introjection that modern psychoanalysis identifies as techniques whereby the mind attempts to control the individual's response to his or her experience. Read in this way, early Tudor literature indicates more clearly than any other sort of evidence the aspects of Tudor policy and political circumstances that caused anxiety. Examination of the ways in which writers tried to allay such anxieties allows one to infer the sources of them.

In the early Tudor period the function of imaginative literature can be classified according to a number of distinct uses to which it was put. Generally, its most important use was to explore the implications of situations that threatened the well-being or peace of mind of the author. John Milton was later to claim that poetry has the power 'to allay the perturbations of the mind, and set the affections in right tune',[10] and in the early Tudor period one can observe authors seeking to achieve this in a number of distinct ways. For example, writers who felt moral doubt concerning the conditions of court service dramatized their feelings in works such as Skelton's *Bowge of Courte* or More's *Utopia*. In each case, these explorations were designed to serve as preliminaries to further action, and one can trace the actions to which they led. Other writers, like Sir Thomas Wyatt, who felt their personal identity threatened by conditions being imposed upon them, used fiction to construct personae that would allow them to present themselves to the world and act in it without loss of face. For this reason, a great deal of early Tudor literature that seems to wear a public guise turns out to be inward looking as well. One needs to distinguish between literature that was designed to work an emotional effect in the writer, and that which was designed to 'move' an effect in others, but the two functions were not mutually exclusive. Works like Stephen Hawes's *The Conforte of Louers* or Wyatt's satires can be deeply personal, while simultaneously serving as generalized moral exempla. This dual function can be seen particularly clearly in Alexander Barclay's *Eclogues*, which seek reassurance for the author by inviting readers to approve the moral superiority of the attitude he has adopted in response to personal disappointment.

The second major use to which fiction was put, was as a means of saying things that otherwise could not be said within the constraints of prevailing social codes.

---

[10] John Milton, *The Reason of Church Government*, in *Complete Prose Works of John Milton*, ed. Donald M. Wolfe and others (New Haven, 1953–82), I, pp. 816–17.

Time and again, writers exploited the displacement for which fictive representation allows, in order to protest against injustices they believed they were suffering. The stereotypical nature of literary conventions made them ideally useful for this purpose. Hawes, in *The Conforte of Louers*, for example, uses the conventional forms of courtly love to warn of treasonous plots on the part of his personal enemies at court, while Wyatt uses the same conventions to express his grievance at losing Anne Boleyn to the king. Other writers used fictive displacement as a means of making approaches to social superiors that decorum would not otherwise allow. When Skelton sought to be readmitted to the favour of an estranged patroness, he did so, in *Speke Parott*, by presenting himself as (among other things) Pamphilus mourning the loss of Galathea, and when Hawes wished to approach Mary Tudor, he did so by projecting himself as Amour seeking the Pucell.

Other writers used fictive representation for a third major purpose: to explore the viability of specific proposals or practices. This can be seen especially in the works of Thomas More. The large degree of imaginative free play required, together with More's constitutional sense of comic irony, meant he could allow doubts and perplexities to surface in the fictional representation that he did not normally permit himself to express, or even admit. He could acknowledge these doubts without committing himself either to negative propositions they implied, or positive propositions they subverted. Hence, his fictive writing is the crucial window into his mind, and no historian can afford to ignore it, if he or she ever wants to understand that enigmatic intelligence. Exactly the same is true for Erasmus. *Utopia, The Praise of Folly*, and *The History of King Richard III* between them, reveal more about the hidden tensions besetting humanism than all the tomes of humanist propaganda taken together.

Finally, imaginative representation was exploited in the period as a means of influencing or expressing public attitudes. The former function is displayed most strikingly in the three satires with which John Skelton tried to sway public opinion against Wolsey in an attempt at personal blackmail, and in the plays written by John Heywood to persuade men to moderation during the crises of the 1520s and 1530s. In other cases, writers used fictive representation to articulate the attitudes of social or political groups. One reason for the spectacular growth of drama during this period was its usefulness as a form of collective representation, capable of uniting individuals with shared interests in a common cause. The effects are shown, for example, in Skelton's *Magnyfycence*, which records the unhappiness of the London merchants at the influence on Henry VIII of the king's 'minions' and the excesses into which they had been leading him, and in the anonymous *Godly Queene Hester*, which expresses the satisfaction of the Howard faction in 1540–1 at having procured the downfall of Thomas Cromwell, and at having arrested the progress of anti-Catholic reform. As the reign of Henry VIII proceeded, this function was taken over by other literary forms, namely propaganda and polemic, but in the early years it was a powerful stimulus to literary invention.

The material to be covered in this study is diverse and disparate. In order to impart coherence to the discussion, I have tried to sustain a sense of chronology by organizing the book around particular political issues that preoccupied writers at each successive stage of the early Tudor period. During the earlier decades of the sixteenth century the need to secure and retain patronage was a major concern, particularly after the accession of Henry VIII in 1509, when the new regime effected sweeping changes of personnel. Once the situation consolidated, the most sensitive minds became preoccupied with humanism as an intellectual force and the implications of its ideas and methods for the reforms that everyone knew had to come in the near future. When, after Cardinal Wolsey had gained ascendancy in Henry VIII's administration, and it had become clear that reform under him would be neither thorough nor adequate, then he in turn became the prime object of authors' concerns. Finally, once the forces seeking radical religious reform broke loose and became enmeshed with Henry VIII's personality and policies during the 1530s and 1540s, the king and the direction of reform dominated the awareness of creative minds. To some extent the organization of the book into four parts focusing on these issues is arbitrary – patronage, for example, remained a concern throughout the early Tudor period – but certain preoccupations dominated at different times, and the four sections try to reproduce the shape that these preoccupations imparted to literary history during the earlier sixteenth century.

The nature of my approach has required some context setting, but as a rule I have kept this to a minimum so that the main emphasis can fall on the literary works themselves. The opening chapter on patronage is an exception. It seemed necessary to describe the conditions governing patronage because many readers are likely to be unfamiliar with them, and there is a paucity of systematic studies of patronage as it affected writers, as distinct from retainers generally. Readers who want more information can consult the work of McConica, Dowling, and Kipling;[11] readers who require less may prefer to skip the first chapter.

It is hoped that this study will draw renewed attention to a literature that has been unconscionably neglected for a very long time. Read without prejudice in its proper context, early Tudor writing offers itself, with its habitual indirection, irony, paradoxicality, and ambiguity, as a distinctively complex form of literature that proves very congenial to the late twentieth century mind. At its best it is capable of providing considerable intellectual and aesthetic satisfaction, and of illuminating the nature of the human condition at large. The present author hopes that, at the very least, readers will find the discussion stimulating, and possibly even true.

---

[11] James Kelsey McConica, *English Humanists and Reformation Politics under Henry VIII and Edward VI* (Oxford, 1965); Maria Dowling, *Humanism in the Age of Henry VIII* (London, 1986); and Gordon Kipling, 'Henry VII and the Origins of Tudor Patronage', in *Patronage in the Renaissance*, ed. Guy Fitch Lytle and Stephen Orgel (Princeton, 1981), pp. 117–64.

PART I

Patronage

1

Literary Patronage: The System and its Obligations

Almost all early Tudor literature, with the exception of popular lyrics, ballads, and prophecies, was concerned with patronage, whether directly or indirectly. It influenced the work of those who were seeking it, just as surely as it conditioned the writings of those who had achieved it. Loss of it, exclusion from it, and mistrust of what it entailed stimulated some of the most inventive literature in the whole period. But before one can understand why, one must grasp the nature of the patronage system itself.

In the reigns of the first two Tudors a network of patronage extended through the whole of society, just as it had done for centuries. The ultimate source of this patronage was the king, who maintained loyalty and rewarded the servants of the crown with titles, property, wardships, church livings, and gifts from the privy purse. Furthermore, this system was repeated at every level down the social scale.[1] Social hierarchy was maintained by it, and the whole government of England depended upon its smooth operation.

The existence of this patronage system had major implications for those who sought to make a career out of their learning or literary talents. Quite a few careers were open to those skilled in the liberal arts: they could aspire to become tutors of the children of royalty or the nobility, legal officers or ambassadors in the crown's administration, or chaplains and secretaries in the royal and noble households. A favoured few could expect to find a place at court as royal musicians, poets, or entertainers. It was absolutely vital, however, to find a patron – either someone who could sponsor the aspiring retainer directly, or else someone in a position to influence others who could. In this respect writing was a critical, almost essential instrument. Through it one could attract the attention of a prospective patron by dedicating or addressing the work to him, and, just as importantly, it was a way of displaying one's credentials. More cynically, it was

[1] See G. R. Elton, *Reform and Reformation: England 1509–1558* (London, 1977), pp. 24–5.

often a quick way of extracting urgently needed cash in the form of a monetary grant given by the patron in appreciation for a literary gift.

The sources of, and routes to, patronage were many and varied. Inevitably, because he sat at the apex of the social pyramid and his bounty was the greatest, the king was the most important patron, as the list of books dedicated to him attests.[2] New Year's Day seems to have become institutionalized as an occasion on which prospective literary candidates for patronage presented themselves. This was especially evident at the accession of Henry VIII, when retainers of the old king desperately hoped to be kept on by his heir, while those who had been out in the cold saw their chance under the new regime. In the former category was Bernard André, who presented to Henry VIII on New Year's Day 1510 a poem called 'Le temps de l'année moralizé sur l'aige et vie de l'home', in the dedication to which he begs Henry to retain his service as an historiographer, citing his 24 years of service to Henry VII in that capacity.[3] It seems to have worked, for André received later payments from the privy purse, and presented Henry with yet another New Year's gift in 1522.[4]

John Skelton, a poet who had been absent from the court from about 1503, also tried to re-enter the royal service through this strategy. Skelton had been tutor to Henry VIII while the latter was Duke of York, but for reasons about which one can only speculate, he retired to a parish at Diss in Norfolk soon after the death of Prince Arthur.[5] At the accession of his former pupil in 1509 Skelton, like others, offered Henry a congratulatory poem,[6] but this seems to have had no effect in achieving him renewed patronage. In 1511 he tried again, this time offering Henry a copy of his *Speculum principis* together with two poems in Henry's praise written out in his own hand. At the end of the collection he ironically laments the oblivion into which he has been cast and his exclusion from the king's munificence.[7] Again, there was no response, and so Skelton tried a third time with a New Year's gift of an old French chronicle, the *Chronique de Raims*, on 1 January 1512. This time it worked, for within several months Skelton had been formally recognized by letters patent as Court Poet to Henry VIII.[8] Others to use the trick of the New Year's gift were Stephen Hawes, who

[2] See Franklin B. Williams, *Index of Dedications and Commendatory Verses in English Books before 1641* (London, 1962).

[3] British Library Royal MS 16 E. xi; see also William Nelson, *John Skelton, Laureate* (New York, 1939), p. 241. Hereafter cited as Nelson, *Skelton*.

[4] See also Nelson, *Skelton*, p. 25; and MS Royal 12 A. x.

[5] For a conjecture that Skelton was replaced as tutor by William Hone, see. H. L. R. Edwards, *Skelton: The Life and Times of an Early Tudor Poet* (London, 1949), p. 77. Hereafter cited as Edwards, *Skelton*.

[6] 'A Lawde and Prayse Made for Our Sovereigne Lord the Kyng' (see *John Skelton: The Complete English Poems*, ed. John Scattergood (London and New Haven, 1983), pp. 110–12). Hereafter cited as Skelton, *Poems*, ed. Scattergood.

[7] Edwards, *Skelton*, pp. 129–30.

[8] Ibid., pp. 131–2.

was rewarded on 10 January 1506 with a payment of 10 shillings from Henry VII's privy purse 'for a balett that he gave the Kinges grace',[9] and John Leland, who presented a New Year's gift to Henry VIII in 1545, briefly describing the aims and methods of his search for English antiquities.[10]

Appeals to the king were not limited to New Year, however. An astonishing array of printed books and manuscripts were dedicated or addressed to Henry VIII throughout his reign, at any time of the year, by those seeking patronage. Stephen Hawes, who had been a groom of the Privy Chamber under Henry VII, tried to stave off his inevitable expulsion from the royal household by offering *A Ioyfull Medytacyon to all Englonde of the Coronacyon of our Moost Naturall Souerayne Lorde Kynge Henry the Eyght*,[11] while Thomas More, who could at last hope for long-withheld royal favour, presented to Henry a specially ornamented manuscript copy of five congratulatory Latin poems soon after his accession in June 1509.[12] One of the most assiduous of Henry's dedicators in the middle period of his reign was Sir Thomas Elyot, who seems to have been obsessed with finding a place on the king's Council. In 1531 he dedicated *The Boke Named the Gouernour* to Henry, and this appears to have achieved for him an appointment as ambassador to the Emperor. Elyot's performance in office, however, was unsatisfactory, and he was soon dismissed.[13] Even after this rejection, Elyot persisted in his hope that he would be called to counsel. Between 1538 and 1541 he made a final concerted bid to attract notice and favour by first dedicating two books to the king, *The Dictionary of Syr Thomas Eliot Knyght* (1538), and a new edition of *The Bankette of Sapience* (1539), and then by dedicating *The Castel of Helth* to Thomas Cromwell, the king's chief minister, in 1539. Once Cromwell had fallen in 1540, Elyot still did not give up, but dusted off the 'actes and sentences notable' of Alexander Severus that he had collected earlier, and dedicated it as *The Image of Governance* to the faction of nobles led by the Duke of Norfolk and Stephen Gardiner, the Bishop of Winchester, which had replaced Cromwell.[14]

As the case of Elyot shows, an alternative to addressing the king directly was to approach those close to him, especially his chief ministers and members of the

[9] *The Dictionary of National Biography from the Earliest Times to 1900*, ed. Sir Leslie Stephen and Sir Sidney Lee, 22 vols (London, 1921–2), IX, p. 188ff. Hereafter cited as *DNB*.

[10] Ibid., p. 892ff.

[11] For further comment on Hawes's political difficulties at the accession of Henry VIII, see Chapter 4 below.

[12] See *The Yale Edition of the Complete Works of St Thomas More*, 15 vols (New Haven and London, 1963–), Vol. 3, Part 2: *Latin Poems*, ed. Clarence Miller and others (New Haven, and London, 1984), pp. 96–115. The Yale edition is hereafter cited as *CW Thos. More*.

[13] See Alistair Fox, 'Sir Thomas Elyot and the Humanist Dilemma', in *Reassessing the Henrician Age: Humanism, Politics, and Reform 1500–1550* (Oxford, 1986), pp. 52–73. Hereafter cited as Fox and Guy, *Reassessing the Henrician Age*.

[14] On the putsch in the household that destroyed Cromwell, see David Starkey, *The Reign of Henry VIII: Personalities and Politics* (London, 1985), pp. 129–33.

royal household. These confidants could then either act as intermediaries in procuring the king's favour, or else were in a position to bestow patronage of their own.

One can reconstruct how this strategy worked from remarks made by Elyot in the preface to his *Dictionary* of 1538, which he dedicated to Henry VIII. Fulsomely praising the king as one whose 'moste noble and beneuolent nature' is declared 'in fauouryng them that wyll be well occupied', Elyot thanks him for his interest in the work, which, he declares, had been brought to Henry's attention by Sir Anthony Denny, chief gentleman in the Privy Chamber, William Tyldesley, keeper of the king's library, and, most especially, by Thomas Cromwell, lord privy seal. As if to prevent Henry from missing the point of the dedication, Elyot reminds him that he is 'myn onely mayster, and styrer of the shyppe of all my good fortune'.[15]

Elyot seems to have cultivated the favour of court officials with unusually dogged determination, having a shrewd eye for who might do him most good. In 1522, for instance (if 'Geminus Eleates' is indeed Elyot's pseudonym, as has been plausibly argued),[16] he dedicated his *Hermathena* to Richard Pace, then the king's principal secretary and one of his most trusted advisors. In 1540 he demonstrated the equal care he took to distance himself from those with whom an association could do him harm. Thomas Cromwell had been one of his chief benefactors, and Elyot reciprocated his generosity by professing eternal friendship, and by dedicating *The Castel of Helth* to him in 1539.[17] Nevertheless, when Cromwell fell in 1540 Elyot dropped him as the dedicatee with remarkable speed; literary affections were often more convenient than real.

Cardinal Wolsey, Cromwell's predecessor as chief minister of the crown, performed an equally important role as patron. Through his sponsorship Richard Pace became secretary to the king in 1515, while both Edward Fox and Stephen Gardiner received their first introduction to court politics as Wolsey's own secretaries. Subsequently, they were to rise to positions of great power, and prove themselves indispensable to the king in engineering and justifying the royal supremacy. Wolsey himself had been advanced at court by his own predecessor as king's almoner and lord privy seal, Richard Fox, Bishop of Winchester. Until he secured Fox's sponsorship, his advancement had been slow, which suggests why scholars and writers found it necessary to cultivate those in positions of influence at court.

The examples of Fox and Wolsey illustrate the importance of eminent

---

[15] Thomas Elyot, *The Dictionary of Syr Thomas Eliot Knyght* (London, 1538), sigs A2ᵛ–A3ʳ.

[16] See C. Bouck, 'On the Identity of Papyrius Geminus Eleates', *Transactions of the Cambridge Bibliographical Society*, 2, Part IV (1958), pp. 352–8.

[17] Elyot's profession of friendship is to be found in a letter inscribed on the flyleaf of a presentation copy of his 1538 *Dictionary* (British Library shelf-mark C. 28 m. 2), for which see K. J. Wilson (ed.), 'The Letters of Sir Thomas Elyot', *Studies in Philology*, 73:5 (1976), pp. 33–7.

churchmen generally in the system of patronage. They tended to have close relations with the universities – Fox and Wolsey both founded colleges – as well as filling many of the chief administrative positions in the realm. They were therefore in a good position to act as talent scouts for aspiring young scholars, and to advance them in the royal service. Polydore Vergil records how, in the reign of Henry VII, Adriano Castelli, a papal emissary, was hired as an ambassador because John Morton, Archbishop of Canterbury, had commended him to the king.[18] Similarly, John Fisher, Bishop of Rochester and chaplain and confessor to Lady Margaret Beaufort, the king's mother, was probably responsible for recruiting John Skelton and William Hone from Cambridge to act as tutors to Prince Henry, and also arranged for Erasmus to succeed him as Lady Margaret reader in Greek.[19] It is not surprising, therefore, to find that after the king, churchmen receive the most literary dedications and commendations during the early Tudor period.

Erasmus was an especially persistent suitor, achieving considerable financial rewards in the form of grants and benefices, although not as many as he would have liked and expected to get. In 1506 he dedicated his translation of Lucian's *Toxaris* to Richard Fox,[20] and a clutch of Lucian translations to William Warham, the Archbishop Canterbury, in 1512, the latter as a gesture of thanks for his presentation to the living of Aldington in March of that year.[21] Warham, indeed, was Erasmus' most munificent patron in England, and Erasmus went to considerable efforts to ensure that he remained so. In January 1506 he presented Warham with his translation of Euripides' *Hecuba*, and was quite put out by the smallness of the sum that Warham gave him in return. On their way home from Lambeth Palace, John Colet, who was riding with Erasmus, explained to him that Warham probably thought he was in the habit of dedicating the same work to several patrons; the practice was quite common: Giovanni Gigli, for example, addressed his treatise *De obseruantia quadragesimali* both to John Russell, Bishop of Lincoln and keeper of the privy seal, and also to Richard Fox, the king's secretary.[22] To correct Warham's supposition Erasmus, after he had returned to Paris, also dedicated the *Iphigenia* to him.[23] Later, when Erasmus was concerned as to whether his English pension would continue to be paid, he dedicated his edition of St Jerome to Warham as a means of retaining the

---

[18] 'Atqui Henricus cum hominem sibi a Mortono commendatum uideret, non minimi esse usus, iam tum mirifice diligere', *The Anglica historia of Polydore Vergil, A. D. 1485–1537*, ed. Denys Hay, Camden Series, Vol. 74 (London, 1950), p. 42.

[19] See Edwards, *Skelton*, p. 56.

[20] P. S. and H. M. Allen (eds), *Letters of Richard Fox 1486–1527* (Oxford, 1929), Letter no. 21, p. 33.

[21] *Collected Works of Erasmus*, 78 vols, various editors (Toronto, 1974–), Vol. 2, p. 229, no. 261. This edition will be referred to henceforth as *CW Erasmus*.

[22] See *Letters of Richard Fox*, ed. Allen, no. 1, p. 5.

[23] *CW Erasmus*, 2, no. 188, p. 208.

archbishop's proprietarial interest.[24] Other churchmen to whom Erasmus dedicated works were John Fisher, to whom he planned to dedicate his New Testament but changed his mind, and Wolsey, to whom he dedicated his translation of Plutarch's *De utilitate capienda ex inimicis* in 1514.[25]

The nobility provided a fourth major avenue to patronage. As members of the king's Council, with substantial households of their own, the Dukes of Norfolk and Suffolk were potential patrons, but so too were the lesser nobles, such as William Blount, fourth Baron Mountjoy, who frequently attended court as friends and confidants of the royal family. Mountjoy, who was first a tutor to Prince Henry and later chamberlain to Katherine of Aragon, was Erasmus' main hope in the first decade of the latter's contact with England. He paid off Erasmus' debt to Bernard André, and persuaded Wolsey to offer Erasmus a prebend.[26] But it was the great nobles who were most worth cultivating. Thomas Howard, the second Duke of Norfolk, was especially well-disposed towards poets. He sponsored Alexander Barclay after the latter had practically despaired of gaining patronage, and encouraged him to write the *Introductory to Wryte and to Pronounce Frenche* and his translation of Sallust's *Jugurtha* (1520–1). His son, the third Duke of Norfolk, continued this tradition of offering patronage to poets and scholars, giving both John Leland and Stephen Gardiner their first positions as tutors in his household. Upon Norfolk's recommendation Leland was appointed royal chaplain, keeper of the library, and king's antiquary, while Gardiner was promoted first as Wolsey's secretary and then as secretary to the king.[27] The nobles' patronage was not just important for immediate rewards, but also for the long-term benefits to which it could lead.

Poets and scholars were not the only ones to benefit; the nobles were major sponsors of play and players. The interlude *Youth* appears to have been composed for Henry Percy, the Earl of Northumberland, to be performed at a major feast, either Christmas or Shrovetide, while the auspices of *Hyckescorner* can be located to Southwark, where Charles Brandon, the Duke of Suffolk, kept his residence.[28] Thus the nobles, along with royalty and the higher clergy, had a significant role to play in the patronage system, and each group had its own expectations of those sponsored by it.

Patronage, because of the very way it was procured and bestowed, had a profound influence on early Tudor writing. Patrons were not primarily altruistic

[24] *Contemporaries of Erasmus: A Biographical Register of the Renaissance and Reformation*, ed. P. Bietenholz and others, 3 vols (Toronto, 1985–7), 3, p. 429. Hereafter cited as Bietenholz, *Contemporaries of Erasmus*.

[25] *CW Erasmus*, 3, nos 314, 432; 2, no. 284.

[26] Ibid., 2, no. 254; 3, nos 360, 388.

[27] *DNB*, XI, p. 892ff.; VII, p. 859ff.

[28] See Ian Lancashire (ed.), *Two Tudor Interludes: The Interlude of Youth; Hick Scorner* (Manchester, 1980), pp. 21–9, 33–4.

in their motivation: they expected certain services in return; the conventionality of much early Tudor literature can be explained in terms of the functions writers had to perform.

Needing to consolidate and legitimize his new dynasty, Henry VII mounted a major campaign to amplify the magnificence of his rule by using artists and men of letters.[29] Apart from expanding the royal library and commissioning tapestries and pageants, Henry VII kept two troupes of minstrels at court and two companies of players. He also retained writers such as Bernard André, Stephen Hawes, Pietro Carmeliano, and Polydore Vergil to celebrate the reign in a variety of ways.

The first use of these writers was to place the Tudors firmly in an historical context. Polydore Vergil was set the task of writing a history of Britain that would show how Henry VII was the prophesied and true heir of the ancient British kings.[30] The new history was not to be like the traditional type of annals, which Vergil described as 'varii, confusi, ambigui, sine ordine (quae in primis abhorret Historia)' ('inconsistent, jumbled, untrustworthy, lacking order – which History particularly abhors'), but polished and refined like the works of the classical historians.[31] Bernard André on the other hand, undertook to write a life of Henry VII and record his acts.[32] For both writers, especially André, history was a species of encomium.

The second function of the court poets was to decorate the reign with complimentary verses for significant occasions. André wrote poems celebrating Henry's victory at Bosworth, the coronation of the Queen, the birth of Prince Arthur, the creation of Arthur as Prince of Wales, and many other events.[33] Giovanni Gigli wrote an epithalamium for Henry's marriage to Elizabeth, Carmeliano produced an epic poem on the birth of Prince Arthur, and Skelton composed an *Epigramma ad tanti principis maiestatem* to celebrate Prince Henry's creation as Duke of York in 1494.[34] The court poets were also expected to rush to the defence of the monarch if his honour was impugned. When a visiting French ambassador, Robert Gaguin, directed some sneering aspersions at Henry after visiting England on a fruitless diplomatic mission, he stirred up a furore, as

[29] For this and much of what follows, I am indebted to Gordon Kipling, 'Henry VII and the Origins of Tudor Patronage', in *Patronage in the Renaissance*, pp. 117–64; and the same author's *The Triumph of Honour: Burgundian Origins of the Elizabethan Renaissance* (The Hague, 1977).

[30] See *Anglica historia*, ed. Hay, pp. 4–5.

[31] Letter to James IV in *Polydore Vergil's English History*, ed. Henry Ellis, Camden Society (London, 1846), I, p. xii.

[32] The *Vita Henrici VII* and *Annales Henrici VII* are printed in *Memorials of King Henry the Seventh*, ed. James Gairdner, Rolls Series, (London, 1858). Hereafter cited as Gairdner, *Memorials*.

[33] Printed in Gairdner, *Memorials*, pp. 35–6, 40, 41–2, and 48–9.

[34] Gigli's poem is British Library MS Harleian 336; Carmeliano's British Library MS Additional 33,736; and Skelton's British Library MS Additional 26787.

André tells us. No fewer than Gigli, Carmeliano, Cornelio Vitelli, Skelton, and André himself raced to reply in kind.[35]

At other times the royal poets were expected to assert the political philosophy of the governing hierarchy on occasions when it was affronted. In 1489 Henry Percy fourth Earl of Northumberland was killed when, as sheriff, he tried to restore order among a Yorkshire mob protesting against high taxes. The official viewpoint was quickly asserted in Skelton's *Upon the Dolorus Dethe and Muche Lamentable Chaunce of the Mooste Honorable Erle of Northumberlande* and André's *Nortumbrorum comitis nece*: the rebels were ungrateful churls motivated solely by malice, and their deed a treacherous breach of natural order.[36]

A third task of the royal literary retainers was to produce pedagogic and morally edifying works. At the request of Lady Margaret Beaufort, Skelton translated Guillaume de Deguileville's *Pèlerinage de la vie humaine*,[37] and also devised for Prince Henry a *Speculum principis* so that he could read therein 'all the demenour of princely astate'.[38] The two chivalrous romances of Stephen Hawes, *The Example of Vertu* and *The Passetyme of Pleasure*, also fall into this category; they are designed to present a pattern the prince should emulate, by depicting a hero on a quest to master both chivalry and the liberal arts. Indeed much of the literary endeavour at court was disguised moral homily, often composed to be recited before the king and his household. The list of works by André includes such edifying pieces as 'Rationis et sensualitatis Dyalogus et coram Regijs maiestatibus recitatus', and 'Item super Egloges Virgilii secundum 4or sensus expositio admirabilis!'[39] This prevailing didacticism extended even to the court pageants and disguisings which the poets helped to devise;[40] the job of the royal poets was to instruct, as much as to entertain.

Under Henry VIII the functions of literary retainers remained much the same as before during the first decade of his reign, but there was a radical change of personnel. For some reason, the circle of younger humanist scholars including More, Linacre, Erasmus, Ammonio, and Colet had been distinctly 'out' during Henry VII's reign.[41] Possibly this was because of ideological conflicts with the older scholars: André certainly intrigued to prevent Linacre from succeeding him

[35] Gairdner, *Memorials*, pp. 56–7; Skelton refers to 'The Recule ageinst Gaguyne of the Frenshe nacyoun' as one of his works (now lost), in *A Garlande of Laurell*, (Skelton, *Poems*, ed. Scattergood, p. 346/1187).

[36] Printed respectively in Skelton, *Poems*, ed. Scattergood, pp. 29–35; and Gairdner *Memorials*, pp. 48–9.

[37] *A Garlande of Laurell*, in Skelton, *Poems*, ed. Scattergood, p. 347/1219–22. The translation is now lost.

[38] Ibid., ll. 1226–32; the *Speculum principis* is printed by F. M. Salter in *Speculum*, 9 (1934), pp. 25–37.

[39] See Nelson, *Skelton*, Appendix 1, pp. 239–40.

[40] See Sydney Anglo, *Spectacle, Pageantry and Early Tudor Policy* (Oxford, 1969); and Kipling, 'Henry the Seventh and the Origins of Tudor Patronage', pp. 150–1.

[41] See Nelson, *Skelton*, pp. 31–3.

as Prince Arthur's tutor by turning Henry against Linacre.[42] Thomas More probably fouled his chances, if Roper can be believed, by opposing the king in Parliament in 1504 over a feudal aid required for the marriage of Margaret Tudor to James IV of Scotland.[43] Generally, it would seem that the More-Mountjoy circle were simply out of sympathy with the prevailing cultural tastes of Henry VII's court, which were Franco-Flemish in imitation of the Burgundian court, rather than humanist in the new guise, and were therefore not used.[44] Whatever the reasons, the progressive humanists had to wait until the accession of Henry VIII in 1509, after which there was practically a cultural purge as well as a political one among the king's servants. Linacre was appointed the king's physician; Ammonio supplanted Carmeliano as Latin Secretary in 1513.[45] Stephen Hawes was swept out in a purge of the household,[46] and his place as court poet was eventually filled by Skelton, who may have been dislodged by William Hone as tutor of Prince Henry after 1502 or 1503.[47] Thomas More addressed a flattering set of Latin poems to Henry VIII, but did not enter the royal service until 1517, either because he was not yet wanted or, which seems just as likely, because his legal career in the City of London was, for the time being, more remunerative.[48]

In spite of the change of personnel, the same types of literary works were manufactured to meet the demands of the patronage system. Poets like Skelton, William Lily, and Leland continued to write encomiastic and propagandistic occasional verse, and historians like Vergil and Edward Hall continued to write encomiastic histories. If anything, Henry VIII was less consciously concerned to amplify the magnificence of his court through literature than his father had been, preferring instead the dramatic spectacle of jousting, pageantry, and entertainments, so vividly described by Hall.

With the onset of the Lutheran business in the mid 1520s and the emergence of the king's 'Great Matter' after 1527, the requirements made of writers changed dramatically, a fact that was reflected in the type of person who was retained. Rather than encomiasts, the king needed propagandists and those skilled in polemic. At first Thomas More fulfilled this role with admirable zeal, if questionable taste, with diatribes against Luther and a number of other reformers.

---

[42] See the letter of Erasmus to Brixius of 30 Jan 1531, in *Opus Epistolarum Des. Erasmi Roterodami*, ed. P. S. Allen and others (Oxford, 1906–47), IX, Ep. 2422, ll. 66–73.

[43] William Roper, *The Lyfe of Sir Thomas Moore, Knighte*, ed. Elsie Vaughan Hitchcock, Early English Text Society, Original Series, no. 197, (London, 1935), p. 7.

[44] A suggestion made by Kipling, 'Henry the Seventh and the Origins of Tudor Patronage', p. 134.

[45] See Nelson, *Skelton*, p. 33.

[46] See below, chap. 4.

[47] See Edwards, *Skelton*, pp. 77–8.

[48] After his selection as Undersheriff, More was earning £400 a year (see J. A. Guy, *The Public Career of Thomas More*, (Brighton, 1980), pp. 4–6.)

Skelton, too, tried his hand at the new form of intellectual polemic, with his *Replycacion Agaynste Certayne Yong Scolers Abjured of Late*. But as the divorce surfaced as the foremost of Henry's concerns, the more urgent need was for writers who were prepared, and had the ability, to argue the justice of the king's cause and assert the doctrine of royal supremacy in church and state. In effect, a whole new set of writers had to be sought, and those who looked likely to satisfy the demands of Cromwell's administration, such as Thomas Starkey and Richard Moryson, were retained at court; those, like Elyot, who could not adapt their knowledge or talents to the partisan cause, were not. The most important figures were not writers of imaginative literature at all, but rather men of letters, like Edward Fox and Stephen Gardiner, who could turn history and canon law to propagandistic uses.

It used to be thought that writers in the 1530s were hired to form a kind of reformist 'think-tank', but any similarity between what they wrote and what was done was coincidental.[49] Elyot was not hired because of his ideas in *The Governour*, but because Cromwell believed his eloquence might be useful in presenting Henry's case to the Emperor. Elyot was quickly dropped when this turned out not to be so.[50] Similarly, there is no evidence that Henry ever saw the enlightened ideas for reform in Starkey's *Dialogue*; much more indicative of what he was expected to produce was *The Exhortation to the People Instructynge Theym to Vnitie and Obedience*. Only if a writer were both a partisan of Henry VIII and also an artist was there any scope for creative literary invention, and the conditions of the time seem to have been inimical to that combination. One isolated exception was John Leland who, in addition to defending the king's supreme dignity in church matters in his *Antiphilarchia*, also found time, and felt the incentive, to compose occasional verses on the coronation of Anne Boleyn, the birth of Prince Edward, and Henry's capture of Boulogne in 1544, and to write *Cygnea Cantio*, a Latin poem celebrating Henry's exploits in the song of a swan swimming between Oxford and Greenwich. Leland's work is quite literally the swan-song of poetry for some time.

When one considers the conditions under which patronage was sought and obtained, it becomes clear that it had a major influence on most kinds of writing in the early Tudor period. The expectations of patrons help to explain the extremely conventional nature of much writing. Having to produce so much complimentary verse to order, poets relied upon a repertory of suitable *topoi*, classical allusions, and imagery, and tended to follow rhetorical models.[51]

A typical pattern for a speech of praise, for example, was prescribed by

---

[49] See W. Gordon Zeeveld, *Foundations of Tudor Policy* (Cambridge, Massachusetts, 1948).

[50] See Fox, 'Sir Thomas Elyot and the Humanist Dilemma', in Fox and Guy, *Reassessing the Henrician Age*, pp. 52–73.

[51] See O. B. Hardison, *The Enduring Monument: A Study of the Idea of Praise in Renaissance Literary Theory and Practice* (Westport, Connecticut, 1973).

Aphthonius in his *Progymnasmata*. After contriving a suitable exordium, the writer should deal in turn with his subject's descent, stressing his forebears and parents, his education, and then his praiseworthy deeds and qualities, subdivided into those of the soul (such as fortitude and prudence), those of the body (such as beauty, speed, and strength), and those of fortune (such as political power, riches, and friends). The encomium should end with an epilogue rather like a prayer.[52] Most writers chose to praise their subjects in terms of these time-honoured *topoi*, with the result that individual characteristics became buried under generalized commonplaces. Kings and queens all tend to excel in virtue, to be terrors to their enemies, yet serene in clemency, and to have inherited the wisdom of their fathers and the beauty of their mothers. They have banished fear, harm, danger and grief from the lives of their subjects and replaced them with peace, ease, joy, and laughter, for which the people feel a joy beyond comprehension and remain undyingly loyal.[53] Inevitably, they have restored, or are about to restore, the golden age, or else mark the return of the Platonic *magnus annus*.[54] To emphasize the virtues of their noble patrons, poets wove in classical comparisons to show how far their subject surpassed the classical exemplars who foreshadowed them. Thomas More's gratulatory poem on the coronation of Henry VIII and Queen Katherine is a typical example. For More, Katherine of Aragon is she 'who could vanquish the ancient Sabine women in devotion, and in dignity the holy, half-divine heroines of Greece. She could equal the unselfish love of Alcestis, or, in her unfailing judgements, outdo Tanaquil . . . The well-spoken Cornelia would yield to her in eloquence; she is like Penelope in loyalty to a husband.'[55] Similarly, in his elegy to decorate the tomb of Lady Margaret Beaufort in 1516, Skelton refers to her as a woman

---

[52] I have paraphrased the translation of Aphthonius' Greek given by Clarence Miller in *CW Thos. More*, 3:2: *Latin Poems*, pp. 43–4.

[53] See, for example, Thomas More's poem on the coronation of Henry VIII and Katherine of Aragon, *CW Thos. More*, 3:2, pp. 100–12.

[54] For examples, see More, Epigram no. 21 ('Cuncta Plato cecinit tempus'), *CW Thos. More*, 3:2, pp. 112–14; Skelton, 'A Lawde and Prayse Made for Our Souereigne Lord the Kyng', Public Record Office MS E. 36/228, fos 7–8, where, in his marginal gloss to the sixth stanza, Skelton writes 'Ecce platonis seculum'; and Leland, verses on the coronation of Anne Boleyn, 'Aurea nunc tandem sunt saecula reddita nobis / Illa, sed auspiciis, Anna serena tuis' (Frederick J. Furnivall (ed.), *Ballads from Manuscripts*, 2 vols (London, 1868–72), Vol 1: *Ballads on the condition of England in Henry VIII's and Edward VI's Reigns, on Wolsey, Anne Boleyn, Somerset, and Lady Jane Grey; with Wynkyn de Worde's Treatise of a Galaunt*, p. 394). Hereafter cited as Furnivall, *Ballads from Manuscripts*.

[55] Illa est, quae priscas uincat pietate Sabinas,
   Maiestate sacras uicerit hemitheas.
Illa uel Alcestes castos aequarit amores,
   Vel prompto superet consilio Tanaquil.

. . .

Eloquio facunda cui Cornelia cedat,
   Inque maritali Penelopeia fide. (*CW Thos. More*, 3: 2, no. 19, pp. 110–111, ll. 166–73.)

Cui cedat Tanaquil (Titus hanc super astra reportet),
   Cedat Penelope, carus Ulixis amor:
Huic Abigail, velut Hester, erat pietate secundi:
   En tres jam proceres nobilitate pares![56]

(to whom Tanaquil must yield (she whom Titus extolled above the stars),
to whom Penelope, the dear love of Ulysses must give way, compared with
whom Abigail, like Ester, was second in piety: Lo! up until now three equal
leaders in excellence!)

Similar clichés recur in the verses Leland wrote for the coronation of Anne
Boleyn:

Heroinarum praeclaras dicere laudes
   Vatibus antiquis maxima cura fuit.
Hinc celebris toties cantatae gloria formae
   Lactea praefulget nunc, Galathea, tuae;
Praenitet hinc etiam Cornelia docta, disertae
   Digna uel aeternis nomen habere libris;
Casta pudicitiae specimen Lucretia magnum
   Praebuit, et meriti carmine fama uiret;
Porcia collucet rigidi famosa Catonis,
   Coniugij cultrix rarior illa fuit;
Maxima nimirum sunt haec praeconia, multo
   Maiora, illustris, sunt tamen, Anna, tibi.
Nam quae tam clare fulserunt singula in illis,
   Omnia nunc in te conspicienda nitent.

(Old bards would tell of their famous heroines. Therefore even now your
beauty dazzles us, Galatea; so your wisdom, Cornelia; so your chastity,
Lucretia; so your wifely love, Portia. These are the most famous praises.
Yet still greater are yours, illustrious Anne; for the virtues which shone
singly in those ladies of old, shine all united in you).[57]

There is some pleasure to be taken in the versification of this kind of poetry, but
thematically it is so conventional that it is difficult to distinguish one poem from
another, let alone feel that any credible portrait is being given of the actual
historical person being praised.

It is almost universally true that whenever writers performed the ritual encomiastic functions of retainers their writing was either excessively conventional or
else perfunctory. The literature of blame and abuse is often more lively than the
poetry of praise, since invective seems to come more naturally to most people

---

[56] *The Poetical Works of John Skelton*, ed. Alexander Dyce, 2 vols, (London, 1843–4), p. 195/7–9.
[57] Furnivall, *Ballads from Manuscripts*, pp. 378, 401. I have quoted Furnivall's paraphrase.

than flattery, but, again, there is little in this kind of literature that is likely to engage the interest of modern readers. Skelton's jingoistic gloating in *Agaynst the Scottes* and More's snarling abuse in the *Responsio ad Lutherum* and *The Confutation of Tyndale's Answer* fail because they become monotonous, and simplify life. When, however, the demands of patronage were disturbed for one reason or another, and writers tended to project personal involvement into their fictions, their works grew more dynamic as a result.

Dissatisfaction with the patronage system was a major stimulus to literary inventiveness throughout the early Tudor period. No man of letters could afford to do without it, yet writers disliked the conditions it imposed. The ideal solution was to be granted church livings or an income with no strings attached, but in practice this turned out to be near impossible. Erasmus tried for this type of patronage most persistently, but the slim pickings he received in England, and of which he complained so bitterly,[58] merely attest to the fact that patrons were less altruistic in their sponsorship of the arts than humanists like Erasmus would have liked to suppose: patrons wanted practical returns for their expenditure in the form of writings that glorified their achievements or advanced their political interests. The jeering invectives that Skelton wrote against the Scots to celebrate the English victory at Flodden, or his diatribe against Thomas Arthur and Thomas Bilney illustrate the kind of thing that was often required.[59]

Men of letters were also perturbed by the apparent injustice of the procedure by which candidates were selected for patronage, especially for positions, or 'rooms', at court. It seemed to depend upon influential connections and a willingness to flatter, rather than upon intrinsic merit, so that most aspirants had to decide between compromising their moral being to become sycophants, or maintaining their integrity at the risk of being shut out from preferment, as was notably the case with two of the most inflexible moralists of the period, Alexander Barclay and, eventually, Sir Thomas Elyot.

Even when a man of letters gained a place at court, he was likely to be appalled at the conditions he found there. Newcomers were resented, and those with learning incurred jealousy from others who lacked it, while the noble members of court despised those of humbler origins, which most literary retainers were. The most acute dangers faced by writers were faction and the persistent efforts of competing individuals to displace their rivals.

Many early Tudor writers found these aspects of the patronage system extremely problematical, and they used literature as an instrument for imaginatively representing, comprehending, and exploring their experience of it. There were

---

[58] See, for example, *CW Erasmus*, 2, nos 281, 283; 3, no. 334.
[59] See *A Ballade of the Scottyshe Kynge; Agaynst the Scottes*; and *A Replycacion Agaynst Certayne Yong Scolers Abjured of Late*, in Skelton, *Poems*, ed. Scattergood, pp. 113–15, 115–21, 372–86.

two main situations that particularly stimulated their imaginations: the first was when those who had gained patronage became disenchanted with it; the second was when people who wanted patronage either failed to attain it, or lost it through reversals of fortune. The rest of the chapters in Part I of this book will focus on three noteworthy examples of writers from the earlier half of the period who became sufficiently disturbed by problems of patronage to seek new ways of expressing their innermost feelings. John Skelton had an honoured place at court, but developed scruples about remaining there. Alexander Barclay would have liked to have been there, but was never fully accepted or acceptable. Stephen Hawes, perhaps the most complex of the three, had a uniquely personal incentive for remaining in the royal household (where he was a groom of the chamber), but got swept out in an unofficial palace purge at the accession of Henry VIII. All three responded to their particular situations by treating conventional literary forms in such a way as to achieve new means of personal expression under the guise of traditional impersonal didacticism. Moreover, the careers of all three were inextricably intertwined: Hawes came into prominence as a court poet only after Skelton had departed, and when Skelton returned in 1512, it was Alexander Barclay whose court hopes he ruined almost beyond the point of recovery. Barclay in turn had his revenge when, in 1521, Skelton fell into disfavour, and it was he, Barclay, who was called upon to supply the offices of court poet. Between the three of them, they laid down the archetypal patterns of a literary response to the problem of patronage that would recur many times in subsequent early Tudor writing, and in different ways each achieved a new type of literature which offered a foretaste of things to come.

2

John Skelton and the *The Bowge of Courte*: Self-analysis and Discovery

Of the three writers under discussion in this section, John Skelton was the most successful in gaining and retaining patronage, especially in the first half of his career. However, that very success brought him face to face with one of the great problems arising from the patronage system – moral scruples. Having risen to a secure and honoured place at court, Skelton became troubled by the corruption he found there, and in *The Bowge of Courte* he sought to work out his reaction to a growing unease. The result is a work of anti-court satire that is startlingly innovative because it is also contrived to serve as an instrument of self-analysis. The poet uses it to explore how he became involved with the court in the past, the implications of his situation in the present, and the actions to remedy it he might be moved to take in the future. To this end he invents a rhetorical strategy that forces the reader to be wiser than the persona who narrates the poem. This, combined with the dramatic mode that Skelton marries to the conventional dream allegory framework, makes the reader a participant in the process by which the poet tries to attain a wise response to his predicament. The poem which results is thoroughly dynamic in its working and complex in its functions, serving both as justification for the poet's stance and also as moral instruction. There had been nothing quite like *The Bowge of Courte* before, but in its representation of the irony, tensions, paradox, and ambivalence inherent in a problematical situation, it was prophetic of much other early Tudor literature to come.

The circumstances in which *The Bowge of Courte* was composed help to explain why Skelton should have contrived it to be simultaneously dramatic, ironic, and open-ended. Skelton had been in the royal service for about ten years, having entered it soon after his laureation by the University of Oxford in 1488.[1] Once in service, Skelton had performed the usual duties expected of a literary retainer: asserting the official line on the assassination of the Earl of Northumberland in 1487; defending the king's honour against the slurs of Robert Gaguin, a French

[1] See Edwards, *Skelton*, pp. 34–8; and Nelson, *Skelton*, pp. 161–5.

detractor, in 1490; writing encomiastic verses on occasions such as the creation of Arthur as Prince of Wales and Henry as Duke of York; and contributing plays and interludes for the entertainment of the court.[2] After about 1496 he managed to consolidate his position at court by becoming first Prince Henry's tutor, and then a chaplain in the royal household once he had taken holy orders.[3] By 1500 Skelton's career at court had all the hallmarks of success, but soon after he suddenly departed from it to become a parish priest at Diss in Norfolk.

Why Skelton should have so suddenly reversed the direction of his career has been the subject of debate. According to the commonly accepted view, he was displaced in the automatic reshuffle that took place when Prince Arthur died on 2 April 1502, when William Hone assumed his position as a new tutor for Prince Henry. The payments to the Duke of York's schoolmaster recorded for the last weeks of April and June 1502, it is argued, were a kind of redundancy settlement when Skelton was dismissed.[4] A newly discovered record for 1503, however, shows that Skelton attended the funeral of Queen Elizabeth in February as a member of 'my lorde prynces houshold seruantes', among whom he is described as a 'scolmaister'.[5] Skelton was not dismissed; he went willingly, and the question is why.

It is at this point that the date of The Bowge of Courte is suggestive. The earliest edition declares that it was 'enprynted at Westmynster by me Wynkyn de Worde'. Considering that de Worde moved from Westminster in 1500, and that he did not use the type in which the poem is set before 1497, The Bowge of Courte must have been printed between those dates, and 1499 has been plausibly suggested as the date on other bibliographical evidence. If we suppose that the work was composed in 1498 as has been proposed,[6] the ramifications are very significant indeed, for that is the year in which he entered the priesthood, being ordained subdeacon on 31 March, deacon on 14 April, and priest on 9 June.[7] His anti-court satire, therefore, is likely to have been very closely connected with the state of mind that led him into the priesthood. Specifically, the perturbation experienced by Drede, the narrating persona, is likely to reflect Skelton's own

[2] Some idea of the range of Skelton's literary activities can be gained from his own account of his works (many of which are now lost) in A Garlande or Chapelet of Laurell. See Skelton, Poems, ed. Scattergood, pp. 345–54, ll. 1170–504.

[3] Edwards, Skelton, pp. 55–7. Edwards dates Skelton's entry to the priesthood to c.1498. For new evidence that Skelton was serving as a chaplain to Prince Henry in 1500, see Arthur F. Kinney, John Skelton, Priest as Poet: Seasons of Discovery (Chapel Hill and London, 1987), p. 34. Hereafter cited as Kinney, Skelton.

[4] Public Record Office MS E 101/415–3, quoted by Edwards, Skelton, pp. 77–8, 288–9; Nelson, Skelton, p. 74.

[5] Public Record Office MS LC2/1, fol. 72 ᵛ, cited by Kinney, Skelton, p. 34.

[6] Helen Stearns Sale, 'The Date of Skelton's Bowge of Court', Modern Language Notes, 52 (1937), pp. 572–4. The many specific references to the fact that the poet is at court suggest that the date of 1480 proposed by Melvin J. Tucker (English Language Notes, 7 (1970), pp. 168–75), is far too early.

[7] Nelson, Skelton, p. 71.

intensifying scruples about the life he was required to lead. Read in this context, the poem helps to explain Skelton's eventual decision not merely to accept a benefice in the country, but actually to reside there – a very unusual practice in those days for someone of his status.[8] He did not go simply because he lost his job, but because genuine scruples, temporarily at least, overpowered his willingness to keep fighting for personal and moral survival in a situation of institutionalized corruption and intrigue. However much he came to regret his decision later (and he did the same thing again under Wolsey's regime), his motives at the time were sincere and unforced.

Growing doubts about the soundness of his career at court, then, moved Skelton into attempting to comprehend how he had come to be there, and to evaluate his motives, prospects, and the implications of remaining there. What is interesting for the critic and historian alike is to see how Skelton created an edifying moral exemplum of *The Bowge of Courte*, while simultaneously turning it into a vehicle for self-analysis and discovery.

He achieves this by investing the timeworn conventions of *The Bowge of Courte* with a personal, rather than simply a general, level of reference. As Heiserman exhaustively established, the poem is constructed of literary *topoi* and themes that had been used since the twelfth century.[9] In genre it is an allegorical dream vision with the sleepless, questing dreamer and personified abstractions to be found from Guillaume de Lorris to Chaucer, Lydgate, and Hoccleve. In content, too, it is highly conventional. Analogues can be found for almost every complaint Skelton levels at court life in the works of Walter Map, John of Salisbury, Aeneas Silvius, and many other authors in a long tradition of anti-court satire.[10] Even the central symbol of court as a ship was drawn from Sebastian Brandt's *Ship of Fools* that had been published in its Latin version the year before Skelton wrote *The Bowge of Courte*.[11] No source or analogue, however, prepares for the way Skelton uses the pretext of anti-court satire to explore a very particular and personal situation.

There is such a clear and explicit correspondence between Drede, the narrating persona, and Skelton himself that *The Bowge of Courte* may be read in part as thinly disguised autobiography.[12] Drede has secured a position at court because of his learning, or 'connynge', which excites the envy of other courtiers.[13] He is

---

[8] Edwards, *Skelton*, p. 52.

[9] A. R. Heiserman, *Skelton and Satire*, (Chicago, 1961), pp. 15–46.

[10] Ibid., pp. 28–42.

[11] Ibid., pp. 26–7.

[12] For a recognition that the main locus of the work is interior, see Stanley Fish, *John Skelton's Poetry* (Hamden, Connecticut, 1965), p. 54.

[13] *The Bowge of Courte*, ll. 148–54, 260–3. All citations are to the edition by Scattergood.

also a poet who can 'make a verse' as well as being a 'clerke'.[14] His rivals wonder at the favour Drede has 'with my lady' and are jealous of it, which suggests Skelton's own favoured relationship with Lady Margaret Beaufort, who presided over the royal nursery at Eltham in which Skelton was a tutor.[15] Drede, then, is not just any neutral court observer; he shares precisely Skelton's own particular situation in a royal household.

The time sequence of the poem reflects this autobiographical relationship between Skelton and Drede. Drede attains favour by stages which are described in a prologue as if they have taken place in the past. When the main body of the work opens Drede is *already* at court. It is a small detail, but one that fits Skelton's own biographical circumstances. At the time of writing *The Bowge of Courte* he, too, was at court, and this explains why there is such a marked change from the narrative mode of the Prologue to the dramatic mode in which the main action, Drede's encounter with the court vices, is presented. The former is treated as if it took place in the past, the latter as if it is taking place in the present.

One other important detail helps to establish the personal level of reference – the setting. Unlike conventional dream visions, which are usually set in an enclosed garden, *The Bowge of Courte* is set in an inn called 'Power's Key' in the East Anglian port of Harwich.[16] The specificity of this location is arresting and suggestive. In the prototype for the whole genre, *Le Roman de la Rose*, the enclosed garden symbolizes the court itself; in Skelton's poem the Harwich inn stands for a time when the poet was far distant from the court, yet desired to be in it. The name of the inn may also contain an autobiographical cipher that makes the link between Drede and the young Skelton closer still. During the 1480s there was indeed an inn in Harwich run by one John Power, and owned by Lord John Howard.[17] By punning on Power's name, Skelton may not merely have been concerned to add local colour, but also to hint that Power's Key (*'quai'*) had also been the '*key* to power',[18] and thus acknowledge that his own advancement was owing to the good offices of its Howard proprietors.[19]

The Bowge of Courte is thus far from being the mere collection of clichéd commonplaces that is sometimes alleged. However universalized it may be, the

---

[14] Ibid., ll. 244–5, 453.

[15] Skelton is most likely the poet referred to in a surviving record of payment of 66s. 8d. 'to my lady the kinges moder poete' on 3–4 December 1497 (Public Record Office MS E 101/414–16); cited by Edwards, *Skelton*, Appendix 1C, p. 288.

[16] *The Bowge of Courte*, ll. 34–5.

[17] See Melvin J. Tucker, 'Setting in Skelton's *Bowge of Courte*: A Speculation', *English Language Notes*, 7 (1970), pp. 168–75.

[18] Skelton was fond of riddling on names; see, for example, his pun on Wolsey's name as '*maris lupus*' in *Why Come Ye Nat to Courte?* (Skelton, *Poems*, ed. Scattergood, p. 311, l. 30).

[19] The setting of the dream at Power's Key lends credence to the conjecture that Skelton had East Anglian connections from an early date. For the debate on Skelton's early life see Edwards, *Skelton*, p. 29, n. 1 (p. 259).

poem nevertheless depicts metaphorically a real, particular, personal experience on Skelton's part.

The Prologue to the poem can be read as an imaginative examination of the impulses that led Skelton to court in the first place. He holds them up for critical scrutiny by adopting a rhetorical strategy that distances both him and the reader from his own earlier self and past actions. Specifically, he creates a double perspective by making his persona, Drede, much more limited in understanding than either the reader or the implied author. Drede, in fact, is an unreliable narrator, and by inviting the reader to see this, Skelton is also inviting him to share in the process whereby he has attained greater wisdom.[20]

Drede's naivety is apparent from the very beginning. Recalling how poets have gained immortal fame in the past by cloaking truths in the garb of poetry, Drede aspires to do the same, yet fears that his reach exceeds his grasp, and does not know what to do for the best. Eventually he falls asleep out of exhaustion, and has the dream which, after he has awoken and recorded it, forms the bulk of the poem. Skelton chooses to set this occasion not in spring, the usual season when such dreams occur, but in autumn:

> In autumpne, whan the sonne *in Vyrgyne*
> By radyante hete enryped hath our corne;
> Whan Luna, full of mutabylyte,
> As emperes the dyademe hath worne
> Of our pole artyke, smylynge halfe in scorne
> At our foly and our unstedfastnesse;
> The tyme whan Mars to werre hym dyd dres.[21]

Although Drede does not realize it, this passage offers a metaphorical comment on the folly of his aspirations. Autumn is a time of deceptive appearances when everything seems at the point of fruition, whereas, ironically, it is on the verge of decline. The reference in the third line to Luna, the moon, picks up and reinforces this idea of mutability, while showing that it is a force that renders human endeavour a vanity. Luna smiles '*halfe* in scorne' because she is not only contemptuous, but also amused at human folly and instability. All the other images in the passage are ominous: the 'pole artyke' has connotations of coldness and sterility, the allusion to Mars suggests violence. Altogether, the opening evokes a situation which Drede should have the good sense to avoid.

Similarly, Drede is unable to recognize the full implications of the symbols that occur in his dream. When he falls asleep the first thing he sees is a ship:

[20] For perceptive comments on this matter, see Fish, *John Skelton's Poetry*, pp. 54–5.
[21] *The Bowge of Courte*, ll. 1–7.

Me thoughte I sawe a shyppe, goodly of sayle,
Come saylynge forth into that haven brood,
Her takelynge ryche and of hye apparayle;
She kyste an anker, and there she laye at rode,
Marchauntes her borded to see what she had lode.
Therein they founde royall marchaundyse,
Fraghted with plesure to what ye coude devyse.[22]

When this ship is named as 'The Bowge of Courte' owned by a lady of estate,
Dame Saunce-Pere (that is, 'Peerless') and the royal merchandise on it 'Favore-
to-stonde-in-her-good-grace', it is absolutely clear that the ship is a symbol of the
royal court and Drede's ambition to find a place in it,[23] but what is not so clear
are the sinister implications inherent in the symbol itself. Just three years before
Skelton's poem was written, Sebastian Brandt's *Das Narrenschiff* (*The Ship of
Fools*) had taken Europe by storm in Locher's Latin version, *Stultifera navis*
(1497). No judicious or well-read reader among Skelton's contemporaries would
have failed to make the equation between the ship and folly – which Drede so
conspicuously does.

Nor does he detect the even more sinister overtones inherent in the number
symbolism of the 'full subtyll persones in nombre foure and thre' whom he meets
on the ship.[24] The names of these personified abstractions show that they
represent vices to be found at court: Favell (flattery), Suspect, Harvy Hafter
(cheating), Disdayne, Ryotte (dissipation), Dyssymuler (dissimulation), and Sub-
tylte (alias Disceyte). But the number seven suggests their close kinship with the
Seven Deadly Sins, which in turn implies the danger that Drede will be courting
by fraternizing with them – damnation. Drede, however, cannot see this. As he
himself tells us:

> . . . oftentymes I wolde myselfe avaunce,
> With them to make solace and pleasure.[25]

The rhetorical distance between the naive Drede and the more perspicacious
reader is consolidated in a number of strategically placed puns. When Drede
looks upon Dame Saunce-Pere, he sees written on her throne the words '*Garder
le fortune que est mauelz et bone.*'[26] This can be translated in two ways; either as
'make sure you *retain* fortune, which is both bad and good', or else, exploiting
the pun in *garder*, '*beware* of fortune, which can be bad as well as good.' The pun
thus picks up all the other warnings in the prologue against the possibility of

[22] Ibid., ll. 36–42.
[23] Ibid., ll. 49–55.
[24] Ibid., l. 133.
[25] Ibid., ll. 143–4.
[26] Ibid., l. 67.

suffering ill fortune: the reference to Luna, the need to have the jewel *Bone aventure* (good luck) if favour is to be gained, and the fact that Fortune herself is the helmsman of the ship:

> Whome she hateth shall over the see-boorde skyp.
> Whome she loveth, of all plesyre is ryche
> Whyles she laugheth and hath luste for to playe.[27]

A second pun occurs when Drede is accosted by Daunger, Dame Saunce-Pere's chief lady in waiting:

> Her chyef gentylwoman, Daunger by her name,
> Gave me a taunte, and sayde I was to blame
>
> To be so perte to prese so proudly uppe.
> She sayde she trowed that I had eten sause;
> She asked yf ever I dranke of saucys cuppe.[28]

The proverb 'to eat sauce' means 'to be unwarrantedly bold'. Skelton, however, draws out of it a further sinister implication which is signalled more clearly in the following line: to drink 'of *saucys* cuppe' is not merely to be excessively bold, but to be so because of having drunk from *Circe's* cup – that is, of having surrendered to a temptation that disfigures the victim. Drede, nevertheless, shows no signs of being aware of this danger.

The ironies generated by the dual perspective serve to expose inadequacies in Drede's earlier attitude, and, perhaps, a degree of hypocrisy, in the light of his later recoil from court. He easily allows his ambition (personified as Desire) to overpower his reticence and prudence. Indeed, Skelton shows that Drede willingly and wilfully connives to gain promotion against all his better instincts and the warnings given him. When, for example, he sees the richness of the royal merchandise to be procured from The Bowge of Courte, he is not at all reticent about competing for it:

> ... than I thoughte I wolde not dwell behynde;
> Amonge all other I put myselfe in prece.[29]

The sardonic pun in this passage on 'prece' meaning 'press' and 'prece' meaning 'price' ('prece' rhymes with 'cese' and 'pece' in the stanza, and hence is aurally indistinguishable from 'price' in early Tudor pronunciation) reveals that he is not unaware of his worth as a potential royal servant either. By the time the prologue

---

[27] Ibid., ll. 3, 97–105, 111–14.
[28] Ibid., ll. 69–73.
[29] Ibid., ll. 43–4.

ends, we can see that Drede is just as eager as anyone else to gain advantage from
the system of patronage he would soon come to fear and despise:

> Thus, in a rowe, of martchaauntes a grete route
> Suwed to Fortune that she wold be theyre frynde.
> They thronge in fast and flocked her aboute,
> *And I with them* prayed her to have in mynde.
> She promysed to us all she wolde be kynde;
> Of Bowge of Court she asketh what we wold have,
> And we asked favoure, and favour she us gave.[30]

At this early point in *The Bowge of Courte*, Drede's name is a misnomer: 'Desire'
would be more appropriate. The rest of the poem is designed to show how he was
jolted into a more sober viewpoint.

When his retrospective glance at the past is over, Skelton constructs a fictive
representation of his situation in the present; that is, as a member of the royal
court competing with other courtiers who resent his presence and feel threatened
by his success. To interpret this experience, Skelton personifies the attitudes to be
found at court that might threaten one such as himself, then places Drede in a
dramatic encounter with them. In this way, he is able to explore the possible
implications of his own predicament.

The shift from the largely narrative mode of the Prologue to a dramatic mode
serves to put the reader in Drede's place, so that he or she can develop a growing
comprehension of what life at court involves at the same time Drede does. In
inducing this reaction, Skelton could look for sympathetic corroboration of his
own developing viewpoint, and give effective moral instruction to his readers.

During his encounter, Drede discovers the envy, malice, hypocrisy, and treachery
at court, generated by the attempts of rivals to try to maintain their place in the
patronage system at each other's expense. While treating these vices as general
moral defects, Skelton also takes care to characterize them as *court* vices, to
evoke the situation in a real (that is, Tudor) court.

To generalize them, he used the traditional allegorical device of emblematic
detail to suggest a correlation between outward appearance and the respective
vices personified. Favell, for example, wears a cloak lined 'with doubtfull
doublenes', Harvey Hafter bears a versing box on his chest and wears a gown 'all
furred wyth foxe', and Disdayne a gaudy garment wrought of scorns and a hood
lined with indignation.[31] The abstract and emblematic nature of their appearance
thus puts them at a remove from reality. Skelton takes care, however, to present

---

[30] Ibid., ll. 120–6. My italics.
[31] Ibid., ll. 178, 231–4, 285–6.

their speech and actions with a verisimilitude that creates the impression of real-life courtiers. The dialogue especially, with its colloquialisms and realistic speech patterns, vividly suggests court intrigue:

> To Hervy Hafter than he spake of me,
> And I drewe nere to harke what they two sayde.
> 'Now,' quod Dysdayne, 'as I shall saved be,
> I have grete scorne and am ryghte evyll apayed.'
> 'Than,' quod Hervy, 'why arte thou so dysmayde?'
> 'By Cryste,' quod he, 'for it is shame to saye,
> To see Johan Dawes, that came but yesterdaye,
>
> How he is now taken in conceyte,
> This Doctour Dawcocke, Drede, I wene he hyghte.
> By Goddis bones, but yf we have som sleyte,
> It is lyke he wyll stonde in our lyghte!'
> 'By God,' quod Hervy, 'and it so happen myghte!
> Lete us, therfore, shortely at a worde
> Fynde some mene to caste him over the borde.'[32]

Likewise, when Suspycyon approaches Drede, 'he came walkynge soberly, / Wyth 'Whom' and 'Ha' and with a croked loke.'[33] Suspycyon's act of clearing his throat reflects the nervous strain he is under because of the need to dissemble his urgent desire to find out whether anything was said about him behind his back. The detail thus not only confirms him as true to the type he represents, but also gives him a psychological realism that contributes to a vivid picture of life at court. This device of generalizing and particularizing at the same time allows the satirical exposé to serve both as an impersonal didactic exemplum, and also as the representation of a personal experience.

Skelton's further purpose in putting Drede into an active encounter with the vices is to show how his exposure to them induces a state of acute paranoia.

Drede's problems stem from the fact that all the vices envy the favour he has gained, and are jealous of the advantage his learning has given him. They also resent him as a social upstart, as Disdayne declares:

> It is greate scorne to see suche a hayne
> As thou arte, one that cam but yesterdaye,
> With us olde servauntes such maysters to playe.[34]

---

[32] Ibid., ll. 295–308.
[33] Ibid., ll. 190–1.
[34] Ibid., ll. 327–30.

Their reaction is to seek his downfall, and their strategy is one of psychological subversion. Some characters, like Disdayne, simply try to intimidate him by creating pretexts to insult him. Others, like Favell and Hervy Hafter, try the more subtle approach of flattering him to his face, while maligning him behind his back. Under the guise of friendly concern, they systematically erode the grounds of his confidence and security. Favell, for instance, having ingratiated himself by flattering Drede on his learning, points out that Drede's 'gyftes of grace' have been lent by Fortune – with the implication that they are liable to be removed just as quickly. Then, having observed that Drede must be worth a thousand pounds to his royal mistress, he adds that he has overheard others libelling Drede to his patroness, 'for here be dyverse to you that be unkynde.'[35] By first reminding Drede of what he stands to lose, and then making him believe that others are plotting to ruin him, Favell cunningly tries to unsettle him so as to make him dependent on the friendship that he offers. Psychologically, it is very similar to the strategy Shakespeare later gave to Iago to subvert Othello, and it is diabolically effective.

No sooner has Drede thanked Favell 'for his grete gentylnes' than Suspycyon destroys Drede's trust in Favell by warning him. 'He wyll begyle you and speke fayre to your face.'[36] And so it goes on: one by one all Drede's props are removed until he is hopelessly overpowered by the anxiety his name signifies.

The whole encounter, in fact, is carefully contrived to dramatize the onset of derangement. To Drede, the experience starts to seem circular as words and events begin to repeat themselves. Suspycyon's words of parting near the beginning of the poem, 'Fare well . . . we wyll talke more of this', are picked up by Dyssymulation near the end: 'Adewe tyll soone, we shall speke more of this.'[37] Dyssymulation also repeats Favell's warning that others are maligning him, and Harvy Hafter who is as 'lyghte as lynde' and in whose presence Drede's purse 'was half aferde' reconstitutes himself in the form of Disceyte, who is also described as a 'lyghte lyme-fynger' whom Drede suspects of designs on his purse.[38] Soon Drede starts to lose his ability to distinguish one character or place from another, as his grip on reality becomes progressively loosened. By the time Disceyte comes to him near the end of the poem, he seems to be being sucked into a mental vortex where events, people, and places have lost all particularity and meaning:

> I have an errande to rounde in your ere.
> He tolde me so, by God, ye maye truste me.
> Parde, remember whan ye were there,
> There I wynked on you – wote ye not where?

[35] Ibid., ll. 148–53, 158–61.
[36] Ibid., ll. 176, 200.
[37] Ibid., ll. 227, 492.
[38] Ibid., ll. 451, 231–8, 503–9.

> In A *loco*, I mene *juxta* B:
> Woo is hym that is blynde and maye not see![39]

By this stage Drede has become so filled with paranoia that his own imagination begins to supply the function of the vices who have been subverting him, and he starts to multiply enemies in his mind:

> And as he rounded thus in myne ere
> Of false collusyon confetryd by assente,
> Me thoughte I see lewde felawes here and there
> Came for to slee me of mortall entente.
> And as they came, the shypborde faste I hente,
> And thoughte to lepe; and even with that woke,
> Caughte penne and ynke, and wroth this lytell boke.[40]

The act of awakening, for the poet, is a way of avoiding the more drastic form of remedy that his nightmare implies. As yet, Skelton was not quite ready to heed fully the dictates of his imagination and leave the court.

The direct address at the end of the *The Bowge of Courte* shows how deliberately Skelton had constructed his rhetorical strategy to involve the reader. Adopting a conventional formula, he pleads for readers not to be offended by anything in the work, on the grounds that it is only a dream:

> I wolde therwith no man were myscontente,
> Besechynge you that shall it see or rede,
> In every poynte to be indyfferente,
> Syth all in substaunce of slumbrynge doth procede.[41]

Immediately, however, he renders this exhortation disingenuous by allowing for the possibility that the dream may be true after all: 'I wyll not saye it is mater in dede, But yet oftyme suche dremes be founde trewe.'

It is at this moment that the underlying purpose of Skelton's strategy becomes clear. He throws the burden of interpretative responsibility wholly on to the reader: 'Now construewe ye what is the resydewe'.[42] What is the 'residue' that the reader is meant to construe? In terms of the possibilities of illusion and truth raised by the final stanza, part of the reader's duty is to determine how far the dream represents actuality. Given the care with which Skelton has planted hints of autobiographical correspondences in the poem, one can fairly assume that

---

[39] Ibid., ll. 513–18.
[40] Ibid., ll. 526–32.
[41] Ibid., ll. 533–6.
[42] Ibid., ll. 537–8, 539.

much of it *is* true in a very real sense. *The Bowge of Courte* is not merely a pious gesture on the part of a priest mildly concerned to feed his sheep with yet another version of tired didactic commonplaces; it is Skelton's representation of his own court position and the threat it poses to his emotional and mental equilibrium.

The second kind of 'residue' that the reader is invited to construe is what a person in Skelton's situation should do about it. In this respect, the outcome of the poem is highly ambiguous indeed. When Drede thinks he sees all the others in a confederacy to destroy him he goes to leap over the side of the ship. Translating the metaphor, one might think that Skelton was signalling his willingness to abandon court. Nevertheless, Drede does not leap; instead he 'wakes up', which may be taken metaphorically as well as literally, and writes his little book. In the course of doing so, ironically, he ends up writing the very work of moral instruction, cloaking truths subtly under covert terms, that he felt he could not write at the beginning. Even though the tenor of the whole work seems to urge the poet not to aim higher than he can attain, and to flee from the court, his persona neither gives up his desire for literary renown (otherwise he would not have written the poem), nor does he, even in his nightmarish fantasy, actually leave the court. *The Bowge of Courte* thus figures forth a very deep-seated ambivalence in Skelton himself. It is one that will be frequently met in other early Tudor authors as they struggle to come to terms with their complex feelings concerning the patronage system and the conditions it imposed.

The Bowge of Courte is our earliest example in the early Tudor period of the complex new type of literature that would emerge as writers began to respond to rapidly evolving political circumstances. In function, it is designed to represent a situation that engages the writer's deepest feelings, for the sake of comprehending it and finding an appropriate response to it. Imaginatively at least, Skelton sought sympathetic corroboration of his own views from readers, and to this end he devised a highly inventive fictive method that involved them as participants. It is also characteristic of other early Tudor literature in that it is thoroughly open-ended and inconclusive. This, too, manifests the deep-seated ambivalence that the most sensitive early Tudor writers felt about the circumstances in which they found themselves, and the problematical issues requiring them to reach decisions for which they lacked either conviction, confidence, or will.

Skelton waited another five years before making his decision, which may, in the end, have been making a virtue of necessity if he were indeed displaced by William Hone as Prince Henry's tutor. In the light of the ambivalence shown in *The Bowge of Courte* this delay is understandable. It was far easier for writers to deal with the consequences of patronage who never became as firmly entrenched in the system as Skelton did, although even here the issue could have interesting effects on literary inventiveness, as the case of Skelton's rival, Alexander Barclay, shows.

3

Beatus ille: The *Eclogues* of Alexander Barclay

The patronage system affected different people in different ways, and these differences conditioned the kind of literature they contrived. Skelton wrote from within the court, having enjoyed the benefits that the system could impart. His problems were not ones of frustration at being excluded from court, but of insecurity and anxiety arising from the need to maintain his position and moral integrity once there. Consequently, he used the fiction of *The Bowge of Courte* to analyse and objectify the sources of that anxiety as a preparation for taking steps to resolve it. The case of Alexander Barclay is quite different, since at the time when he confronted the issue in his *Eclogues*, he had conspicuously failed to gain court patronage, and this is reflected in the nature and function of the work. Whereas *The Bowge of Courte* is an instrument of analysis preparatory to future action, the *Eclogues* are a retrospective justification of Barclay's failure, designed to make a virtue out of necessity; while Skelton narrows the distance between the action in his poem and his personal situation, Barclay seeks to distance it by placing it clearly in the past; and whereas Skelton seeks to involve the reader in deciding what he might do, Barclay instructs him or her on the merit of what he pretends he has already done. The rhetorical strategies of the two works are thus quite different.

There are, nevertheless, striking similarities that show *The Bowge of Courte* and the *Eclogues* to be characteristic of their age. Both seek to confirm their author's viewpoint by exploiting conventional anti-court themes, yet handle them in ways that are innovative in form. Both seek to 'establish the will' of the author,[1] by dramatizing the process through which he evolves towards his final attitude; and both end up being ambivalent in that attitude because of divided impulses in each author that belie his fictional stance. Though a much maligned writer, therefore,

---

[1] I use Barclay's phrase. See *The Eclogues of Alexander Barclay from the Original Edition by John Cawood*, ed. Beatrice White, Early English Text Society, Original Series, 175 (London, 1928), *Eclogue* III, p. 139, l. 820. All references are to this edition.

Barclay takes his place as a genuine contributor to the early Tudor literature of complexity.

Barclay's early career explains the frustration and disappointed expectations that eventually moved him to write the *Eclogues*. Like so many others who sought a literary career, Barclay went to either Oxford or Cambridge, and certainly gained a degree from one of them.[2] From his various references to foreign universities and foreign scholars (particularly French ones), it can be inferred that he travelled to the continent where he may have undertaken further study. Up to this point, Barclay's career is remarkably similar to that of Skelton or Stephen Hawes, and Barclay might well have expected that it would lead to advancement similar to theirs.

On his return to England, Barclay entered holy orders, being ordained by Thomas Cornish, titular bishop of Tyne, and suffragan bishop of Bath and Wells. Cornish was also provost of Oriel College, Oxford (1493–1507), and warden of the College of Saint Mary, Ottery, in Devonshire, between 1490 and 1511,[3] and it was probably through his offices that Barclay gained his first preferment as chaplain at Saint Mary, Ottery, where he combined the duties of librarian and instructor to the choirboys.[4] Saint Mary's was a college of secular priests, and would therefore have given Barclay plenty of scope for further advancement, had he sought it.

There are, indeed, plenty of signs that Barclay wanted to secure promotion to higher positions at this time. The main evidence is provided by the *Ship of Fooles*, the translation of Sebastian Brandt's satire which Barclay completed in 1508, while at Saint Mary's, Ottery. Barclay's verse translation vastly expands on the original, and his periphrastic additions often reveal a great deal of self-projection on his part.

Two specific themes emerge in these additions: resentment at the numbers of unsuitable people gaining promotion, and an implicit assertion of Barclay's own suitability for advancement. Barclay seems particularly resentful of the advantages that those with wealth, noble birth, or powerful connections have over other more worthy aspirants in the competition for promotion. For instance, in the section 'of unprofitable study' he asserts that he dare not let on board 'all the fooles promoted to honours . . . of hye progenitours' because, together with the servants of Cupid and Venus, these would cause the ship to sink.[5] These are the

---

[2] He has been claimed for Oriel College, Oxford, by Wood, and for Cambridge by Watson; see Beatrice White, ed. cit., p. viii.

[3] *DNB*, I, p. 1077.

[4] Ibid., I, p. xiv.

[5] *Stultifera nauis, qua omnium mortalium narratur stultitia . . . The Ship of Fooles, Wherein is shewed the Folly of all States. . . . Translated out of Latin into Englishe by Alexander Barclay Priest* (London 1570), fo. 54[v]. All references are to this edition.

scholars that make good not because of mind or talent, but because of noble lineage. The problem, however, is general in England:

> Eche is not lettred that nowe is made a lorde,
> Nor eche a Clerke that hath a benefice:
> They are not all lawyers that plees do recorde,
> All that are promoted are not fully wise.[6]

> This is the speciall cause of this inconuenience,
> That greatest fooles, and fullest of lewdnes,
> Hauing least wit, and simplest science
> Are first promoted, and have greatest reuerence.
> For if one can flatter, and beare a Hauke on his fist,
> He shalbe made Parson of Honington of Clist.[7]

> The company of men that lacketh witte,
> Is best exalted (as nowe) in every place,
> And in the chayre or hyest rowme shall sit,
> Promoting none but suche as sue their trace.[8]

In the expanded phrasing of passages like these one can detect Barclay's envy at the promotion of others less worthy than he is to positions he feels he is better equipped to occupy. The phrasing with which he proposed the remedy for England's ills (in a section marked '*Anglie defectus*' in the margin) also implies Barclay's belief that he should be among those who are advanced to an honourable office:

> If the noble realme of Englande would aduaunce
> In our days men of vertue and prudence,
> Eche man rewarding after his gouernaunce,
> *As the wise with honour and rowme of excellence,*
> And the ill with greeuous payne for their offence,
> Then should our famous laude of olde obtayned,
> Not bene decayed, oppressed and thus distayned.

> *If men of wisdom were brought out of the scoles,*
> *And after their vertue set in moste hye degree,*
> My ship should not haue led so many fooles.[9]

[6] Ibid., fo. 2^r, paraphrasing 'Seu studiam, seu non, dominus tamen esse vocabor' (fo. 1^v).

[7] Ibid., fo. 2^v. There is nothing in the Latin to suggest this passage, which may refer to an actual incident (See White, p. xix).

[8] Ibid., fo. 235^v, paraphrasing 'Ascendit celebres stultorum turba cathedras, / Stultitia mentes quae violare solet' (fo. 234^r).

[9] Ibid., fo. 235^v, based on: 'Si modo prudentes aleret Germania pugnax, / Et daret ingenuis praemia digna viris: / non sic deserta fluerent praeconia fama, / Parta quidem, quae nunc Theutona terra premit. / Si gradus insignis sophiae cultoribus esset, / Non veheret fatuos tot modo nostra ratis' (fo. 234^r). My italics.

The phrasing with which he translated the Latin here creates an unnecessary repetition, betraying Barclay's conviction that he would benefit from such a reform. *He* is the wise man from the schools that might very profitably be advanced to a 'room of excellence'.

Even though Barclay professes that he translated the book 'neyther for hope of rewarde nor laude of man',[10] there are indications that his motives were rather more practical than he pretends. The work contains a number of strategically placed panegyrics praising the English king, which were manifestly composed with Henry VII in mind. Henry is praised as 'the red Rose redolent' who has quelled insurrection, expelled war and shown exemplary qualities of meekness, chastity, justice and pity, to whom Englishmen are to do obedience 'with faythfull heart'.[11] These encomiastic passages offer exactly the same kind of flattery through which other writers, such as Skelton, Hawes, or More, sought to attract the attention, and hence the patronage, of the current monarch. Having embedded these encomia in the work, Barclay may have hoped that his mentor, Bishop Cornish, to whom *The Ship of Fooles* is dedicated, might bring it to the king's notice to procure him advancement. Henry VII, however, died in 1509 before the work appeared in print. Hasty emendations to the text confirm the idea that Barclay had patronage from the king in mind. In the case of one encomium, a marginal note simply substitutes Henry VIII for Henry VII as the subject of praise:

> But ye proude galants that thus your selfe disguise,
> Be ye ashamed, beholde vnto your prince:
> Consider his sadness, his honestie deuise,
> His clothing expresseth his inwarde prudence
> Ye see no example of such inconuenience.
> In his highnes, but godly wit and grauitie,
> Ensue him, and sorowe for your enormitie.

The marginal comment reads: 'Laus summa de grauitate eximia Henrici Anglorum regis, viij' ('a high commendation of the extraordinary seriousness of Henry VIII, King of England').[12] Whatever else Henry VIII may have been in the early years of his reign, he was not the epitome of *gravitas* and sober dress – but his father was. Another sign of hasty reworking occurs later in the work when Barclay, forgetting that he has already praised Henry VII as the 'red rose redolent' who has been leading England into a state of millenial peace, inserts a long panegyric of the new king who is just beginning a reign of unprecedented glory:

[10] Ibid., sig. ¶¶ 1ᵛ.
[11] Ibid., fo. 127ʳ.
[12] Ibid., fo. 9ᵛ.

One hope we have our enemies to quell,
Which hope is stedfast if we our selfe do well,
For Henry the eyght replete with hye wisedome,
By iust title gideth our scepter of kingdome.
This noble prince beginneth vertuously,
By iustice and pitie his realme to maynteyne,
So that he and his without mo company,
May succour our sores by his manhode souerayne,
And get with his owne hande Jerusalem agayne,
He passeth Hercules in manhode and courage,
Hauing a respect vnto his tender age.[13]

Much of this is simply drawn from Brandt's original praise of the Emperor Maximilian as the leader who will defeat the Turks, liberate Jerusalem, and recover the holy cross, as the marginal note makes clear: 'Mutatur laus Maximiliani Romanorum regis, in laudem Henrici octaui anglorum regis' ('the praise of Maximilian, King of the Romans, is changed into a praise of Henry VIII, King of the English).' However, Barclay praised the young Henry for a virtue that is not mentioned in the source – liberality:

He passeth Achilles in strength and valiaunce,
His fame here as great, but as for his larges
And liberalitie, he showeth in countenaunce
That no auarice can blinde his righteousnes,
Couetice hath left behinde him his riches,
Unto the high possession of liberalitie,
Which with the same shall kepe our libertie.[14]

These lines show Barclay hastening to ingratiate himself with the new regime by (like so many others) attacking the old. He implicitly personifies Henry VII as Covetousness, whose wealth his liberal son, Henry VIII, has inherited, to the happiness of potential beneficiaries – like himself. It is all rather cynical, as Barclay had earlier praised the old king as 'one who spared no expence upon the poore', when it looked as if the father and not the son would be the source of liberality for him.[15] At any rate, these inconsistencies and emendations prove that Barclay was not as disinterested in putting forth his work as he pretended. He hoped to gain preferment and, if he had observed the careers of scholars such as André, Skelton, and Hawes, he might justifiably have expected that it would come his way.

In this hope, however, he was to prove disappointed. Just at the point when

[13] Ibid., fo. 205^r.

[14] Ibid., paraphrasing 'Viribus Alcidem superat, praecellit Achillem, / Caesaris hoc vno est principe, fama minor' (fo. 200, misnumbered 100).

[15] Ibid., fo. 127^r.

Barclay could look to see his literary efforts rewarded, his intended patron, Henry
VII, died, and his successor, Henry VIII, favoured a style of man and writing
which was far removed from anything Barclay had to offer. The new king was
interested in disguisings and joustings, not in didactic treatises – he had enough
of those inflicted on him by his tutors – and in poets who would entertain, not
instruct him. To add to this misfortune, Bishop Cornish, Barclay's old patron,
retired from the wardenship of Saint Mary, Ottery, in 1511 and died shortly
after, thus depriving Barclay of any intercessor with the new regime. And to cap
Barclay's bad luck, just at this time John Skelton decided that he had had enough
of country life as a parish priest, and energetically sought to return to court.[16]
Skelton had the advantage over Barclay in every respect. He was already personally acquainted with the king, having been his tutor, and in spite of a deeply
serious vein of morality, had the wit and racy style to provide Henry with what
he wanted, as his bawdy lyrics and colourful invectives show.

For a number of reasons Skelton became a particular *bête noire* for Barclay,
even before he added insult to injury by gaining the court patronage Barclay
would have liked. Barclay's first attack on his rival came at the end of *The Ship of
Fooles*:

> Holde me excused, for why my will is good,
> Men to induce vnto vertue and goodnes,
> I write no iest ne tale of Robin Hood,
> Nor sowe no sparkles ne sede of viciousnes,
> Wise men loue vertue, wilde people wantonnes,
> It longeth not to my science nor cunning,
> For Philip the Sparowe the *Dirige* to singe.[17]

This reference to Skelton's *Phyllyp Sparowe* reveals not only Barclay's disapproval of the frivolity and sexual lubricity displayed by his rival in that poem, but
also the difference between them as poets. Barclay is unwilling, and unable, to
write jests of fiction for entertainment's sake, preferring instead to write didacti-
cally; Skelton, on the other hand, is both willing and able, and Barclay despises
him for it.

Such an attitude was bound to disqualify Barclay in the eyes of the boisterous
and pleasure-loving young king, and so it eventually proved. Yet Barclay nevertheless appears to have been given a chance to prove his worth at court. One of
Skelton's first tasks as newly appointed court poet was to stage a 'flytyng' or
ritual exchange of verbal abuse, with Sir Christopher Garnesche, one of Henry
VIII's gentleman ushers, for the entertainment of the court in late 1513 or early
1514.[18] Although Garnesche's side of the flytyng does not survive, we can infer

---

[16] See Edwards, *Skelton*, pp. 129–32.
[17] *Ship of Fooles*, fo. 259^r.
[18] See Helen Stearns Sale, 'John Skelton and Christopher Garnesche', *Modern Language Notes*, 43
(1928), pp. 518–23.

from Skelton's, which does, that Garnesche called upon the services of another poet, whom Skelton alludes to sarcastically as 'gorbellyd Godfrey' with 'that grysly gargons face'.[19] There is every reason to suspect that this other poet is not Stephen Hawes, as has been claimed,[20] but Alexander Barclay himself. Gordon adduced that 'gorbellyd Godfrey' was Hawes because of the similarity between that name and the name of a misshapen dwarf, 'Godfrey gobylyue' who occurs in Hawe's *Passetyme of Pleasure*.[21] 'Godfrey', however, is an ironic name that is frequently applied, in various alliterative combinations with adjectives beginning with 'g', to other nefarious types in the early Tudor period. Barclay himself uses it in his *Eclogues* to refer, I believe, to none other than Skelton. Replying to Cornix's assertion that 'a ribaudes blame is commendation', Coridon says:

> Nowe truely my heart is eased with the same,
> For *Godfrey Gormand* lately did me blame.
> And as for him selfe, though he be gay and stoute,
> He hath nought but foly within and eke without.
> To blowe in a bowle, and for to pill a platter,
> To girne, to braule, to counterfayte, to flatter,
> He hath no felowe betwene this and Croydon,
> Saue the proude plowman (Gnato) of Chorlington.
> Because he alway maligneth against me,
> It playne appereth our life doth not agree.
> For if we liued both after one rate,
> Then should I haue him to me a frendly mate.[22]

In late 1513–early 1514, when the *Eclogues* were worked up, the most likely recent occasion for vituperation would have been the Garnesche-Skelton flytyng, and in this passage Barclay seems to be reliving the encounter. Godfrey Gourmand, he says, is unmatched in his dubious ability

> To blowe in a bowle, and for to pill a platter,
> To girne, to braule, to counterfayte, to flatter.

This picks up the level of Skelton's own vituperative manner when, for example, he abuses Garnesche:

> Ye bere yow bolde as Barabas, or Syr Terry of Trace.
> Ye gyrne grymly with your gomys and with yor grysly face.[23]

---

[19] *Agenst Garnesche* (ii), Skelton, *Poems*, ed. Scattergood, p. 123, ll. 29–36.
[20] By Ian Gordon, 'A Skelton Query', *Times Literary Supplement*, 15 November 1934, p. 795.
[21] *The Passetyme of Pleasure*, ed. William Edward Mead, Early English Text Society, Original Series, no. 173 (London, 1928), p. 141/3746.
[22] *Eclogues*, I, ll. 837–48. My italics.
[23] *Agenst Garnesche*, (ii), ll. 11–12.

Barclay is thus purloining Skelton's style and adapting the sobriquet Skelton had given him in order to throw both back in his face. He even alludes to the idea that must have formed the main line of his attack on Skelton, when he declares that his opponent's life-style and his own do 'not agree'. Skelton's own verses confirm that this was one of the main tactics used by his opponent to slander him. Warning Garnesche that he, Skelton, has detected the hand of his 'skrybe' behind his letter, Skelton adds:

> I caste me nat to be od
> With neythyr of yow tw[ey]ne:
> . . .
> Lewedely your tyme ye spende,
> *My lyvyng to reprehende.*[24]

This implies that Garnesche and his poet have singled out improprieties in Skelton's personal life (he kept a concubine) as ammunition for an *ad hominem* attack, which is entirely consistent with the attitude Barclay displays towards Skelton elsewhere. In the *Eclogues* he refers to him in thinly veiled terms as having been 'decked as Poete laureate, / When stinking Thais made him her graduate',[25] and in *The Life of Saint George* he asserts that 'he which is lawreat / Ought nat his name with vyce to vyolate', implying that at least one notable laureate (that is, Skelton) had done so.[26]

One final piece of evidence exists to clinch the identification of Barclay as the poet Garnesche hired to counter Skelton. John Bale attributes to Barclay a work to which he gives the Latin title *Contra Skeltonum*.[27] In the light of the other evidence, it would seem probable that this work, no longer extant, is the missing side of the flytyng, the counterblast to Skelton's *Agenst Garnesche*.

Time has obliterated any further traces of the quarrel between Barclay and Skelton, but we do know that it left him with an abiding detestation of his rival, and resentment at his success. He had good reason to be perturbed. Skelton, the charismatic court wit, was in tune with the times, and Barclay, the sage and serious moralist, was not. If he were indeed the rival poet in the Garnesche flytyng, the whole experience must have shown him that he could not expect to find advancement at court, far less fit comfortably into it. He was left with no option but to seek a living elsewhere, and he found one by becoming a Benedictine monk at the cathedral house of Ely. It was here that he drew breath, and

---

[24] Ibid., (iii), ll. 1–16. My italics. Scattergood prints 'tewyne'.

[25] *Eclogues*, IV, ll. 685–6.

[26] *The Life of Saint George*, ed. William Nelson, Early English Text Society, Original Series, no. 230 (London 1955), p. 14/113–19.

[27] John Bale, *Index Britanniae scriptorum*, ed. Reginald Lane Poole, Anecdota Oxoniensia (Oxford, 1902), p. 19.

chose the moment to reflect on the meaning of his experience in his next major literary work, his five pastoral *Eclogues*.

The first three of Barclay's five *Eclogues* were printed separately by Wynkyn de Worde at an unknown date, and form a discrete group on their own. They may have been written earlier in Barclay's career, for he says in the 'Prologe' that he had first compiled the *Eclogues* in youth; then, having rediscovered them accidentally, has worked them up, 'adding and bating where I perceyved neede.'[28] This protestation closely imitates the Dedicatory Epistle of Mantuan's *Eclogues*,[29] and as such may be largely convention, but references to Henry VII as recently dead and Dudley and Empson as traitors suggest that there may have been some truth in it.[30] Also, whereas Mantuan refers to himself as 'quinquagenarius', Barclay declares that he is 'fortie yere saue twayne'.[31] The more specific age of 38 suggests a particular occasion for the work and, given other internal references dating the *Eclogues* to 1514, it seems likely that the occasion was Barclay's entry into the Benedictine monastery at Ely after his encounter with Skelton in the Garnesche flytyng. Such circumstances would explain the bitterness Barclay still shows towards Skelton, as when he sardonically contrasts his own black monk's robes with the green robe Skelton had been given as *orator regius*:

> No name I chalenge of Poete laureate.
> That name vnto them is mete and doth agree
> Which writeth matters with curiositee.
> Mine habite blacke accordeth not with grene,
> Blacke betokeneth death as it is dayly sene,
> The grene is pleasour, freshe lust and iolite,
> These two in nature hath great diuersitie.
> Then who would ascribe, except he were a foole,
> The pleasaunt laurer vnto the mourning cowle.[32]

While Barclay disavows any ambition to gain the reputation and position that Skelton has, the ironic tone and his insistence on the blackness of his cowl, with its symbolism of mourning, nevertheless betrays more than a hint of sadness and self-pity.

Eclogues I–III translate the *De Curialium Miseriis* by Aeneas Sylvius Piccolomini, later Pope Pius II, but in the course of doing so transforms the original.

Piccolomini's satire on life at the imperial court is written in the form of a Latin prose letter to John Aich. Barclay recasts it as three pastoral dialogues spoken

[28] *Eclogues*, I, ll. 65–79.
[29] Quoted by White, *Eclogues*, p. 220, n. 7.
[30] Ibid., p. lvii.
[31] *Eclogues*, I, l. 69.
[32] Ibid., I, ll. 104–12.

between two shepherds – Cornix, who is old and experienced, and Coridon, who is young, inexperienced, and eager to escape his life of poverty in the country by finding a place at court. Cornix gradually talks him out of this plan by describing to him all the miseries of courtiers.[33]

Barclay's decision to present this anti-court satire in the form of the pastoral dialogue has been denounced as 'ideally unfortunate'.[34] It is no such thing, for the associations inherent in the pastoral conventions meant that Barclay could exploit them as a metaphor for his own situation as a self-imposed exile in Ely. The device of 'shepherds' perfectly suggested the religious vocation of Barclay and his fellow monks, and the traditional setting of the countryside accurately signified his location. Moreover, the countryside had conventionally been attributed with greater innocence, happiness, and virtue than the city, and so the pastoral genre helped Barclay justify his failure to gain preferment at court, on the grounds that his current situation was in any case superior.

The pastoral genre, therefore, helped Barclay to turn Piccolomini's satire into a vehicle for self-projection and self-assertion. The original attack is an extended literary paradox in which Piccolomini proves that all who dwell at court are fools because, in seeking honour, praise, power, wealth, and pleasure, they end up with the opposites of these things. Barclay dutifully reproduces the substance of Piccolomini's proof, while suppressing the element of facetiousness in the original, so that it becomes a serious statement of his own fictionalized reaction to court. *Eclogue I* proves that the honour to be found there is false honour because it arises neither from virtue nor merit – and itemizes the disadvantages of power and riches.[35] *Eclogue II* describes how any pleasures offered to the five senses are outnumbered by unpleasant experiences, such as drinking out of cups 'in which some states or dames late did pis', or eating fish that is 'corrupt, ill smelling, and fiue dayes olde'.[36] *Eclogue III* expands the catalogue of miseries: having to put up with the farting, snorting, and stinking breath of unwelcome bedfellows; the difficulty of getting stipends paid; and the horrors of a troubled conscience.[37] Barclay deliberately obscures the careful structure of the original by introducing Coridon as an interlocutor, who breaks in to voice doubts and queries. His interruptions add a verisimilitude that helps to disguise the rhetorical character of the original, so that its points may be taken more seriously

The dialogue form of the *Eclogues* was just as useful to Barclay as the generic conventions of the pastoral, for he needed not only to justify a life away from court, but also to reconcile himself to his rural existence. By changing Piccolo-

[33] *Aeneae Sylvii Piccolominei . . . opera quae extant omnia* (Basel, 1557), pp. 720–36.

[34] Berdan, *Early Tudor Poetry*, p. 242; cf. C. S. Lewis, *English Literature in the Sixteenth Century*, p. 131.

[35] *Eclogues*, I, ll. 719–910, 911–1072, 1073–308.

[36] Ibid., II, ll. 642, 783.

[37] Ibid., III, ll. 82–112, 265–74, 620–42

mini's epistle into a series of dialogues, Barclay turned the *Eclogues* into an instrument for 'establishing his will', through confronting doubts in order to overcome them. By personifying his own divided impulses as two separate characters, Barclay was able to dramatize as an external action, an internal process of self-persuasion.

Cornix and Coridon both reveal traces of their creator. In a passage that has no source in Piccolomini, Cornix who is old and experienced, says that in youth he dwelt in Croydon, and often brought coals to sell at court, where 'none regarded me'.[38] Barclay mentions Croydon so often that his biographers have supposed that he resided there as a boy. The fact that he was buried in Croydon in 1552 lends some credence to this supposition.[39] In some respects, therefore, Cornix is likely to embody aspects of Barclay's older, disillusioned self. Coridon, on the other hand, the young man who is tired of country life and does not want to live in poverty any longer, shows the same belief in his own worthiness and capacity that Barclay had projected in *The Ship of Fooles*. 'I were a man mete to serue a prince or king', he declares, and later adds:

If I had frendes I haue all thing beside,
Which might in court a rowme for me prouide.[40]

Coridon may therefore represent some of Barclay's own earlier expectations. By setting the two together in a debate, during which Cornix talks Coridon out of seeking a place at court, Barclay attempted to allay doubts about his chosen course that still troubled his mind.

The youthful Coridon acts as the devil's advocate. When Cornix asserts that a life at court is merely vile and full of shame, Coridon asks why, if that is really so, have there been so many 'worthy shepheardes' such as 'the riche shepheard which woned in Mortlake' (John Morton, Archbishop of Canterbury and Lord Chancellor), or John Alcock (the 'cock in the fens'), Bishop of Ely, Master of the Rolls, and also Lord Chancellor.[41] All that Cornix is able to reply, is that things have got a lot worse since they died, and that any good shepherds who resorted to court went there against their will.[42] Here we see Barclay struggling against his fear that virtue and a life at court may not, indeed, be incompatible, as the worthiest churchmen have always enjoyed high rank there. To admit this would be to deprive himself of the comforting thought that it was his virtue that had prevented him from getting court patronage. However lame Cornix's reply, it does show Barclay using the dialogue to confront the sources of lingering perturbation in his mind.

---

[38] Ibid., I, ll. 389–93.
[39] See T. H. Jamieson (ed.), *The Ship of Fools* (Edinburgh, 1874), I, p. xxxi; White, p. viii.
[40] *Eclogues* I, ll. 328, 353–4.
[41] Ibid., I, ll. 494–550.
[42] Ibid., I, ll. 545–6, 557–9.

Another instance occurs when he makes Coridon catch Cornix out on an inconsistency over his attitude to wealth:

> Cornix, thy promise was not to preache,
> But me of the courtiers misery to teache.
> Against thine owne selfe thou speakest nowe perdie,
> For first thou grutched against pouertie.
> Agayne, thou blamest plentie of riches nowe,
> But fewe men liuing thy saying will alowe.
> For without riches, thou sayest openly
> Uertue nor cunning nowe be nothing set by.[43]

The terms in which this paradox is put are not in the source, and reflect Barclay's awareness that he is making Cornix protest too much. In reply, Cornix havers: it is not wrong for a man to possess riches, but for riches to possess the man. The idea is commonplace, but its inclusion at this point dangerously threatens the premise of the case Cornix has been trying to maintain – that a life of poverty in the country is preferable to a wealthy one at court. For the rest of his life Barclay tried energetically to touch money, which exposes a degree of disingenuousness in the attitude propounded in the *Eclogues*.

Indeed, many traces of regret and resentment remain in the *Eclogues*, as when Cornix claims that the kind of power gained at court is worthless:

> There none hath honour by vertue and cunning,
> By maners, wisedome, sadnes nor good liuing.
> But who hath power, hye rowmes or riches,
> He hath moste honour and laude of more and lesse.
> *For what poore man, a playne and simple soule,*
> *Though he were holy as euer was Saint Powle,*
> *Haste thou euer seene exalted of a king*
> *For all his maners and vertuous liuing.*
> These be the wordes of Shepherde Siluius,
> Which after was pope, and called was Pius.[44]

Even though the words italicized in this passage are a fairly close translation from Piccolomini's Latin,[45] Barclay's need to remind the reader that the words are Piccolomini's and not his own suggests that he felt their relevance to his own personal situation was in danger of becoming rather too apparent. Passages in other works too enhance the probability that Barclay was investing these lines

---

[43] Ibid., I, ll. 1123–30.

[44] Ibid., I, ll. 729–38. My italics.

[45] 'Nam quem vnquam pauperem, tametsi praestanti virtute praeditum, Regum aliquis sublimauit?' (White, p. 25).

with more than a little self-interest. In *The Mirrour of Good Maners*, for example, he wrote:

> When from this wretched life at last thou must depart,
> And come to heauen gates to see the eternall king,
> It shall not be asked what countrey man thou art,
> Frenche, English, Scot, Lombard, Picard or Fleming,
> But onely shalbe asked thy merite and liuing,
> *A poore Scot of good life shall find him better then,*
> *Then some riche Lumbarde, or noble English man.*[46]

Barclay, who was a Scot,[47] seems to have thought that his nationality, as well as his poverty, had acted as a barrier to preferment. In spite of the homiletic platitudes Barclay utters in the *Eclogues*, therefore, he was sufficiently honest to allow his grievances and regret to show through.

As a result of Barclay's fictive strategy, a final, perhaps unintended paradox emerges: whereas Barclay wrote the work to warn those seeking court patronage that they were better off without it, his fiction betrays his own ambivalence on that score. Predictably, Cornix ends up voicing the conventional exhortation:

> Flee from the court, flee from the court I crye,
> Flee proude beggery and solemne miserye.[48]

Coridon accepts this as wise advice, but in a passage of Barclay's own invention, he asks about the alternative:

> But tell me Cornix one thing or we departe,
> On what maner life is best to set my harte?

---

[46] *Stultifera nauis . . . The Ship of Fooles . . . Translated out of Latin into Englishe by Alexander Barclay Priest* (1570), ed. Cawood, sig. F6ᵛ. My italics.

[47] For the evidence of Barclay's Scottish origins, see Jamieson, pp. xxv–xxx. It seems not to have been noticed that Skelton corroborates this disputed point. In *Collyn Clout* he criticizes the monks for being slack in refuting heresy, and lists those who could effectively do so. Having scanned the other three orders, when he comes to the black friars he makes the following observation, unquestionably with reference to Barclay:

> Or elles the poore Scot,
> It must come to his lot
> To shote forthe his shot.

(Skelton, *Poems*, ed. Scattergood, p. 265, ll. 749–51.) Either this is an allusion to the passage quoted from *The Mirrour of Good Maners*, or else Barclay's complaint at the discrimination he suffered because he was a Scotsman had become sufficient of a mannerism for Skelton to be able to mock it thus.

[48] *Eclogues*, III, ll. 779–80.

In court is combraunce, care, payne, and misery,
And here is enuy, ill will and penury.[49]

In this passage Coridon is altering the terms on which the attack was predicated: that a life in the country is preferable to one at court. Coridon's words let slip a realization that rural life has its own miseries. All that Cornix can offer, ultimately, is the necessity for stoical endurance:

> CORNIX.
> Sufferaunce ouercommeth all malice at the last,
> Weake is that tree which can not bide a blast,
> But heare nowe my counsell I bid thee finally,
> Liue still a shepheard for playnly so will I.
>
> CORIDON.
> That shall I Cornix thy good counsell fulfill,
> To dye a shepheard established is my will.[50]

Coridon concurs, but it takes an effort of will, suggesting that he, like Barclay, is making the best of a bad deal.

The ambivalence generated in *Eclogues I–III*, shows why fiction was so useful to those who had to confront the realities of early Tudor politics. Because of its capability for representing or figuring forth experience, it could be used as a device for dramatizing and objectifying tensions that arose from personal predicaments such as Barclay's, or Skelton's (as was shown in the previous chapter). The distinctive complexity of early Tudor literature arises from its need to confront such predicaments.

The other one of Barclay's *Eclogues* to have a political bearing, the fourth, serves a completely different function. It is a skilfully contrived bid for patronage which makes the protestations of the first three eclogues seem all the more disingenuous.

Based on Mantuan's fifth eclogue, Barclay's *Eclogue IV* treats of 'the behavour of Rich men agaynst Poetes', in the form of a dialogue between Codrus, who has riches but lacks wisdom, and Minalcas, a poet 'with empty belly and simple poore aray'.[51] In the course of their talk Minalcas laments the difficulty of attaining the kind of financial support that would enable him to write, and then, when he agrees to sing a song for Codrus in exchange for a fee, discovers that even he finds a pretext for putting off the promised payment. The effectiveness of the work depends upon its function as an indirect means of negotiation between Barclay as suppliant and the second Duke of Norfolk as prospective patron.

---

[49] Ibid., III, ll. 811–14. My italics.
[50] Ibid., III, ll. 815–20.
[51] Ibid., IV, l. 26.

As in *Eclogues I-III*, Barclay makes sure that the details of the pastoral context reflect his personal situation. In a long autobiographical insertion of 140 lines he projects his discontent with monastic life at Ely, through the unhappiness of Minalcas with his pastoral lot. Minalcas is 'wery of shepheardes company', hates the isolation, mud, and stink of the fens, and resents being poor when other shepherds are rich:

> Seest thou not Codrus the fieldes rounde about
> Compassed with floudes that none may in nor out,
> The muddy waters nere choke me with the stinke,
> At euery tempest they be as blacke as inke:
> Pouertie to me should be no discomforte
> If other shepheardes were all of the same sorte.
> But Codrus I clawe oft where it doth not itche,
> To see ten beggers and halfe a dosen riche,
> Truely me thinketh this wrong pertition,
> And namely sith all ought be after one.[52]

Minalcas, in fact, has suffered a rude shattering of his expectations:

> When I first behelde these fieldes from a farre
> Me thought them pleasant and voyde of strife or warre,
> But with my poore flocke approching nere and nere
> Alway my pleasour did lesse and lesse appeare,
> And truely Codrus since I came on this grounde
> Oft vnder floures vile snakes haue I founde.[53]

However unpleasant the physical environment may be, 'yet the dwellers be badder then the place.' Minalcas has encountered brawling and envy amongst the shepherds, who have shown hatred and malice towards him because he is a newcomer whose learning they resent. As a result Minalcas is determined 'to seke a newe pasture', so long as he can be assured that it will improve his conditions.[54] If these details are translated into the autobiographical facts they signify, one can infer that Barclay was highly disillusioned with life in the monastery at Ely, and was seeking to change it for something better. In particular, he wanted leisure and material support. When Codrus asks him why he no longer 'endites', Minalcas replies that being a shepherd absorbs all his energy in tending his flock, whereas 'a stile of excellence / Must haue all laboure and all the diligence'; Minalcas cannot do both. Also, a poet needs material comfort to produce good work, for

[52] Ibid., IV, ll. 52, 93–102.
[53] Ibid., IV, ll. 103–8.
[54] Ibid., IV, ll. 123, 124–33, 134–5.

. . . without repast who can indite or sing:
It me repenteth, if I haue any wit,
As for my science, I wery am of it.
And of my poore life I weary am, Codrus,
Sith my harde fortune for me disposeth thus.[55]

Barclay's piety, however genuine, was evidently not strong enough to expunge the wordly ambition that he had earlier shown.

When Codrus advises several remedies, the terms in which Minalcas rejects them imply the particular frustrations Barclay had felt. Codrus suggests, first, that he seek to join the service of a rich prelate:

Thou well perceyuest they be magnificent.
With them be clerkes and pleasaunt Oratours,
And many Poetes promoted to honours,
There is aboundaunce of all that men desire.[56]

Minalcas laments, however, that all the former bounteous ecclesiastical patrons such as Morton, are dead and 'They, nor their like shall neuer returne agayne.' Minalcas, therefore, has given up any idea of finding that kind of patronage, and has now trimmed his sights so that he is prepared to accept a more modest kind of advancement:

Graunt me a liuing sufficient and small,
And voyde of troubles, I aske no more at all.
But with that litle I holde my selfe content,
If sauce of sorowe my mindes not torment.[57]

The fact that these passages are more particular than anything in Mantuan's original makes it probable that they describe Barclay's actual experience.

Barclay also seems to have given up hope of gaining any preferment at court. When Codrus proposes that he seek a place in a prince's court, Minalcas observes bitterly that 'the coyne auaunceth' so that only the rich get promotion, and apart from that, all the 'iugglers and Pipers, bourders and flatterers / Baudes and Ianglers, and cursed aduoutrers' who infest the court 'do good Poetes forth of all courtes chase.'[58] Barclay/Minalcas's special resentment is reserved for the 'rascolde poets' who pander to the vices of princes and get decked as Poet Laureate in return. As usual, he has Skelton in mind, and seems to feel that Skelton's success has hindered his chances:

[55] Ibid., IV, ll. 179–80, 226–30.
[56] Ibid., IV, ll. 498–501.
[57] Ibid., IV, ll. 515–18.
[58] Ibid., IV, ll. 545–52, 665–9.

Thus bide good Poetes oft time rebuke and blame,
Because of other which haue despised name.
And thus for the bad the good be cleane abiect,
Their art and poeme counted of none effect.[59]

As if to illustrate his point, Barclay has Codrus offer Minalcas a payment if he will recite 'some mery fit / Of mayde Marion, or els of Robin hood, / Or Bentleyes ale which chaseth well the bloud.' Minalcas refuses to speak about vice or wantonness, but launches instead into a ballad on the moral maxims of Solomon. Eventually Codrus intervenes to shut him up.[60] The whole episode serves as a dramatic exemplum of the claims Barclay has just made. Princes and courtiers want 'vicious' entertainment – the kind of thing Skelton could produce with gusto – while Barclay was only prepared to offer them poetry 'sownynge in vertu', as Chaucer might have said. In Barclay's own mind, and he was probably right, this essential difference between the two poets had barred him unjustly from court promotion.

Up until his ballad on Solomon's wise saws, Barclay had followed Mantuan's fifth eclogue quite closely, because it served admirably as a disguised representation of his own dilemma. Nevertheless, the fourth *Eclogue* was calculated to remedy the dilemma, not just depict it, and to that end Barclay boldly inserts into his source an elegy on the death of Edward Howard, second son of the Duke of Norfolk, who, as Lord High Admiral, was killed in a naval engagement with the French off Brest in 1513. The elegy itself, 'The Towre of Vertue and Honour', is a chivalric allegory of the Franco-Flemish kind, in which Howard contends with the monster Minerva in order to ascend the Tower of Vertue. By writing the poem, Barclay is offering to immortalize the fame and honour that Howard should have attained, had Fortune not maliciously cut him off at the very moment of his success.

The elegy is an elegant compliment in its own right, but it is even more important for its function within the whole *Eclogue*. Being set into a work complaining of the niggardly behaviour of rich men towards poets, it implicitly invites the Duke of Norfolk, to whom it is explicitly and flatteringly addressed, not to imitate them.[61] The ending is designed to make it even more difficult for Norfolk to withhold his bounty, for Codrus, having promised to reward Minalcas for the poem he has just recited, reneges on the agreement and earns Minalcas's parting curse. In the course of his fiction, Barclay has thus managed to depict his need, offer a sample of the flattering panegyrics he can provide for his intended patron, and give a cautionary exemplum of the obloquy which that patron could

---

[59] Ibid., IV, ll. 711–14.
[60] Ibid., IV, ll. 720–2, 791.
[61] Ibid., ll. 1079, 1120, 1132.

suffer should he withhold patronage. In this way, *Eclogue IV* is not merely a plea for patronage, but also a kind of fictional blackmail by proxy.

It worked. Several decades later William Forrest declares, in dedicating his *History of Joseph the Chaiste* to the fourth Duke of Norfolk, that Barclay had commended *The Mirrour of Good Maners* to his great-grandfather, the second Duke, 'withe other workes mo'. These books, continues Forrest, were received 'in acceptation' for their worthiness and noble fame.[62] We know what some of the other works were. Barclay dedicated both his translation of Sallust's *Jugurthine War*, published by Pynson in the early 1520s, and his *Introductory to Wryte and to Pronounce Frenche*, published in 1521 by Copland, to the second Duke of Norfolk, at whose command he says they were compiled. In the prologue to his French primer, Barclay drops hints that it was the Duke's munificence that had stimulated him to write. He explains that whereas he had once used to write diligently to alleviate the dullness of mind of his native countrymen, some time before he had ceased his literary activity; now, however, he has picked up his pen once more:

> lyke as the naked trees depryued of fruyt and leaf stoppeth
> the byrdes tune: & al that wynter depryueth ye somer
> restoreth agayne / ryght so though dyuers causes have
> withdrawen my pen from my olde dylygence / the mocyon of
> certayne noble gentylmen hath renued and excyted me agayne
> to attempt my accustumed besynesse.[63]

Although Barclay does not say explicitly what the diverse causes of his silence had been, they can be inferred from the symbolism he uses. The images of naked trees deprived of fruit and leaf because of the deprivations of winter suggest the poverty and lack of patronage of which he had complained in the *Eclogues*. Likewise, the idea of summer restoring the dearth of winter suggests that the poet has received new bounty, and that that is why his song has resumed.

Other evidence strengthens the likelihood that Norfolk secured for Barclay some of the advancement he desired. It was probably Norfolk who promoted Barclay's interests at court. In April 1520 Sir Nicholas Vaux wrote to Wolsey from Guisnes begging him to send over 'Maistre Barkleye, the Blacke monke and poete, to devise histoires and convenient raisons to florisshe the buildings and banquet house withal' for the meeting of Henry VIII and Francis I at the Field of Cloth of Gold.[64] For Barclay to have been given this important assignment

---

[62] Quoted by White, pp. xxxi–xxxii.

[63] *The Introductory to Wryte and to Pronounce Frenche*, (London, 1521?), sig. A2^r.

[64] *Letters and Papers, Foreign and Domestic, of the Reign of Henry VIII*, ed. J. S. Brewer and others (London, 1862–1932), III, i, no. 737. Hereafter cited as *LP*.

proves two things: first, that he was not as averse to supplying the offices of a court poet as he had pretended in the *Eclogues*, and, second, that his reputation at court had risen considerably.[65] For that to have happened, he would have needed a mediator, and his patron, Norfolk, was undoubtedly the man. Barclay, in fact, ultimately arrived where he had wished to go all along – at court – if only in a rather minor way. As a final piece of corroborating evidence, we have William Forrest's statements in *The Life of the Blessed Virgin Mary* that 'Alexander Barkeleye . . . to the Cowrte dyd eke beelonge', and that 'hee in Courte had manye freynde.'[66] So much for Barclay's disingenuous assertion of the miseries of courtiers.

Barclay's literary output ceased when the second Duke of Norfolk died. He fell out of favour with the administrations of both Wolsey and Cromwell by managing both to flirt with the new religion and also to oppose the royal supremacy.[67] These attitudes, plus his uncompromising moralism, probably cost him his chance of any further advancement. In any case, it had been the problem of gaining patronage that had excited his literary imagination; once he had tasted it, he abandoned both political aspiration and the literary impulse together.

[65] Significantly, Skelton had fallen into disfavour at this time (see Chapter 8 below).

[66] Quoted by White, pp. xxxiii–xxxv.

[67] See White, pp. xlii; xlviii.

4

Patronage and Pedigree:
The Dream Visions of Stephen Hawes

Patronage caused problems for different people in different ways. Skelton suffered in gaining it, Barclay in being excluded from it. For the third major poet of the early sixteenth century, Stephen Hawes, patronage produced a double misfortune: it elevated him to a position where he fell in love with a girl far above his social station, and he lost his place at court by being caught up in factional intrigues. In so far as he was a victim of faction, Hawes's experience was typical of that of many courtiers, but as far as his love affair was concerned, he was uniquely unfortunate in suffering such an irreconcilable clash between personal and social codes.

What makes Hawes so fascinating for the modern reader is the way he tried to use fiction as a means of confronting his situation. In *The Conforte of Louers*, written sometime between April 1510 and April 1511,[1] Hawes depicted two interrelated quests, one political and one erotic, in a single fable. The work was contrived to be an instrument of intercession through which he hoped to regain his place in the royal household, and make known his passion for his mistress. At the same time, the work serves as an instrument of consolation, by holding out the fanciful possibility that both of the poet's wishes could indeed be fulfilled. To achieve his aims Hawes exploited the stereotypical characters, situations, and events of the traditional romantic-epic dream allegory, turning them into a vehicle for personal expression. The form of *The Conforte of Louers* allows it simultaneously to reveal and conceal the autobiographical intent of its author. As a result, the work is full of emotional and thematic complexity, giving it a life and interest far beyond what one would have thought such a tired old genre could yield. As with other early Tudor writers, Hawes's disturbing experience of political realities stimulated him to write more imaginatively than any other aspect of his experience had done before.

---

[1] The title page of the unique copy extant of *The Conforte of Louers* declares that it was compiled 'in the seconde yere of the reygne of our most naturall souerayne lorde kynge Henry the eyght' (British Library, pressmark C. 57. i. 52).

In reality, the fulfilment of Hawes's desires was impossible, so *The Conforte of Louers* turned out to be merely a wish-fulfilment fantasy; but the very fact that he wrote it shows how important imaginative literature was for writers of this age, as a means of mediating between the inner and outer worlds.

Hawes's near incredible story might very well have passed unnoticed had he not drawn attention to it in *The Conforte of Louers*. Without it, all we would have known about him is what Bale and the early biographers tell us: that he studied in several universities, travelled through England, Scotland, and France, and was made a groom of the chamber in Henry VII's household because of the king's admiration for his exemplary virtue and talent.[2] While a member of the royal household (a status he enjoyed from about 1500 to 1509), Hawes fulfilled the usual function of a court poet. In works such as *The Example of Vertu* and *The Passetyme of Pleasure* he wrote allegorical romances in the Burgundian tradition of learned chivalry, so as to satisfy contemporary taste, glorify the Tudor dynasty, and provide a pattern of exemplary achievement for the young prince Henry to imitate.[3] His *Ioyfull Medytacyon to all Englonde of the Coronacyon of our Moost Natural Souerayne Lorde Kynge Henry the Eyght* also shows that he could supply eulogistic verses when the occasion demanded, although no other examples are extant. Superficially, at least, Hawes's career as a literary retainer looks remarkably similar to those of his peers, Bernard André and John Skelton.

The similarity, however, masks an extraordinary difference; Hawes became involved with the personalities of the court in a far more complex way than either André or Skelton did, and his books had a covert purpose that belied their conventional appearance. In *The Conforte of Louers* he explains, in the person of Amour, that he fell in love with a young lady, and that his books were designed to approach her indirectly:

> Dyuers yeres ago / I dyde in mynde retayne
> A lady yonge / a lady fayre of syght
> Good / wyse / and goodly / an holsome sterre of lyght
>
> I durst not speke vnto her of my loue
> Yet vnder coloure I dyuers bokes dyde make
> Full pryuely / to come to my aboue.[4]

Later in the work he repeats this idea:

---

[2] John Bale, *Scriptorum illustrium maioris Brytanniae* (Basel, 1557–9), p. 632. For an account of the few known facts of Hawes's life, see A. S. G. Edwards, *Stephen Hawes* (Boston, 1983), pp. 1–3.

[3] For the Burgundian sources and analogues for Hawes's works, see Gordon Kipling, 'Henry VII and the Origins of Tudor Patronage', pp. 133–4; and Kipling, *The Triumph of Honour*, pp. 22–3.

[4] *Stephen Hawes: The Minor Poems*, ed. Florence W. Gluck & Alice B. Morgan, Early English Text Society, no. 271 (London, 1974), pp. 95–6/89–94. All subsequent references are to this edition.

> This maye I saye / vnto my owne dere loue
> My goodly lady / fayrest and moost swete
> In all my bokes / fayre fortune doth moue
> For a place of grace / where that we sholde mete
> Also my bokes full pryuely you grete.[5]

The lady herself (Pucell) confirms this, and makes it quite clear that it is Hawes's own books that are being talked about, so that, in case it had not already been made plain, the reader is forced to take notice of their autobiographical relevance:

> PUCELL.
> Of late I sawe a boke of your makynge
> Called the pastyme of pleasure / whiche is wond[rous]
> For I thyn[k]e and you had not ben in louynge
> Ye coude neuer haue made it so sentencyous
> I redde there all your passage daungerous
> Wherfore I wene for the fayre ladyes sake
> That ye dyd loue / ye dyde that boke so make.[6]

By linking his erotic material to elements of political allegory that obtrude from time to time, Hawes audaciously prompts the reader into identifying the conventional mistress of the poem with an actual girl at court. Having confessed his love for the girl, Amour (alias Hawes) tells the sage old lady he encounters in his dream that

> . . . many nyghtes / I watched for her sake
> To her and to hers.[7]

As a result of this vigilance, he discovered that his lady's house had powerful enemies plotting against it:

> I dyde perceyue / somwhat of theyr entente
> As the trouthe is knowen / vnto god aboue
> My ladyes fader they dyde lytell loue.[8]

These enemies, whom he describes as 'aboue .xx. woulues', did so 'touse and rent' the poet, 'delynge moost shamefully', that he nearly lost his life. Fear of their malice forced him to dissemble, and dispraise where he loved best, in order to discover their true intent, even though as he says, 'my herte was trewe vnto my

---

[5] *The Conforte of Louers*, ll. 631–5.
[6] Ibid., ll. 785–91.
[7] Ibid., ll. 95–6.
[8] Ibid., ll. 166–8.

ladyes blood'. Some of his enemies launched an attempt to discredit him by wilfully misconstruing his books, but their attempt failed:

> Som[e] had wened for to haue made an ende
> Of my bokes / before [t]he[y] hadde begynnynge
> But all vayne they dyde so comprehende
> Whan they of them lacke vnderstandynge
> Vaynfull was & is theyr mysse contryuynge
> Who lyst the trouthe of them for to ensu[e]
> For the reed and whyte they wryte full true.[9]

Hawes's references to 'my ladyes fader', and 'my ladyes blood', combined with his allusion to 'the reed and whyte', colours signifying the union of the House of Lancaster and York in the Tudor dynasty, irresistibly propel the reader into identifying the poet's beloved as none other than Mary Tudor herself, Henry VII's daughter, sister to the future Henry VIII, and (briefly) Queen of France. The calculated obliqueness with which Hawes intimates the autobiographical allegory makes other identifications theoretically possible, but no other contemporary girl of high rank answers to the details and hints Hawes supplies. If Mary Tudor were indeed the lady in question, which seems likely, Hawes was playing with fire in entertaining such an impossible suit, given his own relatively humble origins.

A comparison of the *The Conforte of Louers* with Hawes's two earlier dream allegories strengthens the identification of the beloved with Mary Tudor. By viewing *The Example of Vertue* (1503), *The Passetyme of Pleasure* (1506), and *The Conforte of Louers* in chronological order, one can trace a process whereby the general is made progressively more particular and personal, and the conventional more literal and actual. These changes register the development in Hawes of an infatuation with the princess that was real and disturbing to him.

In *The Example of Vertu*, written in late 1503 or 1504, no biographical allusiveness can be detected. It is entirely innocent in its bland treatment of the conventions of the didactic dream allegory. The hero is generalized as 'Youth' who is set on an exemplary path towards the attainment of salvation by wisdom, through conquering vice in the form of a dragon symbolizing the world, the flesh, and the devil. Youth, thenceforth called Vertue, is allowed to marry Lady Clennes [Cleanness], and together the two of them ascend to eternal glory in heaven. Clennes has no particularized attributes and elicits no strong emotional response from the hero. At the time when *The Example of Vertue* was written, Mary Tudor would have been only seven or eight years old – too young to excite erotic devotion, at least in normal circumstances. By 1506, when *The Passetyme of Pleasure* was written, she would have been approaching puberty, and by

[9] Ibid., ll. 183–9.

1511–1512 when Hawes wrote *The Conforte of Louers*, she would have been in the full flush of adolescent beauty visible in the portrait that survives of her. By all contemporary accounts, she was exquisitely beautiful.

One can trace the onset of Hawes's attachment to her in the changes that take place between the merely didactic handling of the conventions of the love allegory in *The Example of Vertu* and the personal overtones with which those conventions are invested in his two later dream visions. In *The Passetyme of Pleasure* the structural ingredients are much the same as in *The Example of Vertu*, but changes occur in the characterization. Both the hero, Graunde Amour, and the heroine, la Bell Pucell, are far less allegorical abstractions than Youth and Clennes in *The Example of Vertu*. Furthermore, there is a new emphasis on their youth. We are told that the Pucell has not yet reached eighteen years, the age of adult womanhood, while Graunde Amour repeatedly excuses his lack of literary expertise on the grounds that he is 'but yonge'.[10] At one point he congratulates himself on having 'past all chyldly ygnoraunce / The .xxj. yere of my yonge flourynge aege', but one senses that if this is so, he is not long past it.[11] More strikingly, there is a new stress on the superior social status of the girl compared with that of Graunde Amour. This is reflected in his despairing cry to Counsel, his guide:

> Alas quod I / she is of hye degre
> Borne to grete londe / treasure and substaunce
> I fere to sore / I shall dysdayned be
> The whiche wyll trouble / all my greuaunce
> Her beaute is / the cause of my penaunce
> I haue no grete lande / treasure and ryches
> To wynne the fauoure / of her noblenesse.[12]

As a groom of the Privy Chamber, coming from relatively humble origins, Hawes was writing from the heart: his dilemma was *real*, not just conventional.

Similarly, the meeting between Graunde Amour and the girl is described in terms that evoke real people in an actual encounter. In *The Example of Vertu* the details of the first meeting of the two lovers are determined strictly according to the poet's didactic purpose, and the underlying *significatio* is made perfectly plain: the 'stormy troublous & wawy water' separating Youth from Clennes signifies the vanities of the world, and the bridge by which he is able to pass over to her signifies the purity and steadfastness of religious belief that are necessary

---

[10] *The Pastime of Pleasure*, ed. William Edward Mead, Early English Text Society, original series, no. 173 (London, 1928), ll. 1868, 2924.

[11] Ibid., ll. 3053–4.

[12] Ibid., ll. 1849–55.

for overcoming those vanities.[13] There is no actual interchange between Youth and Clennes. Sapyence simply puts Youth's case to Clennes's father for her hand; her father, who is King of Love, imposes the condition that Youth must slay the three-headed dragon (whose heads represent the world, the flesh, and the devil); and upon the successful completion of his quest, Youth is married to Clennes with very little ado.[14] Genuine emotion does not appear to enter into this allegorical marriage of virtue and purity.

In *The Passetyme of Pleasure*, the meeting of the lovers is very different. Graunde Amour first meets the Pucell in a temple within the Tower of Music at which a 'great solempnyte' is taking place.[15] As he recounts to Counseyle, Graūnde Amour stood near where she was sitting at the feast, and was later commanded to dance with her. As a result, the lover found himself helplessly trapped in a deep infatuation.[16] These details are far more specific than the allegory requires, which reinforces the possibility that Hawes is drawing upon his own experience. Moreover, the details also correspond to known historical facts. In 1506, about the time that Hawes commenced writing *The Passetyme of Pleasure*, Henry VII mounted a reception for Philip, King of Castile at Windsor, during which Mary Tudor danced, and played the lute.[17] Hawes, as a groom of the Chamber, would have been required to attend the feast, in just the capacity he describes. The reception for King Philip may thus have been the actual model for the fictive episode in Hawes's poem, and even if it were not, it illustrates the kind of experience at court that could have released his infatuation for the young princess.

Other details help to transform the allegorical relationship of lover and beloved into a literal one, and at the same time further point to Mary Tudor as the object of Hawes's passion. The Pucell herself reminds Graunde Amour that she is not free to love as she pleases:

> Yf I drede you / it is therof no wondre
> With my frendes / I am so sore kepte vnder
> I dare not loue / but as they accorde
> They thynke to wedde me / to a myghty lorde.[18]

Even before the reception for the King of Castile, Henry VII had been using his daughter Mary as a pawn in the game of diplomacy. In 1505 he had a report spread that she was sought in marriage by Emmanuel, King of Portugal, for his

[13] *The Example of Vertu*, ll. 1240–81.
[14] Ibid., ll. 1345–72; 1549–611.
[15] *The Pastime of Pleasure*, ll. 1465–72.
[16] Ibid., ll. 1765–85.
[17] *DNB*, XII, p. 1282.
[18] *The Pastime of Pleasure*, ll. 2202–5.

son.[19] Then when Philip of Castile was dead, he arranged a match between Mary and Philip's son, Charles, the future Emperor, with the proxy marriage taking place in December, 1508.[20] It is small wonder, then, that Hawes depicts the Pucell, both in *The Passetyme of Pleasure* and *The Conforte of Louers*, as constrained by marriage arrangements she is powerless to resist. Regardless of any feelings she may have had for the poet, she is clearly beyond his reach, both because of her social status, and also because of contractual arrangements that have already been made for her own marriage:

> PUCELL.
> Ryght lothe I were to se your myschefe
> For ye knowe well / what case that I am yn
> Peryllous it wolde be / or that ye coude me wyne.[21]
>
> It shoulde be harde / to gete to your aboue
> Me for to loue / I dyde not you constrayne
> ye knowe what I am / I knowe not you certayne
> I am as past your loue to specyfy.[22]
>
> But as touchynge your loue and fauoure
> I can not graunt / neyther fyrst ne last
> ye knowe what I am / ye knowe my loue is past.[23]

As before, the lady is not free to marry whomever she pleases:

> I can not do / but as my frendes deuyse
> I can no thynge do / but as they accorde
> They haue me promest / to a myghty lorde.[24]

In *The Passetyme of Pleasure* the Pucell had already warned the poet that these arrangements would mean she would have to travel overseas:

> I must departe / by the compulcyon
> Of my frendes I wyll not you begyle
> Though they me lede / to a ferre nacyon.[25]

Right up until mid 1514, two years after *The Conforte of Louers* was written, it appeared as if the proxy marriage between Mary Tudor and Charles would take

---

[19] *DNB*, XII, p. 1282.
[20] Ibid., pp. 1282–3.
[21] *The Conforte of Louers*, ll. 775–7.
[22] Ibid., ll. 815–18.
[23] Ibid., ll. 831–3.
[24] Ibid., ll. 859–61.
[25] *The Pastime of Pleasure*, ll. 2277–9.

effect, so it seems likely that both *The Passetyme of Pleasure* and the later poem are structured around this possibility.

Comparison of Hawes's three dream visions so far has revealed a progressive particularization of courtly love conventions in order to reflect a real-life situation. One further significant change of detail shows the process at work. *The Passetyme of Pleasure* greatly humanizes Graunde Amour and the Pucell compared with the lovers in *The Example of Vertu*, but their relationship is still too close to the conventional stereotype for it to reflect Hawes's real predicament with sufficient incisiveness. The Pucell reciprocates Graunde Amour's love, and after the overcoming of all obstacles, the two are finally married and live happily together until they die. In terms of autobiographical relevance, this is sheer wish-fulfilment. In *The Conforte of Louers*, however, even though in most other respects the relationship is unchanged, Amour now admits that the Pucell has never shown him any token that could ever have led him to believe his suit would be successful:

> O moost fayre lady / yonge / good / and vertuous
> I knewe full well / neuer your countenaunce
> Shewed me ony token / to make me amerous
> But what for that / your prudent gouernaunce
> Hath enrached my herte / for to gyue attendaunce
> Your excellent beaute / you coude no thynge lette
> To cause my herte vpon you to be sette.[26]

Similarly, the poem ends without showing, or even promising, any future happiness for the two lovers. The Pucell agrees to let Venus and Fortune determine the outcome, and the poet is left with the consolation of a vain hope. As Hawes allowed the conventions he was using to reflect more of his personal situation, they correspondingly lost their power to offer any of the archetypal satisfactions that the courtly love tradition had allowed for.

Hawes's erotic attachment to Mary Tudor might never have passed beyond the bounds of private fantasy into expression had it not become bound up with political problems he suffered as a result of his partisan loyalty to Henry VII. In this respect, too, *The Conforte of Louers* elliptically suggests what those political difficulties were.

At the beginning of the poem, Hawes depicts himself as being 'with sorowe opprest / and grete incombrement' because he has not prevailed with his lady, lacks reward according to his merit, and is in need of protection against enemies who are seeking to destroy him.[27] The reason why he has neither prevailed with

---

[26] *The Conforte of Louers*, ll. 645–51.
[27] Ibid., ll. 32–42.

his lady nor received due reward is hinted at in his dream. When he meets the sage old woman guide figure, she observes to him that 'ye haue caught colde / and do lyue in care', an expression that is totally inappropriate in an erotic context, but one which does suggest that the poet is suffering some sort of political disfavour. It is this disfavour that has caused him to be separated from his lady.[28]

The same idea is expressed in a series of remarkable poems in a manuscript miscellany compiled in the 1520s and 1530s, Bodleian MS Rawlinson C. 813. Poems number 13, 14, 15, and 16 rework stanzas from *The Passetyme of Pleasure* and *The Conforte of Louers* into a series of lover's complaints.[29] One passage in poem number 14 is not in either of the two dream visions, but states more explicitly the situation that is hinted at in *The Conforte of Louers*. The poet declares:

> God gyfe me grace with yow sone to dwell
> lyke as I dyd, for to see yow daylye.
> Your louely chere & gentyll cumpanye
> rejoysyde my hart with foode most delycate;
> my eyes to see yow were insacyatte.[30]

Clearly, the poet has previously been in a position where he had daily contact with the beloved, but no longer enjoys that privilege. If one supposes that Hawes had lost his place at court at the accession of Henry VIII, this particular detail makes sense (and incidentally supports the probability that Hawes himself was the compiler of the centos in the Rawlinson manuscript).

Several further references in *The Conforte of Louers* reinforce the suggestion that Hawes had fallen into some kind of disfavour. At one point the poet wishes that Disdain, Strangeness, and False Report could be restrained just as he has been:

> I wolde they were / in warde all doutles
> Lyke as I was / without conforte.[31]

If not actually in prison, the poet has been put under some form of guard or detention. Perhaps Hawes's wistful comment in the proheme that he writes 'as none hystoryagraffe / nor poete laureate', also betrays his awareness that he has lost the chance to enjoy the kind of court positions currently being held by Bernard André and John Skelton under the new regime. In any case, the poet

---

[28] Ibid., ll. 78–9.
[29] See F. M. Padelford and A. R. Benham (eds), 'The Songs in Manuscript Rawlinson C. 813', *Anglia*, 31 (1908), pp. 309–97, esp. pp. 328–46.
[30] Ibid., No. 14, p. 337, ll. 164–8.
[31] *The Conforte of Louers*, ll. 199–200.

wishes for his lady to know of his grief, and of his need to resist the attempts of his enemies to destroy him.

Who his enemies are and what they have been doing, is obliquely insinuated. Hawes tells his dream guide that his life was threatened by 'aboue .xx. woulues' who hated his lady's father (that is, Henry VII). Having spotted their falsehood and treachery, the poet had dissembled his loyalty in order to know the full extent of their cruelty. What he discovered was that they were planning to interfere with the succession to the throne:

> Some had wende the hous for to swepe
> Nought was theyr besom / I holde it set on fyre
> The inwarde wo in to my herte dyde crepe
> To god aboue / I made my hole desyre
> Saynge o good lorde of heuenly empyre
> Let the mou[n]t with all braunches swete
> Entyerly growe / god gyue vs grace to mete.[32]

The symbolic imagery in this passage is deliberately chosen to recall the pageants Henry VII had presented emblematically celebrating the Tudor dynasty as the 'Rich-mount' (that is, 'Richmond').[33] Implicitly, then, the house that these enemies wish to sweep was the Tudor house itself, and by praying that God would allow the 'mount' to grow with *all* its branches, Hawes is declaring his loyalty to Henry VIII as the heir to the throne, in preference to rival claimants whom these enemies have been plotting to support.

Henry VII was plagued throughout his reign by plots against his dynasty, and the royal household, of which Hawes was a member, was the most fertile seedbed of treachery.[34] In 1487 a statute was passed establishing a jury to enquire whether any household member had conspired to murder the king, or the steward, treasurer or controller of the household.[35] In 1495 Sir William Stanley, the lord chamberlain, and John, Lord Fitzwalter, the lord steward and head of the household-below-stairs, were charged with treasonable communication with Perkin Warbeck, a pretender to the crown.[36] Conspiracies continued into the next decade. A letter to Henry VII from Calais written in 1503 by John Flamank, an informer, describes a conversation had by Sir Hugh Conway and other 'grett personages', speculating on what would happen should the king die:

---

[32] Ibid., ll. 176–82.

[33] For further speculations on the anti-Tudor conspiracy, see Fox, 'Stephen Hawes and the Political Allegory of *The Comfort of Lovers*', *English Literary Renaissance*, 17 (1987), pp. 3–21.

[34] See David Starkey, 'Intimacy and Innovation: The Rise of the Privy Chamber, 1485–1547', in *The English Court from the Wars of the Roses to the Civil War*, ed. David Starkey (London and New York, 1987), pp. 71–118, esp. pp. 75–6.

[35] Ibid., p. 75.

[36] Ibid., p. 76.

... some of them spoke of my lorde of Buckyngham, saying that he was a noble man and woldbe a ryall ruler. Other ther were that spake, he said, in lykewyse of your troytor Edmond De la Pole, but none of them, he said, that spake of my lord prynce [that is, Prince Henry].[37]

One of the worries expressed by Conway was that all those preferred to their offices by Giles, Lord Daubeney, the lord chamberlain, were favourable to the cause of Edmund de la Pole, the Earl of Suffolk, and would therefore be hostile to those that 'folow the kyngis plesure and so wildo'.[38] It is thus entirely credible that Hawes should have found himself directly in the firing line between supporters of Henry VII and those who were treasonously plotting to subvert the succession. As a groom of the privy chamber, attending Henry even in the 'secretum cubiculum', as Bale tells us, Hawes was one of the half dozen personal attendants who were closest to the king. It is easy to see how he might have incurred the enmity of those in the outer chamber, numbering hundreds, who were plotting against the king, and believed that Hawes was in a position to do them harm – especially if they suspected that he discerned their aims.

In *The Conforte of Louers*, Hawes implies that this is exactly what happened. Some enemies to the Tudor house tried to neutralize Hawes's influence by preventing him from writing on one hand, and on the other by maliciously interpreting his books so as to turn them into proof of his disloyalty.

It is in these respects that Hawes's secret infatuation with Mary Tudor became entangled with his political dilemma. As Hawes tells the sage old lady, even though he did not dare to express his love to the Pucell directly, he nevertheless found an *indirect* way of addressing her:

> I durst not speke vnto her of my loue
> Yet vnder coloure I dyuers bokes dyde make
> Full pryuely / to come to my aboue.[39]

For some reason his enemies were able to silence him:

> Thretened with sorowe / of ma[n]y paynes grete
> Thre yeres ago my ryght hande I dyde bynde
> Fro my browes for fere / the dropes doune dyde sweet.
> . . .
> Vnto no persone / I durst my hert[e] vntwynde.[40]

---

[37] *Letters and Papers Illustrative of the Reigns of Richard III and Henry VII*, ed. Gairdner, I, p. 233.
[38] Ibid., p. 232.
[39] *The Conforte of Louers*, ll. 92–4. The sense of these lines may cause difficulty. Paraphrased, they might read: 'I could not express my love directly to my mistress, but nevertheless I managed to contrive various books that enabled me indirectly to address this girl, who is my superior in social status.'
[40] Ibid., ll. 134–8.

The highly metaphoric language here is deliberately obfuscating, yet suggestive at the same time. Hawes picks up and develops this symbolic motif of 'hands' near the end of the work:

> Surely I thynke / I suffred well the phyppe
> The nette also dydde teche me on the waye
> But me to bere I trowe they lost a lyppe
> For the lyfte hande extendyd my Iournaye
> And not to call me for my sporte and playe.[41]

The image of the right hand suggests, proverbially, the act of writing and may (as it did with Milton) signify specifically the writing of poetry. By saying that the left hand extended his journey, in spite of the binding of his right, Hawes is implying that, regardless of being intimidated, he was able to find other means of furthering his aims, although he does not specify what those means were.

The threats that were capable of making Hawes stop writing – as he did indeed do between 1506 and 1509 – must remain a matter of speculation, but the most likely explanation is that someone deciphered the oblique profession of devotion to Princess Mary in *The Passetyme of Pleasure*, and threatened to denounce Hawes (possibly even doing so) should he not desist. As a result, Hawes ended up in a situation where, out of concern for self-preservation, he was blackmailed into dissembling both his devotion to Mary Tudor and his partisan loyalty to the dynasty of which she was a member. Consequently, he found himself running with the hares and hunting with the hounds, mistrusted by both sides.

With some sense of this remarkable context that underlies *The Conforte of Louers*, one can begin to discern its functions, which are complex and varied. As its title makes clear, the purpose of the work is to provide 'comfort', but just what the comfort consists of is difficult to discern.

The difficulties arise from the fact that Hawes deliberately confuses the erotic and political levels of signification, so that one cannot be sure whether the poet is primarily seeking comfort as a disappointed lover, or as a disappointed courtier, or both. Furthermore, he plays upon the conventions of the love vision and dream allegory in such a way as to make it uncertain which are to be read simply as conventions, and which as autobiographical allusions pretending to be stereotyped commonplaces.

According to the conventions of the genre Hawes has chosen – the allegorical dream vision – the lover should expect eventually to be granted his suit by his mistress, in spite of all obstacles and objections put in his way. This is what Hawes had already depicted in both *The Example of Vertu* and *The Passetyme of Pleasure*. In *The Conforte of Louers*, however, this expectation is frustrated. We

---

[41] Ibid., ll. 890–4.

are confronted with the paradox of a work whose title and genre promises comfort, and then denies it. All that the Pucell agrees to, is to abide by the arbitration of Venus and Fortune, allowing for the possibility that 'these two ladyes / maye your mynde fulfyll.'[42] In the light of all the insuperable difficulties the Pucell has painstakingly enumerated, the reader is left feeling that a favourable outcome is highly unlikely. The poet, in effect, is no nearer to obtaining his suit than he had been at the beginning.

The real comfort offered is suggested not by the narrative outcome, but resides in the rhetorical and emotional processes of the work. The poet's primary purpose is to find some way of expressing himself, when the very dangerous political circumstances surrounding him would seem to have made such expression impossible. If, as he says, he had not been able to unburden his heart to any person during three years of enforced silence, the emotional pressure would have been acute. Hawes wanted to tell his story, and used all his literary inventiveness in manipulating generic conventions to do so. Thus we have an example of autobiographical revelation under the guise of a conventional love allegory. Disturbances of tonal register force the reader to take notice of non-erotic elements that signal the presence of a political allegory, while the deliberate linguistic obscurity, often resulting from highly metaphoric and proverbial language for which no key is given, challenges the reader to decipher the allegory.

Both devices were to be used later by other poets for similar purposes. When Sir Thomas Wyatt found himself effectively muzzled from complaining about the desertion of Anne Boleyn to the king, he too used erotic conventions as a vehicle for indirect political and personal protest.[43] Likewise, Skelton, when he felt impelled to denounce the abuses of Cardinal Wolsey (in *Speke Parott*), exploited a deliberate obscurity to make his readers take more notice of what he was saying, through requiring from them an unusual effort to discern it. It is only Hawes, however, who combines both strategies in the one poem.

A second purpose for Hawes in writing *The Conforte of Louers* was to work out the nature of his dilemma, in order to grasp the implications it held for his future. He does this by adopting the same distinctively early Tudor device that we have already seen used by Skelton and Barclay – by dramatizing the internal conflicts of his own mind so as to objectify and resolve them. Specifically, he seeks to work out the relationship between his hopes and his despair.

The first stage in this process of dramatization consists of the dialogue between the poet and the sage old lady he encounters at the beginning of the dream. This dialogue allows the poet to unburden his mind through confessing the causes of his despair: the power of his enemies, the general mistrust towards him they have aroused by their libels, and the fall from place and favour which has removed him

[42] Ibid., l. 917.
[43] See Chapter 14 below.

from contact with his beloved.[44] The old lady's reply is designed to offer some interim comfort to the poet by giving him cause for hope. It takes the form of advice on a prudent course of action that will allow him gradually to improve his position. He is to keep a low profile, but nevertheless take care to display his virtues to advantage:

> Be alwaye meke / let wysdome be your guyde
> Aduenture for honoure / and put your selfe in preace
> Clymbe not to fast / lest sodenly ye slyde
> Lete god werke styll / he wyll your mynde encrece
> Begynne no warre / be gladde to kepe the peace.[45]

In particular, he is to try to mollify his enemies:

> Lerne this she sayd / yf that you can by wytte
> Of foes make frendes / they wyll be to you sure
> yf that theyr frendshyp / be vnto you knytte
> It is oft stedfast / and wyll longe endure.[46]

Above all, he is to hold firm to the scriptural belief that after woe comes joy, and trust that God will put things to rights according to his true desert.[47] In this exchange we can see Hawes reassuring himself that all is not lost: that God's providence together with his own prudence can yet win the day.

The second stage in the objectification of the poet's predicament consists of the extraordinary scene in which he gazes into three crystal mirrors magically showing the past, present, and future.[48] This scene is reminiscent of episodes in traditional romances when the hero is ritually armed in preparation for his chivalric quest, but the symbolism of the three mirrors makes it clear that a *mental* arming is taking place. In the first mirror, showing the past, the poet sees the rashness, wildness, and wilfulness that have led him into his present trouble, imaged as a naked sword hanging point downwards by a slender thread. Chastened by this vision, he takes 'forwytte' (or 'forethought') to be his shield. In the second mirror, showing the present, he sees the true nature of political actions and reactions: how craft and treachery self-destruct, and how excessively rapid ascents can be counterbalanced by equally precipitous falls, unless the ground is sure. This insight is figured forth in the flower made of emeralds and diamonds which enables him to perceive the cunning traps his enemies have laid to destroy him. In the third mirror, showing the future, the poet sees the divine power of the

---

[44] *The Conforte of Louers*, ll. 76–252.
[45] Ibid., ll. 155–9.
[46] Ibid., ll. 211–14.
[47] Ibid., ll. 151, 153, 195–6.
[48] Ibid., ll. 309–602.

Holy Spirit, a sword named 'preprudence' and a shield name 'perceueraunce', and finally a vision of his own future triumph, imaged as a knight overcoming those who 'wolde hym resyst by theyr wronge resystynge.'[49] He reads that the sword has been set in a hand of steel by a great lady long ago, and that only one of her kindred, chosen by God, will be able to grasp it. To the hero's great delight, he finds that the mailed hand relinquishes the sword to him, thereby proving that he comes of the lineage of that lady.[50]

Psychologically, this episode was very important for Hawes. It allowed him to objectify his understanding of the mental conditions, as distinct from the mode of action, that could lead him to success. The whole scene is an allegory of his realization that he needs to shed the indiscretion that had got him into trouble in the first place, and replace it with foresight, perception, extreme prudence, and personal insight.

By using the old motif of a sword which yielded itself only to a divinely elected hero whose quality may have been disguised by humble status, Hawes was giving himself further reassurance. One of the main themes in *The Conforte of Louers* is the idea that true nobility will reveal itself by its own natural properties. The poet uses this idea to explain why he cannot help but love the Pucell:

> For yf there were one of the gentyll blode
> Conuayde to yomanry for nourysshement
> Dyscrecyon comen he sholde chaunge his mode
> Though he knewe not / his parentes verament
> Yet nature wolde werke / so by entendyment
> That he sholde folowe / the condycyons doubtles
> Of his true blode / by outwarde gentylnes.[51]

Hawes, who himself came of relatively humble origin, is here insinuating an a posteriori argument that allows for nobility of action to be accepted as a token of true nobility (the idea was, indeed, a commonplace throughout this period, especially in the drama).[52] Implicitly, this notion justifies his love of Mary Tudor. Even though he is of lower social status, the nobility of his sentiments proves him to be her natural equal. The episode at the third mirror repeats this idea. By showing the royal sword yielding itself up to him, Hawes is providing himself with a surrogate pedigree. He is reassuring himself, in his imagination, of his own worth.

Whereas in the first dialogue Hawes confronts his errors in the past, and in the episode with the mirrors he arms himself with understanding of how he must act in the present, in the second dialogue, this time with the Pucell herself, he

---

[49] Ibid., l. 550.

[50] Ibid., ll. 505–11, 575–95.

[51] Ibid., ll. 113–19.

[52] See, for example, the discussion of John Rastell's *Gentylness and Nobylyte* in Chapter 13 below.

attempts to put his knowledge into action. The purpose of this dialogue is to turn *The Conforte of Louers* into an instrument of intercession. In order to achieve this, Hawes adopts a highly imaginative strategy: he reveals dramatically the way the poem is supposed to work, by depicting it literally in the action that takes place within the dialogue.

Hawes shows himself as Amour, in the act of interceding with his beloved. His first aim is to make her aware that *she* is the object of his affections, and that there is no impediment in nature to prevent their attachment. His cunning method of doing this is to convince her that a suit of this kind should be granted, before she knows that she herself is the object of it:

> [Tho]ughe that I be yonge / yet I haue perceueraunce
> [Th]at ther is no lady / yf that she gentyll be
> [An]d ye haue with her ony acquayntaunce
> And after cast / to her your amyte
> Grounded on honoure / without duplycyte
> I wolde thynke in mynde / she wolde condescende
> To graunt your fauoure / yf ye none yll intende.[53]

Having persuaded her to admit what should happen, he traps her in an inconsistency when, having learnt that she is the beloved, she then goes on to tell him that she is beyond his reach. The situation into which Hawes manoeuvres the Pucell exposes a social irony that gives him an implicit moral advantage.

Can Hawes really have hoped to marry the king's sister? Hardly, and the dialogue acknowledges as much. Even though the Pucell insists that his suit for her is impossible, she observes that with his royal flower and sword and shield he should be able to triumph over his enemies, provided that he conducts himself prudently:

> PUCELL.
> . . . gladde I am / yf prudence be your guyde
> [G]race cometh often after gouernaunce
> Beware of foly / beware of inwarde pryde
> Clymbe not to fast / but yet fortune abyde.
>
> Now of trouthe / I do vnto you tell
> The thynge that to your enmyes is moost dyspleasure
> Is for to gouerne you by wysdome ryght well
> That causeth enuy in theyr hertes to endure
> But be ye pacyent and ye shall be sure
> Suche thynges as they ordayne vnto your gref
> Wyll lyght on them to theyr owne myschefe.[54]

---

[53] *The Conforte of Louers*, ll. 757–63.
[54] Ibid., ll. 870–3, 883–9.

Pucell's words here are very similar to the advice given by the old lady in the first dialogue. The recurrence of this idea – that prudent, judicious conduct will preserve the poet against the malice of his enemies – suggests that it was at least as important in Hawes's mind as the thought of Mary Tudor requiting his love. In the second dialogue, in fact, it is treated as the more realistically attainable option. Hawes does not give over entirely the hope that his dream of attaining the Pucell might be fulfilled, but at the end of the poem he agrees to leave the matter to the judgement of Venus and Fortune, and the poem ends perfunctorily within a few lines.

If Hawes did not really expect his erotic aspirations to be satisfied, why then, did he choose to reveal them in this extraordinary work? The most feasible explanation is that he believed he could elicit the support of Mary Tudor for the restoration of his position at court. He had been a loyal supporter of her father, he had been in close proximity for her for a long time. He may have thought, therefore, that it was not unreasonable to hope that she might support him, should he make his personal devotion to her plain – especially if he could make her feel that the Tudors were under some obligation to him. Viewed in this way, *The Conforte of Louers* resembles the specially contrived entertainments put on before foreign ambassadors that emblematically and symbolically foreshadowed the desired outcome of the negotiations at hand. For Hawes, it was not merely an instrument for attaining emotional and mental equanimity, but also the means by which he hoped to recover his place at court under the new regime.

Significantly, the work is left inconclusive and open-ended. Having made his throw, Hawes was content to wait and see what the dice turned up. The absence of any historical trace of him after *The Conforte of Louers* was written suggests that Fortune may have turned her back on him. In the end, no amount of comfort to be devised in a work of imagination could overcome the cruel reality of Tudor social stratification and court factionalism. In such a situation Hawes was doomed to be a victim not a victor, but in attempting to grapple with it, he produced a literary fiction that is endlessly fascinating in its complexity. It was no mean poet who could have contrived it.

PART II

Humanism

5

Suggestions of Mistrust: Erasmus and *The Praise of Folly*

The second major literary stimulus arising out of early Tudor politics was humanism, which was itself an intellectual movement brought into being by the need for reform. By the late fifteenth century, it had become clear to many people that medieval institutions had degenerated to the point where they could no longer provide the spiritual or intellectual sustenance that men and societies required. Europe had witnessed the onset of a cynical worldliness in the church and the spectacle of the Great Schism, with rival popes at Rome and Avignon, each claiming to be the successor of St Peter. Scholastic learning, too, had in many instances become arid, pedantic, and dehumanized, under the influence of the logical subtlety, not to mention sophistry, of the medieval schoolmen. Across Europe a general malaise was felt, particularly in England, where nearly a century of civil war had attended the breakdown of the old political order, and had left most of society in a state of cultural depression.

It was such a state of moral corruption, civil instability, and spiritual impoverishment that humanism believed it could correct. The movement found its most able spokesman in Erasmus of Rotterdam, the Dutch scholar who made his life's work the promotion of a humanist programme for reform. From the earliest significant work of his career, the *Antibarbari*, begun in 1488,[1] to his latest, the *Ecclesiastes* of 1535, the guiding principles of the Erasmian programme remained constant. The welfare of the commonweal, according to Erasmus, depended upon the degree to which the mental life of its people was nurtured in, and by, those who were in a position to exert influence:

> It seems to me that there are three things above all on which hang the safety or sickness of the state: the good or bad education of the prince, the preachers in public places, and the schoolmasters.[2]

[1] For the date of the *Antibarbari*, see *CW Erasmus, 23, Literary and Educational Writings 1*, ed. Craig R. Thompson, p. xix.
[2] *Antibarbari, CW Erasmus*, 24:1, p. 30/19–22.

The most desirable political goals were impossible to attain without a prior moral regeneration in the individual members of society. To this end, education was crucially important in humanist thinking. Erasmus believed that there was no inclination of the mind that could not be retrained and guided by reason.[3] Moreover, virtue could be increased by learning, and learning was most effective when made most delightful. As *Erasmus* was to explain in defending himself for writing *The Praise of Folly*, 'truth by itself is a trifle astringent, and when ... made palatable finds an easier entrance into the minds of mortal men.'[4] To Erasmus, then, the eloquence of the pagan writers made them delectable, and because he also thought that their morality had been largely in concord with the doctrine of Christ, they featured very prominently in the new educational curriculum he devised. There could be no harm in a man 'exercising and sporting' himself in their works, so long as he did not 'wexe olde and dye in them / as he were bounde to the rockes of Syrenes / that is to put his hole delectacyon in them / and neuer go farther.'[5] Indeed, the classical writers furnished a good preparation for the Christian life, if well used:

> Those scyences fassyon and quycken a childes wytte / and maketh hym apte afore hande meruaylously to the vnderstandyng of holy scripture.[6]

Like Cyprian, one should plunder the Egyptians to deck the temple of God with literary riches, by picking out from pagan books whatever is best, as a bee sips nectar from flower to flower.[7] The prime goal, however, should be to arrive at last by a long circuitous route at the place to which the Spirit led the apostles in a very short time;[8] that is, to the philosophy of Christ which 'renders foolish the entire wisdom of the world'.[9] Ultimately, the 'philosophia Christi' is the whole burden of the Erasmian reform effort. As he declares in the *Paraclesis*, if rulers, teachers, and preachers would perform their duty and spread the true precepts of Christ, peace could be restored to Christendom.[10]

Such was the influence of Erasmus that most of the writing produced by English humanists in the early Tudor period is either largely a recitation of Erasmian commonplaces, as in the case of Richard Pace's *De fructu qui ex doctrina percipitur* (1517) and Sir Thomas Elyot's *Boke Named the Governour*

---

[3] *Enchiridion militis Christiani*, in *The Essential Erasmus*, trans. and ed. John P. Dolan (New York, 1964), p. 45.

[4] 'Letter to Maarten Van Dorp' (1515), *CW Erasmus*, 3, p. 115/109–11.

[5] *Enchiridion militis Christiani: An English Version*, ed. Anne M. O'Donnell, Early English Text Society, no. 282 (London, 1981), p. 46/9–10.

[6] Ibid., p. 46/24–6.

[7] Ibid., p. 46/16–17, also see *Enchiridion, Essential Erasmus*, p. 39.

[8] *Antibarbari*, *CW Erasmus*, 24, p. 121/2–4.

[9] *Paraclesis*, in *Christian Humanism and the Reformation: Selected Writings of Erasmus with the Life of Erasmus by Beatus Rhenanus*, ed. John C. Olin, revised edition (New York, 1975), p. 96.

[10] Ibid.

(1531), or else plods faithfully in the footsteps of Erasmus' typical preoccupations. As such, almost all literary activity is sub-fictional, consisting of translations (such as Linacre's translations of Galen, or Barclay's translation of Sallust's *Jugurthine War*); educational treatises (such as those by John Holt, John Stanbridge, and Robert Whittinton); orations in praise of such things as peace (Pace), marriage (Tunstall), and obedience (Sampson); compilations of adages or aphorisms (Elyot's *Bankette of Sapience*); and advice to princes (Elyot's *Doctrinal of Princes* and *The Image of Governance*, and Starkey's *Dialogue between Lupset and Pole*).

The didactic impulse of Erasmian humanism also meant that far less value was placed on fictive literature by Erasmian humanists than one might have supposed. Erasmus himself viewed 'poetry', or 'fables', as the honey which physicians smear on the cup of wormwood.[11] The poets were valuable chiefly as a source of felicitous phrases and metaphors which could be used to create 'variety', so as not to bore one's audience. They could also provide ethical *sententiae* that could be used to reinforce the teachings of the Gospels.[12] Fictional literature, however, was to be read selectively – and allegorically, if necessary – to prevent dangerous impressions being imparted by the depiction of undesirable aspects of experience. Erasmus, in fact, greatly mistrusted uncensored representations of real experience. This was the reason for his coolness towards historical writings:

> Now I would not deny, to be sure, that very considerable wisdom can be gathered from reading the historians, but you will also take in the most destructive ideas from these same writers unless you are forearmed and read selectively.[13]

Neither fiction nor historical writings that saw life steadily and saw it whole were readily to be countenanced. Hence there is surprisingly little imaginative literary activity in early humanism.

When, however, the two greatest humanists of the northern renaissance, Erasmus and Thomas More, allowed themselves to engage in writing genuine fictions, the results were truly astonishing. Such writing allowed each of them a degree of imaginative play that they normally did not enjoy, and this in turn led them to expose problematical aspects of humanism that otherwise lay deeply concealed. The results, to their own surprise and consternation, threatened to subvert humanism itself by showing that when the ideology of the movement was brought face to face with the real nature of the human condition it was found to be wanting. Fiction for Erasmus and More was an unexpectedly useful tool for enlarging their vision, although this function was not the one Erasmus thought he was invoking when he set out to write *The Praise of Folly*. More, on the other

[11] 'Letter to Dorp', *CW Erasmus*, 3, p. 115/111–12.
[12] See *De copia verborum ac rerum*, *CW Erasmus*, 24, pp. 301–2.
[13] *The Education of a Christian Prince*, *CW Erasmus*, 27, p. 251.

hand, consciously used fictive representation in *Utopia* and *The History of King Richard III* to explore aspects of his subjects that lay outside the boundaries of his peripheral vision. In both cases literature of an extraordinary complexity resulted.

It might seem perverse to deal with the greatest internationalist of his age in a book on early Tudor English literature, but there is a very good reason for it: without the fact of his English experience, Erasmus would never have written *The Praise of Folly*. However international its eventual impact and fame, in genesis and character it was an English book, and once Erasmus was removed from the context that influenced it, he never wrote anything comparable again.

Erasmus' English experience, as many scholars have long recognized, was formative. The humanists he met in London and Oxford on his first visit in 1499 – Colet, Grocyn, Linacre, and More – were the first scholars of repute to take him seriously.[14] Colet in particular, influenced him deeply, reinforcing his natural bent towards piety, and encouraging his bible studies. His second trip to England in 1506 gave him the chance to travel to Italy in the company of the sons of Henry VIII's doctor,[15] and it was the fact of returning to this English ambience in 1509, bringing with him the fruits of his Italian experience, that gave Erasmus the confidence and courage to write *The Praise of Folly*.

Above all, Erasmus' friendship with Thomas More was the crucial determinant. As Erasmus himself says, it was while musing on their friendship during the trip back from Italy to England that the idea for *The Praise of Folly* came to him. The similarity between More's surname and the Greek word for folly, *moria*, sharpened Erasmus' sense of the distance between mere folly, and the wisdom of More.[16] By sheer accident, therefore, this fortuitous aural pun presented Erasmus with a paradox that determined the paradoxical mode of the work. Even so, it might still never have seen the light of day had not More possessed a penchant for humour that fascinated Erasmus and had a powerful effect in releasing his own vein of irony. In his letter to Ulrich von Hutten of July 1519 Erasmus says that More took special delight in declamations and paradoxical themes.[17] In fact it was More himself, Erasmus declares, who persuaded him to write the *Moriae encomium*, and in so doing led Erasmus to perform something against his nature by 'making the camel dance'.[18] *The Praise of Folly* was written while Erasmus was staying in More's house at Bucklersbury in London, in response to More's own proclivity for irony and paradox, and for More's delectation in celebration of their friendship.[19] As such, it can hardly be considered without reference to its specifically English, 'Morean', context.

[14] See Margaret Mann Phillips, *Erasmus and the Northern Renaissance* (London, 1949), p. 43.
[15] Ibid., p. 55.
[16] *The Praise of Folly*, CW Erasmus, 27, ed. A. H. T. Levi, p. 83.
[17] Epistle no. 999, CW Erasmus, 7, p. 23/274.
[18] Ibid., p. 19/124–5.
[19] *The Praise of Folly*, CW Erasmus, 27, p. 83.

It is important to recognize this context because it helps explain why, in writing *The Praise of Folly*, Erasmus found himself doing something that was new and untypical for him. He was lured into attempting a kind of fiction that did not readily lend itself to his usual didactic practices. In Erasmus' other literary works he always took care to assert a norm by which the work could be interpreted so as to yield its morally edifying fruit without any ambiguity. In the dialogue *Julius exclusus e coelis* (1513), for example, Pope Julius II represents the perversion of the norm, while St Peter voices the norm, and what he preaches is the *philosophia Christi*. The presence of these negative and positive antitypes means that the dramatic irony is very simple in its working: what Julius thinks bad is presented for our approval as good, and vice versa.[20] Similarly, in *The Colloquies*, as one critic has ably demonstrated, the speakers very carefully put together the 'vehicle' (the fictive analogue through which meaning is offered) and the 'tenor' (the meaning or *significatio*), so that the representation works very much like an epic simile.[21] The paradoxical mode of *The Praise of Folly*, however, produces a fictive representation that has a very different status, and works in an entirely different manner. Paradox, by its very nature, blurs the outlines and undermines the stability of normal rational categories. In particular, it overthrows the stark opposition between right and wrong and good and bad as they are normally conceived. By choosing to present his views through a paradoxical persona, Erasmus was looking for trouble, and he found it – not so much in the outrage the work provoked, which was severe enough, as in the undermining of some of his most cherished notions. The paradoxical mode awakened his consciousness to aspects of human experience that he ordinarily preferred to overlook.

The problem started with Erasmus' decision to narrate the work through a dramatic persona. According to the laws of dramatic decorum, he was obliged to bind himself to act out the character of his persona, 'Folly', who is imaged as a woman personifying the vice signified in her name. Moreover, he had also chosen to make her deliver a declamation in which she is the subject of her own praise – partly to exploit the grammatical pun of '*Moriae encomium*', in which 'Moriae' is both a subjective and objective genitive, and partly as a self-characterizing device to make the point that this is the kind of foolishness to which 'folly' will stoop. Erasmus does not seem to have foreseen that this narrative strategy would deprive him of his customary authorial control over the moral interpretation of the work.

From Erasmus' statements in his prefatory letter to More and his later letter to Dorp it is fairly easy to infer what he set out to do in *The Praise of Folly*. He was

[20] See for example, Julius' denunciation of the church reforms planned by the Council of Pisa, *Julius exclusus, CW Erasmus*, 27, p. 183.

[21] Sister Geraldine Thompson, *Under Pretext of Praise: Satire Mode in Erasmus' Fiction* (Toronto, 1973), pp. 18–19; 104–5.

aiming to laugh men out of folly by praising it, in the hope that the joke would make his censures less acerbic, and hence more palatable:

> I thought I had found a way to insinuate myself in this fashion into minds which are hard to please, and not only cure them but amuse them too.[22]

Properly read, the mock praise of folly was meant to be inverted so as to reveal the pattern of a Christian life according to the philosophy of Christ: 'Nor was the end I had in view in my *Folly* different in any way from the purpose of my other works, though the means differed . . . the *Folly* is concerned in a playful spirit with the same subject as the *Enchiridion*. My purpose was guidance and not satire.'[23]

Erasmus' expectation that the work would be read this way, however, was naive. Because Folly is 'folly', there is no way that she can give any moral guidance without betraying her own nature.[24] The reader, therefore, can have no certain way of knowing when what she says is being offered by the author for moral approval, or is simply facetious and ironic. Furthermore, by casting *The Praise of Folly* as a declamation, Erasmus was also obliged to frame it as a monologue. He therefore deprived himself of the chance of including any other character in the fiction who could provide the kind of normative guidance that St Peter does, for example, in the *Julius exclusus*. Of necessity, Erasmus found that he had to give Folly too large a degree of independence, and once she had been set free, she showed her author rather more about the human situation than he really wanted to see. The vision of life revealed in her paradoxes was one that could not be interpreted or understood by simply reversing the paradoxes. Many of them turned out to be disconcertingly true, and the fact that they could be made to be so showed Erasmus how unstable any human perspective on the meaning of the human condition is liable to be. Also, he found that once he had allowed Folly to praise her own attributes, he was faced with the task of warding off any excessively favourable response on the part of his readers to her subversive viewpoint. The great danger to which Erasmus had made himself vulnerable, was that folly's virtuosity would work against his moral intent. Unless he were to admit that his own moral vision of life was inadequate, he had to try and find some way of reasserting interpretative control over his runaway fiction, and that is what he chose to do. Having been lured into experimenting with a mode that ran counter to his moral and rational certainties, Erasmus got more than he bargained for.

The volatility of Folly's paradoxes is particularly apparent in the opening of *The Praise of Folly*, in which Folly describes her origins and declares the benefits she

---

[22] *CW Erasmus*, 3, p. 115/124–6; cf. *CW Erasmus*, 27, p. 84.

[23] *CW Erasmus*, 3, pp. 114–13/93–100.

[24] Some critics have argued that it is part of the nature of Folly to be accidentally wise on occasions, but this seems, to me, to be stretching the point.

brings to mankind. Paradoxes can be of two types: either arguments against received opinion, or assertions that seem to say something opposite to common sense or the truth. Folly combines both functions in one long sustained paradox in the first section of *The Praise of Folly*, consisting of the idea that Folly is mankind's best friend and the source of all that is gay and happy on earth. The problem for Erasmus was that the praise he bestowed on Folly turned out not to be easily dismissed.

Much of what Folly says, in fact, is capable of being regarded as irrefutably true, depending upon the viewpoint of the reader. This can be seen when Folly discusses marriage to prove that she brings many benefits to mankind:

> Just tell me, please, what man would be willing to offer his neck to the halter of matrimony if he applied the usual practice of the wise man and first weighed up its disadvantages as a way of life? Or what woman would ever agree to take a husband if she knew or thought about the pains and dangers of childbirth and the trouble of bringing up children? So if you owe your existence to wedlock, you owe the fact of wedlock to madness, my attendant Anoia, and can see how much in fact you owe to me. And if a woman has once had this experience, would she be willing to repeat it without the divine aid of Lethe, who helps her to forget?[25]

Within a few pages, Folly has proven that no alliance or association can be stable without folly: the relationships between ruler and people, master and servant, maid and mistress, teacher and pupil, friend and friend, wife and husband, landlord and tenant, soldier and comrade are all held together by illusions, flattery, or else by turning a blind eye to the human deficiencies of those involved.[26]

The effect on the reader is very dislocating because, in the absence of any possibility of disagreeing with Folly with any confidence, the fiction is implicitly confirming that 'folly' has an integral place in human affairs which reason alone cannot explain.

A further difficulty arises from the terms in which decorum obliges Erasmus to depict Folly. She is intent on praising herself, therefore Erasmus needs to allow her to make all her attributes as attractive as possible. Everything surrounding her, however, threatens to become more dangerously attractive than Erasmus' moral scheme can permit. A good example occurs when Folly describes how her father, Plutus, begot her:

> . . . he didn't make me spring from his brain, as Jupiter did that sour and stern Athene, but gave me Freshness for a mother, the loveliest of all the nymphs and the gayest too. Nor was he tied to her in dreary wedlock like the parents of that limping blacksmith, but 'lay with her in love', as Homer

---

[25] *CW Erasmus*, 27, p. 90.
[26] Ibid., p. 98.

puts it, something much more delightful. Moreover, my father was not the
Plutus in Aristophanes (make no mistake about that), half-blind, with one
foot in the grave, but Plutus as he used to be, sound and hot-blooded with
youth – and not only youth, but still more with the nectar he'd just been
drinking, as it happened, neat and in generous cupfuls at a banquet of the
gods.[27]

The satiric intent in this passage is obvious; Erasmus clearly meant his readers to
render it into its implicit moral allegory: folly results from the immoderate
pursuit of material wealth and the irresponsible indulgence of sensual appetites.
The imagery, however, evokes aspects of life that most human beings are likely to
approve – beauty, youth, freshness, spontaneity, passion, love, and happiness –
so that the emotional impact of the imagery works against the ethical lesson that
one is supposed to derive from the passage. Erasmus realized that his readers
would indeed have a favourable response to much of what Folly says, for he
dramatizes it in the fiction itself. When Folly extols pleasure, her audience
applauds:

What would this life be, or would it seem worth calling life at all, if its
pleasure was taken away? I hear your applause, and in fact I've always felt
sure that none of you was so wise or rather so foolish – no, I mean wise –
as to think it could.[28]

Since Folly addresses her audience directly in the second person 'you', her
listeners in the fiction become, implicitly, her readers. The applause Folly hears,
therefore, is the mental approbation that Erasmus anticipates that his readers will
experience.

By contriving the declamation to have this effect Erasmus was making a serious
point: he was trying to trap readers into an awareness of their own complicity in
folly, as an essential precondition for bringing them to share his belief that 'the
common throng of mortals was corrupted by the most foolish opinions, and that
too in every department of life', as he later described it to Dorp.[29] The strategy
nevertheless, was fraught with risks. Quite apart from making it impossible to
assert a stable norm, the paradoxical mode threatened to promote interpretative
confusion. What edifying moral lesson could be drawn from a demonstration
that what you thought bad could be made to seem good, and vice versa? How
was one to act in the unstable moral environment that the possibility of such
transformations predicated? Erasmus seems to have taken fright at the interpretative indeterminacy of his own fiction, and he decided to reimpose moral order on
a situation in which the validity of moral absolutes had been implicitly denied.

[27] Ibid., pp. 88–9.
[28] Ibid., p. 91.
[29] 'Letter to Dorp', CW Erasmus, 3, p. 115/122–3.

Nevertheless, having once chosen this course, Erasmus found that the cat, once it had been let out of the bag, was not so easily put back in. It was at this point that his control over the fiction of *The Praise of Folly* began to falter.

Erasmus' problem was how to reimpose moral order without disrupting the decorum of his fictional strategy. He had to make his readers aware that they were not to be taken in by the apparently persuasive evidence of the benefits of 'folly' that his persona had presented, but, by limiting himself to a single character, he had eliminated almost every viable way of doing so. One would have thought that it was hardly credible for Folly herself to assert a stable moral norm, given her nature and professed intent,[30] but such was Erasmus' determination to free himself from the tyranny of her vision that this was the course he chose. By degrees, Erasmus makes Folly first spot the flaws in her argument, and then change her own nature in order to repudiate it. This was not so much an integral part of her characterization, I am convinced, as a necessity forced upon Erasmus by his original didactic intent.

The first stage in Folly's transformation occurs when she seems to realize that the happiness she offers men is merely a consolation for their inability to fulfil their desires in an imperfect world:

> Nature, more of a stepmother than a mother in several ways, has sown a seed of evil in the hearts of mortals, especially in the more thoughtful men, which makes them dissatisfied with their own lot and envious of another's. Consequently, all the blessings of life, which should give it grace and charm, are damaged and destroyed. What good is beauty, the greatest gift of the gods, if it is tainted by the canker of decay? Or youth, if it is soured and spoiled by the misery of advancing age?... then what agreeable, pleasant, or graceful act can you perform if you aren't self-satisfied? ... Self-love is her greatest gift.[31]

This first perception prepares her for making a further one: that the alternative happiness men seek is itself an illusion. Life is like a stage play. In pursuing things that seem good according to the values of the world, men are wilfully choosing to trust in something that is deceptive and insubstantial rather than true. They are like an audience at a play whose attention is caught by the illusion and the make-up, and who choose to forget the reality underneath the pretence.[32] Along with this realization that there is a gap between appearance and reality in worldly affairs, Folly also perceives that truth can be found by reversing worldly assumptions about what is valuable or desirable. In another highly symbolic image, Erasmus makes Folly liken human affairs to the Sileni:

[30] For arguments to the contrary see Rosalie Colie, *Paradoxia epidemica* (Princeton, 1966), p. 20.
[31] *CW Erasmus*, 27, pp. 98–9.
[32] Ibid., p. 103.

... it's well known that all human affairs are like the figures of Silenus described by Alcibiades and have two completely opposite faces, so that what is death at first sight, as they say, is life if you look within, and vice versa, life is death. The same applies to beauty and ugliness, riches and poverty, obscurity and fame, learning and ignorance, strength and weakness, the noble and the baseborn, happy and sad, good and bad fortune, friend and foe, healthy and harmful – in fact you'll find everything suddenly reversed if you open the Silenus.[33]

The Silenus image foreshadows what Folly will do in the rest of her declamation: she is going to open up the paradoxical vision of life she had earlier presented as if it were a Silenus. What had *seemed* desirable will be shown to be undesirable or inadequate, and what had seemed to be an obstacle to pleasure and happiness will be shown to be the means for the attainment of true happiness.

By declaring these realizations, Folly is signalling her movement towards a new outlook on life – not that of the life-loving fool she was at the beginning, but that of the severe critic who can see through mankind's self-deception.

At first, she does not acknowledge her new perspective. Indeed, she tries to disguise it by denouncing as a madman anyone who would be so stupid as to declare the truth about the nature of things, and hence disrupt the play:

> ... let us suppose some wise man dropped from heaven confronts me and insists that the man whom all look up to as god and master is not even human, as he is ruled by his passions, like an animal, and is no more than the lowest slave for serving so many evil masters of his own accord. Or again, he might tell someone else who is mourning his father to laugh because the dead man is only just beginning to live, seeing that this life of ours is nothing but a sort of death. Another man who boasts of his ancestry he might call low-born and bastard because he is so far removed from virtue, which is the sole source of nobility. If he had the same sort of thing to say about everyone else, what would happen? We should think him a crazy madman.[34]

The Lucianic wise man from the sky keeps on reappearing in the next few pages, and before long Folly has unambiguously identified herself with his viewpoint.

The change resulting from this radical shift of perspective can be seen almost at once, when Folly takes a second look at some of the 'foolish' aspects of life she had earlier praised as good. Earlier in the piece, for example, she had insisted that the folly of the aged is preferable to wisdom, and that senility is a blessing that she brings to ease the burden of old age:

---

[33] CW *Erasmus*, 27, pp. 102–3. For Erasmus' further explanation of Sileni, see the adage 'Sileni Alcibiades', in Margaret Mann Phillips, *The Adages of Erasmus: A Study with Translations* (Cambridge, 1964), pp. 269–70.

[34] CW *Erasmus*, 27, p. 103.

I see to it that the old man is witless, and this sets him free meanwhile from all those wretched anxieties which torment the man in his senses. He is also pleasant company for a drink, and doesn't feel the boredom with life which a more robust age can scarcely endure. There are times when, like the old man in Plautus, he goes back to those three special letters,[35] but he'd be anything but happy if he still had his wits . . . old age surpasses even childhood . . . they [that is, the old man and the child] are exactly alike: white hair, toothless mouth, short stature, liking for milk, babbling, chattering, silliness, forgetfulness, thoughtlessness, everything in fact.[36]

After she has identified the tragic flaw in the nature of the human condition and discovered the skyman's perspective, Folly returns to the subject of the foolish old man to illustrate her contention that it would be disastrous were wisdom to spread through mankind. As before, she insists that it is only folly that saves men from suffering the miseries that a truly wise insight into the real nature of the human situation would bring. This time, however, there is no geniality or jocularity in her tone:

Thanks to me you can see old men everywhere who have reached Nestor's age and scarcely still look human, mumbling, senile, toothless, white-haired, or bald – or rather, in the words of Aristophanes, 'dirty, bent, wretched, wrinkled, hairless, toothless, sexless.' Yet *they're still so pleased with life* and eager to be young that one dyes his white hair, another covers up his baldness with a wig, another wears borrowed teeth taken from some pig perhaps, while another is crazy about a girl and outdoes any young man in his amorous silliness.[37]

Many of the details in this second portrait of the old man are the same as those in the earlier one – white hair, toothlessness, an amorous predisposition – but the similarities merely serve to emphasize the change in Folly's view. She no longer sees the old man's folly as amusing, but as contemptible, because it springs from self-deception and an unwillingness to see life for what it is – corrupted. The old men in the second portrait are ridiculous, not because they are old, but because, even after a lifetime's opportunity to learn that worldly happiness is hollow, '*they're still so pleased with life*'[38] that they are reluctant to let go of it. Old women are even more disgusting in their reluctance to relinquish sexual pleasure:

They're forever smearing their faces with make-up, always looking in the mirror, and taking tweezers to their pubic hairs, exposing their sagging

---

[35] 'Amo', 'I love', from Plautus, *Mercator*, [II.2], ll. 304–6, in *Plauti comoediae*, ed. Fridericus Leo, 2 vols (Berlin, 1958), I, p. 448.

[36] *CW Erasmus*, 27, p. 92.

[37] Ibid., p. 105. My Italics.

[38] Ibid., p. 105.

withered breasts and trying to rouse failing desire with their quavery whining voices, while they drink, dance among the girls, and scribble their little love-letters.[39]

Folly has ceased to approve folly, because she has become convinced both of its perversity and its futility, and her character has become irrecoverably altered as a result.

For the rest of the middle section of *The Praise of Folly* Folly speaks with the authentic voice of Erasmus himself. The objects of satiric attack are the same as those in any of Erasmus' other reformist works: pedantic grammarians, sophistical lawyers, philosophers, and theologians, corrupt monks, wicked kings, and impious pontiffs, cardinals, and bishops who ignore the teachings of Christ.[40] Likewise, the tone will be instantly recognizable to anyone who has read the *Adages, Colloquies,* or any other of Erasmus' satiric writings. Here, for example, is Folly's denunciation of bad princes:

> Picture the prince, such as some of them are today: a man ignorant of the law, wellnigh an enemy to his people's advantage while intent on his personal convenience, a dedicated voluptuary, a hater of learning, freedom, and truth, without a thought for the interests of his country, and measuring everything in terms of his own profit and desires.[41]

Neither the tone nor the sentiments here differ substantially from those of Erasmus' comparable condemnation of wicked kings in the adage 'Scarabeus aquilam quaerit' (the beetle searches for the eagle'):

> And if these gods, these heroes, these triumphal leaders have any leisure left over from dicing, hunting and whoring, they do give every bit of it to truly regal considerations. Their one and only care is this, to utilise laws, edicts, wars, and truces, treaties and councils, acts of justice, everything sacred and profane, for the purpose of diverting the whole wealth of the whole community into their own treasury.[42]

The mask that Erasmus put on when he began to write *The Praise of Folly* has completely slipped as he has become carried away by the intensity of his own indignation at contemporary abuses. From initially writing a paradoxical mock encomium, he has lapsed into writing his habitual type of unequivocal satire. He admits as much when he makes Folly herself recognize that she has been behaving

---

[39] Ibid., p. 106.
[40] Ibid., pp. 123–39.
[41] Ibid., p. 136.
[42] Adage no. III. vii. 1, in Phillips, *Adages of Erasmus*, p. 234.

uncharacteristically. Arresting her tirade against pontiffs and priests, she declares: 'I don't want to look as though I'm writing satire when I should be delivering a eulogy'[43] – which, of course, she has been doing, and breaching fictive decorum in the process.

It is worth while pondering further the reasons that may have led Erasmus to sacrifice his original conception.

He must have quickly realized that Folly's paradoxes hindered, rather than helped, his didactic purpose. As Folly's demonstration of her benefits showed, 'truth' could not be located simply by reversing the eulogy as in the case of some of the ordinary mock-encomia Erasmus mentions in his preface.[44] With a work like Polycrates' ironic eulogy of the tyrant Busiris, the praise was to be read unambiguously as blame through a process of simple ironic inversion. Paradox, however, does not work like this. By maintaining arguments against received opinion, or else propositions that defy reason, paradoxes show how unstable and arbitrary ordinary conceptions of 'truth' are. Through paradox, Folly is easily able in the first section of her declamation to unsettle ordinary conceptions of what constitutes 'good' and 'bad', 'wisdom' and 'folly', and 'happiness' and 'misery'. The ease with which she does this creates the alarming spectre of a world in which values and even meaning are shifting and indeterminate (as contemporary thought would have them to be). Folly herself plays with this notion at one point, when she ridicules people who believe that it is sad to be deceived:

> They're quite wrong if they think man's happiness depends on actual facts; it depends on his opinions. For human affairs are so complex and obscure that nothing can be known of them for certain.[45]

Men, she implies, conduct themselves according to factitious beliefs designed to make sense of a world in which coherent meaning is absent. This sceptical viewpoint also implies that the moral absolutes Erasmus so cherished throughout his life might similarly be arbitrary fictions, and that a life lived according to Folly's prescription might be just as valid a way of attaining happiness as one lived according to the self-abnegating dictates of conventional wisdom.

This was a possibility too dangerous for Erasmus to contemplate, though his genius had uncovered it, and he moved swiftly to stifle it. His decision to move Folly to the perspective of the wise skyman must have arisen from a desire to sort out what was 'good' and 'true' from what was 'bad' and 'false', and thus to intercept the ambiguity that Folly had let loose. By placing what he took to be

[43] *CW Erasmus*, 27, pp. 140–1.
[44] Ibid., pp. 83–4.
[45] Ibid., p. 118.

positive and negative aspects of human experience into a binary opposition, he could restore a stable moral order and achieve his didactic aim.

The consequences of this revised method are visible throughout the middle section of *The Praise of Folly*, which consists of Folly's enumeration of all those who are slaves to her power. As she runs through each order of society, Folly opposes the ideal against the abuse of the ideal, in a way that reflects Erasmus' concern to restore a fixed, determinate moral norm.

Folly's description of the popes illustrates this strategy. She first specifies the ideal: popes should imitate Christ's life of poverty and toil, his teaching, cross, and contempt for life. Were they to do this, it would involve them in 'vigils, fasts, tears, prayers, sermons, study, sighs, and a thousand unpleasant hardships of that kind'.[46] Having identified the ideal, she then proceeds to compare it with the practice of contemporary pontiffs: they strive ceaselessly after wealth, honours, and countless pleasures; they fight with fire and sword to preserve their privileges and possessions, and instead of being the vicars of Christ, they are, in fact, the deadliest enemies of the church.[47]. At every point, the abuses perpetrated by grammarians, lawyers, philosophers, theologians, kings, and the various orders of the clergy are counterpointed against an ideal standard which their behaviour perverts. This ideal standard, needless to say, embodies the 'philosophy of Christ' which 'renders foolish the entire wisdom of this world'.[48]

By making Folly look at the world from the skyman's perspective, Erasmus has certainly eliminated interpretative ambiguity, but he has created another problem for himself. Folly's opposition of the ideal to the real merely serves to emphasize the existence of a chasm between what should be, and what actually is. By the time she has finished her survey of the various types of folly in human affairs, Erasmus has painted an image of overwhelming perversity in the world of his contemporaries. Even Folly herself no longer takes any joy in the follies she describes, but rather views them with contempt and disgust.

The movement that has taken place within Folly's character reflects an unresolved tension, I believe, in Erasmus himself. As several scholars have recognized, Erasmus never found a way of harmonizing two contradictory convictions: on one hand that mankind had a great capacity for good, and, on the other, that human nature was deeply sinful.[49] Erasmus began to write *The Praise of Folly* under the influence of the first conviction, but ended up under the influence of the second. He had originally chosen the paradoxical mask because he believed that men could be laughed out of folly, but by the time Folly has completed her survey of human perversity, Erasmus seems to have concluded that folly is so deeply

---

[46] Ibid., p. 138.

[47] Ibid., p. 139.

[48] 'Paraclesis' (1516), in *Christian Humanism and the Reformation*, ed. Olin, p. 96.

[49] See Thompson, *Under Pretext of Praise*, p. 165; and Phillips, *Erasmus and the Northern Renaissance*, p. 82.

ingrained in human nature that men will never relinquish it in this world.

The third and final section embodies Erasmus' ultimate response to his own innate pessimism. As a means of bridging the gap between the ideal and the real, he opts for spiritual transcendence. In order to preach this alternative, however, he has to make Folly undergo yet another radical transformation. She now turns into a wise Christian fool who preaches the repudiation of the world in pursuit of mystical ecstacy. According to Folly, those who have been fired by Christian piety are like the man in Plato's myth who, having escaped from the cave where his fellows were chained, returned to tell them that they were marvelling at shadows. The pious recognize that the things of the body are insubstantial compared with true reality, which is spiritual:

> . . . the pious scorn whatever concerns the body and are wholly uplifted towards the contemplation of invisible things. . . . They have no thought for the body, despise wealth and avoid it like trash, and if they are obliged to deal with such matters they do so with reluctance and distaste, having as if they did not have, possessing as if they did not possess.[50]

For the Christian fool who withdraws from the things of the body, the reward is spiritual ecstacy, which is itself a foretaste of the perfect eternal bliss that he will experience after death, when the soul has recovered its former spiritual body.[51]

At this point, one realizes that Folly has undergone a mystical conversion. At the beginning she was a life-loving natural fool. When she started to grow dissatisfied with the happiness that natural folly could bring she changed into a licensed satiric fool. Now, finally having given up any hope of fundamentally reforming the world, she turns into a world-despising, penitent sage, prepared to repudiate the earthly happiness that imperfectly prefigures the ecstacy Erasmus hopes the true Christian will experience in the afterlife. Her conversion is complete when she alludes to Luke 10:42, in affirming her new belief that the reward of blissful immortality 'is the part of Folly which is not taken away by the transformation of life but is made perfect.'[52] The full significance of this allusion is made apparent only in the Latin text: 'Atque, haec est *Moriae* pars, quae non aufertur commutatione vitae sed perficitur.'[53] Luke 10:42 refers to the better part of Mary ('Maria optimam partem'), which Christ said should not be taken from her despite Martha's pleas. In alluding to Luke 10:42, Erasmus substitutes '*Moriae*' for the anticipated '*Mariae*', so as to create an ironic pun: 'Moria' (Folly) has become transformed like 'Maria' (Mary), by repudiating the world, and worldly wisdom.

---

[50] CW *Erasmus*, 27, pp. 150–1.

[51] Ibid., p. 152. For a detailed analysis of Erasmus' concept of ecstacy, see M. A. Screech, *Ecstasy and the Praise of Folly* (London, 1980).

[52] CW *Erasmus*, 27, p. 152.

[53] *Moriae encomion / Stultitiae laus*, (Basel, 1676), p. 234. My italics.

Some critics have argued that Erasmus himself does not approve the Christian-ized Platonism that Folly presents in this final section, and that the ironies of the final part are contrived simply to balance the ironies of the opening section. If the concluding pages of *The Praise of Folly* are compared with the *Enchiridion militis Christiani*, however, it is very hard to see why we should not believe Erasmus when he said that his purpose in the two books was precisely the same: to lay down the pattern of a Christian life.[54] In his declaration of the fifth rule of Christian living in the *Enchiridion*, Erasmus' words echo those of Folly almost to the letter:

> . . . thou [shalt] put perfyt pietie in this thing onely: yf thou shalte enforce alwaye from thynges visyble, whiche almost euery one be imperfyte, or els indifferent, to ascende to thynges inuysyble.[55]

The progressive withdrawal from the world which Erasmus advises is not only consistent with Folly's sermon, but also reflects the pattern of behaviour that she herself has exemplified in the course of the work:

> . . . in this thynge resteth the iourney to the spyrytuall and pure lyfe / yf by a lytell and lytell we shall accustome to withdrawe our selfe from these thynges whiche be not trewly in very dede: but partely appere to be, that they be not / as fylthy and voluptuous pleasure / honour of this worlde, partlye vanysshe awaye, and haste to retourne to naught / and shall be rauysshed·and caryed to these thynges, whiche in dede are eternall, immu-table, and pure.[56]

By opting for spiritual transcendence, Folly has merely followed the dictates of her maker.

It is therefore wrong to argue that the Christian folly of the final section is merely played off against the natural folly of the first section, with no greater or lesser degree of approbation on Erasmus' part.[57] The final section *cancels out* the first section by making a series of substitutions, replacing things of the world with their superior, spiritualized alternatives. Thus the earthly paradise of the Isles of the Blest gives way to an otherworldly Heaven; Jove humbling himself to propagate the human race becomes Christ putting on the nature of man to redeem sinners; the pleasures of sensuality and drunkenness are replaced by the intoxication of spiritual ecstacy; and the witlessness of old men in second childhood is paralleled by the incoherent utterances of Christian ecstatics.[58] By

---

[54] 'Letter to Dorp', CW *Erasmus*, 3, pp. 114–15.

[55] *Enchiridion militis Christiani: An English Version*, ed. O'Donnell, p. 103/25–8.

[56] Ibid., p. 106/9–16.

[57] As does Clarence Miller, in *The Praise of Folly*, trans. and ed. Clarence H. Miller (New Haven and London, 1979), p. xvii.

[58] CW *Erasmus*, 27, pp. 89, 90, 148, 153.

making her audience aware of these spiritual alternatives, Folly has turned herself inside out like a Silenus, to reveal the god within, and in doing so she has at last fulfilled Erasmus' original aim of laying down the pattern of a Christian life.

By the time he had finished *The Praise of Folly*, Erasmus had found that he had created something rather different from what he had set out to write. He had begun with the belief that fiction could be used simply as a means of sugar-coating a didactic pill, but he found in the event that it had a power to show life as more complex than the Christian-humanist rationalization of it could adequately explain. Folly's response to the world in the course of *The Praise of Folly* exactly parallels Erasmus' response to the subversive potentialities he discovered in the paradoxical mode. Both take fright at the refusal of life to conform to the rational categories into which men try to reduce it, in order to understand it.

Thus, in spite of his declared didactic intent, writing *The Praise of Folly* brought Erasmus closer to facing the unresolved tensions in his thought than he had ever come before, or would ever allow himself to come again. The mimetic power of paradox had opened his imagination, against his own expectation or will, to the complexities in human experience that he normally chose not to acknowledge. That is why *The Praise of Folly* has more impact than any of Erasmus' other works. In its heroic attempt to square the author's noble vision with a complex human reality that threatens to subvert it, *The Praise of Folly* serves as an exemplum of men's fundamental preoccupation with deriving a meaning from life that accords with their ideal view of it. As such, this unique work is far more than the sum of its parts, revealing tensions at the very heart of humanism that few others had the daring (or the intelligence) to acknowledge.

6

Paradoxical Equivocation: The Self-subversiveness of Thomas More's *Utopia*

In the course of writing *The Praise of Folly*, Erasmus had discovered that fictive representation was a far more dangerous literary instrument to handle than he had supposed. Whereas he had looked to use it simply as a form of rhetorical enhancement to make his didactic message more palatable, he had found in the event that it uncovered aspects of life he would sooner not have admitted to view. As a form of symbolic representation, fiction requires thought to be translated into images and actions related to, but not identical with, the experience or ideas that it is designed to explore. Inevitably, this process of objectification allows considerable scope for imaginative free-play, and Erasmus discovered that his imagination had grasped aspects of the human situation that frightened him. His attempts to resist the implications of his brilliant mimesis form part of the mimesis itself: *The Praise of Folly* ends up showing the dramatic process with which Erasmus struggled to restore some kind of harmony between his rationalistic sense and what Sir Philip Sidney might have called 'the imaginative or judging power'.

Thomas More, Erasmus' close friend and the only other humanist of the day to have a mind as penetrating as Erasmus' own, also turned to fiction as a means of presenting humanist aspirations. When, in the course of propounding remedies for England's social and political ills, More subjected humanist aspirations to the critical scrutiny of his imagination, fictive representation showed a perspective that destroyed the grounds of his confidence in the reformist aims to which he and Erasmus were most deeply committed. Even more profoundly than in the case of Erasmus, the capacity of his images to take on a semi-autonomous power of suggestion brought More face to face with the equivocal condition of his own consciousness. *The Praise of Folly* and *Utopia* are thus companion works in a far deeper sense than has yet been realized, for the mode of imaginative representation in each work led its author to admit doubts that he would have preferred to keep concealed.

The two authors responded to their discovery of the unstable foundations of their humanist commitments in very different ways. Erasmus, as shown in the previous chapter, reasserted his rationalized ethical norms and Christian piety with even more vigour than before, in order to escape from the ambiguous image of life his fiction was presenting. More, on the other hand, built into his fiction a structure of compounding ironies designed to induce in readers the same degree of ambivalence that he himself felt. In each case, therefore, the author's attempts to respond to his imaginative findings produced a work of extraordinary literary complexity and thematic elusiveness.

The complexity of *Utopia* can only be explained by retracing the stages in which More wrote it, and by matching the shifting character of his fiction with the changes in his circumstances.[1] When More began to write *Utopia*, his commitment both to humanism and also the idea of reform was at its height. Having turned his back on the cloister, he had developed an extremely successful legal career in the City of London as lawyer and Undersheriff.[2] His office brought him into close contact with the plight of the poor and the crime it fostered, so that daily experience impressed upon him the urgent need for new socio-economic measures in England. More's personal friendship with Erasmus was also at its height, as was his commitment to humane letters. He had been at work on his imitation classical history, *Richard III*, since 1513, and was to prove his loyalty to Erasmus by writing an energetic defence of *The Praise of Folly* and Erasmus' New Testament in October 1515, against the attack of Martin Dorp. More's professional and intellectual commitments, therefore, primed him for writing *Utopia*: his experience in the law showed him the need for drastic remedies to alleviate England's ills, and his humanist learning seemed to light the way to them.

He was also, one suspects, not averse to the fame that a well executed literary treatise of this nature would bring, given that he had been working up *The History of King Richard III* in several Latin versions specifically to enhance his continental reputation.[3] More had fallen far behind Erasmus in terms of literary output since they had collaborated on the translation of some of Lucian's dialogues in 1505–6. He had prompted Erasmus to write *The Praise of Folly*, and may have felt mildly envious of its success. Thus, when Erasmus revealed to him in Bruges in June 1515 that he had written a political treatise as well, *The*

---

[1] Hexter followed this procedure with illuminating results (see *CW Thos. More*, 4, Part 1, pp. xv–cxxiv), except that he misses the full extent of More's ambivalence and equivocation.

[2] See Guy, *The Public Career of Sir Thomas More*, pp. 4–7.

[3] See R. S. Sylvester, *CW Thos. More*, 2: *The History of King Richard III*, ed. Richard S. Sylvester (New Haven, 1963), p. lvi.

Education of a Christian Prince,[4] More must have felt that this was a subject on which he was at least as well equipped, given his experience, to write. My guess is that More felt irresistibly drawn to enter into friendly rivalry with Erasmus, just as he had done earlier in answering Lucian's *Tyrannicida*.[5]

More got his chance in July 1515 when negotiations on his diplomatic mission to the Netherlands reached a stalemate. He suddenly found himself with enforced leisure and the chance to visit some notable humanist scholars such as Jerome Busleyden and Peter Giles. This propitious convergence of circumstances seems to have triggered his desire to write his ideal commonwealth: it would prove his worth and enlarge his reputation; it would address some of the problems of English polity; and it would give him a chance to pull his weight in the humanist cause by giving a fictive embodiment to the political idealism of Erasmus and also some practical ideas of his own.

We know from Erasmus that More wrote Book 2 of *Utopia* first.[6] Its earlier composition shows in the relative simplicity of More's thematic conception in the opening section of the work, which describes Utopian socio-economic arrangements. According to Erasmus, More aimed at 'showing the reasons for the shortcomings of a commonwealth', and represented the English commonwealth in particular.[7] Later, in Book 1, written after More had returned to England, he would do this by analysing the causes of English ills directly, but here in Book 2 he does so indirectly by placing England and Utopia in a simple ironic relationship with one another.

Utopian institutions turn it into everything that England's polity is not, but could be. Whereas the whole of life in England is devoted to procuring wealth and property, the Utopians have abolished both money and private possessions. They also ensure that every citizen is taught an essential craft, and have eliminated all types of idleness and vagrancy. With everyone working on fewer commodities, and only those which satisfy the needs of nature, the Utopians not only ensure that there is a plentiful supply of all life's necessities, but also create more leisure for recreation and mental pursuits. Contempt for material ostentation is inculcated from an early age, so that Utopians have no reason to take pride in a superfluous display of possessions. Through these measures, they have rooted out the causes of poverty and beggary, the twin scourges of English society.[8]

[4] Erasmus wrote to Domenico Grimani on 31 March 1515 that he had the work 'in hand' (*CW Erasmus*, 3, no. 334, p. 98/178–80), and described it to Dorp in late May 1515 as if it had been finished (*CW Erasmus*, 3, no. 337, p. 114/95–p. 115/96). It is hardly conceivable that he would not have told More of the work's existence and discussed its ideas with him.

[5] See Erasmus' 'Letter to Ulrich von Hutten' (1519), in *CW Erasmus*, 7, no. 999, p. 23/277–9.

[6] *CW Erasmus*, 7, no. 999, p. 24/282–3.

[7] Ibid., p. 23/280–1.

[8] *CW Thos. More*, 4, pp. 120; 127, 144–6; 130–8; 138; 147.

In addition to these basic policies, More gives Utopia many other practices that give the principles of Erasmus' political idealism a local habitation and a name. The Utopians take special care of the sick and show special consideration for the aged. They eschew luxury, being able to discriminate between true and false pleasures. They pursue humanistic studies, and have developed legal and political institutions that embody the virtues of justice and simplicity.[9]

All these features of Utopian polity are contrived to be in stark contrast with English practice, and the ironic opposition of the two countries is symbolized in the geographical position of Utopia; it is literally opposed to England, being in the southern hemisphere of the globe.[10] Geographical details are also the means by which More suggests that Utopia is a model for what England could be. Like Britain, Utopia is an island, of roughly the same dimensions, separated from a neighbouring continent by a channel, and named eponymously after its conqueror, Utopus, just as Britain was (according to some legends) named after its Trojan founder, Brutus.[11] Accordingly, Amaurotum, its capital city, and the river Anydrus suggest London, and the Thames.[12]

In this earlier section of Book 2 More was doing nothing that would have caused his humanist friends any consternation. He was merely supplying, with unprecedented imaginative brilliance, a fictional body for the idealistic principles to which he, Erasmus, and the whole community of northern humanists were committed. More's humanist friends certainly read the work in this light. Guillaume Budé, admiring More's insights into the economic causes of social malaises, and seeing the Utopian economy as embodying the Christian virtues of simplicity, equity, and justice,[13] viewed *Utopia* as a 'model of the happy life' and a 'rule of living' ('beatae uitae exemplar, ac uiuendi praescriptum').[14] Similarly, Busleyden saw in it 'that ideal of a commonwealth, that pattern and perfect model of morality' ('eam Reipublicae ideam, eam morum formulam, absolutissimumque simulacrum').[15] Most significantly, the marginal glosses, which Peter Giles and Erasmus himself supplied, enthusiastically endorse Utopian policies in the first half of Book 2, and point the contrast between them and European practices. Altogether, the evidence overwhelmingly suggests that More, when he began to write Utopia, set out to create a serious exemplar of what a polity reformed according to idealistic humanist principles might be like – the 'optimus status reipublicae' proclaimed on the work's title-page.

Nevertheless, to write unambiguously in this way was as untypical for More as

---

[9] Ibid., pp. 138–40, 143; 166–72; 158, 180–4; 192–4.

[10] This location is confirmed by the Utopians' description of the Europeans as 'Vltraequinoctialeis' – i.e. those from above the equator (Ibid., p. 108/2).

[11] Ibid., pp. 110–12.

[12] Ibid., pp. 116–20.

[13] See the prefatory letter from Budé to Lupset published in the 1518 edition, ibid., pp. 4–14.

[14] Ibid., p. 12/12–13.

[15] Prefatory letter from Busleyden to More, ibid., pp. 32–5.

to write paradoxically had been untypical for Erasmus. From early in his career More had been filled with contradictory impulses, because of a peculiar condition of consciousness that allowed him to see the positive and negative sides of any issue simultaneously. He seems to have felt the attraction of rival possibilities with equal force, and in his *Life of John Picus* and his translation of Lucian's *Cynicus* he had developed an ironic mode capable of depicting the experience of this type of ambivalence.[16] It is not surprising, therefore, to find that even before the section on the social orders of Utopia has been completed, shifts in tone and perspective begin to appear that threaten to unsettle the equilibrium of More's representation.

Until shortly before More's summary of the advantages of the Utopians' domestic economy ('Iam uidetis quam nulla sit usquam ociandi licentia . . .') ('Now you can see how nowhere is there any licence to waste time . . .'),[17] the account is written almost entirely as if it were an impersonal narration in which Raphael Hythlodaeus, the narrator, did not exist. Indeed, there is no reason to suppose that More had conceived of a narrator having a character and viewpoint different from his own until he had advanced well into the account of his imaginary commonwealth.[18] Such instances of first person verbs as there are (for example, 'uiderim' ('I saw') and 'inquam' ('I say')) do not substantially alter the impression that More, as author, wholeheartedly approves of every aspect of Utopian polity that is being extolled.

When, however, More describes the music, spices, and perfumes with which the Utopians grace their communal banquets, he insinuates a critical judgement on their proclivity towards harmless pleasure that alerts the reader to the presence of a narrator whose view is distinct from both the Utopians' viewpoint and, possibly, the author's own. From this point onwards this narrator's presence obtrudes recurrently in such a way as to stand between More and his fiction, so that, by the end of Book 2, More has so completely detached himself from his narrator that he is able to proclaim his explicit disagreement with him: 'When Raphael had finished his story, many things came to my mind which seemed very absurdly established in the customs and laws of the people described.'[19]

A second sign of More's growing unease is the onset of facetiousness. Until the first rhetorical climax, when he extols the achievement of Utopian socio-economic polity, More's tone has been serious and relatively free of irony.[20] Having finished his demonstration of their achievement in this sphere, however, More almost immediately starts to undermine the seriousness of his exposition by playing fancifully on the ironic consequences of their success. They are such

---

[16] See Fox, *Thomas More: History and Providence* (Oxford, 1982), Chapter 1, esp. pp. 32–3, 41.
[17] *CW Thos. More*, 4, p. 146/15ff.
[18] I am indebted to Dr Brian O'Brien for letting me read his unpublished paper on this subject.
[19] *CW Thos. More*, 4, pp. 244/13–15, 245/17–19.
[20] Apart from the digression on Utopian colonial practices, for which see below, p. 99.

efficient producers of essential commodities that, having far more than they need, they end up with a huge trade surplus and a great quantity of what they value least – gold and silver. Paradoxically, the Utopians, who despise wealth, accumulate a vast treasury. Equally paradoxically (for a nation which believes in peace), they use this treasury for hiring foreign mercenaries and financing the subversion of their enemies.[21] With a brilliance of wit that excites the glossator twice to exclaim 'O Artful Rogue!',[22] More teasingly develops the irony that, by deciding not to want it, the Utopians end up with everything that Europeans do want and expend so much energy in chasing. Ironically, by adopting policies founded upon justice, compassion, and charity, the Utopians acquire the very things that the injustice and callousness of European practices are designed to procure.

Once set loose, More's whimsy takes flight. He proceeds to describe how gold and silver are used to make chamber pots, chains and fetters for slaves, and the insignia of disgrace, while jewels are given as toys to children.[23] This outburst of paradoxical comic irony reaches its climax in the tale of the Anemolian ambassadors, whose fine trappings provoke the opposite reactions to those they were designed to elicit.[24]

Both the introduction of a narrator and the intrusion of comic irony and paradox serve to disguise the extent to which More may have been personally attracted to the vision of the commonwealth he had been presenting. As Book 2 proceeds, More does not merely personalize the narrator, but makes him unreliable as well, which he had not been at the outset. This effectively makes it impossible to detect the degree of More's own approbation of any Utopian practice with any certainty. The comic tone works to obscure the norm from the opposite direction, by altering the reader's perception of Utopia. Whereas the initial presentation of Utopian social orders had invited the reader to take it seriously, the new element of facetiousness warns him or her not to take it too seriously. Thus the fiction works to intercept in the reader the very impulses it induces. Partly this is a result of More's own natural penchant for mirth,[25] but the real reason for it seems to lie much deeper. It is a device for protecting More against potential ridicule, and against deficiencies in his representation. In life certain character types adopt a comic persona as a safeguard against vulnerability of one sort or another; More did so, in literature as in life.

Why should More have felt vulnerable? Apart from a natural fear of self-

[21] *CW Thos. More*, 4, pp. 148–50.

[22] Ibid., pp. 150/6–7, 155/36–7; 151/7–8, 154/28–9.

[23] Ibid., p. 152.

[24] Ibid., p. 154.

[25] In *A Dialogue of Comfort against Tribulation*, More, in the person of Anthony, confesses that he is 'of nature evyn halfe a giglot & more' (*CW Thos. More*, 12, p. 83/3–6), and one of his prayers in the Tower was, 'To abstayn from vayne confabulations/ To eschew light folysh myrth' (*CW Thos. More*, 13, p. 227/11–12).

exposure, which would have been all the more intense the more he felt attracted to his creation (as we know he was),[26] there was another potent cause. Just as Erasmus had been perturbed by what his fictional mimesis was showing him, so, too, was More disturbed by what his imagination was revealing about his ideal rational commonwealth.

Many readers have been repelled by the drabness and uniformity of Utopia, as well as the regimentation and compulsion required to make Utopian society operate.[27] Eliminating ostentation also means suppressing beauty, and eradicating pride also means suppressing individuality. One sign that More may not have been unaware of these consequences of his attempt to curb the natural impulses of human nature is the peculiar reference to the Utopian method of hatching eggs:

> They breed a vast quantity of poultry by a wonderful contrivance. The hens do not brood over the eggs, but the farmers, by keeping a great number of them at a uniform heat, bring them to life and hatch them. As soon as they come out of the shell, the chicks follow and acknowledge humans as their mothers![28]

This detail sticks in the mind not so much because it adds to the verisimilitude or attests to how advanced the Utopians are in animal husbandry, but because it has an emblematic, suggestive power. The eggs are not hatched according to nature, but by artifice, and this artifice involves keeping them at a *uniform* heat. More has, in fact, supplied here an imagistic correlative for what happens in the Utopian commonwealth: the social effects the Utopians seek are achieved against nature, by artificially suppressing the natural instincts of mankind, and they only secure this result by regulating men into a uniformity that deprives them of all individuality. The way that the chicks follow human beings as their mothers symbolizes the blind conformity into which the Utopians are conditioned. More's inclusion of the egg-hatching emblem shows that he knew his ideal commonwealth cut across the bias of human nature.

In short, the image More was creating was turning out to be imbued with characteristics that triggered his natural impulse to equivocate. That is the reason for the high incidence of the rhetorical figure of litotes (the device of affirming something by stating the negative of its opposite) that has been brilliantly

---

[26] This is implicit in the famous daydream he reports to Erasmus in which he fantasized himself as the Utopian king (see *St Thomas More: Selected Letters*, ed. E. F. Rogers (New Haven and London, 1961), no. 11, p. 85.

[27] See, in particular, T. S. Dorsch, 'Sir Thomas More and Lucian: An interpretation of *Utopia*', *Archiv für das Studium der neueren Sprachen und Literaturen*, 203 (1966–9), pp. 345–63.

[28] 'Pullorum infinitam educant multitudinem, mirabili artificio. Neque enim incubant oua gallinae, sed magnum eorum numerum calore quodam aequabili fouentes animant, educantque, hi simul atque e testa prodiere, homines, uice matrum comitantur, & agnoscunt' (*CW Thos. More*, 4, pp. 114/19–24, 115/25–31).

identified by one scholar.[29] Litotes allows for logical ambiguity through not explicitly formulating the positive of what is being affirmed. Thus, as Thomas Wilson says, 'if a cloth be not white, it is no reason to call it blacke. For it may bee blewe, greene, redd, russett.'[30] Accordingly, when More says that the Utopians' clothes are 'not unbecoming to the eye' ('nec ad oculum indecora'), or that their buildings are 'in no way mean' ('neutiquam sordida'), he is not explicitly formulating the extent to which they may be beautiful, which leaves a latitude for doubt that they really are so.[31] The device of litotes is not just symptomatic of More's ability to see two sides of a question, but of uncertainty and a developing lack of trust in the ideal he was presenting.

Another episode in this first section implies More's unease with the way Utopian rationality cuts across the bias of human nature: the description of their methods for regulating the population, and their colonial practices. Some of the details in this description seem designed to provoke a critical reaction in readers, as indeed they have done:[32] the transferring of supernumerary adults between families, cities, and colonies; the way the Utopians colonize uncultivated neighbouring territories and expel the natives who refuse to live according to their laws, waging war against them if they resist; and their willingness to allow any colony on the mainland to perish rather than let any city in Utopia itself be enfeebled.[33] These practices are indisputably rational, and they have good classical precedent in the theory of Plato,[34] but they conflict with some of the deepest instincts of human nature: the bonds of natural affection between members of a family, and the desire to protect territory, both of which More explicitly recognized in his later controversial writings.[35] Although the Utopians believe that they argue from the law of nature and nations ('ex naturae praescripto'), the fact that the Utopians have to wage war on peoples who resist them implies the existence of those to whom neither the naturalness, nor the reasonableness, of Utopian practices is immediately apparent. By thus signalling the possibility of dissent, More was drawing attention to yet another paradox: that

[29] Elizabeth McCutcheon, 'Denying the Contrary: More's Use of Litotes in the *Utopia*', *Moreana*, 31–31 (1971), pp. 107–21; reprinted in *Essential Articles for the Study of Thomas More*, ed. R. S. Sylvester and G. P. Marc'hadour (Hamden, Connecticut, 1977), pp. 263–74.

[30] Thomas Wilson, *The Rule of Reason; Conteining the Art of Logike* (London, 1567), fol. 52^v; quoted by McCutcheon, *Essential Articles for the Study of Thomas More*, ed. Sylvester and Marc'hadour, p. 271.

[31] *CW Thos. More*, 4, pp. 126/5, 120/4.

[32] See, for example, Dorsch, op. cit.

[33] *CW Thos. More*, 4, pp. 134–7.

[34] *Rep.* 2.373 D–E, *Leg.* 4. 707E–736D, 5.735E–736C (see Surtz, *CW Thos. More*, 4, pp. 415–16, note to 136/7).

[35] In *A Dialogue Concerning Heresies*, for example, More declared that it is not merely lawful, but also enjoined by God, that every private person as well as the king should protect themselves against 'losse / bothe of worldly substance / bodyly hurt / and perdycyon of mennys soules' (*CW Thos. More*, 6, Part 1, p. 415/18–22).

the rational law of nature can work directly against the law of human nature. More must have been highly intrigued by this paradox, for he explores it further in the section on Utopian warfare, where, once again, such 'rational' practices as placing the members of a soldier's family on the battlefield to sharpen his incentive to fight seem deliberately designed to outrage human feelings.[36]

Once More allowed irony, paradox, and facetiousness to enter the narrative, the possibility of an unequivocal interpretation vanished for good. The discussion of Utopian moral philosophy appears to offer a serious case for an innocent Epicureanism based upon a Stoic conception of virtue, a distinction between true and false pleasures, and a hierarchy of higher and lower pleasures,[37] but the validity of the case is put in question by the narrator's professed disapproval of Utopian hedonism, and by the questionability of some of the social practices to which it leads, such as the inspection of prospective marriage partners naked, to ensure sexual satisfaction, and licensed suicide to avoid incurable disease.[38] Time and again, More appears to be deliberately unsettling the norm so as to obscure any potential determinacy in meaning.

Just as a radical shift in tone occurred near the end of the description of Utopian socio-economic arrangements, so is there another major tonal shift as the discussion of ethics comes to an end. It commences when the narrator describes the Utopians' attitude towards treaties:

> Treaties . . . they never make with any nation . . . because in those parts of the world treaties and alliances between kings are not observed with much good faith. In Europe, however, and especially in those parts where the faith and religion of Christ prevails, the majesty of treaties is everywhere holy and inviolable, partly through the justice and goodness of kings, partly through the reverence and fear of the Sovereign Pontiffs.[39]

Here, the nature of the irony has changed from whimsy into straightforward satirical irony that is not at all ambiguous; under the pretext of praising Europe, More is condemning it for not adhering to the principles for which it is being praised.

This descent into direct satire leads to the description of Utopian warfare, which shows the fictional perspective of the work to have turned itself inside out. Approval of Utopia has metamorphosed into implicit condemnation, and the contrast between Utopia and Europe has dissolved into an equation between the

---

[36] *CW Thos. More*, 4, p. 211/1–6.

[37] See Edward L. Surtz, *The Praise of Pleasure: Philosophy, Education and Communism in More's Utopia* (Chicago, 1957).

[38] *CW Thos. More*, 4, pp. 160/20–4, 161/25–9; 186–9.

[39] Ibid., pp. 196/14–25; 197/18–30.

two. The rationality of the Utopians has led them to duplicate all the most disgusting of European war practices, and even to invent worse ones of their own: they foster bribery, assassination, sedition, rival claimants to the enemy throne, hire mercenaries, and disregard both kinship and friendship in the ferocity with which they fight.[40] All humour and facetiousness vanishes in this section, and the tone becomes as black as night. Any suggestion that this is the description of an ideal state also vanishes, and it is highly significant that the marginal glosses practically cease through this section. Evidently, even Erasmus and Peter Giles found it difficult to detect any semblance of exemplary behaviour in Utopian war practices.

It is a relief, therefore, when the description moves on to Utopian religion. Although based on reason, Utopian religion allows the findings of faith to modify the absolutes of reason in a way that makes the Utopians far more tolerant and undogmatic in this sphere than they show themselves in any others. They even accept the validity of ascetic religious orders who abstain from sex and the eating of meat, even though such practices flout reason:

> If the latter based upon arguments from reason their preference of celibacy to matrimony and of a hard life to a comfortable one, they would laugh them to scorn. Now, however, since they say they are prompted by religion, they look up to and reverence them.[41]

The more open condition of mind which their religious experience induces in them saves the Utopians from the terrifying rational absolutism that has led them to perpetrate inhuman practices in the previous section. It also makes them responsive to the possibility that in certain respects they may be mistaken, and that there may exist better institutions or beliefs into the knowledge of which God might lead them. In their common prayer, each Utopian prays that,

> If he errs in these matters or if there is anything better and more approved by God than that commonwealth or that religion, he prays that He will, of His goodness, bring him to the knowledge of it, for he is ready to follow in whatever path He may lead him.[42]

By giving them this religious experience, More frees both the Utopians and himself from the despair into which their utopianism could potentially drive them.

---

[40] Ibid., pp. 203–7.

[41] Ibid., pp. 226/12–15; 227/17–21.

[42] 'Qua in re, si quid erret, aut si quid sit alterutra melius, & quod deus magis approbet, orare se eius bonitas efficiat, hoc ut ipse cognoscat. paratum enim sequi se quaqua uersus ab eo ducatur' (Ibid., pp. 236/16–19, 237/17–21).

In spite of all More's efforts to cover his tracks, then, the pattern of tonal shifts in Book 2 makes it possible to infer what had been happening in his mind during the composition of the fable. Initial optimism, signalled in the relative tonal stability of the opening section, gave way to doubt, reflected in the incursion of facetiousness and paradoxical irony. That in turn was displaced by harsh satirical irony as More almost completely lost confidence in the viability of his ideal, seeing Utopian rationality lead to irrationality. Finally, he was able to salvage himself from the black irony of the section on Utopian warfare, by asserting the existence of a dimension of religious experience in which men cease to have to take responsibility for the inadequacy of their own rational vision and the limitations imposed upon them by the paradoxes of the human situation. Readers will observe here much the same pattern of evolving perception and response that was traced in Erasmus' *Praise of Folly* in the previous chapter: initial confidence which gives way to doubt expressed in satire, which in turn finds relief in the affirmation of a religious solution. In the course of seeking to create an imaginative embodiment for his ideal, More had discovered, like Erasmus, that humanist rationality is inadequate for conceiving an ideal that fully accords with either the reality of human desires, or the inherent sinfulness of human nature. Unlike Erasmus, however, he was unable to protect himself from what his mind told him those discoveries ultimately implied. If men could not adequately conceptualize the state that their idealism prompted them to seek, far less could they ever expect to realize it on earth. Nevertheless, even if it could never be attained, perennial human dissatisfaction with the existing condition of life would always impel men to seek something better. 'Utopia', therefore, both existed and was nowhere, as the pun in its names implies. By the end of Book 2, More had realized that men were placed in a situation designed to promote their utopian impulses, but also designed to deprive them of the possibility of fulfilling them on earth. Paradoxically, the Utopians, through experiencing the frustration of their rational efforts to create a perfect society, while refusing to abandon the effort, had indeed worked themselves into the 'optimum statum' of a commonwealth the responsive condition of will that God desires of men, and which the inbuilt imperfectibility of the world had been contrived to induce.[43]

As with Erasmus, the process of imaginative recreation had allowed More to develop a deeper understanding of the status of humanist aspirations than he probably normally entertained. His surrender to the perception that rationalized formulations cannot entirely explain what God requires of men, nor what men themselves desire, filled him with a deep-seated ambivalence about the viability of the whole humanist reform enterprise.

---

[43] For further comment on More's view of providential imperfection, see Fox, *Thomas More*, pp. 147–50.

His ambivalent attitude was complicated still further when he returned to England from his mission to the Low Countries, to find himself offered an annuity by the king. For over a year he refused to accept it. In a letter to Erasmus written in January 1516 he explains this refusal as a reluctance to abandon his position in the City of London and compromise his reputation with the London citizens.[44] In this he was probably quite sincere. By the time More did enter royal service he was earning about £400 per annum in the City, a very considerable sum for those times – his annuity was worth only one quarter of that amount. More's fear of compromising his position with the London citizens also suggests that he discerned Henry's offer as, in part, a bribe. As Roper reports, More had recently defended the pope's interests successfully against the king in a law case involving an impounded ship.[45] It is entirely possible that, as Roper suggests, Henry concluded it would be better to have such a potent advocate representing his own interests rather than those of anyone else, and that More, sensing this covert motive, was cautious. Moreover, an epigram written about this time suggests that More had a healthy instinct for self-preservation. Cautioning an overconfident courtier about the unpredictable rages of kings, he declares:

> Tuta tibi non est, ut sit secura uoluptas.
> Magna tibi est, mihi sit dummodo certa minor.

[The pleasure you get is not safe enough to relieve you of anxiety. For you it is a great pleasure. As for me, let my pleasure be less great – and safe.][46]

As early as 1516, More was under no illusions as to the physical danger in which he would be placing himself should he enter the king's service.

Even this caution does not fully explain why More hesitated to accept Henry's offer, nor does it explain why he allowed Erasmus to believe that he still had not reached a decision long after he had joined the Council.[47] He had, in fact, a much deeper motive still. It is figured forth in the dialogue More wrote in England that became Book 1 of *Utopia*, and it can be ascertained in the light of the conclusions More had reached earlier in the course of writing Book 2.

Book 2 had shown him that human nature and the nature of the human situation were always liable to frustrate Utopianism. He was now being invited to participate in a process, the effectiveness of which he had come to doubt. Yet for More to reject the offer would not only be a snub to the king, but also an admission of defeat, if not of despair. By opting out, he would be repudiating the

---

[44] *CW Erasmus*, 3, no. 388, pp. 234–5.

[45] Roper, *Lyfe of Sir Thomas Moore*, pp. 9–11.

[46] *CW Thos. More*, 3: 2, no. 162, pp. 204/8–9.

[47] See G. R. Elton, 'Thomas More, Councillor', in *Studies in Tudor and Stuart Politics and Government*, Vol. 2 (Cambridge, 1974), pp. 129–33. The usual reason given for this reticence is More's respect for Erasmus' known disapproval of scholars' involvement in political affairs.

positive condition of mind that he had depicted in the Utopians, and to which he believed all men were enjoined by God. Thus, as usual, More could see simultaneously both the reasons why he should not be lured into royal service, and the reasons why he should, and he dramatized them in the form of an argument between two objectified personifications of the contradictory sides of himself: Raphael Hythlodaeus, who is his idealistic, Erasmian self, and 'More', who is his realistic, practical self.

The contents of this debate have been the subject of a huge scholarly literature, and need be only briefly rehearsed here.[48] Hythlodaeus believes that political participation is pointless, because princes and their advisors are not prepared to listen to wise advise. 'More', on the other hand, believes that one can adopt a 'civil philosophy' rather than an absolute academic one, and act indirectly to influence things for the better. Hythlodaeus rejects both policies on the grounds that to bend Christ's teaching to suit human behaviour merely licenses men to be bad in greater comfort, and that the indirect approach leads either to a loss of integrity, or destruction as a traitor.[49] No half-measures will do, he argues; either one should look for a root-and-branch transformation of society, or one should stay clear of politics. Such a transformation can be achieved only through the abolition of private property. When 'More' disagrees, Hythlodaeus appeals to the example of the Utopian commonwealth, where this policy has actually been successfully implemented. He then agrees to give a description of Utopia to prove his claim.

If Book 2 turned out to be ambiguous, it is made even more so by being enwrapped within this dialogue, that sets up two rival positions, both of which the Utopian exemplum can be, and has been, adduced to support. The juxtaposition of the rival viewpoints in Book 1 against the double-sided vision of Book 2 generates an infinite regression that leads only to inconclusiveness. In the face of it, readers are left to make up their own minds as best they can.

The inconclusiveness of More's vision as revealed in *Utopia* makes his eventual decision to join the royal service all the more noteworthy. It was, above all, an act of *faith*. By being willing to participate in the political process, More was putting himself at the disposal of the divine will in exactly the same way as the Utopians do in their common prayer. More had no way of knowing where it would lead, but he was willing to be led. Perhaps his final protestation on the scaffold that he died 'the king's good servant, but God's first' sprang from an ironic recognition of what providence's intentions for him had turned out to be.

It is now possible to see the function of his fictive creation for More, and to speculate on what its processes show about humanism itself as a political force.

[48] For a convenient list of the respective interpretative positions, see the bibliography in Judith P. Jones, *Thomas More*, Twayne's English Author Series, no. 247 (Boston, 1979), pp. 65–8.

[49] See, especially, *CW Thos. More*, 4, pp. 97–103.

Like Erasmus with *The Praise of Folly*, More started off writing *Utopia* to strike a blow in the cause of humanist reform. He planned to present a model for the rational reform of European society according to the ethical values to be found in the classical philosophers, in common sense, and in teachings of the Christian gospels. The suggestive power of fictive mimesis, however, triggered off his instinctive ambivalence, so that what had been an instrument of straightforward exposition gradually turned into a vehicle for interrogating the validity of the ideas it was expounding. When More's own circumstances after his return to England further deepened the ambiguity of his feelings, he wrapped *Utopia* in so many concentric layers of irony that the possibility of a clear norm for interpretation disappeared altogether.

This peculiarly complex evolution turned *Utopia* into the multi-faceted, variegated, and paradoxical text that has baffled commentators for so long. As a piece of political speculation it works both to assert humanistic idealism and simultaneously to temper and limit the possibility of granting full intellectual consent to it. It serves simultaneously to advertise More's enthusiastic commitment to Erasmian humanism, and his sceptical reservations about it. On another level, it is designed to enhance internationally More's personal reputation, while at the same time concealing his personal convictions as completely as possible. On yet another level, because of the addition of Book 1, it is a very private attempt to work out a response to his personal dilemma over whether he should enter royal service. Probably More sought the satisfaction of imagining that his readers might share the experience of his ambivalence as if it were their own. As far as its functions are concerned, *Utopia* thus ends up being paradoxically both a public book and an intensely private one, and More's own vacillations over whether he wanted *Utopia* to be published or not reflect his inability to decide which function, the public or the private, was more important to him.[50]

As with *The Praise of Folly*, the intellectual and emotional processes revealed at work in *Utopia* show why humanism had only a limited impact as a political force. There was a deep-seated fracture at the heart of the Christian-humanist synthesis. Experience, as grasped through the fictive imagination, presented Erasmus and More with an unsettling conundrum. On one hand their humanist enthusiasms tempted them to believe that men could aspire to cultivate their natures and society with an expectation of attaining happiness in this world. On the other hand, Christianity and the findings of their own realistic perception of contemporary circumstances, instructed them to accept that human nature was irremediably sinful. They thus had to admit to themselves the existence of a contradiction between the rational idealism of the pagan philosophers and the Christian view of the world, and of what kind of belief and action each world

---

[50] The relevant letters recording his about-face over the publication of *Utopia* are to be found in *Selected Letters*. ed. E. F. Rogers, nos. 6 (p. 73), 7 (p. 76), 10 (p. 80), 11 (p. 85), 12 (p. 87), 13 (p. 89), 14 (p. 90), and 15 (p. 90). For a fuller discussion, see Fox *Thomas More*, pp. 72–3.

view entailed. Ultimately they, like their contemporaries, either had to choose between them, or find a mode of belief that could license effective action in the world without subverting its premises.

The way that both Erasmus and More move from a satiric attack on human perversity, into a consideration of religious experience at the end of each work is instructive. It shows each writer taking refuge from the tensions inherent in their cast of mind by reaffirming religious faith. Whether they knew it or not, Erasmus and More were asserting religion as a *solution* to the potential breakdown of humanist aspirations. For this reason, both *Utopia* and *The Praise of Folly* turn out to be astonishingly prophetic books, foreshadowing what would soon happen in history itself. Christian-humanism would be given its chance to supply rational remedies for European ills, and then, when it failed to do so, men would look for stronger medicine in the suprarational verities of religion. *Utopia* and *The Praise of Folly* anticipate not merely the Reformation as a response to the frustration of reform, but also the two opposing forms that this religious reaction would take. In its transcendental flight from the world, the closing section of *The Praise of Folly* prefigured Luther's invisible church of the sinless elect; Utopian religion, on the other hand, with its recoil from rationalism into an acceptance of paradox and human fallibility, prefigured More's counter-assertion of a church militant comprising good and bad together in a ceaseless process of lapse and resurgence.[51] The respective solutions of More and Erasmus, therefore, while appearing compatible, in fact looked in opposite directions, and foreshadowed the source of the religious contention to come.

It finally remains to be observed that More's efforts to reconcile his personal doubts, his public aspirations, and the political exigencies of his time produced one of the most complex literary masterpieces the world has seen. In order to give expression to his divided and equivocal consciousness, More was led to devise an ever compounding structure of irony. At first it consisted simply of self-subverting shifts of tone; then it was complicated by the obtrusion of an unreliable narrator onto the narrative, and complicated still further by a dialogue between that narrator and an apparent surrogate ('More') for the disbelieving author (More), whose opinions are not allowed full credibility. Next the dialogue was juxtaposed against the description of the Utopian commonwealth so as first to invite the reader to find in it confirmation of one view or the other, then to show that no confirmation of either can be attained; then the work was surrounded by letters from other humanist authorities who saw in it exactly the proof of those ideas that had been shown to be incapable of being proved, let alone instituted; and finally, belated tampering with some, if not all, of the names

---

[51] On More's view of the church, see Richard Marius, *CW Thos. More*, 8: 3, pp. 1269–1364; and Fox, *Thomas More*, pp. 156–60.

('Nusquama', for example, was turned into 'Utopia', and 'Mentirano' into 'Amaurotum') ensured that any potential determinacy of meaning would dissolve into paradox.[52] Through this process of accretion, More constructed a literary form that was uniquely capable of representing his own peculiar condition of consciousness, and also perhaps the deeper reality of the condition of his times. There had been nothing like it before, and until history produces another individual with More's strange multi-sidedness of vision, and places him or her in comparable circumstances, there is unlikely to be anything quite like it again.

[52] See Arthur E. Barker, 'Clavis Moreana: The Yale Edition of Thomas More', *Journal of English and Germanic Philology*, 65 (1966), pp. 318–330; reprinted in *Essential Articles for the Study of Thomas More*, ed. Sylvester and Marc'hadour, pp. 215–28, esp. p. 222.

7

Thomas More and Tudor Historiography: *The History of King Richard III*

Humanism had a significant bearing on early Tudor politics not only because it offered a coherent programme for reform, but also because it provided a whole new way of looking at things. Based on the rationalized ethics of the pagan philosophers and the practical piety of the Christian gospels, together with a belief that *oratio* (eloquence) and *ratio* (reason) were practically identical in the articulation of truth, humanism proffered itself as a new intellectual system capable of correcting the deficiencies of the older ones that were ceasing to satisfy human needs. In fact, although many of its advocates did not fully realize it, humanism constituted a radical challenge to traditional assumptions about the place of man in his environment; that is why it encountered such fierce resistance on the part of those who, like Martin Dorp or John Skelton, clung to the older intellectual practices and structures of belief.

In England, the potential of the new system for changing the nature of perception itself was displayed most strikingly in the transformation humanism worked on the writing of history.[1] Whereas medieval historians had been content to chronicle the transitory flux of human affairs between the Creation and the foreshadowed Day of Judgement in a relatively formless way designed to persuade men of the mutability of worldly affairs, humanist historians had a more ambitious and specific aim. Under the influence of Italian humanist educators like Vergerius, they believed that history was useful because concrete examples could be drawn from it to illustrate the precepts of moral philosophy. For this reason, it was particularly useful for training rulers, provided that the historical narrative was contrived with sufficient art and eloquence to make these moral truths plain.[2] The formless flux of history needed to be given shape through the employment of

---

[1] See Denys Hay, *Polydore Vergil: Renaissance Historian and Man of Letters* (Oxford, 1952), pp. 145–66; and F. J. Levy, *Tudor Historical Thought* (San Marino, California, 1967), pp. 33–78.

[2] See Levy, *Tudor Historical Thought*, p. 35; and Hay, *Polydore Vergil*, p. 152.

the stylistic and structural devices used by the classical historians. By inventing speeches for historical protagonists and by painting verbal portraits of them, the historian could highlight their essential qualities. The moral significance of historical episodes could be further enhanced by arranging portraits, actions, and events into patterns of comparison and contrast, and by giving the narrative a purposeful beginning, middle, and an end. A historian needed, above all, to adopt a classically rhetorical style, for through the rational control exerted by its syntactical and mental figures, the historian could imply the existence of a stable order of meaning in the universe at large.

Rulers quickly grasped the fact that the new historiography could serve their practical ambitions, and seized the opportunities it held out to them. The humanist habit of partitioning experience into a binary opposition between good and bad, and then of depicting the contrasting qualities in rhetorical stereotypes, held immense implications for the interpretation of history. A present reign, for example, could be favourably contrasted with one in the past simply by invoking a rhetorical contrast between the two. Humanist style, with its propensity to classify experience by division and opposition, would take care of the rest according to the decorum of its own laws.

Among the shrewdest of those monarchs who exploited the potential of the new historiography was Henry VII. From soon after he ascended the throne, he employed historians to celebrate his merit and achievements, so as to justify his tenure of it. By 1500 he had appointed a royal historiographer in the person of Bernard André, whom he commissioned to write a *Vita Henrici Septimi* (in imitation of Tito Livio da Forli's *Vita Henrici Quinti*, written half a century earlier), and a series of annals.[3] Both of André's works had a nakedly panegyrical intent. By his own admission, he wrote the *Vita Henrici Septimi* 'set alight and inflamed by the splendour of his admirable virtues' ('admirabilium virtutum suarum splendore accensus et inflammatus').[4] Accordingly, André's Henry displays all the qualities of a saint, showing exemplary humility, faith, and piety, patience in adversity, and magnanimity in victory. In short, he is presented as the divinely sanctioned saviour of prophecy whose mission is to rescue England from the cruel tyranny of Richard III and the civil strife of the Wars of the Roses. André, however, in spite of his learned references to classical historians such as Plutarch and Sallust,[5] belonged to an older generation of sub-humanists whose vision remained essentially medieval. He was completely untouched by the new theories of historiography that had evolved in Italy during the mid-fifteenth century, so that his *Vita* has a decidedly old-fashioned air about it.[6] Henry VII needed to present English history to the critical scrutiny of Europe, and, in

[3] Gairdner, *Memorials*, p. xi.
[4] Ibid., p. 6.
[5] Ibid., pp. 6–7.
[6] See Hay, *Polydore Vergil*, pp. 149–52.

particular, he needed the sanction of international humanism, if his new dynasty were to be accorded a fully legitimate status.[7] When Polydore Vergil arrived in England in 1502, fully versed in the new Italianate historical doctrines, Henry was quick to commission him to prepare a humanist history of England written in the new vogue.

The first fruits of Vergil's labours appeared in a manuscript version of the *Anglica historia* written in 1512–13, and covering events up to 1513.[8] It manifests all the hallmarks of the new Italianate method, especially in the section dealing with the reign of Edward IV onwards, in which Vergil shaped his own materials rather than relying upon the compilations of other historians.[9]

Chief among these attributes is a concern with formal symmetry. Vergil imposes structural order by assigning (after he has reached 1066) one reign to one book, while each book is shaped according to a similar pattern, beginning with the kings's accession, continuing with his domestic and foreign policies and notable events of the reign, and concluding with a description of the death, character, and family of the king.[10] Vergil also includes digressions to secure the reader's attention and provide essential background, as prescribed by Italian theorists.[11]

Imitating the classical writers, Vergil also imposes verbal order by writing in a highly controlled rhetorical style. Its effects can be seen most strikingly in the formal portraits of the chief historical protagonists, as, for example, in the portrait of Edward IV:

> King Edward was very taule of parsonage, excedinge the stature almost of all others, of coomly vysage, pleasant looke, brode brestyd, the resydew even to his fete proportionably correspondant, of sharp witt, hault corage, of passing retentyve memory towching those thinges which he had once conceavyd, dylygent in doing his affayres, ready in perylls, earnest and horryble to thenemy, bowntyfull to his frinds and aquaytaunce, most fortunate in his warres, geaven to bodyly lust, wherunto he was of his owne disposition inclyned, by reason wherof, and of humanytie which was bred in him aboundantly, he wold use himself more famylyarly emong pryvate parsons than the honor of his maiestie requyryd, wherfor ther was a great rumor that he was poysonyd.[12]

---

[7] Ibid., p. 151.

[8] See *Anglica historia*, ed. Hay, p. xiii.

[9] Up to this point Vergil had relied on writers such as Gildas, Bede, and the medieval chroniclers (see *Anglica historia*, ed. Hay, p. xviii; and C. L. Kingsford, *English Historical Literature in the Fifteenth Century* (Oxford, 1913), pp. 254–5).

[10] *Anglica historia*, ed. Hay, p. xxx.

[11] For example, the digression explaining the background to Buckingham's revolt against Richard III (*Three Books of Polydore Vergil's English History, Comprising the Reigns of Henry VI, Edward IV, and Richard III*, ed. Henry Ellis, Camden Series, no. 29 (London, 1844), pp. 192–3).

[12] *Vergil's English History*, ed. Ellis, p. 172.

This portrait relies for its effect upon its very deliberate syntactical patterning, which, although Vergil originally wrote in Latin, is very faithfully reproduced in the contemporary English translation. Phrases are weighed and balanced, but rhythmically varied to avoid monotony. Furthermore, the huge sentence contains a hidden order as it passes in turn from a description of Edward's physical attributes to his good moral qualities, which are then contrasted with his bad moral qualities. The syntactical order of the style, which in turn mirrors the larger structural order of the whole, is thus designed to give the impression of considered, balanced, impartial judgement, and hence persuade the reader that what it says is 'true'. In striving after these symmetries, Vergil is obeying the injunction of theorists like Guarino who urged that history should convince the reader of the truth by the beauty of its form.[13]

A second distinctive feature of the new humanist approach is revealed in Vergil's attempt to control the reader's interpretative response through rhetorical tricks that direct him or her towards the desired moral conclusion. He does this by combining omniscient authorial commentary that establishes a character's inner motivation with invented set speeches that show that character in action. For example, when Richard Duke of Gloucester arrives in London to assume his role as Protector after Edward IV's death, Vergil attributes to him the direst of secret motives:

> ... yt grevyd him spytefully that he might not receave into his tuition, without some great stere, his brothers other soon Richerd duke of York, whom his mother kept in sayntuarye; for, except he might get them both together into his powr and custody, he utterly despeyrd to compasse that which he longyd for ... And so, as he had purposyd, he laboryd to bring abowt by sleyght which by force he could not ...[14]

Having armed the reader with this insight into Richard's mind – which is, after all, no more than a speculation derived *post facto*, but presented as if it were irrefutably true – Vergil proceeds to give Richard a dramatized speech that displays his hypocrisy in action:

> I pray God that I never lyve yf I be not carefull for the commodytie of my nephews ... But what shall we say of the evell cownsayle which they who most maligne and hate me have geaven to quene Elizabeth? who, withowt any just cause, cownterfayting feare so folyshly, hath enterprysyd to cary in all haste the kings children as wicked, wretched, and desperate nawghtie parsons into saynctuary ... as thoughe we went abowt to destroy them, and that all owr doinges tendyd to violence ... But we are to provyde

---

[13] See R. Sabbadini, *Il metodo degli umanisti* (Florence, [1922]), p. 79, cited by Hay, *Polydore Vergil*, p. 150.

[14] *Vergil's English History*, ed. Ellis, p. 176.

remedy betimes for this womanishe disease creping into owr commonwelthe . . .[15]

The combination of dramatized scene and omniscient commentary by the narrator is marvellously effective in generating irony to sharpen the reader's moral reaction, but it also displays the danger as well as the benefits of the new humanist historiographical method: arbitrary interpretative conjectures could masquerade as truth, whereas in reality they might be little more than fanciful inferences to suit the needs of the author's moral or political vision.

Finally, to ensure that the reader draws the appropriate moral conclusions, already implicit in the rhetorical representation, Vergil employs yet another humanist device, the sententious authorial comment. After describing the murder of the two princes in the Tower, for instance, he continues:

> What man ys ther in this world, who, yf he have regard unto suche noble children thus shamefully murderid, wyll not tremble and quake, seeing that suche matters often happen for thoffences of our ancestors, whose faults doo redownd to the posterytie? That fortunyd peraventure to these two innocent impes because Edward ther father commytted thoffence of perjury, by reason of that most solemne othe which . . . he tooke at the gates of the cytie of York, meaning one thing inwardly and promysyng an other in expresse woordes outwardly, as furthwith appearyd: and for that afterwardes, by reason of his brother the duke of Clarence death, he had chargyd himself and his posterytie before God with dew desert of grevous punysshement.[16]

This *sententia* underlines Vergil's belief that men operate in a moral universe in which offences against moral order cannot escape retribution, even if it means that the sins of the fathers have to be visited on their children. Vergil, as he explained in his dedication of the *Anglica historia* to Henry VIII, expected his readers to learn from history what was good and bad, so that they could imitate virtuous deeds and turn away from evil ones.[17]

Whether Vergil realized it or not, the ultimate effect of his rhetorical method and moral assumptions was to turn history into propaganda validating the new Tudor dynasty. The new historiographical vehicle lent itself to this use because of the humanist habit of interpreting experience by partitioning it according to the

---

[15] Ibid., pp. 176–7.

[16] Ibid., pp. 189–90.

[17] '[History reproduces the past for future ages] ut postea pro se quisque benefacta pariter imitanda, atque malefacta multo diligentissime declinanda curarit: quando historia ut hominum laudes loquitur & patefacit, sic dedecora non tacet, neque operit. quae idcirco ad uitae iustitutionem longe utilissima censetur, quod alios ob immortalem gloriam consequendam, ad uirtutem impellat, alios uero infamiae metu a uitijs deterreat' (*Polydori Vergilii Vrbinatis Anglicae historiae libri uigintisex* (Basel, 1546), sig. a[2]).

concepts of moral philosophy. In particular, humanist historians tended to reproduce a moral opposition between good and bad as a structural opposition between different historical characters and episodes. In spite of Vergil's efforts to appear impartial by including references to the bad qualities of 'good' characters and vice versa, he nevertheless ends up with this dialectical dualism in dealing with the events of the recent past. Henry VII was very fortunate in having a predecessor as susceptible to condemnation as Richard III, for in the very act of identifying Richard as bad, humanist historiography would automatically be predisposed to establish Henry as good. Henry Tudor thus had the advantage of being equated, through humanist rhetoric, with the stable moral order which that rhetoric implied.

Most of those who espoused humanism accepted the postulates of Italian historiographical doctrine without question. There was one humanist, however, who seems to have been fully conscious of the power of humanist history to distort – Thomas More.

More was acutely sensitive to the shortcomings of humanist historiography because he had entertained such high hopes of it. From very early in his career he had been interested in history in general. Stapleton records that 'he studied with avidity all the historical works he could find',[18] and, by piecing together various bits of evidence, one can infer why. In the first place, he believed that the study of history was salutary because, through it, judgement is 'moche ryped' and a wise understanding of human affairs ('rerum humanarum prudentia') imparted.[19] But he also had a more particular reason. By the time he began to write his own exercise in humanist historiography, *The History of King Richard III*, More had come to harbour an intense hatred of tyrants and had deep misgivings about the institution of kingship itself.

This attitude had arisen partly as a result of his observation of the strategies whereby Henry VII had consolidated his power in the previous reign. Whether or not we give credit to William Roper's story of More's opposition to Henry VII in the parliament of 1504,[20] the long poem More wrote to celebrate the coronation of Henry VIII in 1509 leaves no doubt about his detestation of the old king's policies. More hails Henry VIII as a saviour who will deliver England from the long distress it has been suffering as a result of his father's fiscal rapacity and suppression of ancient rights.[21]

It is also possible that by 1513–18, when most of *The History of King Richard*

[18] Thomas Stapleton, *The Life and Illustrious Martyrdom of Sir Thomas More*, trans. P. Hallett (London, 1929), p. 15.

[19] *CW Thos. More*, 6: *A Dialogue concerning Heresies*, I, p. 132/6–16; *CW Thos. More*, 15: 'Letter to the University of Oxford', p. 139/17–21.

[20] William Roper, *The Lyfe of Sir Thomas Moore*, p. 7.

[21] *CW Thos. More*, 3: 2: *Latin Poems*, no. 19, pp. 101–13.

III was written, More had also developed doubts about the evolving tenor of Henry VIII's reign. Even in the midst of his effusive praise of Henry in the coronation poem of 1509, More had reserved sufficient caution to observe: 'Unlimited power has a tendency to weaken good minds, and that even in the case of very gifted men' ('Eneruare bonas immensa licentia mentes / Idque etiam in magnis assolet ingenijs').[22] Even though More does not explicitly say that Henry will be tainted in this way, the fact that he felt moved to mention the idea indicates his awareness that it is a possibility. By the time the first decade of Henry's reign was half-way through, the summary execution of Edmund de la Pole in 1513, which marked the onset of Henry's systematic campaign to eliminate troublesome dynastic rivals, and the unprecedented weight of taxation with which Henry had burdened the country to finance his foreign wars, may well have persuaded More that the new reign might be in the process of manifesting the tyranny of the old. More's hesitation in 1516 over accepting the king's invitation to join the royal service seems as likely to spring from this attitude as any other, as is shown by the reluctance he expressed to Erasmus over compromising his position in the City of London.[23] The fact that he mentions this at all suggests that he could imagine future occasions arising when someone such as himself might be called upon to defend the privileges of the City against the demands of the king. Certainly, More's observation of the oppressive tactics of Henry VII, and his anxiety lest Henry VIII should become tainted by the power he could wield,[24] left him with a highly ambiguous attitude towards kingship.

The *Epigrammata*, written between 1500 and 1518, give the clearest evidence of this perturbation. Kingship in general, and tyranny in particular, form major themes in the collection. In typical humanist fashion, More addresses the problem of bad kings by trying to define the difference between a bad king and a good one. A good king is a father who treats his subjects like children, and holds the commonweal together through the natural affection he elicits from them.[25] A bad king is one who does not respect the laws, rules his subjects like slaves, and who, instead of protecting his flock against the wolf, is the wolf himself.[26] As far as these commonplace definitions are concerned More encountered no intellectual difficulties, but problems arose for him when he tried to consider what could be done to get rid of a bad king.

His natural inclination was to toy with the idea of ascending power. This can be seen in the epigram 'Populus consentiens regnum dat et aufert' ('The consent of a people both gives and takes away royal power'), which clearly implies that

---

[22] Ibid., no 19, pp. 104/90–1, 105.

[23] *CW Erasmus*, 3: 2, no. 388, p. 235/135–45.

[24] William Roper's story that More warned Cromwell against letting the lion know his own power rings true (*The Lyfe of Sir Thomas Moore*, p. 57).

[25] *CW Thos. More*, 3: 2, nos 109 ('Quid inter tyrannum et principem'); 111 ('Bonum principem esse patrem non dominum'); 112 ('De bono rege et populo'), pp. 163–5.

[26] Ibid., nos 109; 115 ('De principe bono et malo'), pp. 162, 164.

despotical rulers can be deposed.[27] More's sense of political reality, however, was always liable to intercept and modify the idealism of his spontaneous reactions, and he could swing violently to the opposite extreme as a result. The epigram 'Sola mors tyrannicida est' ('Death by itself is the slayer of tyrants') shows the far more pessimistic view into which More could lapse in moments when he realized his vision of ascending power was ultimately a wish-fulfillment. Unless Fortune takes a turn for the better, More declares, the only remedy against tyranny is death:

> Versilis in melius uel te Fortuna reponet,
>   Vt solet excussa nube nitere dies.
> Aut libertatis uindex frendente tyranno,
>   Eruet iniecta mors miserata manu.
> Auferet haec (quo plus tibi gratificetur) et illum,
>   Afferet atque tuos protinus ante pedes.

(A turn of Fortune will improve your state, just as daylight shines through scattered clouds, or else Death, the defender of liberty, taking pity, will claim you and snatch you out of the tyrant's grasp while he rages. Death will also carry away him [i.e. the tyrant] (the more to please you), and lay him right at your feet.)[28]

The title of this epigram, 'Sola mors tyrannicida est', in itself contains an ambiguity that epitomizes More's ambivalent cast of mind. It can be read either as meaning 'Death unassisted kills tyrants', or as 'Only Death removes tyrants.' The first reading allows for the comparatively optimistic idea that men do not have to worry about tyrants because nature will take care of them in the ordinary course of things; the second reading negates the first by conceding that, in the face of tyranny, men are ultimately helpless. The only remedy for which they can hope, unless good luck intervenes, is to escape from tyrannical persecution by dying themselves. If this epigram strikes one as alarmingly prophetic of More's own future fate, it is because it expresses the peculiar fascination with death in More that from time to time seems perilously close to a death-wish.[29] In terms of his political philosophy, it shows how he was pulled in two ways at once. The positive side of his mind would propound optimistic solutions based on rational idealism, while his scepticism would prevent him from giving assent to the possibilities in which he wanted to believe. As a result, a profound melancholy often underlies the surface wit of his writing, as in this epigram.

---

[27] Ibid., no. 121, p. 169.

[28] Ibid., no. 80, p. 144/4–9. My translation.

[29] See, for example, More's consideration of 'the very fantasye and depe imaginacion' of death in *De quatuor nouissimus* (*The Workes of Sir Thomas More Knyght, Sometyme Lorde Chauncellor of England, Wrytten by Him in the English Tonge*, ed. William Rastell (London, 1557), p. 77 D).

One final example suffices to illustrate More's capacity to experience simultaneously the pull of mutually contradictory inclinations as far as his political thought was concerned. In the epigram 'Quis optimus reipublicae status' ('What is the best form of a commonwealth'), after weighing the relative merits and disadvantages of rule by a king and rule by a senate, More seems about to come down unequivocally on the side of a senate: the greater good lies in having a greater number of good men, who, being dependent for their election on the people, are less likely to abuse the power they wield, whereas a king is either good or bad, and if he is bad, he is like a leech that never leaves flesh until it is drained. Having suddenly reached this point, however, More arrests himself abruptly with a sceptical disclaimer:

> Quaestio sed tamen haec nascitur unde tibi?
> Est ne usquam populus, cui regem siue Senatum
> Praeficere arbitrio tu potes ipse tuo?
> Si potes hoc, regnas: nec iam cui, consule, trades
> Imperium: prior est quaestio, an expediat.

(– but say, what started you on this enquiry anyway? Is there anywhere a people upon whom you yourself, by your own decision, can impose either a king or a senate? If this does lie within your power, you are king. Stop considering to whom you may give power. The more basic question is whether it would do any good if you could.)[30]

By recognizing that a vast gap exists between the vision that an individual might entertain and his ability to invoke it in reality, More dramatically transforms the quality of the assent he gives to his ideal, without unequivocally abandoning it.

From the evidence of the *Epigrammata* then, one can see why More's interest in history was neither casual nor merely dutiful. Having developed anxieties about the institution of kingship and the possibility that it could become abused in his own time, More looked to history for answers to some of the questions that had formed in his mind. That was why he was intensely interested in the history of Richard III's usurpation and deposition, and, especially, in Polydore Vergil's humanist interpretation of the episode.

More's debt to Vergil has been disputed in the past,[31] but there is much evidence to support the notion. More's commitment to humanism would have predisposed him to welcome the arrival of another humanist scholar even had he not been as interested in historical writings as he was, and, as one would expect, the evidence shows him to have been on intimate terms with Vergil. Guillaume Budé, writing

---

[30] *CW Thos. More*, 3:2, no. 198, p. 230/27–31, 231.
[31] As by R. S. Sylvester, *CW Thos. More, 2: The History of King Richard III*, pp. lxxvi–vii.

to More on 23 May 1521, asks him to pass on his greetings to Vergil, whom he describes as one of More's most devoted supporters.[32] On 3 June 1523, Vergil himself refers to More as 'nostro Moro' ('our More') in a letter to Erasmus, and tells him that he has delivered some writings to More.[33] Given Vergil's close contacts with the international humanist circle and his admiration for More, it is inconceivable that More could have been ignorant of the history Vergil was writing.[34] Indeed, the catalyst that prompted More to begin writing the *History* in 'about the yeare of our Lorde. 1513.' (according to William Rastell)[35] may have been Vergil's completion of the first version of the *Anglica historia* in 1513. Considering that Vergil intended to present a copy to the king,[36] it would have been logical for him to show the work to More in order to gain his opinion before doing so, and the proof that More read it lies in the use he made of the *Anglica historia* in his own work.

The influence of the *Anglica historia* can be seen in the orations of *The History of King Richard III*, all of which are paralleled or adumbrated in the earlier work,[37] and, more particularly, in close correspondences of detail. In the description of Richard III, for example, More duplicates the sequence of details incorporated in Vergil's portrait almost exactly:

VERGIL	MORE
(1) Statura fuit pusilla,	(1) ... habitu corporis exiguo,
(2) corpore deformi,	(2) inaequalibus atque informibus membris, extanti dorso,
(3) altero humero eminentiore,	(3) alteroque humero erectior,
(4) facie breui ac truculentia ...	(4) os inamabile, toruum ...[38]
(1) He was small in stature,	(1) He was small in stature,
(2) deformed in body	(2) uneven and deformed of limbs, with a hunched back,
(3) one shoulder standing out more than the other,	(3) one shoulder higher than the other,
(4) with a sharp and fierce face.	(4) his face unlovable and fierce.

---

[32] *The Correspondence of Sir Thomas More*, ed. Elizabeth Frances Rogers (Princeton, 1947), pp. 252–3.

[33] *Vergil's English History*, ed. Ellis, p. xxxv. For other evidence of the relationship between Vergil and More, see Sylvester, *CW Thos. More*, 2, p. lxxv.

[34] It has been proposed that More was one of Vergil's chief informants for the period 1485–1501 (see *Anglica historia*, ed. Hay, p. xix).

[35] *CW Thos. More*, 2, p. 2.

[36] See Hay, *Polydore Vergil*, pp. 79–81.

[37] See Alison Hanham, *Richard III and his Early Historians 1483–1535* (Oxford, 1975), pp. 146–7.

[38] Vergil, *Anglica historia* (Basel, 1546), Book 25, p. 565; More, *CW Thos. More*, 2: *The History of King Richard III*, p. 7/15–17.

Sylvester argued that the lack of verbal similarities between the two texts showed that More and Vergil worked independently,[39] but in passages like these the almost exact correspondence in the order of the details offers a far more striking proof of influence.

Moreover, verbal echoes do exist, as in the case of the portraits of Edward IV by the two authors:

VERGIL	MORE
(1) Fuit Edouardus corpore procero	(1) Erat corpore procero
(2) animo magno	(2) multum illi animi
(3) promptus in periculis	(3) In aggrediendis periculis promptus
(4) in hostes uehemens, ac horribilis, in amicos & hospites munificus	(4) Aequus in pace clemensque, in bello acer & ferox
(5) libidini indulgens, in quam suapte natura propensus erat.	(5) Caeterum genio ac libidini ab ineunte statim aetate per omnem vitam.[40]
(1) Edward was tall of body	(1) He was tall of body
(2) great of heart	(2) great of heart
(3) resolute in dangers	(3) resolute in facing dangers
(4) violent and dreadful against the enemy, but liberal to friends and guests	(4) just and merciful in peace, but energetic and ferocious in war
(5) given to lust, towards which his disposition naturally inclined.	(5) moreover, from youth onwards inclined to lust through his whole life.

Even though each author amplifies the third and fourth details in their own idiosyncratic ways, and even though the order of details is not as exact as in the portrait of Richard (More reverses the order of the third and fourth detail from that which, for convenience, I have given here), the similarity is too striking to be merely coincidental. The lack of the precise verbal correspondences of which Sylvester complained (although even in this respect there are convincing verbal echoes) can be accounted for by supposing either that More created his English version first, so that his Latin text was at one remove from his imitation of Vergil's, or else that he was concerned to avoid the appearance of outright

[39] CW Thos. More, 2, pp. lxxvi–vii.

[40] Vergil, Anglica historia (Basel, 1546), Book 24, p. 539; CW Thos. More, 2: The History of King Richard III, p. 4/6–17.

plagiarism. In either case, we can be certain that More both knew and used the *Anglica historia*, and kept it astutely in mind while composing his own humanistic history.

The History of King Richard III then, originated in the complex convergence of the personal, political, and intellectual concerns that were uppermost in More's mind around 1513. He was aware of the new type of historiography Polydore Vergil was practising, and once he had read the *Anglica historia*, probably felt a natural desire to try to emulate him. Having also become deeply perturbed by the power of kings to pervert their office, he fixed upon the reign of Richard III as his subject because it would allow him to explore his own perplexities concerning political government, while simultaneously providing a cautionary exemplum against tyranny based on an actual historical event in the recent past.

When More came to compose his *History*, however, he found that his own sense of reality would not allow him to give his full assent to the interpretation of history implicit in the humanistic historiographical forms he was imitating. Specifically, he discovered that the rhetorical, structural, and stylistic devices by which the humanists shaped history inadequately accounted for all the observable facts, and involved the invention of spurious ones. As a result, he was threatened with the realization that humanist history might be little more than a self-deluding fiction, and once he started to suspect this his ironic sense of how easily men deceive themselves led him, as in the case of *Utopia*, to subvert the very vision he wanted to propound, in the act of formulating it.[41]

The doubleness of More's vision generated a profound anamorphism in *The History of King Richard III*; that is, it presents two different appearances, depending upon the angle from which it is viewed, that coexist simultaneously.[42] Most ostensibly, it appears as the kind of neo-classical humanist history practised by Vergil. As such, it seems to reproduce the same structuring devices and moral vision. More unifies the work by organizing it around a central character, Richard, and gives it shape by tracing his rise and (had the work been finished) his fall. He enhances both the structural and moral symmetry by introducing a series of calculated contrasts. At the most general level, More, imitating Sallust, contrasts the virtuous and peaceful past with the corruption that followed. He

---

[41] There have been many fine studies in recent years that identify the external signs of this phenomenon. See, in particular, Patrick Grant, 'Thomas More's *Richard III*: Moral Narration and Humanist Method', *Renaissance and Reformation / Renaissance et Réforme*, New Series, 7 (1983), pp. 157–72; Daniel Kinney, 'King's Tragicomedies: Generic Misrule in More's *History of Richard III*', *Moreana*, 86 (1985), pp. 128–50; and Judith H. Anderson, *Biographical Truth: The Representation of Historical Persons in Tudor-Stuart Writing* (New Haven and London, 1984), Chap. 6, esp. pp. 81–2.

[42] For pertinent comments on More's anamorphic art, see Stephen Greenblatt, *Renaissance Self-fashioning from More to Shakespeare* (Chicago and London, 1980), pp. 18–23.

then develops a number of more specific dialectical contrasts to support the moral distinctions contained within this general one. Richard III as evil tyrant is set in opposition to Edward IV as good king, and the moral difference between them is emphasized by an antithetical physical appearance. Whereas Edward is 'of visage louelye, of bodye myghtie, stronge, and cleane made', Richard is 'little of stature, ill fetured of limmes, croke backed, his left shoulder much higher then his right'.[43] Similar antithetical relationships exist between other characters. For example, Queen Elizabeth and Mistress Shore, the king's concubine, counterpoint one another. Whereas the queen manipulates the king for self-seeking reasons, Mistress Shore intercedes with him to alleviate the plight of those in political disfavour.[44] Bishop John Morton, the other 'good' character, is used as the foil to a whole array of different characters. He contrasts with the improvident Hastings in his shrewdness and foresight; he contrasts with Cardinal Bourchier by remaining determined to resist Richard; and he contrasts with Richard himself in being concerned for the common good rather than with ambition. In developing these dichotomies, More was consciously trying to turn the historical episode into an exemplary illustration of what is right and wrong in political conduct – in accordance with the dictates of humanist historiographical theory.

Nevertheless, More invokes this interpretation of Richard III's reign partly in order to question its truth. Through irony of many different kinds – verbal, structural, dramatic, and cosmic – he systematically undermines almost every interpretative assumption that the historiographical strategy of the work seems to foster.

A major casualty of More's ironic scrutiny is the assumption that history can be soundly interpreted by partitioning its characters and events according to the categories of humanist moral philosophy. The apparent contrast between Edward IV and Richard III is the first such division to crumble. Far from being antitheses, the two brothers turn out to be almost on a par. Edward has committed perjury, suborned murder, deposed a king, ordered summary executions, and even had his own kin assassinated, just as Richard will do. Indeed, Edward has shown Richard the way. Accordingly, when the narrative depicts history beginning to repeat itself, the apparent contrast between their two reigns turns out to have been an illusion.[45]

Having created his *trompe l'oeil*, More exposes the distorting nature of the very rhetorical and stylistic conventions he had used to set it up. In order to turn Edward IV and Richard III into exemplars of moral qualities, More had found himself having to portray them in terms of rhetorical stereotypes. Just as Edward had needed to be 'of hearte couragious, politique in counsaile, in aduersitie

---

[43] CW Thos. More, 2, pp. 4/17, 7/19–21.

[44] Ibid., p. 56/15–24.

[45] For a fuller demonstration of these ironic parallels, see Fox, *Thomas More*, pp. 78–81.

nothynge abashed, in prosperitie, rather ioyfull then prowde, in peace iuste and mercifull' if he were to display the attributes of a good king, so too had Richard needed to be 'malicious, wrathfull, enuious, and from afore his birth, euer frowarde', in order to satisfy his role as Edward's antitype.[46] More undermines the credibility of these characterizations in several ways. In Edward's case he obtrudes unflattering references to his gluttony, corpulence, and 'fleshlye wantonnesse' into the idealized portrait, so as to bring the idealization under check. More also allows the narrative tacitly to question the veracity of the rhetorical portrait, by establishing Edward's reprehensible behaviour in the past. As a result, Edward's status as a good king is seriously put in doubt.[47] In the case of Richard, the procedure is slightly different. Having assembled the picture of a truly grotesque monster by combining the worst details he found in the accounts of Vergil and John Rous,[48] More immediately cautions the reader against believing it to be true by warning that men may 'of hatred reporte aboue the trouthe.'[49] He thus draws attention to the rhetorical contrivance of the portrait and the possibility that it may embody nothing more than a malicious fantasy.

More's ironic vision threatens to dissolve yet another moral dualism upon which the work's ability to serve as an exemplum depends: the apparent contrast between Morton and the tainted characters, especially Richard, to whom he seems set up to be a foil. Near the end of the *History*, More introduces Morton as a major protagonist when he shows him tempting the Duke of Buckingham to rebel against Richard. This episode serves More's aesthetic and moral purposes well, for it initiates a countermovement in the plot that will lead to Richard's fall, and will thus symmetrically balance the action whereby he has risen. The contrast in the direction of the two actions seems to complement the moral contrast between Richard and Morton. As in *Utopia*, Morton is given a marked eulogy. More praises him as 'a man of gret natural wit, very wel lerned, & honorable in behaueor' whose wisdom will lead to the overthrow of Richard and the union of the two rival houses 'wᵗ infinite benefite to the realm'.[50] In typically Morean fashion, however, the striking contrast conceals a more subtle parallel that makes Morton's status as an exemplary representative of good ambiguous. Although their aims seem to be diametrically opposed, the means used by Morton and Richard are practically identical. Morton practises the same kind of Machiavellism

---

[46] CW Thos. More, 2, pp. 4/10–12, 7/22–3.

[47] For the analytical relationship between narrative and the rhetorical interlude, see Richard A. Lanham, *The Motives of Eloquence: Literary Rhetoric in the Renaissance* (New Haven, 1976), pp. 9–12.

[48] From Vergil he takes the description of Richard's bodily deformity and 'hard fauoured' visage (*Vergil's English History*, ed. Ellis, pp. 226–7), and from Rous the suggestion that Richard came into the world with teeth: 'biennis matris utero tentus, exiens cum dentibus' (*Joannis Rossi[js] Antiquarii Warwicensis historia regum Angliae*, ed. Thomas Hearne, 2nd edn (Oxford, 1745), p. 215).

[49] CW Thos. More, 2, p. 7/27–8.

[50] Ibid., pp. 90/21–91/11.

that Richard used to secure the crown. Indeed, many of the terms used to describe Richard at the beginning of the *History* apply equally well to Morton at the end, as the dramatized encounter between Morton and Buckingham reveals. Like Richard he is 'close and secrete' and 'a deepe dissimuler', as far as his real motives are concerned. He is also 'lowlye of counteynaunce', in pretending that he means to 'medle with his boke and his beedes and no farther.' He may even be seen, metaphorically speaking, as 'outwardly coumpinable where he inwardely hated, not letting to kisse whome hee thoughte to kyll', if one thinks of the fate towards which he is luring Buckingham.[51] Similarly, Morton's exploitation of his familiarity with Buckingham in order to sound him out is no different in kind from the way Catesby, on Richard's orders, exploits his familiarity to probe Hastings,[52] and Richard's efforts to elicit spontaneous approval for his pre-arranged plan do not essentially differ from Morton's attempt to 'pricke' Buckingham on, while seeming rather 'to folow hym then to lead him.'[53] We can be forgiven for detecting something sinister in Morton's way of acting, for the psychological strategy he adopts of appealing to Buckingham's vainglory, self-love, and ambition is precisely that which Milton would later show Satan employing to tempt Eve in *Paradise Lost*. More may have initially believed that in Morton he was illustrating the kind of benevolent Machiavellism he had defended in Book 1 of *Utopia*, but, as Hythlodaeus rightly objected, there is a certain moral contradiction in the very concept of such action, and the ironic parallels between Morton and Richard show that More was too honest, ultimately, to disguise the moral ambiguity of his putative hero's behaviour.[54]

His discovery that his historical materials could not be made to conform to a didactic paradigm seems to have led More to an even more disturbing realization: he came to doubt the extent to which men can ever establish the truth concerning human experience in the world, whether their own in the present, or that of others in the past, far less comprehend it. This is because men are always at the mercy either of the limitation of their own powers of understanding, or else of the deceiving images other men construct in order to project themselves.

There are plenty of examples in the *History* of those who believe that they understand the mechanisms shaping events, and that they can remain in control of them. Hastings is the most noteworthy example. Not knowing that within two hours he will have suffered the death Richard has prepared for him, Hastings congratulates himself on the security of his present position, and gloats over the fact that his enemies, Rivers, Grey, and Vaughan, will go to the block that same day. More does not hesitate to make explicit the double irony:

[51] Ibid., p. 8/7–9; cf. p. 92/1–16.
[52] Ibid., p. 46/12–14.
[53] Ibid., pp. 66/15–76/22.
[54] This ambiguous element in Morton has prompted one scholar to see him as More's satiric depiction of a trimmer; see J. C. Davis, 'More, Morton, and the Politics of Accommodation', *Journal of British Studies*, 9: 2 (1970), pp. 27–49.

O good god, the blindnes of our mortall nature, when he most feared, he was in good suerty: when he rekened him self surest, he lost his life, & that w^tin two howres after.[55]

Mistress Shore is another who suffers 'the vain sureti of mans mind' and the unpredictable mutability of the world, in her descent from royal favourite to a 'beggerly condicion, vnfrended & worne out of acquaintance', in which 'shee beggeth of many at this daye liuing', as More says, 'y^t at this day had begged if she had not bene.'[56] Richard himself is a victim of the same self-deception, in believing that he can stage-manage events to his liking without ever having to suffer any retribution. Ironically, he is punished in the mind by the one thing he did not anticipate, torments of conscience, before being punished in the body when he is slain at Bosworth, 'hacked and hewed of his enemies handes, haryed on horsebacke dead, his here in despite torn and togged lyke a cur dogge.'[57] More was acutely conscious of the ironic discrepancy existing between human will and human fate; no man, he seems to be stressing in the *History*, can ever fully understand or control his destiny.

The second impediment to sound knowledge of human affairs – the false appearances men create for themselves – springs from their continual manipulation of language. More demonstrates how this happens by depicting many instances of characters in the process of constructing a persona through which they hope to influence events. We can see this happening when Edward IV delivers his deathbed oration:

My Lordes, my dere kinsmenne and alies, in what plighte I lye you see, & I feele. By whiche the lesse whyle I looke to lyue with you, the more depelye am I moued to care in what case I leaue you, for such as I leaue you, suche bee my children lyke to fynde you. Whiche if they shoulde (that Godde forbydde) fynde you at varyaunce, mxght happe to fall themselfe at warre ere their discrecion woulde serue to sette you at peace.[58]

The king's formal, sententious rhetoric implies an image of himself as a wise, beneficent, provident ruler. It also conjures up a world in which men will be persuaded through reason to conform their actions to ideal moral principles. Neither implied image has any foundation in reality. Edward's past conduct has left him with no right to expect that he can justifiably assume the persona he adopts; to the contrary, his misdeeds and irresponsibility have generated the kind of hatred and rivalry that will ensure his children will not enjoy the ideal world he invents. In spite of Edward's wishful pretensions, his long-winded circumlocu-

---

[55] *CW Thos. More*, 2, p. 52/13–16.
[56] Ibid., pp. 55–7.
[57] Ibid., p. 87/5–21.
[58] Ibid., p. 11/10–18.

tions betray his difficulty in finding a way to bridge the gap between the ideals he wishes to invoke and the reality he is seeking to control.

Richard is more successful in his attempts to manipulate language. He is able to persuade the Council that his motion to have the younger of the two princes taken out of sanctuary is 'good and reasonable', because, by adopting the discourse of deliberative oratory, he is able to project the persona of a statesman who is selflessly concerned at a humane level for the welfare of his nephews, and at a political level for the welfare of the state.[59] There are other instances of the deceitful imitation of particular styles. The conspirators, for example, seek to throw a cloak of legality over their summary execution of Hastings by issuing a proclamation enumerating his crimes 'curiously indited' with the precise semantic and syntactical particularity of a real legal document.[60] Shaa, too, tries to procure a moral sanction for Richard's usurpation by using the language and imagery of a real sermon to allege the bastardy of Edward IV's children.[61] By allowing all these characters to express themselves in direct speech, More paints a picture of linguistic falsification taking place on such a large scale that even though many of the common citizens recognize the sham that is going on, events start to assume the illusory quality of a stage play:

> And so they said that these matters bee Kynges games, as it were stage playes, and for the more part plaied vpon scafoldes. In which poor men be but ye lokers on. And thei y^t wise be, wil medle no farther. For they that sometyme step vp and playe w^t them, when they cannot play their partes, they disorder the play & do themself no good.[62]

As far as their perception of external events is concerned, men are always liable to be faced with appearances that have no real existential status. For this reason, the stage-play metaphor, one of More's favourite images, could serve as a metaphysical symbol for man's situation in the world at large.

As More has shown in his ironic undermining of the humanistic moral stereotypes he has been using, the historian himself is not exempt from this spinning of illusions. He confesses as much by developing an ironic distance between himself and his own narrative persona at certain moments, in order to show how the latter habitually construes things to his liking, just as much as the historical characters themselves do. This can be seen in the narrator's report of the rumour that Richard III was responsible for the death of his brother, Clarence:

---

[59] Ibid., pp. 25–7.
[60] Ibid., pp. 53–4.
[61] Ibid., pp. 66–8.
[62] Ibid., p. 81/6–10. Cf. *Utopia*, CW *Thos. More*, 4, p. 99/14–29; *The Praise of Folly*, CW *Erasmus*, 27, p. 103.

Somme wise menne also weene, that his drifte couertly conuayde, lacked not in helping furth his brother of Clarence to his death . . . *And they that thus deme,* think y^t he long time in king Edwardes life, forethought to be king in case that ye king his brother (whose life hee looked that euil dyete shoulde shorten) shoulde happen to decease (as in dede he did) while his children wer yonge. *And thei deme,* that for thys intente he was gladde of his brothers death ye Duke of Clarence, whose life must nedes haue hindered hym so entendynge, whither the same Duke of Clarence hadde kepte him true to his Nephew the yonge king, or enterprised to be kyng himselfe. But of al this pointe, is there no certaintie, & whoso diuineth vppon coniectures, maye as wel shote to farre as to short. How beit this haue I by credible informacion learned, . . . [63]

The reader is warned of the possibility that the author is wilfully falsifying his evidence, by the sudden descent in the level of style. Whereas More had adopted a style of high solemnity for the portraits and orations, here he casts formal rhetoric to the winds. Instead, the colloquial level of diction, the unnecessary repetitions, the improvised parenthetical statements, the long-winded and clumsy locutions, and the use of syntactical coordination rather than subordination all serve to evoke the voice of someone in the process of responding to, and reporting, information that he is predisposed to hear, and the effect is faintly comic. More is in fact dramatizing men's willingness, including his own, to persuade themselves of the opinions that suit the constructions they desire to make in order to render experience comprehensible. Self-mockingly, he draws attention to this propensity by observing that, in the absence of explicit proof, one may as well 'shoot too far as too short': in other words, fabricate an image to accord with what one wishes to be true. Having admitted this, More audaciously proceeds as if the admission has not already deprived his account of any claim to unconditional veracity. More's habit of juxtaposing this kind of passage against his rhetorical set pieces serves to alert the reader to the way in which the historian himself is perpetually fabricating evidence in the interest of the interpretation he wants to foster. As a result, he intimates the possible existence of an ironic gap between the historian's verbal representation of experience and the experience itself.

By the time More had covered the events of Richard's usurpation, then, he had come to several horrifying realizations. He had uncovered the fictive distortion resulting from the ways men project themselves and interpret the actions both of themselves and of others. Consequently, he had come to doubt that human beings can ever fully grasp the real nature of their situation or the meaning of their experience. On top of everything else, he had discovered that, in spite of the superficial appearance of goodness, all men are fundamentally tainted by sinful-

---

[63] Ibid., pp. 8/22–9/7. My italics.

ness. More knew from treating his historical characters that, as Erasmus had said in the *Praise of Folly*, the appearance of all human affairs can be turned inside out and reversed like a Silenus: the wise King Edward can turn into a gluttonous, murderous lecher; the saintly intercessor, Mistress Shore, is also a whore; and even the politic Morton can be seen as a version of Richard himself. All these realizations together deprived More of any humanist optimism he may have had at the outset, and, I suspect, made it impossible for him to go on. *The History of King Richard III* remained unfinished, in spite of the manifest care More had lavished on it (he developed both an English and a Latin version), and, apart from any other reason,[64] he stopped writing I would suggest, because he could no longer continue with the lie that his historiographical literary form was obliging him to perpetuate. In particular, he could not force himself to tell the final lie required by the dialectic of his *History* – that Henry VII had set everything to rights.

More had begun the *History* in an attempt to allay the perturbations of his mind concerning tyranny. The exercise, however, merely replaced that misgiving with a cause for even greater ones. More was horrified by the perception of the existential instability of human life he derived from his study of history, and the sense of the potential meaninglessness of life that it awakened in him. It is therefore not at all surprising that the next major work he should have written was his meditation on *The Four Last Things* (Death, Judgement, Heaven, and Hell), nor that he should thereafter have committed himself increasingly to the absolutist dogmas of the church. They were the one means to protect himself from the findings of his polyvalent consciousness, and he eventually died to persuade himself of their ultimate truth.

More's *History of King Richard III* marked the end, for the time being, of the efforts of humanists in England to explore, through aesthetic literature, the nature of their own inclinations, methods, and aspirations. The events of the Reformation and Henry VIII's political revolution were soon to overtake humanism and lessen its importance as a force capable of bringing about change. When this happened, the energies of humanist writers were almost completely diverted away from imaginative writing to the compilation of moral, pedagogical, political, medical, and pietistic treatises and translations. Sir Thomas Elyot briefly flirted with the dramatized dialogue in *Pasquil the Playne* and *Of the Knowledge which Maketh a Wise Man* as a means of exploring the implications of his dismissal from office as royal ambassador to Charles V, but Elyot was not by nature an imaginative writer, and his dialogues are only half-realized as fictive representations.[65] Thomas Starkey, too, chose the dialogue form to present his

---

[64] For an earlier speculation that More stopped writing the *History* when the execution of the third Duke of Buckingham made it too dangerous to proceed, see Fox, *Thomas More*, pp. 101–7.

[65] See below, chapter 12.

rational proposals for the reform of English polity, but the fictional form of his *Dialogue* between Thomas Lupset and Reginald Pole is a largely redundant device because, unlike More in *Utopia*, he could have said what he wanted to say without it. Both Elyot and Starkey used fiction largely as a pretext for assertion, not representation, hence their dialogues fall into a different category from those of More and Erasmus. In the brief period between about 1509 and 1518, when the latter were still prepared to experiment with fiction as a means of exploring the nature of the humanist enterprise, the two men produced a literature of unprecedented complexity of form and vision. Its insights were not to be repeated until Shakespeare, too, was moved to explore the polyvalent nature of truth concerning the human condition, and found a new way of depicting it.

PART III
The Cardinal

8

The Bull-calf and the Popinjay: Origins of the Quarrel between Skelton and Wolsey

Humanism was a powerful new intellectual force that promised much, but which by 1515, when More wrote *Utopia*, had delivered very little in the way of actual reform. Radical changes were indeed about to occur in England, but not as a result of the idealistic visions of the humanists. Rather, they were brought about by the personal ambitions of one man – Thomas Wolsey.

The ascendancy of Cardinal Wolsey as chief minister of Henry VIII was one of the most remarkable phenomena of the early Tudor period. From humble beginnings (he was the son of a butcher, as Skelton and other detractors would not cease to remind him), Wolsey rose rapidly to near-supreme power both in church and state. After a period of study at the University of Oxford, Wolsey had been made a royal chaplain by Henry VII, who also used him for minor diplomatic missions, on which his performance had been impressive.[1] When Henry VIII succeeded to the throne, Wolsey was appointed royal almoner and counsellor at the urging of his mentor, Richard Fox, Bishop of Winchester and lord privy seal.[2] Thereafter, he successfully cultivated Henry VIII's favour by throwing his support behind the king's war adventures in France, by catering to his taste for lavish spectacle and entertainment, and by negotiating an honourable peace when Henry's appetite for war was temporarily sated. For these services he was rewarded with the bishoprics of Lincoln and Tournai in 1514, the first of many benefices he would accumulate. When Christopher Bainbridge, the Cardinal-Archbishop of York, died in mid-1514, the bar to further advancement

---

[1] Cavendish, his gentleman usher and later his biographer, reports that Wolsey managed the astonishing feat of travelling to Calais and back on the king's business in three days (see George Cavendish, *The Life and Death of Cardinal Wolsey*, ed. Richard S. Sylvester, Early English Text Society, no. 243 (London, 1959), pp. 8–9.
[2] For a full account of Wolsey's career, see A. F. Pollard, *Wolsey* (London, 1929), pp. 13–23, from which this resumé is largely drawn.

in the church was removed, and with Henry's enthusiastic support Wolsey was made Archbishop of York and in due course cardinal, and the pope's *legatus a latere* in England. Concurrently, he had managed to succeed Warham as lord chancellor in 1515. Thus by 1518 he had become the most powerful man in England, excepting the king himself.

Wolsey's meteoric rise can be ascribed to two things: his influence over the king, which to some of his critics seemed almost the product of witchcraft, and his unusual talent for administration. Exuberant and pleasure loving, the youthful king preferred jousting and pageants to the drudgery of overseeing his administration, and was more than happy to leave matters of detail to his chief counsellor. Above all, he relied heavily on Wolsey because the latter was efficient. Even before he became chancellor, Wolsey had developed the habit of short-circuiting administrative rules to circumvent his official superiors.[3] This was one reason why he could get things done, and the king found his services invaluable, for Wolsey took special pains to make Henry believe that what was being done was what he, the king, wanted done.

The older style of government underwent transformation as a result. On one hand, Wolsey virtually extinguished the influence of the king's continual council – that is, those councillors who attended on Henry VIII at his itinerant court – by pruning it down to two members, and by expanding the activity of the Council in the Star Chamber, over which he himself presided.[4] On the other hand, he manipulated the composition of the Privy Chamber and controlled access to the king, to ensure that no rivals had as much chance of influencing Henry as himself.[5] Once Wolsey had also managed to persuade the pope to appoint him legate *a latere* in 1518, that is, to transfer to him papal authority over the two provinces of the English Church, he had amassed almost all the cards of the power game into his hands – so long as Henry was content to let him retain them.

In exercising this power, Wolsey succeeded in antagonizing nearly everyone. He would interfere constantly in the affairs of the nobility, gentry, and London citizens, while also meddling with ecclesiastical appointments, elections, visitations, and probate jurisdictions.[6] Too often, he refused to delegate authority or business, so that the administrative machine got clogged up and important matters were left unfinished. Faced with the need to finance Henry VIII's adventures in France, he attempted to extract forced loans, subsidies, and even a non-parliamentary tax far in excess of what the country was prepared, or able, to pay. His foreign policy itself became suspect when it was perceived that its

[3] See Pollard, *Wolsey*, p. 15.

[4] See John Guy, *The Cardinal's Court: The Impact of Thomas Wolsey in Star Chamber* (Hassocks, 1977), pp. 23–50; cf. 'The King's Council and Political Participation', in Fox and Guy, *Reassessing the Henrician Age*, pp. 133–4; and Elton, *Reform and Reformation: England*, pp. 59–62.

[5] See David Starkey, *The Reign of Henry VIII: Personalities and Politics* (London, 1985), chaps 3, 4.

[6] For this and much of what follows, see John Guy, *Tudor England* (Oxford and New York, 1988), pp. 85–115.

tergiversations might owe as much to the cardinal's desire to be elected pope in the event of Leo X's death as to diplomatic finesse.[7]

As far as domestic policy was concerned, Wolsey seemed to have many laudable reformist aims. He strove for better law enforcement, sought justice for the poor, especially against enclosing landlords, and attempted to re-endow the monarchy by introducing a new method of assessing taxes. But apart from failing to see many of these schemes brought to a satisfactory conclusion, Wolsey neglected the reform of the one institution most desperately in need of it – the church. Indeed, the cardinal embodied all the worst forms of ecclesiastical abuse in his own person, being a notorious pluralist, a fornicator, grasping and materialistic, and so vainglorious that he set himself above the nobles and presumed to rival the king himself in magnificence. Far from being the church's protector and reformer, he seemed to some to be its very enemy, in his attacks on the privilege of sanctuary and his despoliation of some of its monasteries in order to found colleges to his own glory at Oxford and Ipswich. Edward Hall sums up the disquiet that Wolsey's failure to reform the church, together with his manifest pride and arrogance, provoked in some quarters of the realm:

> When the Cardinall of Yorke was thus a legate, he set vp a court, & called it the court of the legate, and proued testamentes, and hard causes to the great hinderaunce of all the bishops of the realme. He visited bishopes and all the Clergie, exempt and not exempt, and vnder colour of reformacion he gat muche treasure, & nothing was reformed, but came to more mischief: for by example of his pride, priestes & all spiritual persones wexed so proude, that thei ware veluet, & silke, bothe in gounes, iackettes, doblettes, & shoes, kept open lechery, and so highly bare themselfes by reason of his aucthorities & faculties, that no man durst once reproue any thyng in them, for feare to bee called heretike, & then thei would make hym smoke or beare a faggot. And the Cardinall hymself was so elated that he thought hymself egall with the kyng: & when he had said Masse he made dukes & erles to serue hym of wyne with a say taken, & to holde the bason at the lauatories. Thus the pride & ambicion of the Cardinal & clergie was so high, y^t in maner al good persons abhorred & disdeined it.[8]

Any reform Wolsey appeared to be fostering was not the reform for which most people had been waiting, and as future events were to prove, his actions would merely postpone the day of reckoning, while ensuring that when it came its effects would be extreme.

Wolsey's actions, his style of government, and his character provoked a widespread literature of protest. For the most part this consisted of anonymous

---

[7] See Pollard, *Wolsey*, pp. 125–7; cf. Elton, *Reform and Reformation*, pp. 83–6.
[8] Edward Hall, *The Union of the Two Noble and Illustre Famelies of Lancastre & Yorke* (London, 1548), fo. 54^v.

ballads and lampoons of a fairly rudimentary kind that were assiduously collected by, and circulated among, the disaffected citizenry, especially of London.

A representative sample can be found in the manuscript commonplace book of John Colyns, a London mercer.[9] The anti-Wolsey poems range from a generalized complaint about the worsening conditions of the commonwealth ('The Ruyn of a Realm'),[10] to outright attacks on the cardinal, such as 'Of the cardnall Wolse', which supplicates the king and his nobles to set the realm to rights by removing Wolsey,[11] or 'Thomas, Thomas', which draws a contrast between the two Thomases, Wolsey and Becket, and urges Wolsey to repent before he is called to the Day of Judgement.[12]

Two of the most interesting pieces in the miscellany are the lament and supplication put into the mouth of Edward, first baron North, who had been imprisoned by Wolsey in January 1525 for writing a book against him.[13] In the first, 'The complaynte of Northe to the cardinal Wolsey', North laments the unstable fortune that has landed him in prison and, regretting that his inquietude impedes him from plainly showing Wolsey's virtues, beseeches the cardinal to take pity on him.[14] In the second poem ('By Northe to the same cardnall'), which is complementary to the first, North actually delivers the praise that his grief had prevented in the former poem, but in terms so extreme that his sincerity is put in doubt:

> Gouernyd ys this realme by moste nobyll prudens
> of mannes wytte, euer groundyd on reason,
> devydyng, lernyng, myxid with consciens,
> partelye to mytigate all maters in season,
> redressyng wronges, moste hyghest poynte of wysdom.
> Euer more in tyme whate shuld I now sey,
> Surely all Ynglond for hym ys bownd to pray.
>
> Endewyd with grace I thynke that he be,
> remembryng his wytte and goodlye eloquens,
> verrey dèsyrowus of pure humanite,
> enflamyd with vertu and goodly countenaunce,
> that no man, I thynke, hathe bettyr perseueraunce.

---

[9] Now British Library MS Harley 2252. For an analysis of this manuscript, see Carol M. Meale, 'The Compiler at Work: John Colyns and British Library MS Harley 2252', in *Manuscripts and Readers in Fifteenth-Century England: The Literary Implications of Manuscript Study*, ed. Derek Pearsall (Cambridge, 1983), pp. 82–103. The political poems in this manuscript are reprinted in Furnivall, *Ballads from Manuscripts*, I.

[10] British Library MS Harley 2252, fos 25–8.

[11] Ibid., fos 156–156ᵛ.

[12] Ibid., fos 158–159ᵛ.

[13] *LP*, IV, i, no. 1049.

[14] British Library MS Harley 2252, fo. 33.

Hys reasons ar so good that well I may sey,
O Ynglond, Ynglond, for him thou moste nedes pray!

Mervelous hyt were for me now to write,
And yf that I cowde hys famus actes dysclose.
Surely I cannot, yet yf that I myghte,
levyng in this lyfe, hyt were not for my perpose,
Of hys vertue to speke withowte ony glose,
repete hyt I cowde not; wherfor now I sey,
duryng ther lyvys for hym they moste nedes pray.[15]

Viewed together, the two poems dramatize the enforced exaction of contrition, obsequious submission, and the public payment of satisfaction to the offended cardinal. In the context of the other satires surrounding them in Colyns's commonplace book, North's poems acquire a contextual irony. They illustrate (and that is probably why Colyns put them there) the extent of, and the tyrannical effects wrought by, Wolsey's powers of intimidation. Polydore Vergil was forced into exactly the same kind of grovelling apology and self-abasement,[16] and, as we shall see, Skelton himself came near to pretending that he was prepared to do the same. However crude as poetry the anonymous political ballads in Colyns's miscellany might be, they had an important function, serving as instruments for depicting to the London citizens what they feared or despised in Wolsey, and allowing them to relieve their feelings by vilifying and abasing him in their imaginations, in a way they were powerless to do in life. This latter function is well summed up in the invective 'Of the cardinall Wolse'. Having vented his spleen on Wolsey as 'a churle, a bochers curre', and 'as flateryng a vyllane as ever was borne', the anonymous author begs tolerance from the king, whom, in his imagination, he has been addressing:

> Beseechyng your grace, be not dyspleasyd –
> *My mynde ys openyd, my herte ys easyd.*[17]

Wolsey's opponents in the City might have felt helpless, but rail they could with the best of them, and it did their hearts good to do so.

The anonymous ballads are relatively crude as literature, but there was one major writer who was stimulated by the phenomenon of Wolsey to produce his best work – John Skelton. The three satires he wrote against Wolsey, *Speke Parott*, *Collyn Clout*, and *Why Come Ye Nat to Courte?* mark a high point in the earlier English literary renaissance and are milestones in the evolution of the

---

[15] Ibid., fos 33–33ᵛ. I have added punctuation, modernized the capitalization and word-division, and have expanded the contractions in this quotation.

[16] See Hay, *Polydore Vergil*, pp. 10–14.

[17] British Library MS Harley 2252, fos 156–157ᵛ. My italics.

satiric genre. They might never have become so, or even have been written at all, however, had not Skelton been fired by the most powerful of incentives, acute personal self-interest. For a number of reasons that have hitherto eluded satisfactory explanation, Skelton found himself locked into a fight for survival with the all-powerful cardinal, in which his literary skill offered him his only chance of escape. Through a daring combination of appeal, persuasion, and attack, Skelton used his verse to recover the status and protection that he had lost, and to force the cardinal into a position which obliged him to reach a compromise and bring their quarrel to an end. Before this can be appreciated, however, it is necessary to establish the context in Skelton's own career out of which this contention between the poet and the cardinal arose.

History has almost completely obliterated the evidence that might explain the origins of Skelton's confrontation with Wolsey, but not entirely. Traces exist in the form of hints that Skelton supplied in his own works. Because these hints have not been taken into consideration, scholars have, understandably, come up with a variety of conflicting explanations. The quarrel has been explained variously as the outcome of selfless moral indignation on Skelton's part,[18] of a lifelong personal rivalry with Wolsey,[19] and of a misguided attempt to regain Henry VIII's patronage by telling him what he wanted to hear about the corruption of his chief minister.[20] None of these explanations is fully convincing, as each leaves important questions unanswered. If Skelton were acting simply out of moral outrage, why was he prepared, within two or three months of writing his most savage denunciation of Wolsey, to curry favour by greeting him reverently in his next work, and a year later by describing himself as 'obsequious and loyal' in a pamphlet dedicated to the cardinal?[21] If he were truly jealous of Wolsey's advancement, why had he not made a less equivocal effort to develop a court career himself when he had every chance to do so under Henry VII? And can Skelton really have hoped to gratify the king by depicting him as a negligent simpleton who was being tenderly led by the nose as asses are? In order to reconstruct what actually happened, one must first recall Skelton's career following his return to court.

After a lengthy sojourn at Diss as a country parson, during which he had resolved moral qualms about participating in the royal court, Skelton had succeeded in regaining royal patronage in mid 1512 or early 1513, at which time

[18] As by Edwards, *Skelton*, Nelson, *Skelton*, and Ian A. Gordon, *John Skelton, Poet Laureate* (Melbourne, 1943).

[19] Kinney, *John Skelton: Priest as Poet*, p. 133.

[20] Greg Walker, *John Skelton and the Politics of the 1520s* (Cambridge, 1988), pp. 60–94.

[21] See *A Garlande of Laurell*, ll. 1587–93, and *Howe the Douty Duke of Albany*, l, 524 (*Poems*, ed. Scattergood, pp. 356, 372).

he was granted the official title of *orator regius*.[22] For the next few years he seems to have fulfilled his duties as a court poet in the conventional way, writing political propaganda to celebrate the English victory at Flodden in 1513, epitaphs for the new royal tombs in Westminster Abbey, and a flytyng against Sir Christopher Garnesche performed before the court in 1514. After composing his elegy on Margaret Beaufort in August 1516, however, Skelton appears to have written no poem solicited by the king or his administration until late 1523. This sudden dearth of official commissions has not been satisfactorily explained, and has only recently been noticed. It is, however, highly significant.[23] Together with other hints that Skelton himself dropped, it suggests that he may have suffered the consequences of offending Wolsey much earlier than has been supposed.

A lease that Skelton renewed on 8 August 1518 for a tenement in which he had been living within the sanctuary at Westminster Abbey furnishes an important clue.[24] The terms of this lease leave out the customary clause binding the tenant not to harbour fugitives or malignants.[25] While noting this fact, scholars have for the most part not regarded the omission as significant. To the contrary, it is likely that Skelton had a specific reason for wanting the clause obliging him on oath not to harbour fugitives omitted: he had reason to believe that he might soon require refuge for himself, and hence was concerned to avoid committing perjury. Those scholars who are reluctant to believe that Skelton was preparing to use the sanctuary as a refuge argue that there were many other inhabitants of the sanctuary precincts who were not fugitives, and that Skelton probably chose his house at Westminster simply for the convenient access it gave him to court.[26] This may have originally been so when Skelton first rented his dwelling, but it does not preclude the possibility that by August 1518 he was preparing to make use of the sanctuary as a refuge in real earnest.

Indeed, there is plenty of evidence to suggest that this was so. First, there is no doubt whatsoever that at some time Skelton was using his house in the sanctuary as more than a convenient dwelling. Several accounts written within living memory of this period record that he was compelled to remain at Westminster because of Wolsey's antagonism. Edward Braynewode, upon whom Bale relied in compiling his entry on Skelton for his catalogue of British writers, asserted that, 'because of the invectives he wrote against Cardinal Wolsey, he was forced to take refuge in the sanctuary at Westminster Abbey in order to preserve his life,

---

[22] See above, chap. 2.

[23] Walker, *John Skelton and the Politics of the 1520s*, p. 49, was the first to draw attention to this silence. I find his explanation, however, that Skelton was relatively insignificant and therefore simply overlooked, unconvincing.

[24] Edwards, *Skelton*, p. 180.

[25] Ibid.

[26] Nelson, *Skelton*, pp. 121–2.

where he found favour under Abbot Islip.'[27] Another variant of this story occurs in the collection of facetiae, purportedly devised by Skelton, printed by Thomas Colwel in 1567:

> On a tyme Skelton did meete with certain frendes of hys at Charyng crosse, after that hee was in prison at my lord cardynals commaundement: & his frende sayd, I am glad you bee abroade amonge your frendes, for you haue ben long pent in. Skelton sayd, By the masse, I am glad I am out indeede, for I haue ben pent in, like a roche or fisshe, at Westminster in prison.[28]

Both these stories have been discounted because in terms of specific details they are untrustworthy. Skelton was already living in Westminster Abbey *before* he wrote his anti-Wolsey satires, so that the idea of him fleeing there as a result of the cardinal's reaction to them is highly romanticized. Moreover, even if Skelton were forced to seek sanctuary, the notion of him being pent up 'in prison' at the cardinal's commandment is a fanciful exaggeration. Nevertheless, the fact that both accounts agree that Skelton was confined to Westminster, and that Wolsey's anger had something to do with it, suggests some actual situation to which they both, with varying degrees of imaginative elaboration, refer.

Skelton himself makes numerous allusions in his later poems to such a situation. In *Speke Parott*, the first of the satires, written between 1519 and late 1521, the whole framing mythology symbolically figures forth Skelton's predicament. Parrot, Skelton's persona, describes himself as

> . . . a byrde of Paradyse,
> By Nature devysed of a wonderowus kynde,
> Deyntely dyetyd with dyvers delycate spyce,
> Tyll Eufrates, that flodde, dryvythe me into Ynde.[29]

As the rest of the poem gradually makes plain, Parrot is 'my owne dere harte',[30] a symbolic cipher for Skelton himself, and in these opening lines he is giving the reader a thinly disguised allegory of his recent experience and present position. The flood that had driven Parrot from Paradise into India alludes to the flood that Jupiter loosed on the world because of the wickedness of men, especially that of Lycaon.[31] A reference later in the poem to Wolsey as 'Lyacon of Libyk and Lydy',

[27] 'Ob literas in Cardinalem Wolsium inuectiuas, ad Westmonasteriense asylum confugere pro vita seruanda coactus fuit, ubi tamen sub Islepo abbate fauorit inuenit' (Bale, *Index Britanniae scriptorum*, ed. Lane Poole, p. 253).

[28] 'How Skelton was in prison at the commaundement of the cardinall' [Tale xiv], in *Merie Tales Newly Imprinted & Made by Master Skelton Poet Laureat* (London, n. d. [1567]), reprinted in *Poetical Works of John Skelton*, ed Dyce, I, p. lxxii.

[29] *Speke Parott*, ll. 1–4.

[30] Ibid., l. 208.

[31] Ovide, *Les métamorphoses*, ed. and trans. J. Chamonard, 2 vols (Paris, n. d.), I, p. 14, ll. 163–90.

and the mention of 'Dewcalyons flodde' in the refrain of each stanza in Parrot's final complaint, hint strongly at the allegory Skelton wishes obliquely to impart: he has been accustomed to enjoy a privileged existence ('deyntely dyetyd') in the king's court ('Paradyse') because of his status as an inspired poet ('by Nature devysed of a wonderowus kynde'),[32] but now he has been driven from it out of a fear of retributive anger (the 'flodde'), for which Wolsey ('Lycaon') turns out to have been responsible. Wolsey has apparently been able to turn Henry VIII (Jupiter) against him, and has thus managed to have him banished from the king's presence. In *A Garlande or Chapelet of Laurell*, Skelton again refers to this disastrous fact. Approaching a field in which gather those who seek fame, Skelton sees (in his dream) 'a lybbard, crownyd with golde and stones, / Terrible of countenaunce and passynge formydable', who shakes forth this writing:

> Formidanda nimis Jovis ultima fulmina tollis:
> Unguibus ire parat loca singula livida curvis
> Quam modo per Phebes nummos raptura Celeno.[33]

[You bear things to be feared beyond measure, the very thunderbolts of Jupiter. With curved talons he is as ready to go to various dangerous places as was Celaeno the harpy to get treasure from Phoebus.][34]

The leopard was the heraldic beast in the English royal coat of arms. In this passage, therefore, both the leopard and Jupiter stand as figures of Henry VIII, who has taken offence at Skelton. By pursuing such a course of action (that is, by criticizing Wolsey, the king's favourite), Skelton (the unnamed 'he' in the passage) has been risking extreme danger. The king himself has warned the poet that he risks royal displeasure if he continues to harass his chief minister.

There was one other reason for Skelton's loss of favour with the king. Apart from being incensed at the way Skelton had offended his chief minister, in whom he could see no wrong, the king, being enchanted with his 'minions', was no longer prepared to listen to the advice of an ageing poet-buffoon, or defend him against the cardinal. Richard Pace observed in 1521 that 'as old men decay greatly, the King wishes young men to be acquainted with his affairs.'[35] Skelton complained of this situation in *Why Come Ye Nat to Courte?*:

> Helas! sage overage
> So madly decayes,
> That age for dottage

---

[32] Skelton frequently asserts the special nature of the poet; see, for example, *A Replycacion*, in Skelton, *Complete Poems*, ll. 351–88.
[33] *A Garlande of Laurell*, ll. 596–8.
[34] Scattergood's translation, in Skelton, *Complete Poems*, p. 502.
[35] *LP*, III, no. 1437.

Is reconed nowadayes.
    Thus age, (a *graunt domage*),
Is nothynge set by,
And rage in arerage
Dothe rynne lamentably.[36]

In 1521, the situation in which Skelton found himself was unenviable, to say the least.

Parrot refers to Skelton's fall from the king's favour later in the *Speke Parott*:

In Paradyce, that place of pleasure perdurable,
The progeny of Parrottis were fayre and favorable;
Nowe *in valle* Ebron Parrot is fayne to fede:
'Cristecrosse and Saynt Nycholas, Parrot, be your good spede!'[37]

Hebron was one of the 'cities of refuge' mentioned in Joshua 21: 13, which turns it into a cipher for Skelton's dwelling within the Westminster sanctuary. Parrot's statement that he is now obliged to feed there signifies yet again that Skelton has fallen into disfavour. He has lost his privilege of 'bouge of court', that is, his right to eat at the royal tables, which he would have enjoyed as *orator regius*, and is now forced to take his meals at home. Skelton's phrasing in these lines is suggestive. According to the *Oxford English Dictionary*, the adjective 'fain', when used with an infinitive verb, means 'glad or content to take a certain course in default of opportunity for anything better, or as a lesser of two evils.' This fits Skelton's case exactly. He has been accustomed to frequent the king's appartments ('Paradyce, that place [punning on 'palace'] of pleasure perdurable'), but has been obliged to withdraw from the royal presence to avoid trouble which Wolsey ('Lycaon') could inflict upon him. This hint is reinforced in the next line by the reference to St Nicholas, who was the patron saint of captives.[38] Consequently, the 'curiously carven' cage in which Parrot dwells may itself have been chosen to symbolize the restricted scope within which Skelton could move. In *Speke Parott* he depicts himself as being the pampered pet of court ladies:

These maydens full meryly with many a dyvers flowur
Fresshely they dresse and make swete my bowur,
With, 'Speke, Parott, I pray yow,' full curteslye they sey,
'Parott ys a goodlye byrde and a pratye popagay.'[39]

A few lines later, Parrot tells his readers that he is 'a mynyon to wayte apon a

---

[36] *Why Come Ye Nat to Courte?*, ll. 41–8.
[37] *Speke Parott*, ll. 186–9.
[38] See F. W. Brownlow, '*Speke Parott*: Skelton's Allegorical Denunciation of Cardinal Wolsey', *Studies in Philology*, 65 (1968), pp. 124–39, esp. p. 135.
[39] *Speke Parott*, ll. 11–14.

quene' and refers to 'Kateryne incomporabyll, owur royall quene'.[40] This suggests that, although Skelton had been banished the king's presence, or else did not dare to go near it, he was not yet in such disgrace or fear that he could not still frequent the chambers of Catherine of Aragon and her ladies. Indeed, he says that 'with ladyes I lerne and goe with them to scole.'[41] From this we can infer that Skelton was in close collusion with the queen's faction, sharing their growing awareness and experience ('learning and going with them to school') of Wolsey's despotical presumption. Skelton probably had good cause for wishing to have the clause concerning the harbouring of fugitives omitted from his lease.

Further references to Skelton's withdrawal from the king's court occur in the two satires that followed *Speke Parott* the following year. Near the end of *Collyn Clout* (1522), when the poet declares he will lay down his pen, he likens himself to a ship retreating into a safe haven:

> The forecastell of my shyppe
> Shall glyde and smothely slyppe
> Out of the wawes wodde
> Of the stormy flodde,
> Shote anker, and lye at rode,
> And sayle nat farre abrode,
> Tyll the coost be clere
> That the lodesterre appere.[42]

The metaphor effectively intimates where Skelton will be: in sanctuary (out of the 'stormy flodde'), at Westminster ('nat farre abrode').[43] We can infer that by this time he had retreated there near permanently. He has ventured abroad, but having written *Collyn Clout*, he now intends to withdraw into the sanctuary until the storm he knows his satire will create will have died down. In this instance we know almost precisely where Skelton had been – in the dwelling of William Thynne, later the publisher of Chaucer's works, and a reformer whose concern with corruption in the church would lead him to develop Lutheran leanings. Nearly eighty years later, Francis Thynne, his son, claimed that Wolsey had borne a grudge against his father,

> . . . for that my father had furthered Skelton to publishe his Collen Cloute againste the Cardinall, the moste parte of whiche Booke was compiled in my fathers howse at Erithe in Kente.[44]

---

[40] Ibid., ll. 19, 36.

[41] Ibid., l. 21.

[42] *Collyn Clout*, ll. 1251–8.

[43] Skelton would subsequently use the image of a storm-beaten ship twice more to recall his retreat into sanctuary in *A Garlande of Laurell* (see ll. 540–6, 829–35).

[44] Francis Thynne, *Animaduersions uppon the Annotacions and Corrections of some Imperfections of Impressiones of Chaucers Workes*, ed. G. H. Kingsley, Early English Text Society (London, 1865), p. 10.

Francis Thynne may have erred over certain details. Skelton may not have written *Collyn Clout* at the same house in Erith in which Francis grew up, because his father did not rent it until 1531, after Skelton's death.[45] Nevertheless, the story carries conviction. William Thynne was a clerk of the royal kitchen, and had an enthusiasm for poetry. Skelton and Thynne would therefore have had good reason to know each other, both being at court, both sharing a fondness for literature, and both dismayed at Wolsey's perversion of the church. It is entirely credible that Skelton would have been prepared to venture out of sanctuary to concert his attack on the cardinal in the house of a sympathetic friend committed to a common cause. Erith was within easy travelling distance downriver from London, but far enough away to be out from under the cardinal's gaze. Francis Thynne is emphatic in declaring that Skelton wrote *Collyn Clout* at Erith, and that it was in the house of his father that he did so. Whether or not it was in the particular house the elder Thynne rented in 1531, there is no reason to disbelieve him.

By the time of *Why Come Ye Nat to Courte?* (November 1522), it is clear that Skelton was staying away from the court permanently, voluntarily 'pent in' within the sanctuary at Westminster, because he dared not venture outside it. Skelton draws attention to this fact by emphasizing his absence from court in the title. Having propounded the question he wants uppermost in his readers' minds, he proceeds to answer it at length, and spells out more clearly what had already been obliquely insinuated in the two earlier satires. Skelton will not come to court, he declares,

> For age is a page
> For the courte full unmete;
> For age can nat rage,
> Nor basse her swete swete.
>   But whan age seeth that rage
> Dothe aswage and refrayne,
> Than wyll age have a corage
> To come to court agayne.[46]

The old poet, Skelton ('Age'), is staying away from court not only because he is unprepared to muzzle himself and flatter Wolsey, but also because he knows that the cardinal ('Rage') is incensed against him. He will only come back when the cardinal refrains from persecuting his critics. Besides, to which court should he come?

> To the kynges courte?
> Or to Hampton Court?

---

[45] See Edwards, *Skelton*, pp. 209–10.
[46] *Why Come Ye Nat to Courte?*, ll. 32–9.

Nay, to the kynges court!
The kynges courte
Shulde have the excellence;
But Hampton Court
Hath the preemynence![47]

We are confronted, then, with a situation in which Skelton, although not literally 'imprisoned', for he was free to venture outside the sanctuary walls in so far as he dared to, had voluntarily confined himself within Westminster for the sake of preserving himself against Wolsey's wrath. On the evidence of *Speke Parott*, we know that he had already partially been forced to withdraw there *before* he began writing his attacks on Wolsey. The next question to be answered concerns the events that made him do so.

Several scholars have recognized that Skelton was exploiting the potential protection that sanctuary could offer at least as early as 1521, and possibly by 1519–20,[48] but the evidence suggests that he had already begun to foresee that he might need it as a refuge at a much earlier date still. The omission of the clause in Skelton's lease suggests that he may have been in trouble by August 1518, or at least was anticipating it. For this hypothesis to be confirmed, one must find an occasion of enmity between Skelton and the cardinal which predated 1518, and which was sufficiently serious to provoke the king's displeasure.

Such an occasion exists – in the incident alluded to in *Against Venemous Tongues*. From this unfortunate event developed all Skelton's future troubles. As a result of it he lost the support of the noble patrons who had sponsored his return to court, and entered into an antagonism with Wolsey that would become steadily more serious, until he could no longer maintain himself at court with impunity. Skelton eventually would have no option but to withdraw, in the absence of favour, and for the sake of self-protection, into his tenement within the Westminster sanctuary.[49] The three later invectives against Wolsey were not so much the cause of his troubles, as a desperate attempt to get himself out of them.

Against Venemous Tongues was written in 1516. This can be established from the rubric of the title, in which Skelton states that he wrote the piece in the third

---

[47] Ibid., ll. 403–9.

[48] Brownlow, *Studies in Philology*, 65(1968), pp. 124–39, esp. p. 135; cf. Walker, *John Skelton and the Politics of the 1520s*, p. 73.

[49] I am indebted to Dr Greg Walker for first drawing attention to the possibility that Skelton was on the fringes of court life by 1521, not at the centre, although I disagree with his explanation and conclusions (see *John Skelton and the Politics of the 1520s*, pp. 49–51).

year of his appointment as *orator regius*.[50] A reference to the meeting between Henry VIII and his sister, Margaret Queen of Scotland, at Tottenham on 4 May 1516, narrows the date still further. Skelton was in the habit of posing rhetorical questions in his poems concerning topical events.[51] *Against Venemous Tongues* was therefore most probably written about May or June of that year.

This fairly precise dating helps to explain why the incident to which Skelton refers blew up out of all proportion. In the poem itself, Skelton is trying to defend himself against a rumour being spread by a nobleman's retainer that he has criticized the use of armorial devices on the livery of the nobility. In May 1516 this was a particularly sensitive issue, for Wolsey, concerned to keep the nobles in check, had ordered spies to report to him the names of all men who were in livery during Queen Margaret's visit.[52] Skelton himself refers to this fifth-column activity in *Against Venemous Tongues*:

> ... men be now tratlers and tellers of tales;
> *What tidings at Totnam*, what newis in Wales,
> ...
>
> And all is not worth a couple of nut shalis.
> But lering and lurking here and there like spies,
> The devill tere their tunges and pike out their ies![53]

As a result of this intelligencing, Wolsey had a group of nobles, including the Earl of Surrey, the Marquis of Dorset, Lord Abergavenny, Lord Hastings, Sir Richard Sacheverell, and Sir Edward Guilford, called before Star Chamber because they had excessive numbers of men in livery at the meeting with the Scottish queen.[54] It is small wonder then, that Skelton felt a pressing need to pacify any anger on the part of these lords arising from the incautious remark he had obviously made about ostentatious livery. None of the nobles suffering humiliation at Wolsey's hands would have taken kindly to having the situation inflamed by someone with a loud mouth like Skelton, who was in a position at court to do them harm by his meddling.

In his attempt to extricate himself, Skelton was forced into an extraordinary act of double-speak. In *Against Venemous Tongues*, he simultaneously tried to deny the charge that he had criticized the wearing of livery by noble servants, while reiterating the criticism with respect to a different target. Having vented his

---

[50] The date supposes that Skelton's original patent, dated in 'la cinquième année' of the reign of Henry VIII, was issued in 1513 as Du Resnel allows, and not in 1512 as Edwards and Nelson supposed (see Nelson, *Skelton*, p. 122; also Edwards, 'The Dating of Skelton's Later Poems', *Publications of the Modern Language Association*, 53 (1938), pp. 601–11).

[51] See, for example, *Why Come Ye Nat to Courte?*, ll. 233–398.

[52] Pollard, *Wolsey*, p. 76, n. 2.

[53] *Against Venemous Tongues*, ll. 63–8. My italics.

[54] Letter of Thomas Allen to Lord Shrewsbury, 8 June 1516, *LP*, II, i, no. 1959.

spleen against the particular retainer who had reported what he is alleged to have said, Skelton denies that there is any substance in the rumour:

> For before on your brest, and behind on your back
> In Romaine letters I never founde lack
> In your crosse rowe nor Christ crosse you spede,
> Your Pater noster, your Ave, nor your Crede.
> Who soever that tale unto you tolde,
> He saith untruly, to say that I would
> Controlle the cognisaunce of noble men
> Either by language or with my pen.[55]

The pun on the word 'lack' generates a contrived ambiguity, allowing this passage to say two diametrically opposite things, depending upon whom one takes as the object of reference. The first two lines could be paraphrased thus: 'I never had any cause to blame *you* for having Roman letters embroidered on the front and back of your tunic' (that is, because the person being addressed did not have any). Alternatively, it could be paraphrased as meaning: 'I never found any shortage ('lack') of Roman letters on the front and back of your livery' (with reference to an unspecified person who is not present, but to whom Skelton is alluding). If taken as referring to the nobleman's retainer who reported Skelton's supposed slander, these lines disclaim any responsibility for the statement: Skelton had had no occasion to complain of the livery of any noble servants because there were, literally, no 'Roman' letters on it. To this extent he is being entirely sincere when he affirms that he would never presume to 'controlle the cognisaunce [that is, the armorial device] of *noble* men', either by word of mouth or in writing. This disclaimer does not preclude the possibility, however, that he has indeed criticized the livery of someone else who is, implicitly, not a noble. To underline this point, he repeats his criticism, provocatively:

> There is *no noble man* wil judge in me
> Any such foly to rest or to be.
> . . .
>
> But yet I may say safely, so many wel lettred,
> Embraudred, enlasid together, and fettred,
> And so little learning, so lewdly alowed,
> What fault find ye herein but may be avowed.[56]

By avowing that he would never presume to correct a member of the nobility, while nevertheless reiterating his criticism, Skelton is trying to make his intended readers (who almost certainly included the nobles themselves) realize that his

[55] *Against Venemous Tongues*, ll. 16–23.
[56] Ibid., ll. 34–41. My italics.

original barb had been directed at another target, and that the nobles are exempt from his disapproval.

The allusion to 'Roman letters' indicates who and what that target had been. Wolsey had been created a cardinal by the Roman pontiff in September 1515, an honour that was conferred upon him at a ceremony so magnificent that it moved Cavendish to remark that he had never seen the like 'oonlesse it had byn at the coronacion of a myghti prynce or kyng.'[57] Cavendish has also left a description of Wolsey's retinue on one of his departures from London:

> [He had] byfore hyme of gentillmen a great nomber iij^{re} in a rankke in blake veluett lyuere Cottes, and the most part of them w^t great chayns of gold abought ther neckes / And all his yomen w^t noble men and gentilmens seruauntes folowyng hyme in ffrenche tauny lyuere Coottes hauyng embrodered vppon ther bakes & brestes of the same Coottes thes letters / T and C / [short for 'Thomas Cardinalis'] vnder the Cardynalles hatte.[58]

That was in 1527, but there is no reason to suppose that the cardinal, who had taken 'unexampled pains' to ensure a fitting splendour for his investiture, was not already using this livery for his servants in 1516.[59] Such ostentation must have made Wolsey's attacks on the use of livery by the nobles seem all the more intolerable, for he was seeking to diminish their status in order to enhance his own. Skelton obliquely expresses his outrage at this hypocritical presumption in one of the Latin comments he includes in *Against Venemous Tongues*:

> Nobilitati ignobilis cedat vilitas. Etc.[60]

> [Let low-born baseness give way to nobility.]

From this we can infer that Skelton's original satiric remark had been directed at Wolsey for attempting to restrict the numbers of noble servants in livery while presuming to expand the numbers of his own. Skelton's world view was deeply conservative; the nobles were an essential part of the hierarchical social structure that God in his wisdom had bestowed upon humanity, and Skelton's loyalty to them was constant and unwavering. The sight of a base-born commoner elbowing his way past them must have struck Skelton as an affront to the divine order of things. His devotion to the nobility makes it all the more unfortunate, therefore, that in the fraught circumstances of Wolsey's inquisitorial clampdown, in May and June of 1516, his remarks had been reported to some unspecified noble whom Skelton was anxious not to offend. That is the reason for Skelton's

---

[57] Cavendish, *The Life and Death of Cardinal Wolsey*, p. 16/35–6.
[58] Ibid., pp. 44/31–45/1.
[59] Edwards, *Skelton*, p. 165.
[60] *Against Venemous Tongues*, l. 33, gloss.

furious vilification of the unknown informant. The poet feared that he had been compromised with the noble family who had been backing him at court – which was indeed the case. It is doubly ironic that, in trying to repair the damage by writing *Against Venemous Tongues*, Skelton may have betrayed to Wolsey his contemptuous attitude towards him. The calculated obliqueness of the poem shows that Skelton was concerned not to attack the cardinal openly, but he had nevertheless given Wolsey all the evidence he needed to regard Skelton as a malicious enemy. Even after this initial damage had been done, Skelton did everything possible to avoid antagonizing the cardinal further, until Wolsey's assault on the privilege of sanctuary in 1519 forced Skelton into a position where he had nothing further to lose by attacking him, and, indeed, needed to if he were to survive.

By late 1516, therefore, Skelton was in serious trouble. Apart from providing Wolsey with ammunition to use against him, he had also offended the one nobleman whose support he could least afford to lose – Thomas Howard II, the Earl of Surrey and future third Duke of Norfolk.

A determined effort has been made recently to disprove the older view that Skelton enjoyed the patronage of the Howards,[61] but in spite of major modifications that need to be made to the traditional account, the evidence supports it. Edwards, in the standard account of Skelton's life and works, argued that Elizabeth Stafford Howard, daughter of the Duke of Buckingham and wife of Thomas Howard II, was Skelton's patron, and that he wrote the anti-Wolsey satires as her retainer, and at her instigation.[62] The satires are therefore to be seen, Edwards argues, as the Howards attacking Wolsey through their poet in revenge for the execution of Buckingham in 1521. It has rightly been objected that the Howards showed no overt hostility to Wolsey during these years, and that it is unlikely that they would have countenanced such an attack if open sponsorship of Skelton could have allowed its origins to be traced back to them.[63] The Howards were too circumspect in the delicate circumstances of 1521 to risk suffering the same fate as Buckingham. Edwards was wrong, therefore, to conclude that Skelton was an agent of the Howards when he wrote his three invectives, but he was not entirely off the right track.

What those scholars who wish to detach Skelton from the Howards have overlooked is that Skelton himself left several veiled accounts of his relationship to them. One is to be found in *A Garlande or Chapelet of Laurell*, which, in part, forms a retrospective allegory of Skelton's experience from the onset of his

[61] See Walker, *John Skelton and the Politics of the 1520s*, pp. 1–34.
[62] Edwards, *Skelton*, pp. 198, 204–8.
[63] Walker, *John Skelton and the Politics of the 1520s*, pp. 17–18.

troubles at the time of *Against Venemous Tongues*, to his reception back into Howard favour. Before this allegory can be properly assessed, however, it is necessary to establish that the poem was indeed composed in early 1523, not in 1495 as has been recently proposed.

Dyce, Edwards, Nelson all agreed that *A Garlande of Laurell* was written at Sheriff Hutton Castle in Yorkshire sometime during December 1522 and January 1523.[64] Several later scholars, some prompted by doubts as to whether Skelton wrote the anti-Wolsey satires as a Howard agent, have tried to date the poem earlier.[65] Tucker argues that Skelton was unlikely to have been at Sheriff Hutton Castle in 1523 because there is no record of it, a royal castle, being granted to anyone between 1485 and 1525 when Henry Fitzroy, Henry VIII's natural son, took possession, and because there is no evidence that Thomas Howard II stayed there during 1523.[66] He then looked for another occasion on which Skelton could have been there in the company of the ladies named in the poem. Identifying these ladies with women alive in the 1480s and 1490s, and using an astronomical interpretation of the opening *incipit*, Tucker proposed that the poem dates to 8 May 1495.[67]

None of these arguments is very convincing, and they make nonsense of the poem itself. Just because there is no record of Thomas Howard II staying at Sheriff Hutton in 1523, this does not mean that his wife and her retinue did not. The castle had been made available for the use of his father, Thomas Howard I, while he served as lieutenant-general of the north, and there is no reason to suppose that it was not likewise made available to Thomas Howard II, or his family, when he mounted his campaign against the Scots in early 1523, also as lieutenant-general of the north. Indeed, when the Earl of Shrewsbury was appointed lieutenant-general of the north in 1522, he had been expressly granted the use of Sheriff Hutton for a residence.[68] The Countess of Surrey and her household, Skelton among them, may well have preceded her husband to the north to take up residence nearby for at least part of what must have been envisaged as a fairly protracted campaign.[69] Thomas Howard II naturally did not base himself there in 1523 because it was too far from the border, where his brief

[64] See Skelton, *Poetical Works*, ed. Dyce, II, p. 318; Edwards, *Skelton*, pp. 226–7; and Nelson, *Skelton*, pp. 190–7.

[65] See Walker, *John Skelton and the Politics of the 1520s*, pp. 17–23.

[66] Melvin J. Tucker, 'Skelton and Sheriff Hutton', *English Language Notes*, 4 (1967), pp. 254–9.

[67] Melvin J. Tucker, 'The Ladies in Skelton's *Garland of Laurel*', *Renaissance Quarterly*, 22 (1969), pp. 333–45.

[68] *LP*, III, ii, no. 2875 (iii); *LP*, III, ii, no. 2412. I am indebted to Dr. John Guy for drawing my attention to the latter reference.

[69] The king was informed as early as August 1522 that the Duke of Albany was preparing an army royal of Scots and Frenchmen to invade England, upon which Lord Shrewsbury was appointed lieutenant-general as a temporary measure until Thomas Howard II, the lord admiral, was sufficiently free from his engagements in the French war to take over (see Hall, *Union of the Two Noble Famelies*, fo. 102).

was to carry out a series of punitive raids on the Scots. But it was an ideal place in which the countess could reside while her husband was in the field.

Astronomical dating is notoriously unreliable, as poets often used it to satisfy generic criteria rather than to signify an actual date. Given that Skelton sets the poem in winter, refers to Janus making his almanac for the New Year, and published the poem in October 1523, it seems perverse to date it to the summer of 1495, especially when the astronomical data just as readily supports a date of 1523, when Mars was similarly 'retrogradant' and the moon 'plenarly did shyne'.[70]

Indeed, the date of 8 May 1495 creates more problems than it solves. It forces Tucker into identifying the ladies in *A Garlande of Laurell* with the generation that preceded them. This mistake is very easy to make in the early Tudor period because of the prevalence of homonyms; parents tended to name their children after themselves, or grandparents, aunts, and uncles. Tucker's identifications produce some unlikely results. The Jane Blennerhasset he selects died in 1501 at the age of 97; she would therefore have been 91 in 1495 when she is supposed to be stitching Skelton's garland of laurel, which is possible, perhaps, but improbable. Similarly, his Margaret Hussey was dead by 1492, three years before the date when he imagines the poem to have been written, and by 1495 his Margaret Wentworth had changed her name to Seymour. It makes much more sense to identify the names in *A Garlande of Laurell* with the daughters and grandaughters of the women Tucker proposes. Possible identifications can be found for most of them.[71] Elizabeth Howard is the daughter of Thomas Howard I's second marriage (to Agnes Tylney), not of his first; Muriel Howard is not the one who died in 1512, but probably one of the five children of Thomas Howard II, specifically the 'litell lady' whom he was anxious to marry to the heir of the late Lord Mounteagle in April 1523;[72] Anne Dacre is the wife of Thomas Fienes, eighth Lord Dacre of the South, who died in 1534; Margery Wentworth is the daughter not of Sir Henry Wentworth (who died in 1499), but more probably of Sir Richard Wentworth, as Dyce proposed; Margaret Hussey ('As mydsomer flowre, / Jentill as fawcoun / Or hawke of the towre') is not the daughter of Simon Blount who died in 1492, but one of the children of Sir John Hussey to whom Lord Darcy commends himself in a dispatch of August 1523.[73] There is no need, therefore, to opt for earlier identifications that turn the poem into an incoherent mess, when there is plenty of corroborating evidence to support the suggestions that the poem itself makes. In 1523 *A Garlande of Laurell* was a topical poem. In

---

[70] *A Garlande of Laurell*, ll. 3–6; see Nelson, *Skelton*, p. 191; for the counter-argument, see Owen Gingerich, 'The Astronomical Dating of Skelton's *Garland of Laurel* ', *Huntington Library Quarterly*, 32 (1969), pp. 207–20.

[71] See Dyce, II, pp. 321–4.

[72] Letter from Surrey to Wolsey, 15 April 1523, *LP*, III, ii, no. 2960.

[73] *LP*, III, ii, no. 3276.

it, Skelton refers to *Collyn Clout*, which he had written the year before, and which had become sufficiently notorious to cause Wolsey to harbour a grudge against William Thynne for having urged Skelton to circulate it.[74] He sets the poem in Yorkshire, near the scene of a current war being pursued under the leadership of one of the foremost nobles of the day, and when, in this poem, he depicts the Countess of Surrey, he could hardly have expected any contemporary reader not to assume that he was referring to Elizabeth Stafford Howard, the wife of that famous military leader. It is pointless to try to force an improbable early date on *A Garlande of Laurell* when recognition of early 1523 as its true date allows one to trace in it the outline of the missing episodes in Skelton's career.

A Garlande of Laurell is cast as a dream vision in which Skelton witnesses himself being received into the court of Fame by acclamation. This framing action is duplicated by a smaller action within it, in which Skelton is received into the chamber of the Countess of Surrey, who rewards him for his service by giving him a garland of laurel embroidered by her ladies. The two actions are thus mirrored in one another, and the generalized outcome of the larger is translated by implication into the specific outcome of the smaller. In case the reader does not register this suggestion (that is, that Skelton has found favour with the countess because of his outstanding merit as a poet and his past service to her), Skelton adds a rubric to the title informing the reader that the poem was 'studyously dyvysed at Sheryfhotten Castle' in Yorkshire, and depicts himself at the beginning of *A Garlande of Laurell* as being 'in the frytthy forest of Galtres', soaked through with its winter mud ('Ensowkid with sylt of the myry wose').[75] When he wakes up near the end of the poem, he sees 'Janus, with his double chere, / Makynge his almanak for the new yere.'[76] These details are meant to hint to Skelton's readers that he is in the vicinity of the Countess of Surrey's residence at Sheriff Hutton Castle, sometime in the New Year of 1523.

He has not, at this stage, been admitted into the countess's household. We learn this in the earlier part of the poem when Skelton, to magnify the triumph of his elevation at the end of the poem, represents the unhappy situation that had moved him to seek it. As he watches the multitude of poets suing for fame, he sees Apollo with a laurel crown on his head lamenting the loss of Daphne. Given that Skelton is to receive a laurel crown later in the poem, Apollo is a typological figure of himself, which makes Apollo's lamenting words all the more significant:

> 'Daphnes, my derlynge, why do you me refuse?
> Yet loke on me, that lovyd you have so longe,
> Yet have compassyon upon my paynes stronge.
>   . . .

---

[74] *A Garlande of Laurell*, l. 1234. Evidence of the circulation of *Collyn Clout* is provided by its appearance in John Colyns's commonplace book (British Library MS Harley 2252).

[75] *A Garlande of Laurell*, ll. 22–3.

[76] Ibid., ll. 1515–16.

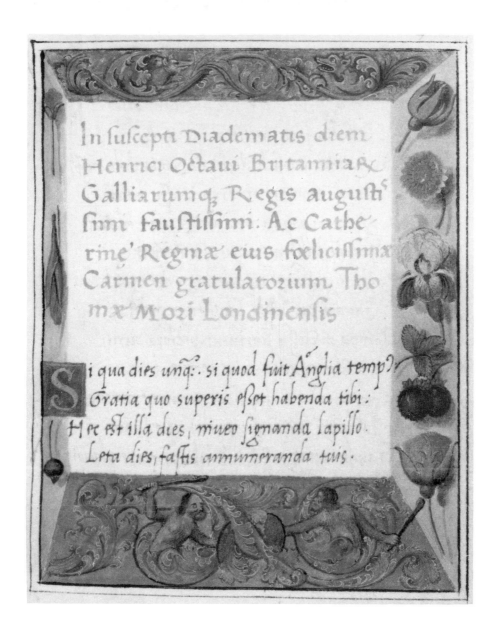

In suscepti Diadematis diem
Henrici Octaui Britanniæ
Galliarumq; Regis augustis
simi Faustissimi. Ac Cathe
rine' Regmæ eius foeliciissimæ
Carmen gratulatorium. Tho
mæ Mori Londinensis

Si qua dies unq̃: si quod fuit Anglia tempo?
Gratia quo superis esset habenda tibi:
Hæc est illa dies, niueo signanda lapillo.
Leta dies, fastis annumeranda tuis.

Page from the presentation copy of Thomas More's congratulatory poems on the coronation of Henry VIII

Title page from Stephen Hawes's *Joyful Medytacion* depicting the coronation of Henry VIII and Katherine of Aragon

The comforte of louers made and compyled by Ste=
uen Hawes somtyme grome of the honourable cham=
bre of our late souerayne lorde kynge Henry þ seuenth
(whose soule god pardon). In the seconde yere of the
reygne of our most naturall souerayne lorde kyge Hen
ry the eyght.

Title page of Stephen Hawes's *The Conforte of Louers*, showing Amour and the Pucell
in the garb of the Tudor court

Sir Thomas More, by Hans Holbein

Mary Tudor (the Pucell of Hawes's *The Conforte of Louers*) with her second husband, Charles Brandon, Duke of Suffolk, by an unknown artist

The Great Seal of Henry VIII. When Wolsey travelled to the Continent in 1521 he took the Great Seal with him, thus hindering legal business at home – a fact to which Skelton alludes in *Speke Parott*

Cardinal Thomas Wolsey, by an unknown artist. The target of John Skelton's satires

Henry VIII, by Joos van Cleve, showing his youthful virility, the subject of much propagandistic literature of the period

Sketch of *The Mount Parnassus*, designed by Holbein for the tableau at Gracechurch Street for the coronation of Anne Boleyn, which provides a visual correlative for the verbal pageantry in Edward Hall's *Union of the Two Noble and Illustre Famelies of Lancastre and Yorke*

Henry VIII dining in the Privy Chamber. This sketch gives some impression of how the 'Minions' (the Vices in John Skelton's *Magnyfycence*) might have been in attendance on the king

The Great Hall, Hampton Court Palace, typical of the kind of venue where *Godly Queene Hester* might have been played

Sir Thomas Wyatt, by Hans Holbein

Hans Holbein, *A Lady of the Cromwell Family* until recently considered to be a portrait of Queen Catherine Howard, the protagonist of the anonymous play *Godly Queene Hester*

Anne Boleyn, by Hans Holbein

Hans Holbein, '*Noli me tangere*'. This painting is recorded as being owned by Henry VIII about the time that Wyatt would have been writing his poems on Anne Boleyn. If the picture were hanging at court, as is likely, Wyatt, in writing 'Who so list to hounte' could count upon the words 'Noli me tangere' to trigger off definite (and ironic) associations in the minds of members of his courtly audience

Henry Howard, Earl of Surrey, by William Scrots, *c.*1550, suggesting the princely affectation that eventually caused his downfall (see p. 289)

Why have the goddes shewyd me this cruelte,
Sith I contryvyd first princyples medycynable?
I helpe all other of there infirmite,
But now to helpe myselfe I am not able.
That profyteth all other is nothynge profytable
Unto me . . .

  . . .

O fatall Fortune, what have I offendid?'[77]

These lines present a symbolic analogue to Skelton's own recent predicament. He, too, had been long devoted to a mistress who had subsequently taken offence at him. He had found this displeasure inexplicable, as the action that had caused it – his contriving of 'princyples medycynable' – had been designed for the benefit of others and not for himself. It had therefore struck him as doubly ironic that what he was doing on behalf of others had been useless as a remedy for his own malaise. We can detect in the Apollo analogue a thinly disguised allusion to the consequences of Skelton's quarrel with Wolsey. He had attempted to cure others (the nobles) of their infirmity (their degradation at the hands of Wolsey), by trying to curb Wolsey's excesses with sharp medicine (his satiric criticisms). Even though he had been able to help them in this way, he had not been able to protect himself from the cardinal's wrath. On top of that, he had offended his mistress (the Countess of Surrey), who had withdrawn her favour from him.

This interpretation of the allegory in this passage is reinforced by the striking resemblance in thought and sentiment it bears to the lines in *Speke Parott*, in which Parrot describes the 'mone' Pamphilus made when he lost his mate:

My propir Besse,
My praty Besse,
Turne ons agayne to me;
For slepyste thou, Besse,
Or wakeste thow, Besse,
Myne herte hyt ys with the.

My deysy delectabyll,
My prymerose commendabyll,
My vyolet amyabyll,
My joye inexplicabill,
Nowe torne agayne to me.

I wyl be ferme and stabyll,
And to yow servyceabyll,
And also prophytabyll,
Yf ye be agreabyll,

---

[77] Ibid., ll. 297–316.

My propyr Besse,
To turne agayne to me.

Alas, I am dysdayned,
And as a man halfe-maymed,
My harte is so sore payned,
I pray the, Besse, unfayned,
Yet com agayne to me![78]

As in *A Garlande of Laurell*, the poet laments the onset of disdain in his mistress, and pleads with her to restore her former favour. That this mistress is to be identified with Elizabeth Stafford Howard, the Countess of Surrey, is made practically certain by Skelton's strategic substitution of 'Besse' (Elizabeth) for 'Galathea', which is the name of Pamphilus' actual mistress in the pseudo-Ovidian myth upon which Skelton is drawing.[79] Skelton chose this myth in order to depict his loyalty to the countess in terms of a lover ('Pamphilus' = 'Totus amor' = 'All-loving') who is concerned to recover the love of a mistress from whom he has become estranged. As with Phoebus' lament in *A Garlande of Laurell*, Pamphilus' moan in *Speke Parott* is designed to serve as a symbolic analogue expressing Skelton's own desire to recover the patronage he had once enjoyed, but had lost.[80]

A Garlande of Laurell contains further confirmation of the relationship between Skelton and the Countess of Surrey. In the lyric poem he addresses to her, Skelton likens her to 'Pamphila', who, he declares, 'Habillimentis royall founde out industriously.'[81] Not only does the allusion link her associatively with 'Pamphilus' in *Speke Parott*, like a kind of mythological Papagena to Skelton's Papageno, but it also clearly implies that the countess had been the one responsible for helping Skelton to acquire the green and white robes of the *orator regius*, of which he was inordinately proud.[82] In other words, it was she who had helped him return to court in 1513, as would be appropriate for the wife of the leading magnate in the shire where Skelton served as rector of Diss, in Norfolk.

Apart from confirming that Skelton was trying to repair an estrangement from the Howards, *A Garlande of Laurell* also reinforces the possibility that this estrangement had been caused by consequences arising from the incident re-

[78] *Speke Parott*, ll. 235–56.

[79] The edition Skelton was using was probably the anonymous *Pamphilus de amore cum commento familiari: recenter ac vigilanter impressus* (Rouen: Raulinus Gaultier, 1508), which contains the learned gloss that Skelton facetiously imitates in the version of *Speke Parott* to be found in British Library MS Harley 2252. Edwards correctly guessed that 'Besse' was the Countess of Surrey, but missed the point of Pamphilus' lament by interpreting it in terms of the moralized version of an early Tudor lyric, 'Come over the burne, Besse', suggesting that Pamphilus stands for Christ and Besse for erring mankind (pp. 191–3).

[80] See below, chap. 9, pp. 165–9.

[81] *A Garlande of Laurell*, ll. 850–1.

[82] See *Calliope*, in *Poems*, ed. Scattergood, pp. 112–13.

corded in *Against Venemous Tongues*. Half-way through the poem, Dame Occupacyon leads Skelton out of the forest of Galtres (a symbol of the poet's melancholy because of the emotive associations inherent in its literal etymology, 'gall-trees') to the Countess of Surrey's 'pile' (a fictive image of the castle of Sheriff Hutton). This action is symbolic as well as literal, signifying Skelton's return to favour with the countess. Just as he is about to enter the castle, Skelton sees a personal enemy playing a fiddle. The sight of this antagonist prompts Skelton to unleash a virulent tirade of abuse at him that seems to clash discordantly with the ethos and tone ordinarily required by the decorum of a courtly dream vision. In the course of his outburst, Skelton reveals his enemy's name in numerical cipher. Decoded, the cipher spells 'Rogerus Stathum', whom scholars have identified as a Cambridgeshire man who, in 1482, married Gertrude Anstey, one of the ladies depicted in the poem among the Countess of Surrey's retinue. Edwards speculated that Skelton had been an unsuccessful rival for Gertrude Anstey's hand, but it hardly seems credible that Skelton would harbour feelings of jealousy sufficiently intense to motivate, forty years later, an attack as fierce as the one he delivers:[83]

> His name for to know if that ye lyst,
> Envyous Rancour truely he hight.
> Beware of hym, I warne you; for and ye wist
> How daungerous it were to stande in his lyght,
> Ye wolde not dele with hym, thowgh that ye myght,
> For by his devellysshe drift and graceles provision
> An hole reame he is able to set at devysion.
>
> For when he spekyth fayrest, then thynketh he moost yll;
> Full gloryously can he glose, thy mynde for to fele;
> He wyll set men a feightynge and syt hymselfe styll,
> And smerke, lyke a smythy kur, at sperkes of steile.[84]

Far from being a rival lover, Stathum is more like one of the sinister vices in *The Bowge of Courte*. As Skelton describes him, he is someone who is envious of those who overshadow him in status and preeminence ('stande in his lyght'), and who feigns friendship in order to gain confidences that he can then betray. In this way he is able to get his rivals into trouble, and so diminish them. He is so skilful at such 'devellysshe' drifts that he is able to stir up contention through a whole realm. Skelton speaks as if he is warning his readers against this man, having personally experienced the damage he can cause. There is only one known event in Skelton's career that matches up with such a situation, and it is the rumour spread by a nobleman's retainer that provoked Skelton to write *Against Venem-*

---

[83] Edwards, *Skelton*, pp. 237–8.
[84] *A Garlande of Laurell*, ll. 752–62.

ous Tongues. Indeed, the language and imagery of Skelton's warning against Stathum links it associatively with the similar warning he utters in *Against Venemous Tongues* against the damage caused by malicious informing:

> Such tunges unhappy hath made great division
> In realmes, in cities, by suche fals abusion.
> Of fals fickil tunges suche cloked collusion
> Hath brought nobil princes to extreme confusion.[85]

In the slander he had suffered, Skelton detected the same kind of hellish malice that he would attribute to Stathum in *A Garlande of Laurell*:

> A fals double tunge is more fiers and fell
> Then Cerberus the cur couching in the kenel of hel.[86]

In 1516 Skelton did not know the identity of the malicious informer who had ruined his credit with Thomas Howard and his countess:

> But if that I knewe what his name hight,
> For clatering of me I would him sone quight;
> For his false lying, of that I spake never,
> I could make him shortly repent him for ever;
> Although he made it never so tough,
> He might be sure to have shame ynough.[87]

I am quite convinced that by 1523 Skelton *had* learnt the identity of the person who had betrayed him: it was none other than this same Roger Stathum, a Howard retainer who had seized upon an injudicious remark by Skelton, actually directed against Wolsey, as a means of compromising him either with the Earl of Surrey, or the countess, or both. Having found out who his detractor was, Skelton interpolated his satire on Stathum into *A Garlande of Laurell* to deliver the long-delayed retribution he had promised in *Against Venemous Tongues*. In the light of this background, Skelton's intense bitterness is readily understandable. The man who had informed against him had succeeded in destroying his powerbase just when he most needed it, and we now know what Skelton meant when he claimed that Stathum, 'by his devellysshe drift and graceles provision / An hole reame he is able to set at devysion.' He had helped to exacerbate the contention between Surrey and the cardinal, and at the same time had set Skelton on a path that would force him into direct confrontation with the cardinal and wreck his career for over half a decade. Skelton had a lot to pay Stathum back for, and had he not needed to tread carefully – because Stathum and his wife were

---

[85] *Against Venemous Tongues*, ll. 55–8.
[86] Ibid., ll. 79–80.
[87] Ibid., ll. 73–8.

still in the Howard household, to which Skelton had been labouring for several years to return – his satiric lash would doubtless have been even less temperate.

We are at last in a position to begin to appreciate the true context of the three satires against Wolsey. They were not written on behalf of the Howards, nor were they designed to tell the king what Skelton imagined he wanted to hear. They were a desperate attempt to remedy a situation that had been growing steadily worse for Skelton since 1516. He had lost his Howard patrons; the king had become incensed against him and was totally under the sway of Wolsey, who was his 'derlyng / And his swete hart rote', in any case.[88] It is possible, too, that Wolsey had already set his sights on Skelton after the appearance of *Against Venemous Tongues*, which probably fooled nobody as to its real target, in spite of the poet's efforts to keep this obscure. Prudently, Skelton decided to stay away from court until the coast was clear. The absence of any ostensible attack on Wolsey in his next work, the morality play *Magnyfycence*, shows that Skelton was determined to mollify Wolsey if at all possible. But Wolsey was not a man to be mollified, nor was Skelton a man who was able indefinitely to bite his lip. Once Wolsey had launched his assault on sanctuary in 1519, and had set off on his self-aggrandizing progress through Europe in 1521, the lid must have come off Skelton's patience. Thus, when in 1521 Wolsey left on his embassy to sort out the problems of Europe (and incidentally to nurture his chances of being elected pope), Skelton, motivated by a genuine and deep abhorrence of all that the cardinal stood for, and a fear that even his refuge in Westminster might not ultimately protect him from the long arm of the cardinal, seized his chance. He exploited Wolsey's absence to try to strengthen his position. On one hand he appealed to the Howards for restored patronage, and on the other he tried to turn the nobles against Wolsey by frightening them with a satiric image of the supreme power Wolsey was being allowed to exercise. In this way, he hoped not only to recover his status and livelihood, but also to awaken the moral conscience of the nation.

Initially, Skelton's success was limited, but he did succeed in regaining the Countess of Surrey's favour. Moreover, the old laureate's constant attacks soon had an inflammatory effect, especially in the City, already bristling with discontent over the enforced loans Wolsey had exacted to finance his foreign policy. Eventually, the cardinal must have felt that his position was sufficiently vulnerable for it to be in his interests to silence Skelton. This he did in late 1522 or early 1523, when he reached an accommodation with Skelton in which he promised him a prebend in exchange for his silence and obsequiousness. Even if the price of this compromise was to be a servility enforced upon the old poet for the rest of his life, he had brought about, through daring exploitation of the affective power of fiction, one of the most astonishing coups in literary history.

[88] See *Why Come Ye Nat to Courte?*, l. 666.

9

From Allegory to Action: Skelton's
Speke Parott

By 1521 Skelton's position had become increasingly precarious. His incautious tongue had purchased him an untenable position at court. He had offended Thomas Howard II and his countess with an injudicious remark about livery that had been maliciously reported. In trying to exculpate himself with them, he had merely succeeded in antagonizing Wolsey and, as a result of that, had incurred the displeasure of the king himself. Consequently, at court he dared move only in the circle of the queen and her ladies. He had also lost his privilege of eating at the king's tables, and in the absence of royal favour and noble patronage may have been finding it increasingly difficult to support himself solely on his income from his benefice in Diss, out of which he also had to find the fee to pay his deputy in Norfolk.

For five years after 1516 he tried, as far as we know, to prevent himself from provoking Wolsey any further, but as Wolsey's pride and presumption grew, Skelton found it more and more difficult to remain silent. He had only been doing so out of a fear of punishment and, one suspects, a belief that the storm would blow over and that things would change for the better. As it became obvious that neither was going to happen, Skelton found himself in a position where he had to make a bid to restore his fortunes, or else accept that he was ruined. By 1521 he was ready to exploit any occasion that might allow him to improve his lot.

His opportunity came in late July 1521, when Wolsey set off for Calais on a grand embassy to negotiate peace between Francis I and Charles V. Skelton seized upon his absence as a chance to tip the balance of the scales in his own favour. Apart from being out from under the cardinal's intimidating gaze, Skelton had a second good reason for believing that he might have some success. On 17 May 1521 Edward Stafford, Duke of Buckingham, the Countess of Surrey's father, had been stripped of his dignity and executed as a traitor. Many contemporaries believed that the duke had been convicted on trumped up charges that had originated in Wolsey's malice. Skelton could expect, therefore, that the countess would be particularly receptive to an attack on Wolsey at this time, and that if he could play upon her natural feelings of grievance, it might help restore him to her favour. Having experienced personally the consequences of the cardinal's arrogance and vindictiveness, the countess might now see that Skelton had been right to attack him back in 1516, and that it could be convenient to have his satiric voice attacking Wolsey once again, in the interests of the nobility.

Skelton's appeal to the countess was the linchpin of his whole strategy, and any future moves would be contingent upon her reaction to this first one. *Speke Parott* was initially designed to be a tentative feeler. His approach to the countess and his attack on Wolsey would be very oblique, veiled by allegory, metaphor, and extreme allusiveness. If the countess responded favourably, he could afford to speak out more plainly thereafter. Furthermore, if he were to be received back into Howard favour as a result, that in turn would embolden other nobles to acknowledge their own grievances against Wolsey. In this way, Skelton could hope to recover some of his power and simultaneously activate the moral conscience of the nation.

His plan worked. The successive parts of *Speke Parott* trace the reaction of Elizabeth Howard to his initial plea, and show the encouraging effects of her response on its author. Because it records the dynamic interaction between the poet's interior emotions and external political circumstances as they changed around him, *Speke Parott* demonstrates the instrumental effectiveness of different fictive strategies with unusual clarity and vividness. At first, Skelton uses devices of extreme indirection as a means of feeling his way. The successive stages of the work, composed at chronological intervals, show him casting off indirection in ratio to the degree that his confidence and security was growing. As this occurs, the fictive mode correspondingly changes. Skelton replaces the collection of evocative fragments of the first part with a less impenetrable symbolic projection of the relationship he desires to have with his patroness, drawn from a popular erotic poem used as a subtext. That, in turn, is replaced by the wholly unambiguous mode of the final complaint, in which Skelton at last speaks out 'trew and playne'. The poem thus illustrates perfectly the dynamic interface that can exist between evolving political circumstances and the imagination of the literary artist as he struggles to use the affective power of fiction to grapple with them.

The fictive mode of *Speke Parott* is so complex that it prompted C. S. Lewis to wonder whether Skelton were not the first of the nonsense poets.[1] Once the context of the poem is properly understood, however, its complexity of form can be seen as arising out of the complexity of Skelton's motives. He wished simultaneously to persuade Elizabeth Howard to restore her patronage, to warn people about the dangers of Wolsey's misgovernment, to work out what he himself felt about his own predicament, and to make some active protest while nevertheless avoiding, as he put it, 'the checkmate'. *Speke Parott* therefore

[1] C. S. Lewis, *English Literature in the Sixteenth Century Excluding Drama*, p. 141.

springs from a private, almost subconscious motive, as well as a more public and conscious one. This means that the poem is just as much analytical and reflective for Skelton himself, as it is expressive or generative of meaning that he desires to impart to his readers.

Speke Parott falls into four main sections written at chronological intervals. The strategy of each section derives from Skelton's perception of how the previous section had been received, as well as the effect he desired the next to procure. In the way that the successive parts of the poem are adjusted to take account of past reactions and future purpose and audience, *Speke Parott* foreshadows the process that would take place in the anti-Wolsey satires as a whole.

In the first section of the poem, Skelton, tentative and uncertain of the response he might meet, apparently considered it discreet to advertise himself to the countess in a manner that was indirect, but which would nevertheless arrest her attention and elicit her sympathy. To these ends, he opted for presenting himself through a persona, and the persona he chose was, of all things, a parrot. It was a brilliant stroke. Jean Lemaire de Belges had recently used a parrot to present his suit to Margaret of Burgundy in *L'epître de l'amant vert*, which meant that Skelton's main purpose, though veiled in obscurity, would more readily be discerned, should the Countess of Surrey be disposed to notice it. Also, the well-known talent of parrots for imitating snatches of human speech allowed Skelton to disguise his subversive statements as a nonsensical collection of fragments that the bird has picked up in its mimicry.

There was an even greater advantage to be had from choosing Parrot as a persona; Skelton could exploit both the natural characteristics of parrots and the mythology surrounding them to turn Parrot into a symbolic figure of himself – 'the royal popagay', as he terms himself several times in the poem.[2]

At the simplest level, he invokes the literal image of Parrot in his cage to reflect his own position at court. Parrot's green feathers serve as a correlative for the green of his laureate's robes, while Parrot's status as a caged ladies' pet signifies his own diminished status within the royal household. Skelton is no longer in the king's retinue, but is restricted in his movements to the queen's appartments. A variant reading in the surviving manuscript version of the text shows that Skelton was concerned to reinforce this hint. Originally he wrote that Parrot was sent from Ethiopia 'to grece [i.e. Greece] to *lordes* of estate', but he later changed this to 'greate *ladyes* of estate'.[3] The emendation prepares the reader more effectively for registering the full import of Parrot's statement that he is 'a mynyon to wayte apon a quene'.

At a more profound level, Skelton invokes the myth of Psyttacus, as recorded by Boccaccio in *De genealogia deorum*, in order to suggest further details of his past history and present predicament. Boccaccio records that

[2] See *Speke Parott*, ll. 217, 262a, 357, 404, 446.
[3] British Library MS Harley 2252, fo. 133ᵛ.

Psyttacus, the son of Deucalion and Pyrrha (as Theodontius says), having steeped himself in the learning of his grandfather, Prometheus, went to the land of the Ethiopians where he was held in great veneration. When he had advanced greatly in years, he prayed that he might be withdrawn from human affairs. Agreeing to his request, the gods turned him into the bird bearing his name. The cause of this legend, I believe, is the fame of his name and virtue, which endures perpetually green in this dead, grey-haired old man, just as those birds are green.[4]

Skelton was able to draw upon this myth to establish several symbolic parallels between Psyttacus and himself. Like Psyttacus, he had been steeped in learning, and had also been forced to withdraw from human affairs just as Psyttacus had withdrawn to Ethiopia.[5] Moreover, just as the green colour of a parrot's feathers symbolized to Boccaccio the eternal fame of Psyttacus' name and virtue, so too did it signify the fame of Skelton and his verses. This is what Skelton implies in Parrot's boast that 'When Parrot is ded, he dothe not putrefy.'[6]

Psyttacus' filial relationship to Deucalion made it possible for Skelton to draw still more symbolic autobiographical parallels from the myth, by reaching back into the legend of the father. In De genealogia deorum, Boccaccio describes how a huge flood inundated the world, killing everyone except Deucalion and Pyrrha, who escaped in a boat and landed on Mount Parnassus when the flood receded.[7] There is no mention of Psyttacus being born when this happened. Skelton, however, inventively combines the two legends to suggest that it was Deucalion's flood that drove Psyttacus into Ethiopia:

> My name ys Parott, a byrde of Paradyse,
> By Nature devysed of a wonderowus kynde,
> Deyntely dyetyd with dyvers delycate spyce,
> Tyll Eufrates, that flodde, dryvythe me into Ynde,
> Where men of that contre by fortune me fynde,
> And send me to greate ladyes of estate.[8]

As suggested in the previous chapter, Skelton's reworking of these mythological

---

[4] 'Psytacus Deucalionis & Pyrrhae filius: ut ait Theodontius: Promethei aui sui doctrinis imbutus ad aethiopas abiit: ubi in maxima ueneratione habitus cum in longissimum euasisset aeuum: orauit ut rebus subtraheretur humanis. cuius precibus dii faciles eum in auem sui nominis mutauere. Huius ego fictionis causam credo sui nominis & uirtutis phamam: sunt eo cano mortuo uiri ditate durauit perpetua: uti sunt uirides aues illae' (Giovanni Boccaccio, *Genealogiae Ionnis Boccatii* [*De genealogie deorum*] (Venice, 1494), lib. IV, cap. xlix, fo. 36). See also Nelson, *Skelton*, pp. 182–3; Nelson was the first to identify the Psyttacus myth as one of Skelton's sources.

[5] See above, chap. 2.

[6] *Speke Parott*, l. 213.

[7] *Genealogiae Ionnis Boccatii* (Venice, 1494), lib. IV, cap. xlvii, ('De Deucalione filio Promethei'), fo. 35ᵛ.

[8] *Speke Parott*, ll. 1–6.

allusions serves to create an allegory of his own recent past. Unlike Psyttacus, who withdrew from human affairs voluntarily, Skelton has been driven out of Paradise to Ethiòpia against his will. This alteration alerts the reader to the fact that 'Paradise' signifies the king's court, and Ethiopia ('Ynde') Skelton's retreat to Westminster because of the king's displeasure. From there he is sent to 'greate ladyes of estate', namely, the queen and her ladies, who are still willing and able to receive him. Skelton thus transformed the Psyttacus-Deucalion myth into an ideal vehicle for the kind of indirect autobiographical self-projection and advertisement he wanted.

Having announced who he is, Skelton's next step in *Speke Parott* is to insinuate the idea that Wolsey is the person responsible for all England's ills, including his own. For this purpose he uses Parrot as an instrument for creating a new kind of allegory – one that is not sustained or continuous, but fragmentary and intermittent, being generated by suggestions inhering in snippets of phrases that Parrot pretends to be mimicking.

Parrot's seemingly inconsequential chatter includes fragments of quotations in a variety of foreign languages, proverbs and *sententiae*, and biblical allusions. Given the hints that Skelton has already supplied in describing Parrot's background, these snippets all acquire a contextual significance that progressively and cumulatively conveys what Skelton wants to say, but dares not make explicit. One can see how this tactic works in the passage where Parrot describes how he has come to know so many languages:

> My lady mastres, Dame Phylology,
> Gave me a gyfte in my neste when I lay,
> To lerne all langage and hyt to speke aptlye.
> Now *pandes mory*, wax frantycke som men sey;
> Phronessys for frenessys may not hold her way.
> An almon now for Parott, delycatelye dreste;
> In *Salve festa dyes, toto* ys the beste.
>
> *Moderata juvant* but *toto* dothe exede;
> Dyscrecion ys modyr of nobyll vertues all;
> *Myden agan* in Grekys tonge we rede,
> But reason and wytte wantythe theyr provynciall,
> When wylfulnes ys vicar generall.
> *Hec res acu tangitur*, Parrott, *par ma foye* –
> *Tycez-vous*, Parrott, *tenes-vous coye.*[9]

Parrot is pretending, innocently, to be merely repeating some of the phrases he has learnt to display his learning in foreign tongues. But the actual meaning of the

[9] Ibid., ll. 43–56. I have added italics to 'phronessys' since it is a Greek word, and have omitted the quotation marks printed in Scattergood's edition, as these imply the presence of interlocutors, which is a dubious editorial inference.

phrases implies the existence of a person whose actions fill Parrot with indignation. *'Pandes mory'*, French for 'grow mad', suggests the effects of the emotional pressure Skelton feels at witnessing Wolsey's outrageous conduct without being able to speak out against it. Later in the poem Parrot again refers to the mental instability that the pressure of his insights has provoked:

> Now a nutmeg, a nutmeg, *cum gariopholo*,
> For Parrot to pyke upon, his brayne for to stable.[10]

The cause of that pressure is more clearly indicated in the wordplay of the next line of the stanza quoted above. *Phronesis* is Greek for 'understanding', whereas *phrenesis* means 'madness' or 'frenzy'. In typical Skelton style, the line can be interpreted in two different ways. If 'phrenesis' is translated as 'madness', the line refers yet again to Skelton's own loss of rational control through indignation at Wolsey's behaviour. If, however, it is read as 'frenzy', the line suggests the frenzied activity of Wolsey himself, in his diplomatic manoeuvres on the continent that fly in the face of all sound judgement or policy. Skelton draws out this second implication more explicitly several lines later:

> Besy, besy, besy, and besynes agayne!
> *Que pensez-voz* Parrot? What meneth this besynes?[11]

Similarly, the proverbs that Skelton sprinkles through the passage add to the growing sense of what is wrong in Wolsey's conduct. *'Moderata juvant'* and *'myden agan'* mean respectively 'moderation gratifies' and 'nothing in excess', but the statement immediately following, that 'reason and wytte wantythe theyr provynciall, / When wylfulnes ys vicar general', suggest that moderation is precisely what is lacking. The imagery also identifies Wolsey specifically as the individual responsible for the excess. A 'provincial' is the leader of a province of the church, in this case the *ecclesia Anglicana*; by saying that reason and wit lack their provincial, Skelton is alluding to how Wolsey managed to usurp the authority of William Warham, the Archbishop of Canterbury and true head of the English church, by having himself made the pope's *legatus a latere*, or permanent deputy. Thus, by saying that 'wylfulnes ys vicar generall', Skelton is audaciously identifying Wolsey as the personification of that vice. The final two lines show that Skelton knew full well that in verging upon such explicitness he was taking a great risk:

> *Hec res acu tangitur*, Parrott, *par ma foye* –
> *Tycez-vous*, Parrott, *tenes-vous coye.*

---

[10] Ibid., ll. 183–4.
[11] Ibid., ll. 57–8.

[You have hit the nail on the head, Parrot, on my word –
Shut up, Parrot, be more discreet].

From this it can be seen that in this first section Skelton's method is indirect in
the extreme. Parrot himself confesses as much in order to signal to interested
readers how they should read the poem:

> ... of that supposicyon that callyd is arte,
> *Confuse distrybutyve* ['ordered confusion'], as Parrot hath devysed,
> Let every man after his merit take his parte;
> For in this processe, Parrot nothing hath surmysed,
> No matter pretendyd, nor nothyng enterprysed,
> But that *metaphora, alegoria* withall,
> Shall be his protectyon, his pavys and his wall.[12]

Skelton has deliberately written the poem so that no one can pinpoint any
statement that can be unambiguously read as derogatory or malicious. It is up to
those with sufficient cause to want to know what he is insinuating to figure it out,
and among those people he included the Countess of Surrey and any others who
might feel that Wolsey was becoming a tyrant.

As the poem proceeds, more and more details materialize that gradually build
up a satiric portrait of Wolsey. Parrot draws upon biblical allusions, in particular, for images and analogues to suggest the nature of Wolsey's corruption. A
reference to the episode of the golden calf in Exodus 32 deftly alludes to the
bovine corpulence evident in the surviving portrait of Wolsey, directs a sneer at
his lowly origins as a butcher's son, and intimates the false god that materialistic
greed is leading him to worship – again, with a passing reference to the mental
perturbation these things stir up in Skelton's (Aaron's) mind:

> *Vitulus* in Oreb troubled Arons brayne;
> Melchisedeck mercyfull made Moloc mercyles.[13]

The image of the 'vitulus' (calf) is picked up in the reference to Moloch, who
was the bull-god of the Midianites, and initiates a whole string of bovine images
that will signify Wolsey through the rest of the work. Melchizidek is a figure for
Henry VIII, whose excessive tolerance has been responsible, Skelton thinks, for
Wolsey's excesses.

Wolsey's own self-seeking ambition is cannily exposed in some punning lines
dense with implication even by Skelton's standards:

> Jereboseth is Ebrue, who lyst the cause dyscus.

---

[12] Ibid., ll. 197–203.
[13] Ibid., ll. 59–60.

Peace, Parrot, ye prate as ye were *ebrius*!
Howst the, *lyuer god van hemrik, ic seg*;
In Popering grew peres, whan Parrot was an eg.[14]

In the lines immediately preceding this passage, Skelton has just implied that Wolsey is a traitor who has formed a league with the enemy, just as the descendants of Lot sought support from Assur and the Assyrians. Ironically mocking his pretended pendantry as a bible-clerk with a pun on '*ebrius*', as meaning alternatively 'Hebrew and 'drunk', he now breaks into a phrase of Dutch. In doing so, he is cunningly alluding to Wolsey's presence in Bruges in August 1521, negotiating with the emissaries of Charles V. Wolsey's true purpose is exposed in the extraordinary puns of the next line: 'In Popering grew peres, whan Parrot was an eg.' Poperinghe was a town in Flanders famous for its pears ('peres').[15] 'Peres' can also mean 'peers', while 'Popering' also plays upon the word 'pope'. The line thus insinuates that Wolsey is not engaged in diplomacy for the good of the nation, but because he is concerned to further his own papal ambitions and so become the equal ('pere' = 'peer') of the king himself.

By the time Skelton has come to the end of the first section, in spite of the obscurity of his method, he has amply demonstrated why he thinks Wolsey has been such a disaster for England. The cardinal has brought the church into disrepute and misery, profaned its sanctuaries and dissolved its abbeys, and all to furnish knacks for ladies and found chairs and colleges to foster a new type of education that marked a sad decline from the old.[16] For Skelton, Wolsey could do no right, and his loathing of him was unfeigned.

At the same time as Skelton was insinuating his objections to Wolsey in this first part of the poem, he was also depicting complex feelings about where he himself stood. This was partly a rhetorical device to persuade readers to take his side by eliciting sympathy, but it was also a psychological device to enable him to explore the implications of his own feelings as a preparation for action.

For this purpose, the Psyttacus myth again proved useful. Psyttacus had asked to be removed from human affairs, and was turned into a parrot when the gods granted his request. By depicting himself as a parrot, Skelton is suggesting that he, too, is withdrawn from human affairs, a condition that is symbolized in his confinement within a cage. In one half of his mind, Skelton finds this situation quite comfortable. Even though he has been driven from the king's quarters ('Paradyce'), the royal ladies still make the most of his remaining connections with the court. He has lost favour and influence with the king, and the right of bouge of court, but is still held in regard by the queen and her ladies, who are happy to be entertained by him. Parrot depicts the temptation Skelton felt simply to reconcile himself to this situation:

[14] Ibid., ll. 67–70.
[15] See Skelton, *Poems*, ed. Scattergood, p. 455, note to l. 70.
[16] Ibid., ll. 141–82.

'Moryshe myne owne shelfe,' the costermonger sayth;
'Fate, fate, fate, ye Irysh water-lag.'
In flattryng fables men fynde but lyttyl fayth;
But *moveatur terra*, let the world wag,
Let Syr Wrig-wrag wrastell with Syr Delarag:
Every man after his maner of wayes,
Pawbe une aruer, so the Welche man sayes.

Suche shredis of sentence, strowed in the shop
Of auncyent Aristippus and such other mo,
I gader togyther and close in my crop.[17]

Parrot's 'shredis of sentence' suggest the idea that one should let the rest of the world crumble and look after oneself. 'Moryshe myne owne shelfe' is mock Irish dialect for 'Morris for my own self'. 'Fate, fate, fate' is a dialect imitation of the Irish pronunciation of 'water, water, water', but also contains a pun on 'fate', with the suggestion that what has happened was predestined, and that there is nothing Skelton can do about it. 'In flattryng fables men fynde but lyttyl fayth' embodies Skelton's favourite trick of working two distinct meanings into the single line or phrase. It can suggest either that people like the countess are not liable to be impressed by the kind of flattering fable he is attempting to concoct for her, or, alternatively, that he is deceiving himself if he thinks he can offer *himself* the flattering illusion that there is some remedy for his situation. In either case, the statement reflects Skelton's inclination to accept that it is better for him to do nothing: '*moveatur terra*, let the world wag, / Let Syr Wrig-wrag wrastle with Syr Delarag' – let the nobles fight their own battles with Wolsey; the world can crumble, for all Skelton cares. Nevertheless, even as Skelton propounds these escapist sentiments, his statement that he has gathered them out of the shop of Aristippus shows that his conscience will not really allow him to accept them. Aristippus was the Epicurean philosopher who argued that immediate pleasure is the only end to action. By invoking him, Skelton is confessing that his instincts are unconscionably selfish.

The poet-moralist, therefore, feels obliged to speak out – 'I pray you, let Parot have lyberte to speke' – but no sooner does he acknowledge this impulse, than discretion urges him to restrain it:

But ware the cat, Parot, ware the fals cat!
With, 'Who is there? A mayd? Nay, nay, I trow!
Ware, ryat, Parrot, ware ryot, ware that![18]

Again, the thought and emotions in these lines betray ambivalence and indeci-

[17] *Speke Parott*, ll. 85–94.
[18] Ibid., ll. 99–101.

sion. The cat of whom Skelton must beware is Wolsey, who might destroy the poet should he openly challenge him, as a cat consumes a mouse or bird. On the other hand, Parrot thinks he senses the presence of a maid who, implicitly, might help him. This is the first reference he makes, obliquely, to Elizabeth Howard and the possibility that he might be able to enlist her support. For the time being, however, he depicts himself as being unable to trust in this hope: 'Nay, nay, I trow!'

It soon becomes clear what, in general, Parrot/Skelton is after. He wants encouragement and support to embolden him to take the next step and attack Wolsey directly, and also protection against the cardinal's wrath if he does:

> Support Parrot, I pray you, with your suffrage ornate,
> Of *confuse tantum* avoydynge the chekmate.[19]

Above all, he needs to be cherished and appreciated as he was formerly:

> Parrot is a fayre byrd for a lady;
> God of his goodnes him framed and wrought;
>
> . . .
>
> Make moche of Parrot, the popegay ryall.

> For that pereles prynce that Parrot dyd create,
> He made you of nothynge by his magistye.[20]

Skelton is reminding his readers here of the status to which he had been elevated by the king. In doing so he is also reminding the Countess of Surrey that it would not be beneath her dignity to sponsor him once again.

Speke Parott shows every sign of having originally ended after the first 230 lines of the poem in its present form. It has Skelton's usual valedictory Latin tailpiece, containing verses in which the *vates* celebrates his song as 'full of the god' ('*plena . . . deo*'), extols the fame of Skelton, who is numbered in the catalogue of the muses ('*Skeltonida famigeratum, / In Piereorum cathalogo numeratum*'), and beseeches his readers to understand carefully and cherish their parrot ('*Candidi lectores, callide callete, vestrum fovete Psitacum*').[21] We can therefore suppose that Skelton circulated the poem around the court in this form, and also sent it to the Countess of Surrey.

He was not content to leave it at that, however, for he evidently followed it up with a further instalment specifically addressed to the countess, to make it clear

---

[19] Ibid., ll. 195–6.
[20] Ibid., ll. 211–19.
[21] Ibid., ll. 229–32b.

that his plea for support and protection was aimed at her in particular. This is the section in which a new character, Galathea, appears and presents Parrot with a specific request:

> Speke, Parotte, I pray yow, for Maryes saake,
> Whate mone he made when Pamphylus loste hys make.[22]

These lines mark Skelton's switch to a new strategy. Instead of relying upon the cumulative effect of a bundle of evocative fragments, he now invokes a subtext as an essential key which indirectly explains the full import of what he is saying.

The text in question is *Pamphilus de amore*, a pseudo-Ovidian love story enormously popular at the time, as a marginal comment in MS Harley 2252 makes clear: 'Hic occurrat memorie Phamphilus de Amore Galathee' ('Let here be remembered *Pamphilus de Amore Galatheae*).[23] The marginal note, one of many which could only have been supplied by Skelton himself (as a mock-imitation of the pedantic commentaries used to explicate difficult texts),[24] is a clear signal to the reader to keep the subtext in mind as he or she reads the verses Skelton next gives to Parrot.

The printed edition of *Pamphilus de amore* which Skelton and his readers were almost certain to have known was that published by Raulinus Gaultier in Rouen, in 1508. The work opens with the situation to which Galathea refers: Pamphilus 'bewailing and grieving on account of the violent ardour of his love':

> Vulneror et clausum porto sub pectore telum
> Crescit et assidue plaga: dolorque michi
> Et ferientis adhuc non audeo dicere nomen
> Nec sinit aspectus plaga videre suos
> Unde futura meis maiora pericula damnis
> Spero: salutis opem nec medicina dabit
> Quam prius ipse viam meliorem carpere possim
> Heu michi: quid facio: non bene certus eo
> Conqueror: estque mee iustissima causa querele
> Cum sit consilii copia nulla michi.[25]

---

[22] Ibid., ll. 233–4.

[23] See Skelton, *Poems*, ed. Scattergood, p. 460, note to 233–4.

[24] The Latin glosses are published by Dyce in his edition of Skelton's works. They are not included in Scattergood's edition.

[25] 'I am wounded, and I carry love's weapon out of sight in my breast. The wound constantly grows, causing me to suffer pain, and still I do not dare to pronounce the name of the striker. Nor does the wound allow its face to appear, from which I anticipate that greater dangers will arise in the future to my harm. Neither will medicine give a means of health until I am able to take a better way. Alas! What am I doing? I lament, lacking certainty, and there is a very just cause for my complaint, since I lack any source

Pamphilus is suffering from unrequited love, and feels as if he has a dagger concealed within his breast that keeps wounding him. Lacking advice that can help him, he despairs of being cured, and does not know what to do. Apart from the text of *Pamphilus*, this edition also included an interpretative commentary that is just as important for understanding *Speke Parott* as the text of *Pamphilus* itself. The commentary on the second part of Pamphilus' opening speech reads:

> Pamphilus deliberates on what to do and argues on both sides of the question. At first he thinks that he ought not reveal his love to Galathea, for he fears that if she knew of it, the girl would be ashamed, and, being displeased, would respond harshly and reject him altogether.

At length, however, he invokes the aid of Venus, and decides to take his chance.[26] Skelton plainly wants his reader to bear in mind this subtext so that he or she can recognize that he is developing an implicit parallel between Pamphilus and himself. Just as Pamphilus wants to secure Galathea's favour but fears rejection, so, too, does Skelton wish to approach the Countess of Surrey, but fears incurring her displeasure and being rebuffed.

The plea that Parrot substitutes for Pamphilus' actual complaint in the source, goes a step further in making the allegory explicit, and there can be no doubt that Elizabeth Howard would have recognized herself as the lost mistress whom Parrot/Skelton was entreating:

> My propir Besse,
> My praty Besse,
> Turne ons agayne to me;
> For slepyste thou, Besse,
> Or wakeste thow, Besse,
> Myne herte hyt ys with the
> . . .
> Be love I am constreyned
> To be with yow retayned,
> Hyt wyll not be refrayned:
> I pray yow be reclaymed,
> My propyr Besse,
> And torne agayne to me![27]

---

of counsel' Anon, *Pamphilus de amore cum commento familiari: recenter ac vigitauter impressus* (Rouen, 1508) fo. A1^v.

[26] 'Pamphilus deliberat quid agendum et argumentat ad vtramque partem. Prio quod non debeat suum amorem gallatee reuelare. Nam timet si amorem ipsum puelle reuelauerit: ipsa puella verecundata et male contenta durius respondeat & eum penitus repellar . . .' (ibid., fo. A2^r).

[27] *Speke Parott*, ll. 235–62.

Skelton makes two significant changes to his source that would have jolted the countess into recognizing instantly that these lines expressed Skelton's desire to recover her patronage. First, Parrot-as-Pamphilus moans not for Galathea, his real lover in the source, but for 'Besse', or 'Elizabeth', Skelton's former patroness in real life. Second, there is no suggestion in the source that Galathea has loved Pamphilus before. The refrain of Parrot's entreaty, however, emphasizes the fact that Pamphilus (alias Skelton) wishes to *restore* a relationship that has existed in the past, but has been damaged by some disdain the poet had incurred. As an incentive for the countess to take him back into her household ('To be with yow retayned') Skelton promised to serve her interests:

> I wyl be ferme and stabyll,
> And to yow servyceabyll,
> And also prophytabyll,
> Yf ye be agreabyll,
> My propyr Besse,
> To turne agayne to me.[28]

Implicitly – since he has already demonstrated his willingness to expose Wolsey's abuses in the first part of the poem – Skelton is here promising to use his satiric powers to stir up political opposition to the cardinal on her behalf. Finally, Skelton now describes himself as '*thy* popagay royall', thus emphasizing the personal loyalty he is offering to the countess.[29] This second instalment of *Speke Parott* concludes with yet another of Skelton's typical *explicits*, which suggests that he sent it off to Elizabeth Howard to see what response it would elicit.

The next section, extending from line 265 to line 277a, dramatically records within the fiction itself that Skelton's entreaty was successful. Once again, he picks up the subtext of *Pamphilus de amore* to suggest what has happened – with yet another significant change to the source. In the original, Galathea is not at all pleased with Pamphilus' proposition ('galatee est minime concordans', as the commentary euphemistically declares), and does indeed reject him. This contrasts strikingly with the reaction Skelton depicts in Galathea to what Parrot has said:

> Now kusse me, Parot, kus me, kus, kus;
> Goddes blissyng lyght on thy lytell swete musse!
>
> *Vita et Anima* ['Life and soul' (Latin)]
> *Zoe ke psiche.* ['Life and soul' (Greek)]
>
> *Concumbunt Grece. Non est hic sermo pudicus.*
> [They lie together in Greek. This is not a modest way of speaking.][30]

[28] Ibid., ll. 246–51.
[29] Ibid., l. 262a. My italics.
[30] Ibid., ll. 265–9.

Galathea responds rapturously, as is signified in her kisses, and instead of rejecting Parrot-Pamphilus-Skelton, at once sleeps with him. Unlike Pamphilus in the source, therefore, Parrot is gratified immediately. By this we can understand that 'Besse' (alias Elizabeth Howard), with whom Galathea is to be equated, liked what she read in the earlier part of *Speke Parott* and fell into an immediate complicity with Skelton, appreciating that he could indeed be useful to her were he to be offered Howard patronage. Skelton expresses relief at the successful outcome of his ploy by concluding this section with a prayer:

> Amen
> Amen, Amen,
> Amen, Amen,
> And sette to a D,
> And then hyt ys 'Amend',
> Owur new-founde A.B.C.

> *Candidi lectores calide callete; vestrum fovete Psitacum.*
> [Honest readers, understand craftily; cherish your Parrot.][31]

Having recovered the support of a powerful noble faction, Skelton now at last felt sufficiently secure to launch the full-scale assault on Wolsey that he thought necessary were England to be pulled back from the ruin into which he was convinced it was falling.

Emboldened by his newly restored alliance with the Howards, Skelton continued to augment *Speke Parott* in the form of a series of envoys that he dated according to his private system of chronology.[32] As Nelson demonstrated, these envoys trace the movement of Wolsey and his agents on the continent as well as the diplomatic shuffling between the three monarchs, Francis I, Charles V, and Henry VIII, with considerable exactitude.[33]

Parrot's satiric denunciation of Wolsey is still very elliptical and oblique, but far less obscure than in the first part of the poem. He attacks Wolsey for hindering legal business at home by taking the great seal of England with him, while exposing the pompous pride that has motivated Wolsey to keep it with him:

> With porpose and graundepose he may fede hym fatte,
> Thowghe he pampyr not hys paunche with the grete seall;

---

[31] Ibid., ll. 273a–77a.

[32] See Nelson, *Skelton*, pp. 161–3.

[33] For a detailed explication of all the topical allusions in the envoys, see Nelson, *Skelton*, pp. 165–73; see also Scattergood's notes in Skelton, *Complete Poems*, pp. 461–4.

We have longyd and lokyd long time for that,
Whyche cawsythe pore suters have many a hongry mele;
As presydent and regente he rulythe every deall.[34]

These lines again demonstrate Skelton's extremely subtle and skilful economy
with language. The puns on 'porpose' [porpoise]/'purpose', 'graundepose'
[grampus]/'grand-posturing', and 'seall' as referring bothe to the animal and the
chancellor's seal, enable him to capture Wolsey's self-indulgent hedonism, his
self-importance, and his political irresponsibility all at once. Skelton then
strengthens his indictment by contrasting the luxurious food of Wolsey's banquets with the starvation rations to which his absence condemns poor people
who have suits pending in Chancery, unable to sue for the money that could feed
them. As far as Wolsey's efforts at shuttle-diplomacy are concerned, Skelton's
message is simple: come home. The mission itself is pointless, 'For Jerico and
Jerssey shall mete togethyr as sone / As he to exployte the man owte of the mone',
and, in any case, Wolsey's real motive is simply to serve papal interests in the
hope of increasing his chances of becoming the next pope: 'Of Pope Julius cardys,
he ys chefe Cardynall' [punning on 'card-in-all'].[35]

In spite of the fact that the envoys are still couched in allusive and symbolic
cipher, Skelton nevertheless manages to become increasingly explicit. He does
this chiefly by reiterating significant motifs with increasing insistency. One such
motive is that of the *vitulus bubali*, or bull-calf, which had first appeared in the
early part of the poem in a reference to the golden calf that 'troubled Arons
brayne'.[36] By the time of the fourth envoy, Skelton's reiteration of the motif is so
insistent that no one can fail to discern what it means:

Sicut Aron populumque,
Sic bubali vitulus,
Sic bubali vitulus,
Sic bubali vitulus.

(Like Aaron and the people,
So the bull calf of the ox,
So the bull calf of the ox,
So the bull calf of the ox.)[37]

Just as Aaron took the people's gold to make a false image, so too has Wolsey
plundered the English people to pander to his own greed for glory and luxury.
Even worse, 'vitulus bubali fit dominus Priami!' ('the bull-calf of the ox has

---

[34] *Speke Parott*, ll. 308–12.
[35] Ibid., ll. 306–7; 418–31.
[36] Ibid., ll. 1–59.
[37] Ibid., ll. 377–80.

become the master of Priam'). It is at this point that Skelton makes his most daring challenge. Addressing Henry VIII directly, he declares:

Dum foveas vitulum, rex, regeris, Britonum;
Rex, regeris, non ipse regis, rex inclite, calle;
Subde tibi vitulum ne fatuet nimium.

(As long as you cherish the bull-calf, king of Britain,
you are ruled; learn this, king, you are ruled, you
do not rule yourself, celebrated king;
subdue the bull-calf under you, lest he grow too foolish.)[38]

While Skelton knew this exhortation was not likely to make him popular with the king, far less with Wolsey, what he had been wanting to say all along was now out. There was no longer any reason for Skelton to stay in his cage, protected behind his shield of allegory, because in making this statement he had gone beyond the point of discretion, and committed himself to an irrevocable course in which any further efforts at self-protection were pointless. If Wolsey and the king were going to take offence, they were going to do so on the basis of what he had said already.

It is not surprising, therefore, that when, near the end of the poem, Galathea begs Parrot to 'Sette asyde all sophysms, and speke now trew and playne',[39] he willingly complies. Skelton, metaphorically speaking, has been drawn like Parrot out of his cage, and has allowed conscience and indignation to outweigh his instinct for self-preservation. He now recites a litany of complaints in the manner of popular contemporary ballads such as the anonymous poem, *Now a Dayes*:[40]

> So many trusys takyn, and so lytyll perfyte trowthe:
> So myche bely-joye, and so wastefull banketyng;
> So pynchyng and sparyng, and so lytell profyte growth;
> So many howgye howsys byldyng, and so small howse-holdyng;
> Suche statutes apon diettes, suche pyllyng and pollyng –
> So ys all thyng wrowghte wylfully withowte reson and skylle.
> Syns Dewcalyons flodde the world was never so yll.
>
> So many vacabondes, so many beggers bolde,
> So myche decay of monesteries and relygious places;
> So hote hatered agaynste the Chyrche, and cheryte so colde;

<hr>

[38] Ibid., ll. 350–2.
[39] Ibid., ll. 447–8.
[40] See Furnival, *Ballads from Manuscripts*, I, pp. 93–100.

So myche of my lordes grace, and in hym no grace ys;
So many holow hartes, and so dowbyll faces;
So myche sayntuary brekyng, and prevylegidde barryd –
Syns Dewcalyons flodde was nevyr sene nor lyerd.[41]

As Parrot's roll-call of England's ills unfolds, he makes clear what has been covertly implied from the outset of the poem: decay and corruption are rampant in England, and Wolsey's flawed character and misgovernment are responsible for all of it. By saying so Skelton had unequivocally compromised himself, and whether he liked it or not he was just as unequivocally committed to continue on his chosen course. His next move was to press home audaciously his campaign against the cardinal by appealing to a wider audience. The need to do this stimulated him to further heights of imaginative invention, as *Collyn Cloute* and *Why Come Ye Nat to Courte?*, the next two poems he wrote, will show.

[41] *Speke Parott*, ll. 491–504.

10

Widening the Audience: *Collyn Clout*, and *Why Come Ye Nat to Courte?*

Although *Speke Parott* regained a patron for Skelton, it did not have as wide-spread an effect in militating opinion against Wolsey as Skelton may have hoped for. This was inevitable, given the extreme obscurity wrought by its literary method. The inclusion of some parts of the poem in John Colyns's commonplace book shows that it did arouse the attention of some interested parties, but for the most part his readers simply did not understand it.

Skelton acknowledges the unfavourable reaction *Speke Parott* had received and defends himself against hostile criticism in the envoys to that poem itself:

> . . some folys say ye arre furnysshyd with knakkes,
> That hang togedyr as fethyrs in the wynde;
> But lewdlye ar they lettyrd that your lernyng lackys.[1]

Some of his readers had dismissed the work as mere childish trifling, which stings Skelton in turn to accuse them of having insufficient learning to discern its symbolic allusiveness. He must have been even more disturbed by the derision some of his readers had expressed at the very fact that he was presuming to take on Wolsey. Skelton reserves the full weight of his contempt for this type of detractor:

> Helas! I lamente the dull abusyd brayne,
> The enfatuate fantasies, the wytles wylfulnes
> Of on and hothyr at me that have dysdayne.
> Som sey they cannot my parables expresse;
> Som sey I rayle att ryott recheles;
> Some say but lityll and thynke more in there thowghte,
> How thys prosses I prate of, hyt ys not all for nowghte.

---

[1] *Speke Parott*, ll. 292–4.

O causeles cowardes, O hartles hardynes,
O manles manhod, enfayntyd all with fere,
O connyng clergye, where ys your redynes
To practise or postyll thys prosses here and there?
For drede ye darre not medyll with suche gere,
Or elles ye pynche curtesy, trulye as I trowe,
Whyche of yow fyrste dare boldlye plucke the crowe.[2]

In Skelton's view, attempts to decry his efforts sprang merely from a desire on the part of his detractors to justify their own pusillanimity; they dared not tackle Wolsey themselves, and so, feeling their cowardice exposed by Skelton's own brave attempt, tried to ridicule it.

In spite of his bravado in these passages, the string of *exclamationes* in the final one suggests, in its exaggerated emphasis, that Skelton was seriously worried that these charges might be true. If he wished to make his attack on Wolsey effective, he had to do two things: on one hand he had to make his message more persuasive by making it more coherent, and on the other he had to reach a wider audience. To further these aims he renewed his attack on the cardinal in 1522.

His new assault was launched on several fronts at once, being directed at three main audiences. *Collyn Clout*, written about July 1522, was directed largely at the higher clergy. *Why Come Ye Nat to Courte?*, written about November 1522, was aimed mainly at the nobles. Both poems together were also designed to marshal the opinion of the London citizens against the cardinal. If Skelton's three satires are viewed together, one can see how he deliberately tried to contrive a different fictive strategy in each poem, appropriate to his intended audience and purpose.

In *Speke Parott* he had sought to excite the Countess of Surrey's curiosity by depicting his personal situation obliquely through symbolism and allusion. He had dramatized his reluctance to speak out and his reticence in approaching her, as a means for eliciting her sympathy in the hope that she would encourage him. At the same time his obliqueness functioned as a dramatic representation of the repressive effects of Wolsey's misgovernment on such a one as himself. This, too, was a device calculated to arouse sympathy, this time among a wider audience of nobles at court where, one supposes, *Speke Parott* was circulated in the first instance.

Realizing that this method had failed to arouse many other than the countess, Skelton chose a completely different style in *Collyn Clout*. He still presents himself indirectly, through a persona, but this persona is calculated to procure a more favourable reaction from a different audience – the prelates. Colin Clout is a pastoral character drawn from the tradition of popular complaint.[3] By making

---

[2] Ibid., ll. 383–96.

[3] For the conventions of this genre, see John Peter, *Complaint and Satire in Early English Literature* (Oxford, 1956).

Colin supplicate the bishops on behalf of the common people, to redress their grievances, Skelton was seeking simultaneously to prick the conscience of the prelates, while objectifying the thoughts that the common people had, or ought to have, in order to ensure that such thoughts were uppermost in everyone's mind.

Why Come Ye Nat to Courte? is designed to function as a still more provocative goad. Turning yet again to the nobles, Skelton tries to shock them out of complacency by forcing them to undergo an interior catechism, in which they are brought to face their own realization of the damage Wolsey has been inflicting on them. Skelton invented certain techniques of dislocation to achieve this shock-value: abrupt transitions between different perspectives, the interpolation of dramatized 'voices', and above all a dramatized depiction of the disturbed processes of his own mind. In this way, he sought to overcome the combination of ignorance and complacency in the nobles that had prevented them from registering what he had been trying to say in *Speke Parott*. As Skelton warns Wolsey in *Collyn Clout*:

> For lordes of noble bloode,
> ˙Yf they well understode
> Howe connynge myght them avaunce,
> They wolde pype you another daunce.
> But noble men borne,
> To lerne they have scorne,
> But hunte and blowe an horne,
> Lepe over lakes and dykes,
> Set nothynge by polytykes.[4]

In *Why Come Ye Nat to Courte?*, Skelton tried to ensure that, in spite of their lack of learning, the nobles had all the understanding they needed to take action against the cardinal, and plenty of motive for doing so.

The entire strategy Skelton adopts in *Collyn Clout* is governed by his desire to make his criticisms more effective through making them more palatable. The actual abuses he identifies are much the same as those Parrot denounces in *Speke Parott*: the clergy have grown venal, abuse their legal jurisdiction, neglect preaching, break their vows, indulge in lechery, luxury, and simony, have plundered the monasteries, exacted excessive taxes, promoted division between the spirituality and temporality, and, generally, have brought the church into disrepute. Taken altogether, these charges amount to a very harsh indictment, but Skelton seeks to prevent as much antagonism on the part of the clergy as he can by presenting the

---

[4] *Collyn Clout*, ll. 615–23.

criticism in a very different manner. It is the manner, not the matter, that has changed between *Speke Parott* and *Collyn Clout*.

Skelton's main device for making his satire more persuasive is his choice of Colin Clout as a persona. He characterizes Colin as a man who is extremely diffident about undertaking the task of complaining about the faults in the church and its clergy. People will accuse him either of being a dunce, or of meddling out of tainted motives:

> Sey this and sey that:
> 'His heed is so fat
> He wottyth never what
> Ne whereof he speketh.'
> 'He cryeth and he creketh,
> He pryeth and he preketh,
> He chydeth and he chatters,
> He prayeth and he patters;
> He clyttreth and he clatters,
> He medleth and he smatters,
> He gloseth and he flatters.'
> Or yf he speke playne,
> Than he lacketh brayne.[5]

Even those who do see that he is speaking the truth will not see any need to do anything about it:

> And yf that he hytte
> The nayle on the hede
> It standeth in no stede:
> 'The devyll', they say, 'is dede,
> The devyll is dede.'[6]

By making Colin anticipate that he will meet with the same kind of dismissive reaction that Skelton had already aroused with *Speke Parott*, Skelton is seeking to disarm it in advance. Because Colin knows that his action will be disparaged, his willingness to undertake it serves to enhance the importance of what he has to say. In this way, Skelton hopes to intercept the reactions of his readers, and to make them question the justice of the dismissal to which they may be tempted.

The character he gives Colin also serves this purpose. Colin is a humble unlettered man of simple virtue from the country, as his imagery implies:

> And yf ye stande in doute
> Who brought this ryme aboute,

[5] Ibid., ll. 15–27.
[6] Ibid., ll. 33–7.

My name is Collyn Cloute.
I purpose to shake oute
All my connynge bagge,
Lyke a clerkely hagge.
For though my ryme be ragged,
Tattered and jagged,
Rudely rayne-beaten,
Rusty and mothe-eaten,
Yf ye take well therwith
It hath in it some pyth.[7]

The contrast between this simple rustic and the learned prelates whom he is supplicating is designed to arouse shame. If such a man can see what is wrong with the church, and risk opprobrium to bring it to light, what should they, the true shepherds of the flock, be doing? The character and behaviour of Colin constitutes an implicit rebuke.

Indeed, Skelton exploits the personality of his invented character to invest everything he says with moral authority. Colin is a loyal son of the church who is 'lothe ... to offende', and speaks only out of sorrow ('ruthe') at what he sees happening to the church around him.[8] Besides, he is merely reporting what many other people around the countryside are saying:

Thus I, Collyn Cloute,
As I go aboute,
And wandrynge as I walke,
I here the people talke.[9]

Just as Christopher St German would later find in his polemical battle with Thomas More, the device of 'some say' implies that discontent is widespread, and that what the writer says represents only the tip of an iceberg. Skelton is thus setting up Colin as the voice of the people at large.[10] That is why his choice of the populist complaint genre was especially appropriate. There was one risk in this strategy: Lollards had used the genre of pastoral complaint to spread heretical notions. Skelton takes care to neutralize any suspicion that his anti-clerical satire had heretical overtones, by making one of Colin's main motives for speaking out his fear that the negligence of the bishops was allowing heresy to flourish. Declaring how sad it makes him to see how glad the people are 'the churche to deprave', Colin observes:

---

[7] Ibid., ll. 47–58.
[8] Ibid., ll. 186, 343.
[9] Ibid., ll. 285–8.
[10] See Robert S. Kinsman, 'The Voices of Dissonance: Pattern in Skelton's *Colyn Cloute*', *Huntingdon Library Quarterly*, 26 (1963), pp. 99–125.

.. some have a smacke
Of Luthers sacke,
And a brennynge sparke
Of Luthers warke,
And are somewhat suspecte
In Luthers secte.
And some of them barke,
Clatter and carpe
Of that heresy arte
Called Wytclyftista,
The devylyshe dagmatista.
And some be Hussians,
And some be Arryans,
And some be Pollegyans,
And make moche varyans
Bytwene the clergye
And the temporaltye.[11]

In making Colin shudder at the prospect of heresy spreading, Skelton was able to have it both ways: he could exploit the full force of anticlericalism, without suffering the taint of heterodoxy. Again, his tactical instincts had proved unerring.

Apart from using a more appropriate persona, Skelton tried to render his assault on Wolsey persuasive to a wider audience by making it seem less like a merely self-interested, vindictive attack. To this end, he experimented with a new technique – that of evoking an array of different 'voices' in the poem. As Kinsman first pointed out, 'one ... can hear voices directly or indirectly sketching a pattern of desired conduct'.[12] Among these voices are the unnamed detractors who, Colin imagines, will ridicule his efforts, the subversive utterances of those who are seizing the chance to sow heresies, and the concerned colloquial tones of Colin himself. Above all, there are the voices of the laity as they trade their anticlerical discontents with one another, talking 'lyke tytyvylles' and harming their souls in the process.[13] The cumulative effect of these voices is to sketch in a far wider context, out of which Skelton's present complaint is arising. In *Speke Parott* the reader's attention was focused narrowly on Skelton's personal predicament and on Wolsey as the sole bogey who animates him. In *Collyn Clout* Skelton prompts the reader to imagine a panoramic display of all the actions and counter actions that are taking place in England as a result of Wolsey's abuses. In one corner of the field of vision we can see Skelton musing despondently at the lack of positive response to *Speke Parott*. He intimates the tone of his own voice in

[11] *Collyn Clout*, ll. 540–56.
[12] See Kinsman, 'The Voices of Dissonance: Pattern in Skelton's *Colyn Cloute*', p. 293.
[13] *Collyn Clout*, ll. 330–42, 415.

the poem through the words of yet another voice – that of the Psalmist, from whom he draws the Latin motto placed at the beginning of the poem:

> *Quis consurget mihi adversus malignantes,*
> *aut quis stabit mecum adversus operantes*
> *iniquitatem? Nemo, Domine!*

> [Who will rise up with me against the evil-doers, or who will stand with me against the workers of iniquity? No-one, Lord!][14]

Skelton's voice is heard again in the Latin verses at the end of the poem, lamenting the decline of the esteem in which poets were once held.[15] This intimation of the poet's real state of mind adds piquancy to his efforts to try, once again, to rouse the sleeping consciences of his audience through the words of his persona. In the background we see the discontent and seditious anarchy of thought and speech spreading through the common people, in the absence of spiritual sustenance from the clergy in the form of sound preaching. At the opposite end of the field of vision, one gains glimpses of scenes that are taking place in the royal palace itself. Colin's warning to the prelates to 'beware of a quenes yellynge' conjures up an image of angry words exchanged between Queen Catherine, renowned for piety, and an unspecified person concerning some action or lack of action by the clergy that has upset her.[16] It is a small detail, but one which evokes the divisive tensions that have afflicted even the royal household. Most vividly of all, one hears the arrogant and intimidating tones of the one prelate, Wolsey, who is responsible for the whole mess, as he sits in Star Chamber, having had a detractor hauled before him:

> 'Shall they taunt us prelates,
> That be theyr prymates?
> Nat so hardy on theyr pates!
> . . .
> How darest thou, daucocke, mell?
> Howe darest thou, losell,
> Allygate the gospell
> Agaynst us of the counsell?
> Avaunt to the devyll of hell!

> Take him, wardeyn of the Flete,
> Set hym fast by the fete!

[14] Ibid., p. 246.
[15] Ibid., p. 278.
[6] Ibid., l. 987.

I say, lieutenant of the Toure,
Make this lurdeyne for to loure![17]

This is the fate Colin fears for himself, and which Skelton knew that he, too,
would suffer were he to fall into Wolsey's hands once he had circulated *Collyn
Clout*. Through interpolating into the poem these 'dissonant voices', as Kinsman
has termed them, Skelton conjures up the whole atmosphere of fear, concern, and
repression that he hopes will explain and justify his attack on Wolsey.

Skelton takes a long, circuitous route to arrive at the point he really wants to
make in *Collyn Clout*: that Wolsey must be removed. At first the 'ye' to whom the
poem is addressed refers to the higher clergy in general, but almost from the
outset there are subtle hints implanted in Colin's narrative to suggest that Skelton
has one particular prelate in mind. The first such hint is an allusion to Wolsey's
concubine, Joan Larke:

> .. some say ye hunte in parkes
> And hauke on hobby larkes
> And other wanton warkes
> Whan the nyght darkes.[18]

The puns on 'larke' meaning 'Larke' and 'hobby' meaning 'hobby-horse' (with its
obscene innuendo), suggest the notorious sexual immorality of one particular
prelate, as well as the worldly propensity of prelates in general for hunting. A
third of the way through the poem Skelton delivers a prophecy, again concerning
the fall of one particular individual:

> Some men thynke that ye
> Shall have penalte
> For your iniquite.
> *Nota* what I say
> And bere it well away.
> Yf it please nat theologys
> It is good for astrologys,
> For Tholome tolde me
> The sonne somtyme to be
> *In Ariete*
> Ascendent a degre.
> Whan Scorpyon descendynge,
> Was so then pretendynge
> A fatall fall for one

---

[17] Ibid., ll. 1150–68.
[18] Ibid., ll. 192–5.

> That shall sytte in a trone
> And rule all thynges alone.[19]

There was only one prelate who could be charged with aspiring to rule the realm alone, and that was Wolsey. Skelton warns him a second time of aspiring too high, later in the poem:

> It is a besy thynge
> For one man to rule a kynge
> Alone, and make rekenynge ·
> To governe over all
> And rule a realme royall
> By one mannes wytte.
> Fortune may chaunce to flytte,
> And whan he weneth to sytte
> Yet may he mysse the quysshon![20]

Just before this, Skelton had included an accurate description of Hampton Court and its erotic hangings as a clue for members of the court circle as to his victim's identity, so that by the end of the poem no reader could seriously doubt whom he meant. Skelton has progressively narrowed the field of the reader's vision from the general to the particular, until it is focused squarely on Wolsey himself as the source and epitome of all clerical corruption. To underscore this point, Skelton places at the climax of the work the dramatized scene in the Star Chamber, graphically showing the despotical cardinal in action.

Collyn Clout thus turns out to be just as much an *ad hominem* attack on Wolsey as *Speke Parott* had been, but Skelton has taken pains not to let it appear as such – for reasons that were tactical rather than charitable. He had come to realize that if he were to attack Wolsey in too specific a manner, people would be too scared to side with him, even if they wanted to. A generalized complaint delivered by an apparently harmless rustic, on the other hand, might well embolden them to acknowledge their own grievances against the cardinal. Skelton had reason to hope that his artful tactics in *Collyn Clout* would not only prick the conscience of the clergy, but also persuade the common people that Colin had been articulating their own interests.

There is evidence that the new strategy worked. In his next work Skelton refers to himself as the bard '*de quo loquntur mille*' ('of whom thousands are speaking').[21] If we can believe him, the popular response to *Collyn Clout* had

---

[19] Ibid., ll. 460–75. This passage was recorded along with other prophecies in a contemporary manuscript entitled 'the profecy of Skelton' (British Library MS Lansdowne 762, fo. 75).

[20] *Collyn Clout*, ll. 988–96.

[21] *Why Come Ye Nat to Courte?* ll. 29–30, and again at the very end of the poem.

indeed been widespread. The presence of *Collyn Clout* in several commonplace books of London citizens would tend to confirm this, as would Wolsey's enduring hostility towards William Thynne for having urged Skelton to circulate it. Nevertheless, in spite of the success of *Collyn Clout* with the commonalty, Skelton still had to goad the nobility into waking up to the danger posed to them by Wolsey. It was to this end that, several months later in 1522, he wrote *Why Come Ye Nat to Courte?*

In Skelton's final satire against the cardinal, designed specifically to activate the nobles, he changed his fictive strategy yet again. Given the complacency in the nobility Skelton had encountered when he wrote *Speke Parott*, he realised that this time shock tactics were required. His new strategy consisted of a number of devices designed to arrest attention, and a number of other devices to bring to the surface of the minds of the nobles the thoughts Skelton believed they should have.

Instead of seeking to elicit sympathy through gentle pleading as he had done in *Collyn Clout*, Skelton arrests attention from the outset by adopting the oracular manner of the true *vates*, or seer:

> All noble men of this take hede,
> And beleve it as your crede.
>
> To hasty of sentence,
> To ferce for none offence,
> To scarce of your expence,
> To large in neglygence,
>
> To slacke in recompence,
> To haute in excellence,
> To lyght intellegence,
> And to lyght in credence;
> . . .[22]

The rhetorical heightening of the opening passage by the anaphoric repetitions at the beginning of each line and the repetitions of the rhymes at the end impart to this gnomic utterance the quality of an oracular summation that should command the same credibility as a religious creed.[23] This oracular manner, in fact, is sustained throughout the whole poem by Skelton's use of a principle of repetition that manifests itself in many different forms. It is seen in small instances such as the repetition of individual words, for example, when Skelton gives his reasons for not coming to court:

---

[22] Ibid., ll. 1–10.
[23] On this point, see also the pertinent comments of Kinney, *John Skelton: Priest as Poet*, pp. 151–4. Kinney sees the opening of *Why Come Ye Nat to Courte?* as a parody of the Nicene Creed.

> For *age* is a page
> For the courte full unmete;
> For *age* can nat *rage*,
> Nor basse her swete swete.
>   But whan *age* seeth that *rage*
> Dothe aswage and refrayne,
> Than wyll *age* have a corage
> To come to court agayne;

or, in an even more striking form when he denounces Wolsey's wilfulness:

> For *Wyll* dothe rule all thynge,
> *Wyll, Wyll, Wyll, Wyll, Wyll!*
> He ruleth alway styll.[24]

It is seen, too, in instances of concatenation when the concluding line of one verse paragraph recurs as the opening line of the next:

> I drede, by swete Jesu,
> This tale will be to trew:
> 'In faythe, Dycken, thow krew,
> In fayth, Dicken, thou krew, etc.'

> Dicken, thou krew doutlesse!
> For trewly to expresse,
> There hath ben moche excesse.[25]

On a larger scale, it is seen in the repetition of whole sections. Having listed Wolsey's misdeeds once, Skelton begins, at line 399, to list them all over again as a kind of theme with variations. This amplifying duplication is signalled with a repetition of the words which prompted the first instalment:

> Ones yet agayne
> Of you I wolde frayne
> *Why come ye nat to court?*[26]

Finally, the whole work is sewn together by the repetition of symbolic motifs. Chief among these is the constantly recurring image of the cardinal's red hat, which is designed to alienate the reader from the cardinal further by representing him as a cipher of his office rather than fully human.[27] Altogether, these manifold

---

[24] *Why Come Ye Nat to Courte?*, ll. 32–9, 105–7. My italics.
[25] Ibid., ll. 64–70.
[26] Ibid., ll. 399–401; c.f. l. 31. My italics.
[27] See Ibid., ll. 175, 238, 281, 283, 388.

repetitions serve to drive Skelton's message home with a battering insistent force.

Skelton's further strategy for raising certain ideas to the surface of his readers' minds consists of inducing them to undergo a psychological catechism.[28] He does this by dramatizing a dialogue between the speaking voice of the poem and an unnamed, friendly interlocutor.

The effect of this device depends upon the shifting referentiality of the second person pronoun 'ye', to whom the various questions and statements are addressed. Sometimes this 'ye' is Skelton himself, as in the opening question when the interlocutor asks: 'Why come ye nat to court?' Apart from the biographical parallels between Skelton and the narrator that become clear in his answer, we know that 'ye' in this case is Skelton, the writer, because of the way he varies the pronoun in this phrase later on:

> I have told you part, but nat all.
> Herafter perchaunce I shall
> Make a larger memoryall
> And a further rehersall
> And more paper I thinke to blot
> To the court why I cam not.[29]

Sometimes 'ye' is the interlocutor, as when Skelton reverses the situation and asks him a question:

> But harke, my frende, one worde
> In ernest o[r] in borde:
> Tell me nowe in this stede,
> Is maister Mewtas dede,
> The kynges Frenshe secretary
> And his untrew adversary?[30]

This obscure passage alludes to John Meautis, French secretary to Henry VIII, who lost his job and was replaced by Brian Tuke. Skelton depicts him as someone upon whom the king has depended, but also as someone who has not served the king's interests. He thus establishes a loose parallel with Wolsey. By asking his interlocutor to consider whether Meautis is dead (in fact he is not, but is 'so payned in the hede / that he shall never ete more bread'), Skelton is inviting him to realize that Wolsey could be brought to suffer a similar fate. We can see, therefore, that Skelton reverses the direction of the questions in order to make his

---

[28] I am indebted to Kinney (*John Skelton: Priest as Poet*, p. 154) for the notion of a catechism, but interpret it less literally than he does.

[29] *Why Come Ye Nat to Courte?*, ll. 822–7. My italics.

[30] Ibid., ll. 784–9. Scattergood's edition prints 'of' for 'or'.

readers aware of their potential power, and the effects that could be brought about if they exercised it.

This is the purpose of Skelton's most significant use of the second person pronoun. For much of the time, 'ye' refers to the nobles themselves and, in the second instalment of the poem (from line 841 onwards), to the citizens of London. We can see this in the 'creed' in which Skelton invites the nobles to believe at the opening of the poem. Noting, with particular reference to the Duke of Buckingham who had been executed in May 1521: 'A noble man may fall, / And his honour appall', Skelton adds:

> And yf *ye* thynke this shall
> Not rubbe you on the gall,
> Than the devyll take all!
>
> All noble men of this take hede,
> And beleve it as your crede.[31]

Clearly, in this instance, 'ye' refers to the members of the nobility, who are being addressed directly.

The shifting referentiality of the second person pronoun is crucial to Skelton's fictive strategy, because it enables the dialogue within the poem to serve not only as a catechism undertaken by the author with himself, but also by any reader of the poem. The dramatization of the poet's own mental processes, therefore, becomes that which the poem is designed to induce in Skelton's readers, so that they may be primed for action.

Skelton tries to ensure that his readers do enter into this process of examining their potential feelings and insights about Wolsey's misrule, by seeking to jolt them out of their complacency. To this end he alters his persona once more. The 'Skelton' who narrates *Why Come Ye Nat to Courte?* is no longer the withdrawn, self-protective bird of *Speke Parott*, nor the humble, ingratiating rustic of *Collyn Clout*, but is now an impatient and exasperated seer who has wasted enough time on bringing the nobles to their senses, and who will simply abandon them to shift for themselves should they fail to heed this final warning. Skelton also characterizes his persona as someone who knows far more than he is prepared to say. When the interlocutor asks him for news of the king's Council, for example, he replies:

> I coulde say some what,
> But speke ye no more of that,
> For drede of the red hat
> Take peper in the nose;

[31] Ibid., ll. 24–8. My italics.

> For than thyne heed of gose.
> Of! by the harde arse![32]

In terms of the likely psychological effect on Skelton's readers, these are shrewd tactics. Being made to feel that anyone is about to give you up as a lost cause is a powerful incentive for most people to wonder why. Similarly, withholding information is a sure way of arousing most people's curiosity as to what is being withheld. Skelton is thus trying to focus the minds of his noble readers on their past inaction and present causes for action. The point that he is withholding, but means his readers to recognize, is that Wolsey has diminished the size and stature of the king's Council to the point where the nobles have lost most of their power and their right to participate in government.

Another of Skelton's goading techniques is to disrupt the smooth continuity ordinarily expected from the kind of narrative he is presenting. He frequently moves abruptly from one form of consciousness to another, juxtaposing his own meditations against the enquiring voice of his interlocutor, and switching perspectives with unnerving rapidity, and without warning. The effect of these abrupt transitions is to jangle the nerves and trigger anxiety in his readers, so that their complacency is shattered.

A different type of disruption occurs when, as in *Collyn Clout*, Skelton interposes dramatized voices into the narrative. These include anonymous voices reciting snatches of songs, ballads, and proverbs which have, in their tenor, a sinister relevance to the present situation Skelton is describing:

> We may blowe at the cole!
> Our mare hath cast her fole,
> And, 'Mocke hath lost her sho;
> What may she do therto?'
> An ende of an olde song:
> 'Do ryght and do no wronge.'
> As ryght as a rammes horne![33]

Such snatches of phrases imply a moral order that is being betrayed, and also evoke the actual circumstances of the present situation, which are made more visible by being objectified in the form of images drawn from the world of common experience.

Other voices concern more readily identifiable historical characters. We hear the thick dialect of the Scots massing on the border to invade England because Wolsey has sent the English army on a futile mission into France:

[32] Ibid., ll. 381–86.
[33] Ibid., ll. 84–90.

> Twit, Andrewe! Twit, Scot!
> Ge heme! ge scour thy pot,
> For we have spente our shot![34]

We hear the treasonous words of the self-serving Lord Dacre, lieutenant of the north, as he makes a dishonourable pact with the Scots:

> With, 'Do thou for me,
> And I shall do for the'.[35]

And, of course, we hear the voice of the cardinal himself, engaged in the actions that give men cause for dismay. We hear him on a visit to 'the naked stewes', grunting in the very act of copulation with, 'Gup, hore, gup! Now gup.'[36] We hear his pompous tones in the Star Chamber as he bullies the other councillors to agree with him, and the sycophantic agreement he extracts from those whom he intimidates:

> . . . in the Chambre of Sterres
> All maters there he marres,
> Clappyng his rod on the borde.
> No man dare speke a worde,
> For he hathe all the sayenge
> Without any renayenge.
> He rolleth in his recordes,
> He sayth, 'How saye ye, my lordes?
> Is nat my reason good?'
> Good evyn, good Robyn Hode!
> Some say 'yes', and some
> Syt styll as they were dom.[37]

We hear the offensively disparaging terms in which he presumes to address his social betters:

> He hath dispyght and scorne
> At them that be well borne;
> He rebukes them and rayles,
> 'Ye horsons, ye vassayles,
> Ye knaves, ye churles sonnys,
> Ye rebads nat worth two plummis!
> Ye raynbetyn beggers rejagged,

[34] Ibid., ll. 125–7.
[35] Ibid., ll. 279–80.
[36] Ibid., ll. 240.
[37] Ibid., ll. 188–99.

Ye recrayed ruffyns all ragged!'
With, 'Stowpe, thou havell!
Rynne, thou javell![38]

As in *Collyn Clout*, the interpolation of voices vividly conjures up images of events that have actually taken place. Furthermore these dramatized 'scenes' serve to induce the reader to grasp their relevance at an experiential level; that is, they move the reader affectively to *feel* what the situations intimated by the voices mean. As with every other of Skelton's devices, this is meant to induce anxiety as a spur to action.

The rest of *Why Come Ye Nat to Courte?* is rich in Skelton's more customary forms of satiric diminution. He is particularly fond of animal imagery, as he was in *Speke Parott*. Wolsey is described variously as 'the mastyve cur', 'the bochers dogge', a 'hogge', a bear, 'an oxe or a bull', and so on.[39] The lords, both temporal and spiritual, are also referred to in animal images, but to very different effect and purpose. Victims of Wolsey's ambitions such as William Warham, Richard Fox, Thomas Grey, and Buckingham, are alluded to as the hare, the fox, the gray, the buck respectively. Skelton also prays that Christ might grant Henry VIII the grace to know 'The faucon from the crow, / The wolf from the lam', and that the 'mastyfe' might never confound 'the gentyll greyhownde'.[40] Skelton uses these animal images as far more than convenient ciphers; he is juxtaposing animals that feature in heraldic symbolism against animals without heraldic associations. This is yet another way in which he tries to arouse the nobles' awareness of their own superior status, in the hope that they will act to restore it.

Skelton's suggestion as to how they should do this is clear: the nobles must reassert themselves by restoring a conciliar form of government, and thus redress the ill effects of allowing one man to govern alone:

> It is a nyce reconynge
> To put all the governynge,
> All the rule of this lande,
> Into one mannys hande;
> One wyse mannys hede
> May stande somwhat in stede.
> But the wyttys of many wyse
> Moche better can devyse
> By theyr cyrcumspection,
> And theyr sad dyrection,
> To cause the commune weale
> Longe to endure in heale.[41]

[38] Ibid., ll. 599–608.
[39] Ibid., ll. 295–308.
[40] Ibid., ll. 772–9.
[41] Ibid., ll. 760–72.

Skelton's position had changed somewhat from the one he had espoused in *Speke Parott*. There he had urged the king to wake up and seize the reigns of power himself. A year later, he seems to have given up on the king, and pinned his hopes on a consensual form of government based on the central role of the council. In this he was ahead of his time. It would not be until the mid 1530s that the conciliar ideal would be proposed with such fervent conviction, by such men as Christopher St German, Thomas Starkey, and the leaders of the Pilgrimage of Grace.[42]

Skelton could have ended *Why Come Ye Nat to Courte?* at this point, having done all he could to goad the nobles into action, and having suggested what that action should be, but he chose to write a further 360 lines addressed mainly to the London citizenry. The reason is obvious: Wolsey, having already raised in April 1522, a considerable sum of money from the City of London to finance civic celebrations for the visit of Charles V, had demanded a forced loan from the City in May of that year to finance the war in France.[43] Both the loan and the manner in which the citizens had been assessed for their ability to pay it, had aroused great dissatisfaction. Having said all he wanted to say to the nobles, Skelton seized the chance of exploiting this disaffection to fuel the opposition of the citizenry, too, against Wolsey. Consequently, the second instalment of *Why Come Ye Nat to Courte?* (which Skelton had foreshadowed at lines 823–6), harps incessantly on the penury the citizens have suffered as a result of the forced loan:

> ... howe comme to pas
> Your cupbord that was
> Is tourned to glasse,
> From sylver to brasse,
> From golde to pewter
> Or els to a newter,
> To copper, to tyn,
> To lede, or alcumyn?[44]

The remedy Skelton proposes to the citizens is less subtle than that which he suggested to the nobles:

> Suche a prelate, I trowe,
> Were worthy to rowe
> Thorow the streytes of Marock

---

[42] See John Guy, 'The King's Council and Political Participation', in Fox and Guy, *Reassessing the Henrician Age*, pp. 121–47; also Thomas F. Mayer, 'Faction and Ideology: Thomas Starkey's *Dialogue*', *Historical Journal*, 28: 1 (1985), pp. 1–25.

[43] See Walker, *John Skelton and the Politics of the 1520s*, pp. 103–8.

[44] *Why Come Ye Nat to Courte?*, ll. 900– 7.

To the gybbet of Baldock.

. . .

For els by and by
He wyll drynke us so drye,
And suck us so nye,
That men shall scantly
Have peny or halpeny.[45]

By shifting the second person pronoun in this part of the poem to refer to the London citizens (whom he explicitly apostrophizes in the Latin verses at the conclusion of the work), Skelton is able to subject them to the same psychological process he had forced the nobles to undergo – to confront their own awareness of how much reason they have to detest and resist this man with the red hat. After a final reprise of Wolsey's misdeeds, Skelton tells them, too, what they must do – in a jeering poem that ridicules the mock-humility of Wolsey's custom of riding a mule:

Excitat, en, asinus mulum, mirabile visu,
Calcibus! O vestro cives occurite asselo
Qui regnum regemque regit, qui vestra gubernat
Predia, divitias, nummos, gasas, spoliando!

[See how the ass rouses the mule, a marvellous sight, with
his heels. O citizens, oppose your little ass who rules the
realm and the king, who governs your estates, your wealth,
your treasures, by plundering.][46]

The derisive, jaunty tone of Skelton's parting jibe suggests that he was fairly assured of the Londoners' readiness to back the cause. If his satire worked as he meant it to, he could confidently expect that it would help to bring both the nobility and the citizenry into an alliance of common interest against the man he believed to be his and the nation's deadly enemy. As events were soon to prove, he was not mistaken.

[45] Ibid., ll. 953–68.
[46] Ibid., p. 311, 'Apostropha ad Londini cives', ll. 1–4.

11

The Aftermath: *A Garlande of Laurell* and Skelton's Later Poems

By the end of 1522, Wolsey had had enough. He could not silence Skelton forcibly, because the old poet was safe behind the walls of the Westminster sanctuary. On the other hand, he needed urgently to stop Skelton's satiric attacks, because the latter had succeeded in putting a voice to the rising discontent the cardinal's actions had occasioned in the nobility and commonalty. To make matters worse, Skelton had regained the favour of the Howards. The very fact that they were prepared to offer Skelton patronage, while he was delivering himself of such open attacks on the cardinal, must have signified to Wolsey that his position was no longer as invulnerable as it had once seemed. In short, the cardinal found it prudent to temporize.

We can infer quite clearly from Skelton's own writings what happened. At the end of *A Garlande or Chapelet of Laurell*, written a month or so after *Why Come Ye Nat to Courte?* in early 1523, Skelton commands his poem to perform a specific mission:

> *Cardineum dominum . . . venerando salutes,*
> *Legatum a latere, et fiat memor ipse precare*
> *Prebendae, quam promisit mihi credere quondam,*
> *Meque suum referas pignus sperare salutis.*
>
> [Greet with reverence the lord cardinal, *legatus a latere*, and
> beg him to remember the prebend he promised to commit to
> me, and give me cause to hope for the pledge of his favour.][1]

There had been a trade-off: Skelton had agreed to cease writing satires against the cardinal in exchange for a more lucrative benefice than the one he had. Nevertheless, while Skelton had shown himself willing to fulfil his side of the bargain by writing the innocuous *A Garlande of Laurell*, Wolsey still had not, up to the time of its publication, honoured his pledge:

---

[1] *A Garlande of Laurell*, ll. 1589–92.

Twene hope and drede
My lyfe I lede,
But of my spede
Small sekernes;
Howe be it I rede
Both worde and dede
Should be agrede
In noblenes:
Or els &c.[2]

Skelton's final 'or else' conveys a thinly veiled threat to the cardinal that, if he does not deliver the prebend as promised, Skelton would give him another dose of the same sour medicine he had previously dispensed.

A Garlande or Chapelet of Laurell, the last imaginative fiction Skelton wrote in response to political circumstances, only becomes fully comprehensible when it is viewed in this context. It is far more than a simple exercise in self-glorification as is usually claimed. After half a decade of worsening tension with the almighty cardinal, during which he had been brought to the brink of ruin, Skelton, once the quarrel had been resolved, had a lot to be thankful for and a lot of ground to catch up. *A Garlande of Laurell* was written to serve three main purposes. At one level, it was a courtly compliment to the Countess of Surrey, designed as a gesture of thanks for the crucial part she had played in his rehabilitation. Had she not responded favourably to his desperate plea in *Speke Parott*, he would have had neither the heart nor sufficient prospect of success to go on. At another level, the poem was contrived to serve as a means of keeping Wolsey honest. Skelton's public compliment to the countess was not intended solely to gratify her, but also to flaunt Skelton's new-found power source at the cardinal – to remind him that the poet was not so completely at his mercy as he had been in the days of his estrangement from the Howards. At the most important level of all, however, Skelton wrote *A Garlande of Laurell* to achieve an emotional purgation and retuning, by reliving imaginatively the distress he had been through, 'trying on' his new status as a Howard retainer, and contemplating what the future held out for him. In devising a fiction that was capable of performing all these functions, Skelton produced what may be justifiably considered his masterpiece.

As he had done nearly thirty years earlier in *The Bowge of Courte*, Skelton turned once again to the dream vision genre in order to allay the perturbations of his mind and set his affections in right tune. With great inventiveness, he was able to rework the conventions of the genre to turn it into a vehicle for exploring his past, present, and future experience, through the symbolic images and actions of the dream he constructs in *A Garlande of Laurell*.

[2] Ibid., ll. 1594–602.

The first alteration he makes is to change the traditional setting of the dream. From *Le Roman de la Rose* down, it had been customary to set the dream vision in spring. When, as in Chaucer's *House of Fame*, or Skelton's own earlier *Bowge of Courte*, this commonplace was modified, it usually signified that the conventional erotic focus of the dream was being replaced with one that was either political, or personal in some non-erotic sense. So, too, in *A Garlande of Laurell*: Skelton chooses a setting that provides a symbolic commentary on his present political situation and the disturbed personal feelings which it has left him.

The astrological *incipit*, conventional in such poems, serves far more than merely to indicate the time of year and season in which the poem was written:

> Arectyng my syght toward the zodyake,
> The sygnes xii for to beholde a farre,
> When Mars retrogradant reversed his bak,
> Lorde of the yere in his orbicular,
> Put up his sworde, for he cowde make no warre,
> And whan Lucina plenarly did shyne,
> Scorpione ascendynge degrees twyse nyne;
>
> In place alone then musynge in my thought
> How all thynge passyth as doth the somer flower,
> On every halfe my reasons forthe I sought,
> How oftyn fortune varyeth in an howre,
> Now clere wether, forthwith a stormy showre;
> All thynge compassyd, no perpetuyte,
> But now in welthe, now in adversyte.[3]

As Skelton tells us in his reference to 'Janus, with his double chere, / Makynge his almanak for the new yere' near the end of the poem,[4] *A Garlande of Laurell* was written in January. The *incipit* is therefore highly appropriate at a general level. Mars, the god of war, is 'retrogradant' and has 'reversed his bak . . . for he cowde make no warre' because the campaign planned against the Scots for early 1523 had been unable to get under way. It could not commence in earnest until the Earl of Surrey was able to disengage himself from the debacle in France and return to England to lead the English forces. At a personal level, however, the astrological detail is even more relevant. Mars is Wolsey, whom Skelton had forced into a stalemate with his three hostile satires of 1521 and 1522. He, too, had 'put up his sworde', for he had found himself powerless to silence Skelton. After long misfortune, Skelton's circumstances had taken a turn for the better with his restoration into the favour of the Countess of Surrey. He alludes to this fact in the other astronomical symbol of the opening, Lucina, the moon, who 'plenarly did

---

[3] Ibid., ll. 1–14.
[4] Ibid., ll. 1515–16.

shyne'. Traditionally, the moon was a symbol of grace; so in having it shine fully, Skelton is not only signifying literally the full moon of January 1523, but also symbolically the renewal of his good fortunes under the patronage of the countess, whom he is attending at Sheriff Hutton castle in Yorkshire.

Given such a radical revolution in his fortunes, therefore, it is not surprising that Skelton shows himself to be musing about the mutability of life. One thing in particular worries him: the fact that mutability means that there is 'no perpetuyte'. Specifically, as it turns out, he is worried that his recent troubles will have so damaged his reputation that it will be impossible for him to secure the status and fame he has long desired.

Skelton objectified his emotional disturbance at this prospect in the form of symbolic correlatives included in details of the setting:

> Se depely drownyd I was in this dumpe,
> Encraumpysshed so sore was my conceyte,
> That, me to rest, I lent me to a stumpe
> Of an oke, that somtyme grew full streyghte,
> A myghty tre and of a noble heyght,
> Whose bewte blastyd was with the boystors wynde,
> His levis loste, the sappe was frome the rynde.
>
> Thus stode I in the frytthy forest of Galtres,
> Ensowkid with sylt of the myry wose,
> Where hartis belluyng, embosyd with distres,
> Ran on the raunge so longe, that I suppose
> Few men can tell where the hynde calfe gose.[5]

Skelton characterizes himself as being sunk in a depression so deep that even his imagination seems helpless to act. The winter mud of the forest of Galtres with which Skelton is soaked through serves as a fitting symbol for this melancholy, while the pun on 'hart'/'heart' suggests that the bellowing deer signify his own inner anguish. The blasted oak against which he leans is more complex in its suggestiveness. At one level, it suggests the successful career for which Skelton had hoped, but which had been blasted 'with the boystors wynde' of his recent contention with Wolsey, but other details imply a further level of signification. The tree was once 'a myghty tre and of a noble heyght', but has now been reduced to a 'stumpe', 'his levis loste, the sappe . . . frome the rynde'. In *Why Come Ye Nat to Courte?* Skelton had noted how 'Unto great confusyon / A noble man may fall, / And his honour appall.'[6] In that instance he had been referring to the Duke of Buckingham. The image of the blasted oak in *A Garlande of Laurell*, too, seems to be alluding to the fall of the duke. In showing himself leaning

---

[5] Ibid., ll. 15–26.
[6] *Why Come Ye Nat to Courte?*, ll. 21–3.

against the stump, Skelton is signifying yet again his dependence on the favour of the duke's daughter, Elizabeth Stafford Howard, the Countess of Surrey. All the images of the opening to *A Garlande of Laurell*, therefore, work together to give an accurate impression of Skelton's situation at the time of writing the poem, and also how he felt about it.

Having sketched these things in evocative images, Skelton then explores them further by developing a symbolic action. Once he has fallen asleep, the first thing he sees in his dream is an externalization of his fear that the loss of time and favour in the past six years will have irreparably harmed his reputation as a poet. This is imaged in the form of a debate between the Queen of Fame and Dame Pallas (or Wisdom), as to whether Skelton should have a place in the court of Fame. Fame recalls to Pallas that Pallas herself had given a royal commandment that Skelton should have a place in Fame's court, and had prompted Fame to advance him to the office of laureate ('the rowme of laureat promotyve') as a preparation for greater things. Skelton, however, has given the appearance of being 'sum what to dull'.[7] This whole exchange dramatizes a dialogue within Skelton's mind as to whether he has really made as good a use of his poetic gift as everyone had a right to expect. He knows that wisdom had provided for him to be advanced to the highest rank in the pantheon of the muses, but he suspects his performance may have fallen far short of what he was capable of achieving. In effect, he is suffering the doubt of someone who feels he has not lived up to the career expectations people had for him, and the result is a paralysing depression.

Skelton attempts to grapple with his melancholy by giving himself some cause for reassurance. In his dream, this materializes in the form of a vision he has of the poets laureate of all the nations. Among them are Gower, Chaucer, and Lydgate, who come up to Skelton and embrace him, telling him that, because he has increased and amplified English poetry, he does indeed deserve the chance to make a plea for admission to their 'collage above the sterry sky', for a permanent place in the court of Fame.[8] They then take him to the pavilion of Dame Pallas, who commands that he should be led to the court of Fame, where he is to answer for himself.

In another sudden, dream-like transition, Skelton finds himself before the palace of Fame, but here the course of the action takes an unexpected turn. Skelton's mentors have delivered him to the palace too early, so that he is obliged to kill time until the ceremony is due to commence.

At this point, Skelton introduces the traditional guide figure of dream vision poems, here taking the form of Dame Occupacyon. He uses her as a means for reliving his recent past experience up to the time of the present action. Such a narrative digression is unusual, to say the least, but as it proceeds one can see

---

[7] *A Garlande of Laurell*, ll. 58–9, 115–16, 79.
[8] Ibid., ll. 386–434.

Skelton attempting to come to terms with the emotional scarring that his fall into political disfavour and contention has produced.

Dame Occupacyon first reminds him of the onset of his troubles, and of how she has assisted him to overcome them:

> Of your acqueintaunce I was in tymes past,
> Of studyous doctryne when at the port salu
> Ye fyrste aryvyd; whan broken was your mast
> Of worldly trust, then did I you rescu;
> Your storme dryven shyppe I repared new,
> So well entakeled, what wynde that ever blowe,
> No stormy tempeste your barge shall overthrow.[9]

This passage recalls the ending of *Collyn Clout*, where Skelton declares that he is going to withdraw 'Out of the wawes wodde / Of the stormy flodde' and direct his ship 'towarde the porte salue', by which he means that he will retreat behind the walls of the sanctuary at Westminster. Here, as there, Skelton is using the image of 'the port salu', or 'safe port', to signify the sanctuary, which he had used as a refuge when his 'mast of worldly trust' was broken – that is, when he had neither the protection of the king nor of the nobles against the rage of Wolsey.[10] By making Occupacyon remind him how she had repaired his storm-driven ship with such strong tackling that no wind or tempest would thereafter ever be able to overthrow it, Skelton is recalling the studious way he had devised his satires there against Wolsey, and how these had succeeded in restoring him to an unassailable position.

This recollection sets the context for the next stage in Skelton's imaginative re-enactment of the past. Dame Occupacyon leads him to a field surrounded by a thousand gates symbolizing the different nations. At the gate engraved 'A' (for 'Anglea'), he sees images of the main protagonists involved in his past disputes who have been responsible for all his misfortunes. At the gate itself he sees a leopard, 'crownyd with golde and stones, / Terrible of countenaunce and pas-synge formydable', who frowns fiercely at Skelton and shakes forth a writing warning him of the thunderbolts of Jove.[11] The leopard, an heraldic beast in the English royal coat of arms, symbolizes Henry VIII, who, one can infer, had taken offence at Skelton, at Wolsey's instigation, for having libelled his chief minister and 'his darling'. In the field itself, Skelton hears an outburst of cannon fire, and sees amongst those wounded by it, one in particular who has suffered major injuries:

---

[9] Ibid., ll. 540–6.
[10] *Collyn Clout*, ll. 1251–61.
[11] *A Garlande of Laurell*, ll. 589–601.

> And one ther was there, I wondred of his hap,
> For a gun stone, I say, had all to-jaggid his cap,
>
> Raggid, and daggid, and cunnyngly cut;
> The blaste of the brynston blew away his brayne;
> Masid as a Marche hare, he ran lyke a scut.[12]

The allusion to the 'cunningly cut' hat of the cardinal allows the reader to infer that it is Wolsey who is being signified here, however obliquely, and that the cannonade Skelton hears ('Bowns, bowns, bowns!') is an emblem of the satiric salvos Skelton fired at him in his three invectives. Skelton's bombardment has left Wolsey as disorientated as a March hare, and he has been forced to run for cover. Finally, Skelton sees two others who had been instrumental in his downfall:

> The one was a tumblar, that afterwarde againe
> Of a dysour, a devyl way, grew a jentilman,
> Pers Prater, the secund, that quarillis beganne.[13]

The first is some other figure at court who presumably bore Skelton malice; the second is the person who began the whole quarrel with his tittle-tattling. Both are described as 'titivyllis', which suggests that they informed against Skelton. As Skelton soon makes explicit, the second of the pair is Roger Stathum who, as suggested already, was the retainer in the Howard household who got Skelton into trouble with the Howards by misreporting his satiric jibe about livery.[14] The first one, the former court entertainer who had tried to turn himself into a gentleman, may have been someone else who had fuelled the hostility of either Wolsey or the king towards Skelton.

Skelton evokes these main actors in his personal tragedy in order to juxtapose them against the Countess of Surrey and her ladies, to whom Occupacyon next leads Skelton. Psychologically, this serves to enhance Skelton's sense of happiness and relief at having been rescued from what had seemed an impossible situation. The happy change in his fortunes set in train by the countess is signified in the phoenix Skelton sees at the top of 'a goodly laurell tre, / Enverdurid with levis contynually grene', symbolizing his own political resurrection.[15] Furthermore, the paradisal arbour in which Skelton finds himself, itself a symbol of the countess's court, offers the prospect of a substitute for the king's court, from which Skelton had been banished. He suggests as much in an observation that he makes to Occupacyon:

---

[12] Ibid., ll. 628–32.
[13] Ibid., ll. 634–5.
[14] See above, Chap. 9.
[15] *A Garlande of Laurell*, ll. 665–8.

Jupiter hymselfe this lyfe myght endure;
This joy excedith all worldly sport and play,
Paradyce this place is of syngular pleasure.
O wele were hym that herof myght be sure,
And here to inhabite and ay for to dwell![16]

Henry VIII himself ('Jupiter') could be satisfied by the countess's court, which is a worthy substitute for 'paradise' – or, as Skelton had described the king's own court in *Speke Parott*, 'Paradyce, that place [palace] of pleasure perdurable'. Skelton's wistful sigh at the thought of how happy a man could be who was able to stay at the arbour indefinitely, implies that although his restoration to favour had made him welcome to visit the Howard household, he had not formally been taken into their retinue.

Skelton, nevertheless, had a lot to be thankful to the Howards for, and in the middle section of *A Garlande of Laurell* he proceeded to repay his debt. Occupacyon leads him into the presence of the Countess of Surrey and her ladies, who are embroidering a spectacular garland of laurel for him to wear when he presents himself before the jury of laureates in Fame's court later that day. This action in itself signifies the countess's role in preparing the way for Skelton's reputation to be restored. In return, Skelton advances himself, 'sum thanke to deserve', and offers them a poetic garland of verses that he has devised. Each of the ladies in the countess's retinue is eulogized in turn, with varying degrees of ornateness, depending upon their relative precedence and age. For several of the younger women Skelton wrote some of the most exquisite lyric poetry he ever devised, as for example in the (often anthologized) verses he addresses to Margaret Hussey:

Mirry Margaret,
As mydsomer flowre,
Jentill as fawcoun
Or hawke of the towre;

With solace and gladnes,
Moche mirthe and no madnes,
All good and no badnes,
So joyously,
So maydenly,
So womanly
Her demenyng
In every thynge,
Far, far passynge
That I can endyght,
Or suffice to wryght

[16] Ibid., ll. 715–19 Scattergood prints 'wordly' for 'wor[l]dly'.

Of mirry Margarete,
As mydsomer flowre,
Jentyll as fawcoun
Or hawke of the towre.[17]

This was a side of Skelton that had not been exercised for many years. No wonder he says, having witnessed the vision of his polemical encounter with his enemies, 'wele may ye thynk I was no thyng prowde / Of that aventuris, whiche made me sore agast.'[18] Skelton knew that there was more to his poetic gift than a talent for satiric diminution, however skilfully contrived, and it must have been with relief that he felt able to express the gentler side of his nature once more. In seeking to convey his gratitude to the countess and her ladies, he gave them the best he had.

Skelton's final innovation to the conventional elements of the dream vision is to adapt the topos of the *cour amoureuse* to a new purpose. In traditional romantic dream allegories, the quester is often brought before the court of a queen and her ladies to solve an erotic riddle, or *demande d'amour*. Skelton makes use of the same device but adapts it to his present purpose – that is, to justify his claim to fame as a poet. The conventional court consisting of a queen and her ladies is transmuted into the court of the Queen of Fame, and the jurors are all those laureates whose company Skelton aspires to join. Fame asks Skelton to justify how he has deserved the place in her court that has been reserved for him, and in reply he asks Occupacyon to read out a list of his works. A precedent for this existed in Chaucer's 'Prologue' to his *Legend of Good Women*, where a list of the poet's work is recited to determine whether he has committed heresy against love. But that is on a modest, selective scale compared with the exhaustive list of Skelton's works read by Occupation. It is small wonder then, that at the end of this recitation, which includes everything from scurrilous lyrics such as 'Manerly Margery Mylke and Ale' to *Collyn Clout* and works of religious contemplation, the assembled laureates and orators should cry out 'Triumpha, triumpha!', and clarions and trumpets sound so loudly that 'the noyse went to Rome', the starry heaven shakes, and the ground trembles.[19] Skelton had made his point.

The final triumphal acclamation at the end of the poem marks a successful transition in Skelton himself, from the emotional perturbation of the opening to a state of renewed calm and confidence. In the very last lines of the poem proper, he observes 'Janus, with his double chere, / Makynge his almanak for the new yere', and expresses his newly allayed and retuned state of mind in a significant wish:

---

[17] Ibid., ll. 1004–22.
[18] Ibid., ll. 648–9.
[19] Ibid., ll. 1505–9.

Good luk this new yere, the olde yere is past.[20]

Skelton was now ready to put the upsets and disappointments of the past behind him and look forward to what he might achieve in a happier future. As if to confirm this resolution, he leaves a final hint to the reader that he has made it:

> *Mens tibi sit consulta, petis? Sic consule menti;*
> *Emula sit Jani, retro speculetur et ante.*

[Do you wish your mind to be skilful? In that case pay attention to your mind; let it be like that of Janus which looks backwards and forwards.][21]

Here, Skelton is hinting to his readers that, if they wish to understand the poem, they should imitate what he has been doing in the poem itself: they should look back over his past in order to comprehend what makes possible the transformation in his behaviour that will henceforth be manifest.

Taken as a whole, *A Garlande of Laurell* fulfils its manifold functions with remarkable skill: it purges Skelton of the emotional dross left over from his personal tribulations; it offers a very courtly and decorous compliment to the Countess of Surrey in repayment of his debt to her, and it becomes both the means for justifying the reward of the fame Skelton desires, and a means of perpetuating it. There can be few other, if any, poems in which the poet bestows and receives poetic immortality with such perfect reciprocity. It truly is, metaphorically speaking, a 'garland of laurel' in more senses than one.

A Garlande or Chapelet of Laurell was the last imaginative fiction that Skelton, to our knowledge, wrote. There are only two later works of his extant, and each is a fairly crude sort of versified propaganda.

The first of them, *Howe the Douty Duke of Albany . . . Ran Awaye Shamfully*, was written, as Skelton tells us, at Wolsey's request, to mark the ignominious withdrawal in November 1523 of the combined force of Scots and Frenchmen with which John Stewart, the Duke of Albany and regent of Scotland, had laid seige to the castle of Wark in Northumberland. The intent is crude, and is aptly summed up in Skelton's own words. Having urged England to rejoice at these new tidings, he adds:

> . . . to jeste
> Is my delyght
> Of this cowarde knyght,
> And for to wright

[20] Ibid., ll. 1515–18.
[21] Ibid., ll. 1519–20.

In the dispyght
Of the Scottes ranke.[22]

In the poem that results he fulfils this promise to the letter. As one historian has
recently shown, the poem is effective as a piece of propaganda designed to raise
morale in England in the face of what was, and remained, the threat of a Scottish
invasion supported by the French, and which England was ill equipped to
withstand, having exhausted its men and financial resources in pursuing the war
in France.[23] That does not make it any more satisfying, however, as poetry.
Skelton is content to repeat the official line, spiced with a bit of invective and
delivered in the first person plural pronoun 'we', to suggest that what he voices
are the sentiments shared by every loyal Englishman. Accordingly, the Scots are
described as 'puaunt pyspottes', and Skelton hopes that they, being the most
treacherous, vermin-ridden, and vicious nation in Christendom, might ever
remain 'In wretched beggary / And maungy misery, / In lousy lothsumnesse, / And
scabbed scorffynesse'.[24] The Duke of Albany himself is presented as a travesty of
a true knight:

> Syr Duke, nay, syr ducke,
> Syr drake of the lake, sir ducke
> Of the donghyll, for small lucke
> Ye have in feates of warre.[25]

Conversely, the Earl of Surrey, who had led the English forces who relieved
Wark, is described as being

> Of chivalry the well,
> Of knighthode the floure
> In every marciall shoure.[26]

Finally, Skelton eulogizes 'our moost royall Harry' as the true type of the ideal
king, of which Francis I is merely a parody. Whereas Henry is like Hercules in
martial prowess, like Solomon in prudence and wisdom, like Absolom in loyalty
and fidelity, and so on, Francis is merely an effete 'losel'.[27] The mere sight of
Henry would be enough to make him 'defoyle the place'.[28] Skelton knew that this
perfunctory jingoism was hardly showing him at his best, and felt moved to utter

---

[22] *Howe the Douty Duke of Albany*, ll. 13–18.
[23] See Walker, *John Skelton and the Politics of the 1520s*, p. 198.
[24] *Howe the Douty Duke of Albany*, ll. 120, 137–40, 219–20.
[25] Ibid., ll. 222–5.
[26] Ibid., ll. 238–40.
[27] Ibid., ll. 430–45.
[28] Ibid., ll, 351–3.

a semi-apology for it in the envoy he appended to the work. Addressing his poem, he says:

> Though your Englishe be rude,
> Barreyne of eloquence,
> Yet, brevely to conclude,
> Grounded is your sentence
> On trouthe under defence
> Of all trewe Englyshemen.[29]

The barbarousness of the style, he hoped, would be justified by the truth of his matter, and one senses that his belief even in that lacked a certain degree of commitment and enthusiasm.

If *Howe the Douty Duke of Albany* marks a sad falling-off of Skelton's imaginative powers, the underlying cause is not hard to discern. At the conclusion of the poem, Skelton dedicates it to Wolsey, describing himself as '*obsequious et loyall*'. He then addresses a second envoy to his work, this time telling it to prompt the cardinal 'In his mynde to comprise, / Those wordes his grace dyd saye / Of an ammas gray.'[30] Wolsey still had not delivered to Skelton the prebend he had promised him, and Skelton was therefore reduced to the obsequious performance of anything that the cardinal required, in the hope of gaining his benefice. That is why the poem is so perfunctory and uninspired; Skelton no longer had any need to protect his own person, nor were his circumstances sufficiently desperate to require from him a strenuous effort to amend them. In the absence of a profound motive, therefore, he lacked any incentive to find a truly imaginative or inventive way of making his poem convey what Wolsey had instructed him to say. Consequently, instead of a genuine fictive representation, *Howe the Douty Duke of Albany* is merely a polemic, rhetorically enhanced by the figurative devices of poetry. There is no tension, no drama, no dialogue, and no thematic complexity. Not only is the work entirely monological, but the logic is not even Skelton's own: it comes from the king's chief minister, Wolsey, who was masterminding the propaganda initiative concerning the Scottish war. It is small wonder, then, that Skelton's heart was hardly in the venture.

Much the same is true of Skelton's last work, *A Replycacion Agaynste Certayne Yong Scolers Abjured of Late*, again written at Wolsey's command as part of the concerted campaign to arrest the spread of heresy. Skelton genuinely disapproved of heresy (just as his literary partner in this enterprise, Thomas More, had), and his committed orthodoxy lends a certain linguistic force to his denunciation of the two young Cambridge scholars, Thomas Arthur and Thomas Bilney, who

---

[29] Ibid., ll. 516–21.
[30] Ibid., ll. 524–31.

had been forced to recant their Lutheran beliefs in December 1527. Predictably, they have 'lyppes polluted', are 'blowen with the flye / Of horryble heresy', and prate like 'poppyng dawes'.[31] Skelton's message to them is simple:

> ... mende your myndes that are mased;
> Or els doutlesse ye shalbe blased,
> And be brent at a stake,
> If further busynesse that ye make.[32]

The short length of *A Replycacion* is striking considering the seriousness of the topic, especially if one thinks of the exhaustive lengths to which Thomas More pursued the same issues in *A Dialogue Concerning Heresies*, written at the same time. Skelton simply did not have much to say because his imagination was not genuinely engaged in the matter with which he was obliged to deal.

By far the most interesting part of the poem is the concluding digression into which Skelton was drawn, defensively, to try to forestall the objection that he knew would inevitably be made – that poetry was an unsuitable vehicle for confuting heresy, as, indeed, his own performance in *A Replycacion* tended to confirm. He has no real answer to the objection that 'poetes do but fayne' (Tyndale would level the same charge against More), beyond asserting that because David had used poetry for spiritual matters, no other poet should be blamed for seeking to do likewise. His real defence lies in his belief that poetry has a mystical affective power which makes it useful for God's persuasive purposes:

> ... there is a spyrituall,
> And a mysteriall,
> And a mysticall
> Effecte energiall,
> As Grekes do it call,
> Of suche an industry
> And suche a pregnacy,
> Of hevenly inspyracion
> In laureate creacyon,
> Of poetes commendacion,
> That of divyne myseracion
> God maketh his habytacion
> In poetes whiche excelles,
> And sojourns with them and dwelles.[33]

---

[31] *A Replycacion*, ll. 29, 85–6, 39.
[32] Ibid., ll. 293–6.
[33] Ibid., ll. 365–78.

In the case of his own *Replycacion* this protestation amounts simply to wishful thinking, but there are signs that Skelton, especially in the remarkable prose *incipits*, tried to invest his writing with an energic force as if to prove his statement true. Both in the Latin dedication to Cardinal Wolsey and in the English prose sections of the *Argumentum*, Skelton indulges in a bizarre linguistic excess that is not called forth by any exigencies of the matter, and which is wholly inappropriate to it in terms of the mock-serious tone it generates. Skelton addressed Wolsey, for example, in superlatives so excessive, even by the standards of ritual humanist praise, as to induce laughter:

> *Honorificatissimo, amplissimo, longeque reverendissimo in Christo patri, ac domino, domino Thome, etc. . . . Cardinali meritissimo, et apostolice sedis legato, a latereque legato superillustri, etc. Skeltonis laureatus, orator regius, humillimum dicit obsequium cum omni debita reverentia, tanto tamque magnifico digna principe sacerdotum, totiusque justitie equabilissimo moderatore . . .*

> [To the most honourable, most mighty, and by far the most reverend father in Christ and lord, Lord Thomas . . . the most meritorious cardinal, legate of the apostolic see, the most superillustrious legate *a latere*, etc. the laureate Skelton, orator of the king, makes known his most humble obeisance with all the reverence due to such a magnificent and worthy prince among priests, and most equitable dispenser of every justice . . .][34]

Wolsey had bought Skelton, and the only way the old poet had of expressing his discontent at his own venality was to give Wolsey the flattery he craved in terms so extravagant as to turn compliment the seamy side out for anyone who cared to notice.

Something similar happens when Skelton declares what the subject of his poem will be:

> Howe yong scolers nowe a dayes enbolned with the flyblowen blast of the moche vayne glorious pipplyng wynde, whan they have delectably lycked a lytell of the lycorous electuary of lusty lernyng, in the moche studious scolehous of scrupulous philology . . . [tumble into theology].

He will also touch upon

> the tetrycall theologisacion of these demy divines, and stoicall studiantes, and friscajoly yonkerkyns, moche better bayned than brayned, basked and baththed in their wylde burblyng and boyling blode, fervently reboyled with the infatuate flames of their rechelesse youthe and wytlesse wonton-

[34] Ibid., p. 372.

nese, enbrased and enterlased with a moche fantasticall frenesy of their
insensate sensualyte . . . [and so on][35]

The excessive alliteration, the doublets, and the inkhorn polysyllabics of these
passages create an overblown linguistic effect equivalent to that found, for
example, in the later burlesques of Swinburne. It undermines the satiric point
Skelton wants to make by refusing to allow the reader to take the whole matter
seriously. It is almost as if Skelton, having lost his genuine inspiration, is
attempting to generate some kind of substitute for true poetic creation in mere
linguistic virtuosity, regardless of its appropriateness.

If one were to be less kind, it could be claimed that A Replycacion shows signs
of a mild form of derangement settling in upon the old master (he was within a
year of his death). The fact that his creative energy had to find such a bizarre
outlet suggests that he had begun to turn inward, seeking a substitute satisfaction
for that which the nature of his official commissions would not allow him to
achieve through fictive invention.

The pattern to be observed in Skelton's later career was not peculiar to him alone.
Indeed, it was prophetic of a wider trend that would set in after about 1525,
when the issues first of the Reformation, and then of Henry VIII's desire for a
divorce, forced writers to become far more ideologically committed than they
had been during the first two decades of the sixteenth century. When this
happened, there was a general movement away from the kind of complex,
inventive, exploratory and analytical fictions that are so characteristic of early
Tudor literature, towards propaganda and polemic in which imaginative play has
little part. The personal motive was replaced by a public one, and as this
happened literature tended to become increasingly monological, didactic, tendentious, and rhetorical. The story of the radical transformation this process
wrought on the literature of the final years of Henry VIII's reign will form the
subject of the fourth and last part of this book.

---

[35] Ibid., pp. 373–4.

PART IV

Reform and the King

12

Propaganda and Polemic: The Retreat from Fictive Literature after 1525

Up until the mid 1520s, the two main stimuli to the invention of politically orientated fiction had been humanism as an intellectual force, and Cardinal Wolsey as the presiding force in government. Neither had had much of an influence on English life in terms of tangible political reforms.

Humanism failed to live up to the hopes of its apostles. It did have a considerable impact on education, producing the revised grammar school curriculum used, for example, in Colet's school at St Paul's, as well as encouraging the endowment of lectures, chairs, and colleges in Oxford and Cambridge designed to promote humanistic learning.[1] It also fostered a new approach to the study of scripture once Erasmus' exposure of mistranslations in the Vulgate text had weakened the church's claims to absolute authority in its interpretation. But humanism, although outwardly confident, contained unresolved tensions between the competing claims of faith and reason, idealism and realism, and contemplation and action. This meant that humanists, while they entertained a noble vision, never found an effective way of translating their theoretical knowledge into practical action.[2] Men who actually held the reins of power paid lip-service to humanist moral idealism while proceeding as if it did not exist. If they hired humanists as secretaries and ambassadors, it was because the latter were articulate and therefore useful in expediting the crown's business, not because their ideas were valued. Richard Pace came closest to admitting the truth in his extraordinarily self-subverting treatise *De fructu qui ex doctrina percipitur* when, after having tried bravely to extol the benefit of a liberal education, he ended up by confessing that the arts were considered worthless by society, and that the honourable pleasure to be derived from them only partially compensated

---

[1] See Kalyan K. Chatterjee, *In Praise of Learning: John Colet and Literary Humanism in England* (New Delhi, 1974); and Maria Dowling, *Humanism in the Age of Henry VIII*, chaps 3, 4.

[2] For a fuller exemplification of this view, see Fox, 'Facts and Fallacies: Interpreting English Humanism', and 'English Humanism and the Body Politic', in Fox and Guy, *Reassessing the Henrician Age*, pp. 9–51.

for the beatings, poverty, and other miseries that the youth who studied them would incur on the way.[3] Humanists who did enter royal service found that they had to forget the moral idealism learnt from their studies, and give up any flattering notions that they could indirectly guide the prince by offering him wise counsel. Instead, they discovered the cruel reality that they were there to further the will of those in power above them. More found himself obliged to justify the judicial murder of the Duke of Buckingham to a disquieted City of London in spite of his qualms of conscience over it;[4] Pace, during the very time he was writing De fructu, was pursuing diplomatic negotiations to open a war against France, in spite of his humanist belief in the need for peace;[5] and Thomas Elyot was sent to Spain to justify a divorce in which his ethical idealism would not let him believe.[6] If moral scruples impeded the efficiency with which a humanist was able to perform his brief, he was quickly dropped, as in Elyot's case,[7] or was liable to suffer a worse fate, as More's tragedy demonstrated.

Wolsey, on the other hand, made plentiful changes to administrative procedures and initiated many reformist schemes, but his motivation was too impaired by self-interest for him to be really effective. Cynical onlookers viewed his pretended concern with reform as merely a pretext on the cardinal's part for extending the range of his personal power.

Significant change, when it came, was much more radical than anyone could have envisaged in the first two decades of Henry VIII's reign and proceeded from a new set of social, intellectual and political mechanisms. Specifically, it developed from two main causes: first, the efforts of religious dissidents to procure reform of the church, and, second, Henry VIII's determination to secure a divorce.

Widespread anticlericalism, exacerbated by the failure of the English church under Wolsey to reform itself, proved a fertile seedbed for heterodoxy in the early 1520s. In spite of the cardinal's holocaust of Luther's books in May 1521, Lutheran doctrine had won many converts, and the publication of William Tyndale's tendentious translation of the New Testament in 1525 was followed by a flood of heretical books printed on the continent and smuggled into England.[8] Many of these books had an overt political aim. If the reformers were to make

---

[3] See De fructu qui ex doctrina percipitur (On the Benefit of a Liberal Education), trans. and ed. Frank Manley and Richard S. Sylvester (New York, 1967), pp. xx–xxiii.

[4] See Fox, Thomas More, pp. 103–4.

[5] See Jervis Wegg, Richard Pace: A Tudor Diplomatist (London, 1932), pp. 65–113.

[6] See Fox, 'Sir Thomas Elyot and the Humanist Dilemma', in Fox and Guy, Reassessing the Henrician Age, pp. 52–73.

[7] Ibid.

[8] See Anthea Hume, 'English Protestant Books Printed Abroad, 1525–1535: An Annotated Bibliography', in CW Thos. More, 8: The Confutation of Tyndale's Answer, Part 2, Appendix B, pp. 1065–91.

any headway, they had to weaken the church's power to repress them, and the only way of achieving this was to win the support of the king. Much early protestant literature, therefore, is aimed at turning Henry VIII against the church, in the hope that he would (as soon, indeed, he did) curtail its wealth and independence as a means of recovering the sovereignty that reformers claimed the church had usurped from him. While Henry remained obdurately opposed to heretical theology, he was highly responsive to calls upon him to enlarge his sovereignty. Of Tyndale's *Obedience of a Christian Man* (1528), he is purported to have said that 'this is a book for me and all kings to read', and Foxe reports that he kept Simon Fish's *A Supplicacyon for the Beggers* (1529) in his bosom for three or four days, being so delighted with its contents that he offered Fish his personal protection to encourage him to return to England.[9]

Henry had a pressing personal reason for his interest in the appeals the Lutheran writers were making to him. By the spring of 1527, he had developed doubts about the validity of his marriage to Katherine of Aragon and, having canvassed the opinion of various individuals and the foreign universities, began proceedings to secure a divorce. At first the king pinned his hopes upon Wolsey to gain him the divorce through his legatine court, but by 1529 it had become clear that the cardinal was a broken reed, especially after Katherine's nephew had been elected Pope Clement VII. If Henry were to secure his divorce, some other means would need to be found. Through a strange twist of fate, therefore, the king and the Lutheran reformers found themselves pursuing a common cause, and for the next few years literature was to be dominated and conditioned by issues arising from the nexus of their convergent interests.

A veritable explosion in the number of books produced, increasingly in printed form rather than manuscript, occurred as writers responded to the exigencies, opportunities, and dangers of the new situation. These works can be divided into a number of distinct categories. The first wave to appear comprised of works of religious polemic by Lutheran writers such as Tyndale, Fish, Frith, Barnes, Barlowe, and Joye, together with counterblasts by defenders of the Catholic position such as More, Fisher, and Rastell. A second wave of tracts appeared as the king's 'great matter' gave rise to two major pamphlet debates, the first on the issue of the divorce itself, with partisans arguing both the king's case and the queen's case, and the second on the royal supremacy, once it had been reasserted in Henry's break with Rome. Apart from those directly involved in the propaganda and polemical campaigns occasioned by these issues, there was a third class of writers, like Elyot and Starkey, who, knowing that reform was in the

[9] John Strype, *Ecclesiastical Memorials; Relating Chiefly to Religion and the Reformation of It, and the Emergencies of the Church of England, under King Henry VIII, King Edward VI, and Queen Mary I*, 6 vols (Oxford, 1822), I, i. p. 172. Foxe's story of Henry VIII's reception of Fish's book is reprinted in *A Supplicacyon for the Beggers*, ed. Frederick J. Furnivall, Early English Text Society, Extra Series, no. 13 (London, 1871), p. vi. See also Foxe, *Acts and Monuments*, IV, p. 659ff.

offing, sought to promote their own ideas in tracts like *The Governour* and *A Dialogue between Lupset and Pole*, while simultaneously declaring their credentials for office in the royal service. Yet a fourth class of writers comprised courtiers, who like Sir Thomas Wyatt and, later, Henry Howard, the Earl of Surrey, became victims of political manoeuvring partly beyond their control during these years, and sought to express their feelings in works of disguised literary protest. Presiding over all this literary activity, whether directly and knowingly, or indirectly and unknowingly, was Henry VIII himself. Almost every writer was seeking either to influence him, impress him, do his bidding or that of his ministers, or protest against him in various ways. No one was free of the awareness that the welfare of England depended upon what he decided to believe, and how he decided to act, or had acted. In short, the king's response to the evolving situation potentially affected everyone, and no one appears to have allowed that fact to stray far from the forefront of their mind. As far as the present study is concerned, therefore, Henry must be considered the presiding genius of the final phase of early Tudor literature; he was the focus of the epoch-making crisis that determined the predominant mode of literature for many years to come, and transformed it in the process. The rest of this chapter will sketch in the main features of that transformation.

All the literary works surveyed so far display the distinctive early Tudor tendency to represent thought in the form of dramatized situations. The most striking aspect of the writings that followed in this next period is the almost universal flight from the creation of imaginative fictions to which they attest.

In the first religious polemics of the reformers the tendency to dramatize can still be seen, especially in two of the earliest and most devastating, Jerome Barlowe's *Rede Me and Be Nott Wrothe* (known to contemporaries as *The Burying of the Mass*), and Simon Fish's *A Supplicacyon for the Beggers*, both of which were written in 1528. Barlowe's dialogue is a virulent attack on the clergy in England as a 'cruel generation of vipers' who have usurped the dignity and power of the nobles, oppressed the poor, indulged in every conceivable vice, and persecuted the faithful. Predictably, Cardinal Wolsey becomes the focus of an especially scathing attack. The dialogue begins by being cast as a fictive invention. Its status as such is signalled by the mock coat of arms for Wolsey which prefaces the work, in which six bloody axes signify his cruelty, six bulls' heads his 'sturdy furiousness', a mastiff cur in the middle gnawing a king's crown his base origins and arrogant presumption, and a club covered by a cardinal's hat his tyranny.[10] The author then supplies a context for the work in a prefatory epistle which pretends that the work has been sent out of England by one of the

[10] J. Barlowe and W. Roye, *Rede Me and Be Nott Wrothe, For I Saye Nothinge but Trothe*, ed. Edward Arber, English Reprints (London, 1871), pp. 19–20.

evangelical brethren. It was, in fact, written in Strasbourg; the prefatory epistle, therefore, serves not only as a blind, but also to dramatize as an actual event what is really only a desired analogue of probability. In this way, Barlowe hopes to create the impression that the anticlerical views he depicts are far more entrenched than they may actually have been.

The satiric attack itself is couched as a fully dramatized dialogue between two servants, Watkin and Jeffray, who are downstairs mulling over events while their master, a papist priest, is upstairs lamenting the decease of the mass (which had been suppressed after the Berne disputation) along with others of his persuasion. Each side contemplates the effect it will have on them. The papists bewail that they will no longer be able to keep their whores and palaces, nor pay for their luxuries, hold the nobility at bay, or maintain their status and authority. Watkin and Jeffray, on the other hand, decide to look for new employment in anticipation of being masterless. The satiric effectiveness of the work derives almost wholly from the comic irony generated by this dramatized context, and the way that Barlowe exploits the analogy between the suppression of the mass and the death of a real man. Watkin is able to report that the Mass was slain like a common vagabond with a sharp, two-edged sword drawn out of the gospel. Not all the worldly riches and substance of the priests could save him. When Jeffray asks how long it will be before the Mass is buried, Watkin replies that there is still debate on the matter. England would be the most suitable place, but they suspect that the prelates there will resist this prospect furiously, as they have already burnt the gospel and banned unlicensed preaching.[11] This idea leads naturally into an attack on Wolsey as being the prelate most responsible for England's ills, in which Barlowe reiterates all the complaints familiar from Skelton's satires against the cardinal, with plenty of lurid embellishments of his own.

The original fictional conception is remarkably appropriate for scoring the satiric points Barlowe wants to make, because it represents the polemical situation in experiential terms that invoke common sense on the side of the author. Within 30 pages, however, this dimension has receded in importance to be replaced by simple polemic. Watkins and Jeffray lose any vestiges of personality and become mere prompts for one another to unleash anticlerical diatribes.

This relinquishing of fictional decorum and verisimilitude indicates a salient new feature of literature in the later 1520s and the 1530s: any fictive elements in it tend to be used merely as pretexts for ideological assertion. Instead of being a vehicle for exploration, analysis and assessment, fiction is emptied of any potentiality for imaginative free play; its dialogical properties, in other words, had become translated into monological ones, so that writers began to use fiction almost exclusively as a rhetorical device by limiting the full scope of its representational potential.

Simon Fish's *Supplicacyon for the Beggers*, printed in early 1529, illustrates

11 Ibid., 30–45.

this bias towards assertive rhetoric even more clearly. Addressed to Henry VIII himself, Fish's pamphlet seeks to persuade the king that the clergy have impoverished the realm by their exactions and usurped much of his own temporal power. The author's remedy is simple: Henry should strip the clergy of their independent legal jurisdiction, expel the regular clergy from the monasteries, and enforce them to obey his own authority.

Once again, Fish obeys the early Tudor instinct to dramatize, by inventing a fictive framework for his polemic. He casts the work as a supplication addressed by the poor beggars of the realm to the king, in which they beg him to alleviate the misery they are suffering as a result of clerical rapacity. It was a cunning ploy, for Fish was able thereby to exploit the supposed misery of the beggars as a pretext for indulging in heightened affective rhetoric.

Given such a good pretext, he pulls out all the rhetorical stops. Among his favourite figures of speech are metaphors arranged in antithetical sets. The clergy, for example, are 'rauinous wolues' devouring 'the flocke'. Similarly, the pope is 'a cruell, deuelisshe bloudsupper, dronken in the bloude of the sayntes and marters of christ'.[12] Fish reinforces this emotive imagery with equally highly charged figures of sentence, especially *exclamationes* that are linked to strings of rhetorical questions. Perhaps the best example occurs in a passage that particularly incensed Thomas More, who had undertaken to refute the treatise:

> . . . who is abill to nombre the great and brode botomles occean see, full of euilles, that this mischeuous and sinful generacion may laufully bring vppon vs vnponisshed? where is youre swerde, power, crowne, and dignite become, that shuld punisshe (by punisshement of deth, euen as other men are punisshed) the felonies, rapes, murdres, and treasons committed by this sinfull generacion? where is theire obedience become, that shulde be vnder your hyghe power yn this mater? . . . Oh the greuous shipwrak of the common welth, whiche yn auncient time, bifore the coming yn of these rauinous wolues, was so prosperous, that then there were but fewe theues![13]

Yet another of Fish's favourite syntactical figures is the redundant amplification and repetition of specifics in lists, so as to create an exaggerated impression through the sheer accumulation of detail, of clerical rapacity. We see this when the beggars describe the possessions that the clergy have gathered into their hands:

> The goodliest lordshippes, maners, londes, and territories are theyrs. Besides this, they haue the tenth part of all the corne, medowe, pasture, grasse, wolle, coltes, calues, lambes, pigges, gese and chikens. Ouer and

---

[12] *A Supplicacyon for the Beggers*, ed. Furnivall, pp. 1, 5.
[13] Ibid., pp. 7–8.

bisides, the tenth part of euery seruauntes wages, the tenth part of the wolle, milke, hony, waxe, chese, and butter.[14]

Perhaps the most extravagant flourish of all occurs in the repetitions of the final climactic drumroll with which Fish ends the *Supplicacyon*. Should the king dissolve the monasteries and set the monks to work, the advantages to the whole realm, he suggests, would be immense:

> Then shall, aswell the nombre of oure forsaid monstruous sort, as of the baudes, hores, theues, and idell people, decrease. Then shall these great yerely exaccions cease. Then shall not youre swerde, power, crowne, dignite, and obedience of your people, be translated from you. Then shall you haue full obedience of your people. Then shall the idell people be set to worke. Then shall matrimony be moche better kept. Then shal the genera-tion of your people be encreased. Then shall your comons encrease in richesse. Then shall the gospell be preached . . .[15]

It is small wonder, given this rhetorical overkill, that More was roused to denounce the *Supplicacyon* as 'florishing without fruite, sutteltie without sub-stance, rethorike without reason, bold babling without learning, and wylines without wit', containing 'not halfe so many leaues as lyes, but almost as manye lyes as lynes'.[16] Be that as it may, the effectiveness of Fish's rhetoric is attested in the way that More, in denouncing it, was led, ironically, to write rhetoric of his own. And can he have been aware of the irony that the very matter and manner of Fish's proposed remedy echoed the style and substance of Raphael Hythlodaeus' summary of his reformist vision, in the peroration to More's own *Utopia*? Perhaps that explains some of the vehemence of his animus against 'the beggars' proctour'.

Fish gained one further advantage from casting his diatribe as a dramatized fiction. The particular fiction he chose gave him the change of playing upon the psyche of the king. To have the beggars supplicate Henry in trustful humility was to place him in an implicitly flattering position. Henry was being invited to consider himself as the protector of his people, and hence to identify the enlargement of his regal sovereignty as an altruistic act. Moreover, the beggars' rhetorical questions were designed to fill his mind with notions that would incense him against the clergy and move him to take action against them out of wounded pride and indignation. In inventing a dramatized situation that he claimed had come about because of the misdeeds of the clergy, and then focusing

[14] Ibid., p. 2.
[15] Ibid., p. 14.
[16] *The Supplicacion of Soules*, in *The Workes of Sir Thomas More Knyght . . . Wrytten by Him in the Englysh Tonge* (London, 1557), p. 291 F-G. Hereafter cited as More, *Workes in the Englysh Tonge (1557)*.

attention on the implications of that situation by posing rhetorical questions, in the hope that his audience would be moved to do something about it, Fish was adopting almost exactly the same strategy that Skelton had used so effectively in *Why Come Ye Nat to Courte?* He tried to nudge the king further towards such a response by drawing an unfavourable comparison between Henry and his 'nobill predecessours' who, the beggars declare, had 'euer stode fre' of the exactions England was now obliged to pay to the church.[17] As Henry's keen interest in the book confirmed, Fish had shrewdly gauged the psychology of his man.

Fish's choice of fiction, therefore, was ideal for his purpose, but, as in the case of *Rede Me and Be Nott Wrothe*, the fictional decorum of *A Supplicacyon for the Beggers* is not sustained. It soon becomes obvious that the beggars, given their plight and status, could never have gained the knowledge of half the things they allege. The fiction, in fact, is merely a pretext for Fish's rhetoric, which is developed in exactly the same way as it would have been had not Fish's personae existed. In the case of *A Supplicacyon for the Beggers* the match between the fictional conception and the polemical intent was happier than in most other instances of reformist literature, but the underlying problem remained the same: writers were ceasing to trust that fully realized fictive representations could communicate their message, and a retreat from such representations of experience was underway.

The two pieces by Barlowe and Fish show that ideological fervour was one threat posed to fiction writing in the late 1520s. Other early Protestants, however, recoiled from fiction for another, equally strong reason. It is revealed in the strictures against William Roye and Jerome Barlowe with which Tyndale prefaces his *Parable of the Wicked Mammon* (1528). After warning the reader against the untrustworthiness of Roye (who had been his assistant in the preparation of his New Testament), Tyndale denounces *Rede Me and Be Nott Wrothe*, which Barlowe had written at Roye's instigation. His grounds are as follows:

> It becommeth not . . . the Lordes seruaunt to vse rayling rymes, but Gods worde, which is the right weapon to slay sinne, vice and all iniquitie . . . The weapons of our warre are not carnall thynges (sayth he [i.e. St Paul]) but mighty in God to cast downe strong holdes, and so forth, that is, to destroy high buildings of false doctrine . . . with that sword [i.e. the word of God] ought men sharply to fight, and not to rayle with foolishe rymes.[18]

For Tyndale, the word of God revealed in the scripture had become an absolute and self-sufficient authority rendering obsolete any possible function that fiction

---

[17] *Supplicacyon for the Beggers*, ed. Furnivall, p. 3.
[18] *The Parable of the Wicked Mammon*, in *The Whole Workes of W. Tyndall, John Frith and Doct. Barnes* (London, 1573), p. 60. This edition is hereafter cited as Tyndale, *Workes* (1573).

could perform. That is why he dismissed More's attempt to confute him as mere 'poetry', by which he meant that More's arguments were a form of sophistical 'feigning' designed to obscure the truth, a charge that would later be repeated by John Foxe.[19] 'Poetical' fictions were to be dismissed because they belonged to the order of carnal seductions that led men into the maze and darkness of error. They were comparable, for Tyndale, to the images, rituals, and ceremonies of the Catholic church, which he saw as sinister forms of 'juggling' to keep impression-able minds in a state of superstitious credulity. Only the clear light of scriptural truth, he believed, could dispel this darkness.

This attitude left a very marked impression on Tyndale's own writings and those of his followers. As a rule, Tyndale mistrusted figurative imagery and symbolism except where it could be used to illuminate the meaning of the scripture, or heighten the contrast between truth and error by furnishing analo-gies. As he explained in *The Obedience of a Christian Man*, 'similitudes proue nothyng, but are made to expresse more playnly that which is contayned in the Scripture and to lead thee into the spirituall vnderstanding of the text.'[20] Characteristically, this restriction of figurative language to an expositional func-tion rather than a representational one in the works of Tyndale and other early English Protestants, produces a limited range of imagery in which the basic dualisms of Lutheranism are expressed as sets of contraries. Figurative language tends to fall into a class of apocalyptic images designating truth, and an opposing set of demonic images that signify error. Images of light are opposed to images of darkness, the fire of truth against the smoke of error, cleanness against pollution, health against disease, the temple against the synagogue, the true church as a spouse against the papist church as a whore, plainness against convolution, lambs against foxy hypocrites and wolves, and so on.

The Lutherans' tendency to interpret experience according to a binary division between truth and falsehood, and goodness and evil reaches its apotheosis in John Frith's treatise called *An Antithesis betweene Christ and the Pope* (1529), the very title of which suggests the massive structure of contraries that Frith erects in this work. His method is first to take an attribute of Christ as described in the New Testament, and then to supply images of worldliness and corruption to show that the pope is Christ's antithesis; for example:

Luke. 2   12. Christ lay in a stable, with few clothes, betwixt an Oxe and
an Asse for the place was narrowe.
The Pope, in rich chambers, with quiltes, curtaines, carpettes

---

[19] See *An Aunswere vnto Syr Thomas Mores Dialogue*, in Tyndale, *Workes* (1573), pp. 250–1; cf. *The Acts and Monuments of John Foxe*, ed. Josiah Pratt, 4th edn, 8 vols (London, n. d.), IV, pp. 643-6. Hereafter cited as Foxe, *Acts and Monuments*.
[20] Tyndale, *Workes* (1573), p. 170.

quishyons spread all about with sweete smelles and paynted walles.[21]

The images referring to both Christ and the pope are literal, but those associated with Christ are made to evoke a spiritual order of experience, while those associated with the pope are meant to signify a worldly level of experience that perverts and parodies the former. As a result, the true life of the spirit is signified in images of simplicity, plainness, and privation, while images of sensual beauty and richness are reserved for the carnal level of experience that must be rejected:

John. 19.   19. Christ had a crowne of thorne thrust vpon his head, so
                  that ye bloude ranne downe vpon his amiable counte-
                  naunce, and sharpe nayles thorow his precious handes.

Ca. Constãt.   The Pope must weare three crownes of golde, set with
dist. xcvi.   riche precious stones, he lacketh no Diademes, hys handes
                  and fingers with owches and ringes are royally dight, he
                  passeth poore Christ farre.[22]

Their theology and their rhetoric thus trapped the early Lutheran reformers into a wholesale rejection of huge areas of human aesthetic and emotional experience, the complexity (and ambiguity) of which imaginative fiction was capable of capturing. It is not surprising, therefore, that after the abortive experiments of Barlowe and Fish with fiction, the early Protestants should quickly have settled into using as their favourite literary vehicles the treatise of exposition, and the selective analysis of an opponent's work.[23]

If the retreat from fully realized imaginative representation in the 1520s and 1530s could be isolated as exclusively a protestant phenomenon, it could be explained as the by-product of Lutheran theology. The matter is not that simple, however, for exactly the same phenomenon can be observed in writers of the opposite persuasion, most strikingly in the controversial writings of Thomas More.

In the first of his polemics, More tried to refute heresy by contriving fictive representations. *A Dialogue Concerning Heresies* (1529) begins as a fully dramatized dialogue, just as *Utopia* had been. More invents an apt situation, and tries to invest his characters with credible personalities and motives appropriate to his persuasive purpose. A 'ryght worshypfull frende' of More's has sent a young university student to More as an emissary, to resolve certain doubts that are in

[21] *The Workes of the Excellent Martyr of Christ, John Frith*, in Tyndale, *Workes* (1573), sig. QQ2[r].
[22] Ibid.
[23] See Rainer Pineas, *Thomas More and Tudor Polemics* (Bloomington and London, 1968), p. 216.

the air arising from the suppression of Luther's and Tyndale's books by the authorities. More perceives that, 'as yonge scolers be sometym prone to newe fantasyes', the Messenger may himself have fallen into Luther's sect, and he suspects that his friend has sent the Messenger to him in order that he should be 'somwhat answered and satysfyed'.[24] There were many advantages to this fictive strategy. More could exploit the character of his young interlocutor to discredit the heretical opinions to which the latter is susceptible. By depicting him as impetuous, rather conceited, and 'of nature nothynge tonge tayed', as young scholars brimming with the intellectual stimulation of their studies tend to be, More could hope to pass off the heretical opinions as fashionable newfangledness that would fade away as their adherents matured into wisdom. The fictive framework of the dialogue was useful for another reason; it avoided the appearance of coercion, by depicting the discussion as taking place among people linked together by bonds of friendship and good will. In the 'letter of credence' which More's friend sends to him, he recalls that in the past they had spent time 'in famylyer communycacyon', and hopes that More will be able to spare some time to engage the Messenger in similarly relaxed, discursive enquiry.[25] The phrase recalls More's reference in Utopia to the kind of philosophical debate that is appropriate 'apud amiculos in familiari colloquio' ('among close friends in familiar conversation'), and which he represents taking place between himself, Peter Giles and Raphael Hythlodaeus in that book.[26] In choosing to show doubts concerning heresy being resolved through a similar process of 'familiar colloquy', More was trying to reproduce the process that takes place in Plato's philosophical dialogues, in which disputation leads progressively to the revelation of the logos, or innate truth about the nature of things. In this way, he could hope to create the impression that unfettered rational enquiry, pursued with good will, would always arrive at the same conclusion: that the heretics were wrong.

This was bound to prove a futile expectation, for More in A Dialogue Concerning Heresies was fundamentally dishonest – dishonest, that is, in pretending to depict a dramatized representation of a free, objective process of philosophical enquiry. The Messenger, brilliantly characterized at the beginning, soon grows unconvincingly pliant as More becomes progressively more dogmatic and assertive. Tyndale, in rebutting the work, hit the nail on the head:

M. More throughout all his booke maketh, quoth he [i.e. the Messenger], to dispute and moue questions after such a maner as he can soyle them or make them appeare soyled, and maketh him graunt where he lysteth and at the last to be concluded and lad whether M. More will haue him.[27]

---

[24] A Dialogue Concerning Heresies, in CW Thos. More, 6, Part 1, p. 34/29–33.
[25] Ibid., p. 24/28–9.
[26] Utopia, CW Thos. More, 4, p. 98/5.
[27] An Aunswere vnto Syr Thomas Mores Dialogue, in Tyndale, Workes (1573), p. 330.

In spite of More's good intentions, therefore, the pressure of ideological commitment led him, just as surely as it did Barlowe or Fish, to desert the fictive representational mode in which he had so deeply believed.

It takes More even less time in his next polemical work, *The Supplicacion of Soules*, to abandon his initial conception. Taking his cue from Fish, whom he had set out to rebut, More contrived the work as a plea from the souls suffering the 'hote clensing fyre' of purgatory (which Fish had denounced as a papist invention) for 'help, coumforte, and reliefe' on the part of kindred and friends on earth, who may be tempted to forget them because of the mischief being sown by the heretics.[28] The device was promising, potentially, at least. More could hope to persuade readers to his viewpoint by playing upon their natural affection for dead relatives and friends, especially if he could depict the suffering of the souls in purgatory with convincingly affective verisimilitude. In the event, however, he ruined his opportunity by overdoing the suffering of the souls on one hand, and by forgetting that the work was supposed to be being narrated by them on the other. John Foxe's later critical remarks on *The Supplicacion of Soules* are most apposite, for he rightly observes that More failed to keep 'decorum personae', as a perfect poet should have done:

> They that give precepts of art, do note this in all poetical fictions, as a special observation, to foresee and express what is convenient for every person, according to his degree and condition, to speak and utter.[29]

According to the decorum of More's conception, Foxe adds, the souls should not have so soon forgotten their charity as to rail 'so fumishly' against Fish and the other Lutherans. What Foxe is identifying, is the destructive effect More's intense hatred of heresy had had on his fiction. Having commenced the work by trying to objectify his thoughts in a dramatic situation, More's animus against the heretics soon overpowered his self-control, so that once again he jettisoned the fiction in favour of a diatribe in his own voice. This allowed Foxe easily to reverse More's charge that Fish's *Supplicacyon* had been inspired by men's 'gostlye enemy the deuyll':

> Now, as touching the manner how this devil came into purgatory, laughing, grinning, and gnashing his teeth, in sooth it maketh me to laugh, to see the merry antics of Master More. Belike then this was some merry devil, or else had eaten with his teeth some nasturcium before; who, coming into purgatory, to show the name of this man, could not tell his tale without laughing ... So then, here was enmying, envying, laughing, grinning,

---

[28] *The Supplicacion of Soules*, More, *Workes in the Englysh Tonge* (1557), pp. 288–9.
[29] Foxe, *Acts and Monuments*, IV, p. 665.

gnashing of teeth, puling, scoffing, railing, and begging; and all together to make a very black 'sanctus' in purgatory.[30]

Allowing for the excess of Foxe's remarks, he nevertheless accurately identifies the problem with The Supplicacion of Soules: it fails because More, by shattering the fictional decorum of the work, fails to sustain dramatic credibility, so that his satiric vehemence becomes counterproductive with those readers who are not already persuaded to his position. The more strident and forceful he becomes, the more his assertions seem like the wishful thinking of an excessively anxious man.

The onset of the deterioration in More's personality and his decline as a writer can be dated from his loss of faith in imaginative representation. His ensuing works reveal a progressive loss of control and sense of proportion. In The Confutation of Tyndale's Answer (1532–1533), More's desperation had grown so intense that he made the fatal error of copying his opponent's method of systematic quotation and rebuttal. The result is horrifyingly demonstrated in the huge sprawl of the work, so long that the Lutherans could boast that no one could be bothered to read it.[31] More does make some effort in The Confutation of Tyndale's Answer to retain some element of fictive representation by including 'merry tales' sprinkled through the work. These are designed to invest the argument with an experiential quality, to persuade readers that what More says is confirmed by the verities of their own common experience of life, but being few and far between in More's later polemics, these facetiae, although a welcome relief from the harangue, are a poor substitute for the real thing. Significantly, when More recovered his mental and emotional equilibrium after he had been imprisoned in the Tower, his recovery was accompanied by a renewed desire to write fiction. A Dialogue of Comfort against Tribulation shows More once again trusting to imaginative representation as a means not only of coming to terms with his own troubled situation, but also of persuading others to accept it without fear.

The truth of the matter is that as the reformation conflict escalated in England, neither side could sustain the fictive impulse with any conviction. Many polemicists tried, but without notable success. The anonymous author of The Image of Ypocresye (1533) aspired to imitate Skelton's Collyn Clout, but managed to produce only a sprawling, rambling, 'treatise' which embodies no dramatized situation, has no characterized persona, and ends up being a simple compendium of the familiar anticlerical complaints.[32]

Many works begin quite promisingly. William Turner's The Huntyng and

---

[30] Ibid., IV, pp. 665–6.
[31] See The Apology of Sir Thomas More Knight, CW Thos. More, 9, pp. 7–11.
[32] The Image of Ypocresye is reprinted in Ballads from Manuscripts, ed. Furnivall, 1, pp. 181–266.

Fyndyng out of the Romishe Fox (1543) makes very effective use of an extended metaphor based upon natural lore (Turner was himself a naturalist) and one of the favourite scriptural texts of the radical reformers: 'Foxes haue holes and byrdes of the ayer haue nestes / but the son of man hath not where he may rest hys hede in.'[33] Turner, along with other evangelicals, was dismayed at the lack of progress in doctrinal reform after Henry VIII's break with Rome, and in this work aims to persuade the king to extirpate the remaining traces of papist doctrine in the English church. To present his plea, Turner develops an extended analogy between papism, which he likens to a cruel but cunning fox that has found a hole in the church in which to take refuge, and Henry as a hunter who must chase this beast out of his realm. Turner is able to exploit his knowledge of the way real foxes behave to develop the analogy. He is certain, for example, that the Romish fox has hidden in the church:

> for as it is a good coniectur of a man be in a wod & se a great hole in the gronde to thynk that theyr haunteth or hath haunted a fox / and if theyr be / by thys hole many peces of lambes skynnes / many chekynges fethers, that at that praesent tyme ther is a fox hauntyng that hole / so i thynk that if i coniecture that theyr is a romishe fox in the chirche / i shall not coniecture amis / for i saw when i was in Englonde in a certayne chirche a great hole in the hie aultare which i could not tell for what purpos the gentle men of the chirche haue ordened it except it be to hyde theyr father the fox in . . .[34]

The effectiveness of this device comes from the way Turner is able to create an image with great particularity and realism, of an experience with which many of his readers would have been familiar. He is then able, by shifting the level of representation from a literal to an allegorical one, to transfer the reader's feelings of familiar recognition from the fox to the idea of papist doctrine. Here, indeed, is an example of the 'juggling' that made Tyndale so mistrustful of fiction, and from one of his own collateral descendants – but it was potentially very effective as a persuasive device. Predictably, however, Turner does not sustain it, and within several pages the fictive element drops away to be replaced by a bare catalogue of the superstitious 'errors' of the Henrician clergy.

The Plowman's Tale, purportedlly written by Geoffrey Chaucer, but in fact written by Thomas Godfray in 1535, is another work that betrays its early promise. Godfray's choice of a ploughman for a persona was highly appropriate because Chaucer's original ploughman had been one of two characters of exemplary, humble virtue in the 'General Prologue' to *The Canterbury Tales*. A ploughman was also bound to be associated with the long tradition of pastoral

---

[33] *The Huntyng & Fyndyng out of the Romishe Fox* (Basel, 1543), sig. A1[r]. The biblical text is from Matthew 8. I am indebted to Mr John Benger for allowing me to read the chapters on Turner in his unpublished doctoral dissertation on radical protestant writers of the mid-sixteenth century.

[34] Ibid., sigs A3[v]–A4[r].

complaint of which *Piers Plowman* was the supreme exemplar. The author could thus hope to attract to himself some of the immense authority and respectability of Chaucer and Langland, and the earlier traditions to which they had given voice.

The beast fable that constitutes this tale also holds considerable promise. The Ploughman tells how he set out to discover which was the falser of the two, the papist clergy or the Lollards. On his travels he saw two birds, a griffin, representing the papist, and a pelican, representing the Lollards. The pelican preaches of mercy and meekness, and denounces the worldliness of the clergy, and eventually the enraged griffin goes off to plot revenge. When it returns with other birds of prey to kill the pelican, a phoenix, signifying alternatively Henry VIII or Christ, depending upon which level of the allegory one prefers, drives all the birds of prey under the earth, and the tale ends.[35] As with other polemics, the characterization of the personae is not sustained. The pelican becomes increasingly intemperate to a degree that conflicts with its supposed attributes of mercy and meekness, and the griffin remains unbelievably passive until its final fit of fury at the conclusion of the work. Exactly the same thing has happened, therefore, as occurred in Barlowe's *Rede Me and Be Nott Wrothe* or More's *Supplicacion of Soules*: the fictive conception, being essentially a rhetorical pretext, drops away to be forgotten once the writer warms to his premeditated theme.

If religious literature written during the Henrician revolution shows that ideological commitments were inimical to fiction in the circumstances of the 1520s and 1530s, non-religious literature shows the destructive effects even more graphically. England witnessed two major pamphlet debates during these years, one concerning the king's divorce, and the other concerning the royal supremacy. In works such as the exposition accompanying *The Determinations of the Moste Famous and Mooste Excellent Uniuersities of Italy and Fraunce* (known in its Latin version as the *Gravissimae censurae*) by Edward Fox, John Stokesley, and others, or Fox's *De vera differentia* and Stephen Gardiner's *De vera obedientia*, there is not the faintest pretence at fictive invention – quite the contrary. The reason for this is revealed in one of the 'king's books' that preceded the *Gravissimae censurae*. Henry VIII recounts how several months earlier he had described the reasons that were prompting him to seek a divorce. He goes on to explain that certain men desired in that earlier work 'minus eloquentie maiorem autem rationem, et argumentorum lucem, fidem, pondus quoque et auctoritatem' ('less eloquence, and, on the other hand, more reason and arguments that were lucid, credible, and of weighty authority').[36] For better or for worse, this

---

[35] *The Plouuman's Tale Compylled by Syr Geffray Chaucher Knyght* (London, [? 1545]), sigs A2–D7.
[36] Public Record Office SP 1/63, fo. 244; quoted in *The Divorce Tracts of Henry VIII*, ed. Edward Surtz and Virginia Murphy (Angers, 1988), p. vi.

statement sums up the attributes of Henrician propagandistic writing precisely: it is weighty, rationalistic, and laden with references to sources so as to acquire authority. Such works are of minimal relevance to this study.

The literature of religious and political propaganda and polemic shows a relentless, if reluctant, retreat from fiction under the pressure of ideological commitments. As the case of More shows, humanists were just as affected by these pressures as anyone else. Most humanists who found themselves actively involved in Henrician politics, like More or Stephen Gardiner, abandoned their humanism in order to serve the immediate interests of the cause to which they were committed. Nevertheless, the fictive impulse survived fitfully among several of the younger humanists who wished to participate in the action, but for one reason or another found themselves excluded from government.

The most interesting of these younger humanists was Sir Thomas Elyot, a committed Erasmian who, believing that a wise man should offer the fruits of his wisdom in the service of the commonweal, desired above all to become a royal counsellor. After years of serving in a minor post as assistant to the clerk of the Council, Elyot was given a chance to prove his worth when he was made ambassador to Charles V in 1532. Within months, however, Henry VIII and Cromwell had grown dissatisfied with his performance, and he was recalled to England, to be replaced by Thomas Cranmer.[37] Thereafter, he remained permanently excluded from the role in politics he desired, embittered and highly disgruntled.

Elyot's immediate response to his dismissal from office was to write two dialogues in quick succession in early 1533: *Pasquil the Playne*, and *Of the Knowledge which Maketh a Wise Man*. The fact that he turned to a fictive literary mode for the first time in his life shows yet again, as in More's case, that descent into personal tribulation provided a singularly powerful incentive for writers to use imaginative representation as a means of confronting their dilemmas.

In *Pasquil the Playne*, Elyot sought to justify himself and explore his own feelings concerning his past and present motives. As an instrument for achieving this purpose he contrived a dramatized dialogue in which Pasquil, a stone statue in Rome, encounters two cousins, Gnatho, a courtier, and Harpocrates, a priest-confessor, both of whom have been called to counsel.[38] The encounter dramatizes three different forms of political conduct: plain-speaking, represented by Pasquil, obsequious flattery, represented by Gnatho, and hypocritical dissemb-

---

[37] For a full account of the events leading to Elyot's appointment and dismissal, see Fox, 'Sir Thomas Elyot and the Humanist Dilemma', in Fox and Guy, *Reassessing the Henrician Age*, pp. 52–73, esp. pp. 56–62.

[38] *Pasquil the Playne*, in *Four Political Treatises by Sir Thomas Elyot*, ed. Lillian Gottesman (Florida, 1967), pp. 42, 62.

ling, represented by Harpocrates (alias Cranmer). In the course of the dialogue Pasquil rejects Gnatho's sycophancy out of hand, on the grounds that it is morally repellent, and gets Harpocrates to confute himself by having him answer a string of leading questions that destroy the validity of his own argument: that in silence is surety.[39] In this way Elyot tries to justify the plain-speaking with which he had 'remonstrated' with the king over the divorce in June 1532, and implies that he was dismissed because of it.[40]

As a fictive device, Elyot's symbolic fable is pretty crude, not least because it requires a stone statue to talk, but it was nevertheless useful for Elyot in that it allowed him to acknowledge a deep-seated ambiguity he felt concerning the ironic position in which his own moral absolutism had placed him. Because of it, as Gnatho points out, Pasquil (alias Elyot) has 'professed to stande style in the rayne', and is doomed to remain a stone statue, that is, immobilized, helpless to act, and permanently excluded from the counsellor's role he seeks. Elyot knows that he is the author of his own misfortunes, and has the honesty to question the real motives behind his satiric pasquillade when he makes Harpocrates accuse Pasquil of simply chewing sour grapes: 'thou that art nat called to counsayle, arte full of bablynge.'[41] This is close to an admission on Elyot's part that his satire might be motivated by little more than envy. Nevertheless, he counters this possibility by asserting another motive. When Harpocrates asks why he is so busy since he profits so little by it, Pasquil replies: 'To thintent that men shal perceiue, that theyr vices, whiche they thinke to be wonderfull secrete / be knowen to all men.'[42] Elyot's attempt to repress the possibility of a morally ambiguous personal motivation by asserting this altruistic public one suggests that he was not fully in control of the implications of his fictional creation. Pasquil the Playne, in fact, embodies a pervasive irony of which Elyot may not have been aware: it extols plain-speaking by using its very opposite, indirect representation. In order to speak his mind, Elyot was forced to translate his thoughts into a dramatized situation that would protect him by preventing his meaning from being too nakedly apparent. Paradoxically, Elyot was a victim of the discretion and prudence which, in Gnatho and Harpocrates, he was making Pasquil denounce. The dialogue thus vividly illustrates the complex emotional and intellectual reactions into which the Henrician crisis forced those who were political casualties of its processes.

Elyot displays the same paradoxical attitude in his second dialogue of 1533, *Of*

---

[39] Ibid., pp. 70–1.

[40] For Elyot's remonstrance, see the letter of Chapuys to Charles V, 5 June 1532, *Calendar of Letters, Dispatches and State Papers, Relating to the Negotiations between England and Spain, Preserved in the Archives at Vienna, Brussels, Sumancas and Elsewhere*, ed. G. A. Bergenroth and others, 13 vols (London, 1862–1954), IV, ii. 453. Hereafter cited as *Cal. SP Spanish*.

[41] *Pasquil the Playne*, p. 97.

[42] Ibid., p. 99.

the Knowledge which Maketh a Wise Man, in which he again tried to justify his actions through fiction. This time he chose an episode from history to serve as an analogy to his own experience, namely, Plato's fall from grace with Dionysius, the ruler of Sicily. As the dialogue opens, Plato, dressed in rags, is travelling along the road with Aristippus, a voluptuary, and recounts to him how he was sold into slavery for having told Dionysius that the latter was turning into a tyrant. The rest of the dialogue consists of Plato's systematic philosophical proof that he could not have acted in any other way. He argues that wisdom consists of knowledge, which in turn consists of understanding, that must in turn be expressed in action. When Dionysius desired to see whether Plato's countenance, speech, and form of living expressed his reputed wisdom, Plato had been obliged either to speak the truth and incur the king's wrath, or else to prove himself a fool, and so destroy his credibility with the king.[43] By making Plato develop this line of argument, Elyot thus brought himself face to face with the same tragic paradox he had uncovered in *Pasquil the Playne*: to maintain his moral integrity would mean his permanent disqualification from office, because of the gap between moral ideals and political realities. While he affirms in *Of the Knowledge which Maketh a Wise Man* his determination to maintain his integrity, the fictional form of the work allows him simultaneously to express doubts as to whether he should. The doubt surfaces in Aristippus' response to Plato's exposition. Although Aristippus has somewhat modified his initial opinion – that discretion is the better part of valour – and although he admires Plato's heroism, he declares that he will not follow Plato 'in such experience of wysdome'.[44] The dialogue thus admits an element of realistic common sense which, because most ordinary readers are more likely to identify with it than with Plato's high-flown philosophizing, tends to undermine the moral absolutism that Elyot is professing to assert. The presence of such ironic tensions makes one suspect, yet again, that Elyot's defiant Stoicism may have been a compensation for having failed to attain the office he craved. In this respect, the two dialogues of 1533 can be seen as serving for him the same function that the *Eclogues* did for Alexander Barclay: they provided reassurance and self-justification as a protection against the pangs of frustrated hopes.

As fiction, however, Elyot's dialogues are not entirely satisfying. Ordinarily, Elyot preferred straightforward theoretical exposition to fictive invention. He was only moved to attempt it by pressures arising from his personal crisis in 1532, and once he had come to terms with his situation, he reverted to his customary non-fictive mode of writing. Elyot's lack of comfortable familiarity with fiction meant that his representations are rather gauche. His devices serve as pretexts for talk, and more talk, and as with More's *Dialogue Concerning*

---

[43] T. Elyot, *Of the Knowledge which Maketh a Wise Man*, ed. Edwin Johnston (Oxford, Ohio, 1946), p. 226.
[44] Ibid.

Heresies, it is the matter, not the manner, that turns out to be important. Consequently, Elyot's dialogues are really 'incomplete fictions', to echo a term that has been used to characterize the dialogue genre as a whole in the English renaissance.[45]

The other humanist among the younger generation who deserves attention for his writing is Thomas Starkey. He, too, attempted to use fiction for the presentation of his ideas, but for motives that were very different from those of Elyot. A member of the circle of scholars who gathered around Reginald Pole in the 1520s, Starkey, anticipating that Pole would be persuaded to participate in the major reform programme which had commenced in 1529 with the opening of the Reformation Parliament, prepared a long dialogue between 1529 and 1532 outlining his own reformist theories. In effect, *A Dialogue between Thomas Lupset and Reginald Pole* was designed to display Starkey's own credentials, so as to strengthen his chances of riding into the king's service on Pole's coat-tails.[46] As a persuasive fiction, the *Dialogue* begins promisingly. Starkey cunningly dramatizes what he hopes will happen as being in the process of actually happening: he shows Pole, who is reluctant to abandon the contemplative life, being persuaded by Lupset through 'resonyng and dowtyng for cleryng of the truth', to accept that the perfection of man stands in both action and contemplation, the former being the true end of the latter.[47] In this way he could hope simultaneously to move Pole into agreeing to undertake a role in government, while also encouraging the king or his ministers, to whom Starkey must have anticipated presenting the *Dialogue*, to exploit the opportunity of taking Pole on.

The influence of More's *Utopia* is evident throughout the work, with the opening section recalling the debate over whether a philosopher should enter a king's service in Book 1 of *Utopia*, and Pole's ensuing declaration of the nature of a true commonwealth paralleling and reproducing many of the ideas of Book 2. A comparison between the two works, however, reveals a striking difference. Whereas More took care to translate his ideas into an imagined situation in which the ideas were exemplified in a sustained image, Starkey soon abandons any pretence at a comparable imaginative translation. The respective viewpoints of the protagonists quickly get lost once Pole begins to expound his theory of the commonwealth. Indeed, Pole starts to sound just like Lupset did at the beginning, and it becomes clear that it does not matter which character voices the exposition. Neither dramatic nor psychological credibility are important. Starkey's *Dialogue*, therefore, turns out to be yet another 'incomplete fiction', just as

---

[45] See K. J. Wilson, *Incomplete Fictions: The Formation of English Renaissance Dialogue* (Washington, 1985).

[46] See Thomas F. Mayer, *Thomas Starkey and the Commonweal: Humanist Politics and Religion in the Reign of Henry VIII* (Cambridge, forthcoming), chap. 3.

[47] *A Dialogue between Thomas Lupset and Reginald Pole*, in *England in the Reign of King Henry the Eighth*, ed. Sidney J. Herrtage, Early English Text Society, Extra Series, nos 12, 32 (London, 1871, 1878), Part 2, pp. 2–26.

Elyot's dialogues are. In Starkey's case, his burning zeal 'to lyue in a polytyke lyfe' that he later confessed to Cromwell in 1534,[48] overpowers his interest in sustaining the imaginative integrity of his invention. He is simply eager to expound his ideas in the hope of being noticed and appreciated. Starkey's *Dialogue* thus shows yet again the difficulty writers experienced during these years in fully trusting that fiction could achieve their most pressing ends.

Fully realized fictive invention did survive in the later half of Henry VIII's reign, but away from the main focuses of literary attention. The following chapters will show how imaginative representation continued sporadically in the drama and the verse of the courtly writers, but before moving on to those topics there is one more writer showing fictive talent who fits into neither category and needs to be considered briefly – Edward Hall.

Although *The Union of the Two Noble and Illustre Famelies of Lancastre and Yorke* (1542) is generically a chronicle history compiled from many sources, there is more genuine fictive representation in the part which Hall himself composed, 'The Triumphaunt Reigne of Kynge Henry the VIII', than in most of the other texts surveyed in this chapter put together. Hall's 'Triumphaunt Reign', in fact, shows literary method moving in the opposite direction, from non-fiction towards fiction, and shows Hall to have been a precursor of Shakespeare. Whereas writers in the native chronicle tradition had, for the most part, been content to assemble a bare recitation of facts in annalistic form, Hall sought to create heightened pictorial images of the splendour of Henry's reign, and to dramatize some of its most significant moments. Consequently, one gets an extraordinarily vivid evocation of Henry at play, Henry at war, Henry as a dispenser of justice, and the magnificence, generally, of Henry's court.

The coronation of Henry and Katherine of Aragon provides a good example. Having described how the royal couple passed through the London streets, which were draped with tapestries and cloth of gold, with all the different social orders dressed in their appropriate liveries, and priests and clerks censing them with silver censers as they passed, Hall rises to a climactic description of the king himself:

> The features of his body, his goodly personage, his amiable visage, princely countenaunce, with the noble qualities of his royall estate, to euery man knowen, nedeth no rehersall, considerynge, that for lacke of cunnyng, I cannot expresse the giftes of grace and of nature, that God hath endowed hym with all: yet partly to discriue his apparell, it is to bee noted, his grace ware in his vpperest apparell, a robe of Crimosyn Ueluet, furred with Armyns, his iacket or cote of raised gold, the placard embrowdered with Diamondes Rubies, Emeraudes, great Pearles, and other riche Stones, a greate Bauderike aboute his necke, of great Balasses. The Trapper of his

---

[48] Ibid., Part 1, p. x.

Horse, Damaske gold, with a depe pursell of Armyns, his knightes and Esquires for his body, in Crimosyn Ueluet, and all the gentlemen, with other of his chappell, and all his officers, and household seruauntes, wer appareled in Skarlet.[49]

This is far more than mere objective reporting: it is the method of Chaucer in his description of the Canterbury pilgrims, in which outward appearance is used to suggest inner moral qualities. Hall invokes the modesty *topos*, professing to be unable to do justice to Henry's gifts of grace and nature, in order to allow his lavish description of Henry's apparel to imply them. The sequence of amazingly rich and vivid descriptions of pageants, tournaments, disguisings, and state occasions, perhaps finding their most magnificent expression in the description of the meeting between Henry VIII and Francis I at the Field of Cloth of Gold in 1520, all serve this purpose. The colour, opulence, and spectacle translate into qualities that are morally, emotionally, politically, and nationally laudable in Hall's eyes. Like renaissance Italian devotional paintings, Hall's pictorial evocations are designed to stimulate an emotional condition of reverence in the beholders towards the subject depicted, in this case Henry VIII, whom Hall regarded as the saviour of England and the embodiment of its national pride and achievement.

Hall's arsenal of fictive devices consists not only of lavish visual description. He also invents orations, and even letters, in the manner of humanist historians like Vergil and More, to heighten the solemnity of moments of national importance, as when, for example, Henry replies to the Scottish herald in response to the letter he receives from James IV declaring the latter's intention to invade England,[50] or when the Reformation Parliament opens with a key speech by Thomas More.[51] Most effectively of all, Hall narrates certain events as if they are taking place before the very eyes of the reader. To create this effect, he makes skilful use of the novelist's technique of interweaving narrative reporting with dramatized scene and dialogue. Furthermore, he adds to it the dramatist's technique of using symbolic stage groupings and symbolic actions. As a result, many episodes could almost be lifted from the history and enacted, as if they were scenes in a stage play.

A striking example of this form of semi-dramatic recreation occurs in Hall's account of the events following the riot of London apprentices on Evil May Day, 1517. Hall describes how, after the rioting had been quelled, the prisoners were led through the streets tied in ropes, 'some men, some laddes, some chyldren of .xiii. yere', with 'a great mourning of fathers and frendes for their chyldren and kynsfolke'. Thirteen of them were sentenced to be hanged, drawn, and quartered,

---

[49] *The Union of the Two Noble and Illustre Famelies of Lancastre & Yorke* (London, 1548), sig. AAa2^v.

[50] Ibid., fos EEe5^r–FFf1^v.

[51] Ibid., fos JJJ1^r.

and were executed with 'extreme cruelty' on gallows set up in various places around the City for the purpose. Hall then reveals the skill with which the king psychologically manipulated the dismayed London citizens back into an attitude of affectionate loyalty towards him. Having filled them with pity, fear, and apprehension with the barbarous punishment inflicted on a select number of victims chosen for the purpose, Henry allowed himself to be 'coaxed' by stages into granting a general pardon to the others. Hall manages to show all this in the course of being enacted, by dramatizing the key episodes. The first occurs when three further prisoners, Lincoln, Sherwin, and Betts, are dragged on hurdles through London to be executed on 7 May. After a short speech Lincoln is, in fact, hanged, but as the other two have 'the rope about their neckes' there arrives a commandment from the king to stay execution. The second episode occurs when the recorder and alderman of London, dressed in gowns of black, visit the king at Greenwich on 11 May and supplicate him on bended knee to relinquish his displeasure towards the City. This ritual wooing of the king culminates in the grand scene in Westminster Hall on 22 May, when Henry finally grants pardon to all. Here, we see Hall's talents as a dramatist at their height, with the whole scene contrived to present a vivid stage picture. At the upper end of the hall, set with 'clothe of estate, & the place hanged with Arras', is the king himself, flanked by Cardinal Wolsey and the Dukes of Norfolk and Suffolk, together with other members of the king's Council. Before this assembly are led in the prisoners, 'the poore younglinges & olde false knaues bounde in ropes all along, one after another in their shertes, & euery one a halter about his neck.' After the cardinal has berated them, the prisoners together cry 'mercy gracious lord, mercy', and the lords also plead for mercy on their behalf, upon which the king pardons them all. When the king finally pronounces his pardon (which presumably he had intended all the time), 'all ye prisoners shouted at once, & altogether cast vp their halters into ye hall roffe, so y^t the kyng might perceaue they were none of the discretest sorte.' The gallows are taken down, with 'many a good praier saied for the kyng', and 'the citezens toke more hede to their seruauntes thereafter.'[52] In recreating this sequence of events with such immediacy, Hall was trying to impress his readers with Henry's virtues as a ruler who could temper justice with mercy, but wittingly or unwittingly, he also constructed a revealing image of one of the key mechanisms of social control used up by the early Tudor monarchs. In so doing, he created an Act worthy of Shakespeare.

In his account of Henry VIII's 'triumphant' reign, Hall rose to considerable heights as an imaginative writer because of his desire to recreate for posterity the experience of the things in Henry's reign that impressed him. Thus, although he betrays an intense partisan bias (Henry, in Hall's eyes, is unquestionably justified, for example, in his attitude to his marriage with Katherine of Aragon, and his suppression of dissent to the royal supremacy), Hall's history is not assertively

[52] Ibid., fos LL12^r–3^r.

tendentious in the way that other propagandistic or polemical writing in these years tended to be. This is because Hall gives the reader, through his evocations, the chance to reach the same conclusions as he has, on his or her own initiative. In short, he is sincere and ingenuous, so that the fictive elements in his work have their own integrity, and are not merely employed for rhetorical enhancement or as a pretext. The problem with Hall's *Union of the Two Noble and Illustre Famelies*, however, is that although it reveals the writer's genuine fictive talent, it also lacks the artist's shaping hand. Hall's imaginative inventiveness occurs only sporadically, and in between the passages of pictorial or dramatic representation lie long stretches of bare factual narrative in the manner of the older annalistic historians. For this reason, 'The Triumphaunt Reigne of Kyng Henry the VIII' ultimately falls far short of, for example, More's *History of King Richard III* as literary art. The dramatic qualities found in Hall's work do, nevertheless, indicate one area where fully realized imaginative invention still occurred during these years, and it is to the drama that we must now turn.

13

Acting in the Play at Hand: The Political Role of Early Tudor Drama

Drama was one of the most important forms of fictive representation throughout the Tudor period. The splendours of Elizabethan and Jacobean drama have tended to obscure the achievement of the earlier tradition, but if it is viewed in its own context, without the erroneous presupposition that it is chiefly important for the ways in which it foreshadowed what was to come, early Tudor drama at its best displays a high level of accomplishment, and is never less than fascinating in its workings.

Dramatic enactments or displays were ubiquitous during the reigns of the first two Tudors. At the simplest level, these comprised pageants, tournaments, and spectacles that were devised as an essential part of early Tudor policy.[1] Edward Hall's account of the early years of Henry VIII's reign astonishes, with its testimony to the sheer frequency of such enactments. From the coronation onwards, every significant occasion was marked by some kind of spectacle. The coronation feast itself was contrived like an episode from a medieval romance, with a strange knight on horseback entering the hall after the second course, to act as the king's champion in issuing a ritual challenge to anyone doubting his rightful inheritance of the crown.[2] Thereafter, Henry's reign seems like one endless sequence of tourneys, disguisings, entertainments, and pageants. Through Hall's eyes we see, for example, the king and his men disguised as Robin Hood and his outlaws bursting into the queen's chamber, as Turks, Russians, and Prussians leading in a mummery, jousting before the Spanish ambassadors, and

---

[1] See Sydney Anglo, *Spectacle, Pageantry, and Early Tudor Policy* (Oxford, 1969); also Gordon Kipling, *The Triumph of Honour: Burgundian Origins of the Elizabethan Renaissance* (The Hague, 1977).

[2] Hall, fos 3^v–4^r.

going a-Maying.[3] When the queen was delivered of a prince in January 1511, a solemn joust was held to mark the occasion in which the king, masquerading as '*Cure loial*', together with the Earl of Devonshire as '*Bon voloire*', Sir Thomas Knyvet as '*Bon espoir*', and Sir Edward Neville as '*Valiaunt desire*', rode against all comers as '*Les quaters Chiualers de la forrest saluigne*'.[4] Henry and his court engaged in these feats not only because they were fun and the king was youthful, exuberant, and pleasure loving, but also because they declared to his subjects the ideal image that the Tudor dynasty had of itself. The true age of chivalry had long passed, but by dressing up for such occasions, Henry and his nobles could appropriate – at least for appearance's sake – the virtues of chivalrous romance.[5]

Those enactments seem to have had a profound effect on people, and were important in reinforcing loyalty to the dynasty. Through them, the king was able to translate his personal beauty, muscular vigour, and taste for sumptuous apparel into political virtues. For example, when he went Maying in 1510, he dressed himself and his knights in white satin to go into the forest, and each man returned with a green bough in his cap. The whole entourage thus presented a symbolic emblem of the Tudor dynasty, the heraldic colours of which were green and white. When the people heard the king had gone Maying, Hall declares, they 'were desirous to se hym shote', which gave Henry a further pretext for displaying his prowess.[6] Such dramatic representations helped Henry to persuade the people that he was the king they had always wanted.

The more elaborate pageants staged on state occasions had a further function: they expressed the official view of the significance of the occasion so as to guide onlookers into the response to it that the administration desired from them. When Charles V visited London in June 1522, for instance, one of the most splendid of all the pageant series was mounted for him as a means of proclaiming the importance of the alliance between England and the Empire to Wolsey's foreign policy at that time. At every important place along the route, pageants had been erected by different groups in the City, according to an overall design.[7] Each of the pageants symbolically depicted how the alliance between the two kings was to be regarded. The first, mounted at the City gate at London Bridge, showed Hercules with a mighty club on one side, and Sampson with the jawbone of an ass on the other, as two giants.[8] Beneath a tablet held by the two giants proclaiming the extent of the Emperor's suzerainty, were the words:

> Carolus Henricus uiuant. Defensor uterque.
> Henricus Fidei. Carolus Ecclesiae.

---

[3] Ibid., fos 6[r], 7[r]–7[v].
[4] Ibid., fo. 9.
[5] See also Arthur B. Ferguson, *The Indian Summer of Chivalry* (Durham, North Carolina, 1960).
[6] Hall, fos 7[v]–8[r].
[7] See Anglo, *Spectacle, Pageantry and Early Tudor Policy*, p. 187.
[8] Hall, fo. 95[v].

[Long live Charles and Henry. Both a defender: Henry of the faith, Charles of the church].[9]

Although simple in construction, the pageant is quite complex in its working. The giant figures representing the two kings invited the onlookers to assume that they had a special preeminence in Europe, which, flattering to the Emperor but possibly wishful thinking on Henry's part, was nevertheless designed to impress the Londoners with their king's importance. The specific choice of Hercules and Sampson was designed to impart a religious sanctification to the political league between the two kings by investing them with the qualities of Christ, whom Hercules and Sampson typologically prefigured. This religious implication is made explicit in the concluding verses, which depict Henry and Charles as equal co-defenders of Christianity. Thus, the burden of the whole pageant is the idea that the might of the Anglo-imperial alliance is on the side of right, and, therefore should be supported ungrudgingly by the nation, regardless of the financial exactions and warfare that it might subsequently entail – both perennially unpopular with Londoners.

Plays, as distinct from these other forms of dramatic entertainment and spectacle, performed an equally important role in politics. Only a fraction of the enormous number of plays written in this period survive intact, but enough do to allow the range of their types and their functions to be inferred.

At the simplest level were satirical farces, presented to score points at the expense of opponents – usually already discredited, and therefore easy game and safe to attack. Such a farce, showing Cardinal Wolsey going down to hell, is recorded as being acted before Claude de la Guiche, the new French ambassador, at the London house of Thomas Boleyn, the Earl of Ormond and Wiltshire, in January 1531.[10] We can presume that this play was designed to incline the French ambassador towards supporting the divorce, given its sponsorship by the father of Henry VIII's prospective new wife.

At a more sophisticated level were plays that sought to attack opponents more obliquely. It is interesting to compare the farce put on by the Boleyns with another play attacking Wolsey presented before he had fallen from power. During Christmas 1526, a play was acted at Gray's Inn showing Lord Governance ruled by Dissipation and Negligence, and Lady Public Weal put from Governance by their misgovernance and evil order. As a result, Rumour Populi, Inward Grudge, and Disdain of Wanton Sovereignty rose up with a multitude and expelled Negligence and Dissipation in order to restore Public Weal. Wolsey, imagining that the play had been devised about him, was so furious that he imprisoned the author and one of the actors in the Fleet, and severely repri-

[9] Quoted by Anglo, *Spectacle, Pageantry, and Early Tudor Policy*, p. 191.
[10] *Cal. SP Spanish*, IV, ii[1882], no. 615, pp. 40–1.

manded the rest.[11] The play, in fact, had been composed twenty years earlier in 1506 or 1507 by John Roo, and so initially was entirely innocent of any satiric reference to Wolsey, being a didactic moral work in the tradition of *Mankind* or *Mundus et infans*. The whole episode demonstrates strikingly, nevertheless, how an apparently innocent play could be invested with political topicality by its context and auspices. Although Hall himself did not believe that the play had been specifically aimed at Wolsey, there is every reason to suspect that it had been. Foxe reports that Simon Fish had acted the part touching Wolsey, and given Fish's connections with Barlowe and Roye on the continent, and the scurrilous anti-Wolsey invectives that the three of them would soon unleash against the cardinal, Fish's participation in the play is unlikely to have been innocent.[12]

The Gray's Inn play also demonstrates why so many specimens of early Tudor political drama are extremely oblique in their topical allusiveness. It was dangerous to meddle in politics, particularly in matters concerning the king, his ministers, or his policies. Yet those were the very subjects that writers most urgently wanted to address as Henry VIII's reign progressed. The potential of dramatic forms for oblique political comment made them extremely useful to writers from about 1515 onwards, once the pressures for reform began to mount in real earnest.

Native English drama had developed into two main types: the moral interlude and the biblical mystery play. Both lent themselves ideally to political expression. In the typical morality play, such as *Mankind* or *Everyman*, personified moral abstractions representing virtues and vices usually competed for control over man's soul as he made his way through the different stages of life. The plots of these plays were equally stereotyped, usually involving either a rise to felicity followed by a fall into misery through misfortune or surrender to vice, or a fall into despair followed by spiritual recovery, or a combination of all these possibilities. They thus furnished an exemplary model that could be used simultaneously to suggest the behaviour desired from a political figure, such as the king, and the dire consequences that might befall him should he fail to adopt it. This function can be seen in the anonymous interlude *Youth* (c.1513) which, in its warning against dissoluteness and pride, is probably directed both at Henry VIII and his ardent supporter, Henry Percy, heir to the fifth Earl of Northumberland.[13]

Moreover, by associating moral abstractions with literal historical figures, the writer (or in the case of the Gray's Inn play, the actors) could imply a moral interpretation of contemporary political events, and thus turn the play either into

[11] Hall, fo. 154^v.
[12] See Foxe, *Acts and Monuments*, IV, p. 657.
[13] See Ian Lancashire (ed.), *Two Tudor Interludes: The Interlude of Youth; Hick Scorner* (Manchester, 1980), pp. 26–9.

a polemical instrument, or else into an expression of a common attitude towards a contemporary situation shared by members of the audience. We can see this in the anonymous *Hyckescorner* (*c*.1514), in which morality figures are used to express a generalized complaint about the unreformed state of contemporary England, while the topical identification of the vice figure, 'Hick (alias 'Dick', alias the Devil) Scorner', with the pretender Richard de la Pole, who had amassed an army to invade England in 1514, warns Englishmen against being tempted to seek reform by supporting him.[14]

Mystery plays, which dramatized episodes from the Bible for the sake of moral instruction, could be used for much the same purposes. By creating a parallel between the scriptural episode and a past or contemporary historical one, the writer could impart an archetypal significance to those events in order to give weight to a particular moral interpretation.

These two native forms of drama served more than merely a polemical or propoganda purpose. Their conventional morality, the generalized nature of their personified abstractions or archetypal characters, and the universality of their stereotyped plots imparted to them a show of objective truth. This meant that they could be used by different social groups with a common viewpoint to serve as a representation of their collective attitude or understanding. Hence, they are closely related to other forms of social ritual in the early Tudor period. Any group could feel that their viewpoint was sanctioned and morally justified, when they saw it identified with the exemplary and archetypal patterns of the morality and mystery plays. The politically orientated play thus became a prime means of activating and expressing such shared awarenessess concerning important contemporary issues. Because of this social function, however, plays based on the morality or mystery models are almost invariably proclamatory and homiletic rather than deliberative or exploratory.[15]

For the political function of any early Tudor play to be fully appreciated, it is essential to establish the date of performance, the auspices, and the topical level of reference with some precision, yet these facts are notoriously difficult to ascertain, and in some cases impossible. In the following pages I shall attempt to analyse the relationship between content and context in the most important extant plays of the period with a political bearing.

John Skelton's *Magnyfycence* used to be thought an anti-Wolsey play, and is usually assumed to have been written in 1515 or 1516.[16] It can be dated with

---

[14] See Lancashire, *Two Tudor Interludes*, pp. 23–4.

[15] For a similar distinction between the two main types of early Tudor play, see Joel B. Altman, *The Tudor Play of Mind: Rhetorical Inquiry and the Development of Elizabethan Drama* (Berkeley, 1978), p. 26.

[16] See, for example, *Magnyfycence*, ed. R. L. Ramsay, Early English Text Society, Extra Series, no. 98 (London, 1908).

much greater certainty, however, to the period between May 1519 and mid 1521, and its auspices can be established as most probably the Merchant Taylor's Hall in the City of London.[17] At one level it is a typical moral interlude, providing an exemplary warning against the destructive effects of excess, and urging that liberty be restrained by temperance. This moral allegory operates throughout, and its presentation is the ostensible pretext of the play.

Skelton obtrudes a second, topical level of reference subtly, but firmly, into the moral one. The central character over whom the Vices and Virtues fight is not any ordinary Everyman, but Magnyfycence, the personification of the Aristotelian virtue associated with rulers in Skelton's time, and particularly sought after by the Tudors. At the topical level, Magnyfycence, in fact, is none other than Henry VIII. He is described as 'a noble prynce of myght', and repeated reference is made to his household which the Vices aspire to join.[18] He is shown as casting off the restraint of wise counsellors in favour of riotous and irresponsible companions who tempt him into a life of intemperate pleasure and profligacy, until their influence is replaced by that of four sad and sober advisors who instruct Magnyfycence on the means of attaining a moral recovery.

The number and groupings of the Vices and Virtues suggest the specific event to which the play alludes: the expulsion of the king's 'minions' in May 1519. Soon after Wolsey's ascent to power, a group of youthful royal favourites in their mid to late teens emerged, led by Sir Nicholas Carew and Sir Francis Bryan.[19] Being elevated to places in the king's Privy Chamber, the 'minions', as they were known, 'wer al Frenche, in eatyng, drynkyng and apparell, yea, and in Frenche vices and bragges.'[20] Hall records the consternation in the Council at the deleterious influence these young favourites were having on the king, and describes the measures that were finally taken against them in May 1519:

> In whiche moneth the kynges counsaill secretly communed together of the kynges gentlenes & liberalitee to all persones: by the whiche thei perceiued that certain young men in his priuie chamber, not regardyng his estate nor degree, were so familier and homely with hym, and plaied suche light touches with hym that thei forgat themselves.

Accordingly, the Council requested the king to redress these 'enormities and lightnes', at which Henry entrusted the whole matter to their care. As a result, the minions were denounced before the Council, expelled from the court, and

---

[17] Paula Neuss in her Revels edition of *Magnyfycence* (Manchester, 1980), correctly identifies the auspices (p. 42), but, still believing the play to be about Wolsey, dates it far too late (p. 34).

[18] *Magnyfycence*, in Skelton, *Complete English Poems*, ed. Scattergood, ll. 166, 509, 613, 640.

[19] See David Starkey, *The Reign of Henry VIII: Personalities and Politics* (London, 1985), pp. 67–81. Others in the group included Henry Norris, Anthony Knyvet, William Coffin, William Cary, and Sir John Peachy.

[20] Hall, fo. 67ᵛ.

replaced by 'foure sad and auncient knightes, put into the kynges priuie chamber' – namely, Sir Richard Wingfield, Sir Richard Weston, Sir Richard Jerningham, and Sir William Kingston.[21]

The rise and fall of the minions clearly provides the topical subject matter in *Magnyfycence*.[22] In number unusually large for a morality play, the Vices match the minions, and reproduce some of their known attributes and circumstances. Fansy is temporarily banished from Magnyfycence's presence by his 'counsell', just as Nicholas Carew was briefly banished to the country in early 1518.[23] Courtly Abusyon is presented as a dandy who has fetched his 'newe fonne jet / From out of Fraunce', just as the minions had after their sojourn in the court of Francis I:

> My heyre bussheth
> So plesauntly;
> My robe russheth
> So ruttyngly;
> Me seme I flye.
>
> . . .
>
> Beyonde measure
> My sleve is wyde;
> Al of pleasure
> My hose strayte tyde;
> My buskyn wyde,
> Ryche to beholde
> Gletterynge in golde.[24]

Part of the value of using personified abstractions lay in the difficulty of pinning them down to a precise identification with any real person. It would be rash, therefore, to try to equate any of the Vices with any particular minion. Nevertheless, one can intermittently detect the shadowy outline of the actual personages involved, and identifications could have been easily reinforced by details of costume and gesture in the performance itself.

Similarly, while the four figures who enter to help Magnyfycence after his fall, Good Hope, Redresse, Sad Cyrcumspeccyon, and Perseveraunce, are exactly those required by the conventional moral scheme Skelton is using, one can also detect in them the shadowy identity of the 'foure sad auncient knightes' that were put into the king's Privy Chamber to replace the minions.

---

[21] Ibid., fos 68^r–68^r.

[22] A fact noted by Ian Lancashire, *Dramatic Texts and Records of Britain: A Chronological Topography to 1558* (Toronto, 1986).

[23] *Magnyfycence*, l. 306. For Carew's temporary exile, see the letter of Richard Pace to Wolsey of March 1518 (*LP*, ii, no. 4034); see also Starkey, *The Reign of Henry VIII*, pp. 74–6.

[24] *Magnyfycence*, ll. 835–90.

It only remains to determine the auspices before the functions of the play can be ascertained. A string of references to merchants and mercantile matters in *Magnyfycence* makes it practically certain that the play was performed in the hall of the Merchant Taylors' Company, off Threadneedle Street in the City of London. These references make best sense if they are seen as in-jokes designed to appeal to an audience of London guildsmen. In tempting Magnyfycence to repudiate Measure, for example, Fansy declares:

> Measure is mete for a marchauntes hall
> But largesse becometh a state ryall.[25]

At the climax of the play, when Felycyte makes a final bid to persuade Magnyfycence to restrain Lyberte with Measure, Magnyfycence exclaims:

> What! Wyll ye waste wynde and prate thus in vayne?
> Ye have eten sauce I trowe, at the Taylers Hall.[26]

By showing the Vices and Magnyfycence rejecting the virtues that the merchants stand for, Skelton is not only sharing a joke with them, but also objectifying the grounds of their concern. More than that, in having Magnyfycence accuse Measure of having 'eten sauce' at the Merchant Taylor's Hall, he is inviting his audience of guildsmen to identify the present performance as just the kind of sauciness to which Magnyfycence refers – and thus to revel in their own daring and impudence.

The function of the play now becomes clear. It was written to represent to the London citizens their common concern with, and understanding of, recent events. The City had been understandably worried by the king's extravagance because, as the forced loans of 1522 and 1523 would soon prove, in the event of war (always on the cards given Henry's proclivity for chivalrous war-games), the London citizens had largely to foot the bill. By showing the king reduced to poverty and despair through the profligacy into which the minions had tempted him, Skelton, on the City's behalf, was expressing their anxiety as to what might happen should he not rein in the largesse with which he had been pursuing pleasure and magnificence. To complement this, in showing Magnyfycence's willingness to undergo reformation under the guidance of wise counsellors, Skelton was sending Henry the citizens' message. The play thus focuses public opinion into a common attitude, and it does this in order to strengthen the will and potency of a political pressure group. There is no evidence that the king attended a performance of *Magnyfycence* – whenever a character addresses the members of the audience, he refers to them as 'syrs', which implies the absence of the higher nobility – but he would have heard of it, and the City of London had

[25] Ibid., ll. 382–3.
[26] Ibid., ll. 1403–4.

every right to expect that he should listen to what it had to say. Indeed, he seems to have made some show of doing so.

The other striking example of a declaratory play that uses a traditional dramatic form for political purposes is the anonymous *Godly Queene Hester*, written twenty or so years after *Magnyfycence*. Instead of the morality form, the author took the biblical mystery play as his model (although moral personifications briefly appear in one episode).

As with *Magnyfycence*, the false assumption that *Godly Queene Hester* is about Wolsey has hitherto obscured its true function and effectiveness. It used to be thought that the biblical account of Esther's intercession with King Ahasuerus to save the Jews referred topically in the play to Katherine of Aragon's efforts to foil Wolsey's attempt to undermine her position in the period between 1527 and 1529.[27] In this reading, the ending of the play, with the execution of Aman (alias Wolsey) and the ascendancy of Hester's virtuous counsel is 'prophetically hopeful', like the ending of *Magnyfycence*.[28] Changes to the biblical source and precise topical allusions, however, prove conclusively that the play refers to the triumph of the conservative faction over Thomas Cromwell in 1540, which is attributed to the influence of Catherine Howard over the king.[29]

The author's handling of the source shows him adjusting it to enhance the parallel between the biblical story and the events of 1540. In the Book of Esther, Mordecai brings up Esther, who is 'his uncle's daughter', whereas in the play, Mardocheus declares that Hester is 'my brothers daughter.'[30] This change was made so that the audience would recognize in Mardocheus the Duke of Norfolk, Catherine Howard's uncle, who pushed for her marriage to Henry VIII after the Cleves fiasco. Another significant change concerns the depiction of Aman. In the scriptural account Haman is promoted after Esther has been made queen, but in the play Assuerus makes Aman his 'chaunceloure' before he decides to look for a new queen, and before Hester is chosen.[31] Were Katherine of Aragon to be represented by Hester and Wolsey by Aman, there would have been no reason to make this change, as the topical allegory would have been better suggested by the original biblical version. The inversion of chronology does, however, fit an identification between Aman and Cromwell, and allows for Hester to be pre-

---

[27] See, for example, *A New Enterlude of Godly Queene Hester*, ed. W. W. Greg, in *Materialien zur Kunde des älteren Englischen Dramas*, ed. W. Bang, vol. 5 (Louvain, 1904), p. x. All references to the play are to this edition.

[28] David Bevington, *Tudor Drama and Politics: A Critical Approach to Topical Meaning* (Cambridge, Massachussets, 1968), p. 94.

[29] This suggestion was first made by Kathy Pearl. See Lancashire, *Dramatic Texts and Records of Britain*, p. 22.

[30] Esther 2:7; *Godly Queene Hester*, (in Bang) l. 149.

[31] Esther 3:1; *Godly Queene Hester*, (in Bang) ll. 106–10.

sented as locked in rivalry with Aman for influence over the king from the very beginning. Cromwell had been promoted from the king's Council to become chancellor of the exchequer in April 1533, and within a year he had become the king's principal secretary. By January 1535 he had been named the king's vicar-general in religious matters; In 1536 he became lord privy seal; and in 1540 he assumed the office of lord great chamberlain. His extraordinary advancement, therefore, fits the presentation of Aman in the play far better than the career of Wolsey. Moreover, the disaffected members of the Pilgrimage of Grace had already made the topical identification between Cromwell and Aman as an enemy of true religion, as witnessed by the seditious ballad written by an anonymous author soon after Cromwell's fall. This ballad relates so closely to *Godly Queene Hester* that the relevant lines deserve to be quoted at length. Having complained of the 'turkes' in England who have been 'spoilyng crist churche', the author launches into an attack on 'nowghty Cromwell', developing an analogy between him and Haman:

XIII.

Alter Aman he is, as ys mayde mention
   in the booke of Hester – yt doth ther appere –
whome Assuere exaltyd to hye promotion,
   makyng hym cheff ruler of all ys empire
     Thys Aman, in mynd repleit with vaynglore,
     of euery man dyd coveit honored to be.

XIV.

Thys for to do, non durst yt rekewsse,
   better ne worsse, thorowe all the cowntre,
Saue only Mardoche, who dyd refusse
   hym for to honore in any degre.
     this knawne to Aman, repleit with furie,
     in myde dyde imagyne howe Mardoch shulde dye;

XV.

And with that noit content, hys mallys put in vre:
   agaynes the trew Iewes of hys propagation
Sent wrytyng a heide brode with his besy cure,
   all his pepull to be browght to gret desolacyon;
     but yet noit-with-standyng, gode dyd so provyde:
     he myst of hys purposse: gode was ther gyde.

XVI.

The chaunche fortonyde so, (this ys no fable,)
   the gallous apone, prepared for Mardoche,
hanged he was, as a theiff notable, –
   Assuere commandyng that so it shuld be, –

> And hys rommys ryall, no fardell delay,
> were gyven onto Mardoche in that same day.[32]

The similarity of the allegorical parallels developed in this ballad with the biblical narrative and Cromwell's contest with Norfolk is so close that either the anonymous poet was also the author of *Godly Queene Hester*, or else the biblical allegory had become so widespread among the disaffected conservative Catholic faction that it could be used by anyone who cared to exploit it.

Further specific topical allusions put the identification of Hester with Catherine Howard and Aman with Cromwell beyond question. The arguments that Aman presents to Assuerus for the suppression of the Jews go far beyond anything that Wolsey ever contemplated or would have countenanced, as such measures would inevitably have destroyed the basis of his own power. Aman denounces the Jews (alias the Catholic clergy) because they seek to subvert Assuerus' subjects by drawing them 'vnto theyr ceremonyes and faction', on the grounds that they refuse to be bound by the king's laws, and because their possessions are so great that they are capable of subduing the king by force. One can detect in Aman's arguments the anti-papist doctrinal bias that Cromwell's enemies attributed to him, something which Wolsey never shared, and also the arguments put by Cromwell and his team to justify the Royal Supremacy after Wolsey had fallen..

Similarly, the depiction of the dissolution of the monasteries is clearly more appropriate to the major dissolution of 1535–6, than to Wolsey's relatively minor dissolutions of the 1520s. Aman promised the king that, if he suppressed the Jews, he would win 'to your treasure .x. thousande pound of golde', and in response the king deputizes him to 'quenche' them, in token of which he gives him 'a ringe and seale'.[33] The bestowal of a ring and seal to Aman clearly refers to Cromwell's appointment as vice-gerent in spirituals in late 1534. Predictably, the effects of the dissolution of the monasteries, referred to several times in the play,[34] are far more severe than anything Wolsey accomplished in the 1520s. One of the vices, in fact, alludes to the earlier despoliations as paling into insignificance compared to the new measures enforced by Aman.

> AMBITION
> . . . I Ambytion, had a commission,
> By force of a bull,
> To gett what I could but not as I wolde,
> Neyther of lambe nor woll.
>   The bull nor the calfe, coulde please the one halfe,
> Of my feruente desire.

---

[32] See Furnivall, *Ballads from Manuscripts*, pp. 307–8. I have modernized the capitalization of proper names in this passage for the ease of the reader.

[33] *Godly Queene Hester*, (in Bang) ll. 728–71.

[34] See, for example, ibid., ll. 465–80.

> But euer I thought by god, there was I woulde haue had
> when I was neuer the nere.
>   Therfore all my ambition, to gether in a comission,
> Vnder my seale,
> I geue it to Aman, to the intent that Sathan,
> Maye loue hym well.[35]

As the satirical writings directed against Wolsey by Skelton and Barlowe illustrate, it had become customary to refer to him alternatively as '*vitulus bubali*', or a 'bull', or a 'bull's calf'. In this passage, Ambition attributes the vice he represents both to Wolsey (the 'bull') and to Aman (Cromwell), with the difference that he transfers all his power to Aman, so that the latter can accomplish fully what was only partially achieved by his predecessor.

The topical identification of Hester with Catherine Howard is equally definite. Like Assuereus, Henry VIII in 1540 was 'comfortles, for lacke of a Queene', having found Anne of Cleves unacceptable.[36] In July 1540 the Duke of Norfolk and the Council supplicated Henry 'to frame his most noble heart to love, in order to secure some more store of fruit and succession', to the comfort of the realm.[37] This plea is echoed in the play in Assuereus' agreement to marry according to his advisors' 'counsells', 'leaste defaulte of issue shoulde be, whiche God defende'.[38] Accordingly, he despatches officers to 'peruse this realme' to find the virgin who is fittest to be queen. Again, the identification fits Catherine Howard, who was English (of the 'realme'), rather than Katherine of Aragon, who was a foreigner.

Later in the play, having swayed Assuerus to grant a reprieve to the Jews, Hester causes Aman to be brought to execution by exposing his ambition and treachery in terms that closely parallel the charges levelled at Cromwell in his Attainder. The grounds upon which Cromwell was condemned included, among others, that 'being a person of as poor and low degree as few be' within the realm, he said publicly 'that he was sure of' the king; that he was also a destestable heretic who dispersed books to the discredit of the blessed sacrament of the altar and other articles of religion; that he had abused his office as the king's vice-gerent to foster heresy; and that by bribery and extortion he had obtained innumerable sums of money, and, being so enriched, had held the nobles of the realm in great disdain.[39] All these charges find echoes in the play, especially in Hester's disclosure of Aman's 'falsed, fauell and fraude'.[40]

The final parallel between Catherine Howard and Hester is seen when, after

---

[35] Ibid., ll. 546–57.
[36] Ibid., l. 117.
[37] See J.J. Scarisbrick, *Henry VIII* (London, 1968), p. 429.
[38] *Godly Queene Hester*, (in Bang) ll. 121–2.
[39] *LP*, XV, no. 498 (60).
[40] See *Godly Queene Hester*, (in Bang) ll. 867, 924–42.

Aman's fall, Hester is rewarded with 'the house of Aman with all his treasure', just as Catherine was given Cromwell's lands after his execution in July 1540.[41] And to top off her good deeds in the eyes of the Catholic Howard faction, Hester persuades Assuerus to instigate a purge of all those who have offended against the laws of the Jews, and to restore the 'holy ceremonies' of their religion to the realm.[42] This addition to the biblical source refers to the renewed persecution of heretics after Cromwell's fall, which commenced with the burning of Robert Barnes, William Jerome, and Thomas Garret at Smithfield on 30 July 1540, two days after Cromwell's execution.[43] In my view, there can be no doubt whatsoever that *Godly Queene Hester* was written between August 1540 and Catherine Howard's own fall in October 1541, to celebrate the triumph of the conservative faction that had accomplished Cromwell's ruin.

As in the case of *Magnyfycence*, the play's function can only be properly grasped when its topical allegory and auspices are understood. Several stage directions survive in the text that furnish clues as to how and where it was performed. At one point a Purseuaunt enters 'with manye maydens', who later depart with the queen and Aman.[44] This suggests that the play was closely associated with the queen's side of the royal household, from which the retinue of maidens was likely to have been drawn. Another important stage direction occurs when Hester is fortifying herself to denounce Aman to Assuerus. Turning to Mardocheus, she orders him: 'Call in the chapell to the intent they maye / Syng some holy himpne to spede vs this day', and the stage direction reads: 'than the chappell do singe.'[45] The presence of the chapel choir could imply that *Godly Queene Hester* was actually performed in a chapel, but this is unlikely, as Henry VIII did not own any palace in which the queen's side had its own chapel, and it is hard to imagine that the Howard faction would risk showing the play at a venue where the king might be present, since it depicts him as a gullible and pliable weakling. More probably, the play was performed in the queen's own chambers, with the choir called in for the occasion, or else in the great hall of one of the royal palaces while the king was away. We may suppose, therefore, that the play was presented before the assembled members of the Howard faction at court, including such figures as the Duke of Norfolk himself, Catherine's brother Charles, who was a member of the Privy Chamber, her uncle Lord William Howard, the Dowager Duchess of Norfolk, her cousin, Henry Howard, the Earl of Surrey, and Stephen Gardiner, Bishop of Winchester – that is, those people who had been responsible for Cromwell's fall.

In this light, the purpose of the play becomes clear. It was to serve primarily as

---

[41] Ibid., ll. 1062–3; Scarisbrick, *Henry VIII*, p. 430.
[42] *Godly Queene Hester*, (in Bang) ll. 1077–102.
[43] See Scarisbrick, *Henry VIII*, pp. 379–82.
[44] *Godly Queene Hester*, (in Bang) stage directions at ll. 188, 335.
[45] Ibid. ll. 860–1.

a celebration of the faction's triumph. After years of antagonism with Cromwell,[46] Norfolk and Gardiner had dangled Catherine as bait before the king following his disillusionment with Anne of Cleves, and the ploy had worked. The choice of the biblical parallel between Catherine and Esther was designed to impart righteousness to the deed, and provide moral fortification for the faction. Finally, given the scriptural fable and the presence of the chapel choir singing a solemn hymn, it was also an act of devotion, marking the commitment of the conservative faction to continue resisting anti-Catholic measures and to maintain the old religion. Even more than in the case of *Magnyfycence, Godly Queene Hester* was an instrument for focusing the understanding and aspirations of an entire community, united in a common political and spiritual cause.

While conservative authors like Skelton and the writer of *Godly Queene Hester* continued to apply the old morality and mystery forms to political uses, a radically different type of drama was being developed by members of the circle connected to Sir Thomas More.[47] Rather than being merely homiletic, these plays sought to dramatize a question in the form of a debate, conducted according to the dialectical habits of mind acquired from training in humanist rhetoric.[48]

The first example of this new type, Henry Medwall's *Fulgens and Lucres*, showed that the new form could be put to political use just as readily as the older mystery and morality forms. Arguing whether a woman should have the right to self-determination in marriage, the play was performed in the house of John Morton, Archbishop of Canterbury and lord chancellor, before the Flemish ambassadors at Candlemass, 1497. At this time negotiations were under way for the Spanish marriage between Prince Arthur and Katherine of Aragon. Lucrece's agreement to marry Gaius Flamineus for his natural nobility, rather than Publius Cornelius for his hereditary nobility, was clearly aimed at encouraging the Spanish to accept a Tudor husband for Katherine, in spite of the dubious lineage of the king and the existence of rival pretenders to the throne.

The political potential of the new humanist-inspired drama, however, was only fully developed by those who came under the influence of the genius of Thomas More. More himself had been a page in Morton's household, had taken part in some of the dramatic performances that had been mounted there, and would have observed the use to which Morton put such plays as *Fulgens and Lucres*. It is not surprising, therefore, to find that in announcing the mode of political

---

[46] See Norfolk's letter to the Council of December 1546, in which he describes the continual attempts of his enemies, including Cromwell, to procure his destruction (*LP*, XXI, ii, no. 554).

[47] See A. W. Reed, *Early Tudor Drama: Medwall, the Rastells, Heywood, and the More Circle* (London, 1926); also Pearl Hogrefe, *The Sir Thomas More Circle: A Programme of Ideas and their Impact on Secular Drama* (Urbana, Illinois, 1959).

[48] See Altman, *The Tudor Play of Mind*, pp. 7–8.

action he himself would adopt for the next decade and a half, More should have drawn upon stage-play metaphors.

The passage in Book 1 of *Utopia* where 'More' instructs Hythlodaeus on his 'civil philosophy' enunciates, in fact, the ethos underlying the whole dramatic enterprise of his kinsmen, John Rastell and John Heywood. Rejecting Hythlodaeus' academic philosophy, 'More' adds:

> There is another philosophy, more practical for statesmen, which knows its stage, adapts itself to the play in hand, and performs its role neatly and appropriately.

'More' postulates that, just as it would be absurd for a philosopher who entered the stage while a comedy of Plautus is being performed to begin reciting a tragic speech from Seneca's *Octavia*, so one must not force upon people new and strange ideas that will carry no weight with those of opposite conviction. Instead, 'by the indirect approach' ('obliquo ductu conandum est'), one must seek and strive to the best of one's power 'to handle matters tactfully', with the aim of making as little bad as possible that which cannot be made perfectly good.[49]

Not surprisingly, dramatic representation, whether in the form of prose dialogues or of stage plays, constituted one of the chief strategies of the indirect approach used by members of the More circle. The debate form of the dramatized dialogue was designed to avoid arousing antagonism by an appearance of objectivity, while the comic element built into these plays was calculated to generate good humour and charity so as 'to laugh men out of folly' – as Erasmus would have put it.

John Rastell, More's brother in law, was the first to attempt to put the Morean prescription into practice, in *Gentylnes and Nobylyte*, written about 1519–1520. Some scholars have ascribed this play to John Heywood, but its consistent argument from 'natural reason', its lack of Heywood's characteristic verbal irony, the static nature of its action, and the comparative rhythmic monotony of the verse bear the unmistakable stamp of Rastell's authorship.[50] Rastell was in the habit of expropriating humanistic ideas with embarrassing zeal, as his ill-conceived Utopian-style expedition to the New World in 1517 illustrates.[51] *Gentylnes and Nobylyte* shows him trying to promote humanist political ideals according to the Morean prescription with equal alacrity and clumsiness. Although he uses the form of the dramatized dialogue, in which a Knyght,

---

[49] *Utopia, CW Thos. More*, 4, pp. 99–101.

[50] Rastell would again argue from 'natural reason and philosophie' ten years later, in attempting to prove the existence of purgatory in his *A New Boke of Purgatory, whiche is a Dyaloge betwene Comyngo & Gyngemyn* (London, 1530). For the case for Heywood's authorship of *Gentylnes and Nobylyte*, see K. W. Cameron, *Authorship and Sources of 'Gentylnes and Nobylyte'* (Raleigh, North Carolina, 1941); for Rastell's authorship, see Reed, *Early Tudor Drama*, pp. 104–17, with whose judgement I concur.

[51] See Reed, *Early Tudor Drama*, pp. 11–12.

Marchaunt, and Plowman dispute whether true nobility springs from lineage, wealth, or virtue, Rastell manages to turn the dialogue into near monologue. The Plowman is allowed to win the debate through the crude expedient of having the Knyght and Marchaunt simply give up the argument on the grounds of Cato's dictum, 'Contra verbosos noli contendere verbis' ('Contend nor argu never in no matter / With hym that is full of wordys and clatter'), which rather defeats the whole point.[52] In spite of the objections that he allows the Knyght and Marchaunt to make once the Plowman has gone, Rastell's authorial complicity with the Plowman is plain, and to make sure that the reader does not miss it, he introduces a Phylosopher who delivers an epilogue unequivocally approving the Plowman's arguments. The Phylosopher's references to 'soferayns' ('citizens') who are present in the audience suggest that Gentylnes and Nobylyte was not a court play, but one performed in the City.[53] Thus the play may be seen as the work of someone concerned to publish his own opinions and show his commitment to humanism, rather than as an instrument designed to serve a specific political end.

Rastell admits as much in his epilogue. Having proposed the Utopian measure of rotating administrative positions – about as likely in the England of the 1520s as Henry abdicating – Rastell concludes:

> ... untyll that such orders be devysd
> Substauncyally, and put in execucyon,
> Loke never to see the world amended
> Nor of the gret myschefes the reformacion.
> But they that be bounde to see the thynges done,
> I pray God of his grace put in theyr myndys
> To reforme shortly such thynges amys.[54]

Gentylnes and Nobylyte, then, displays the wishful thinking of an enthusiast who is safely remote from the actuality of political affairs. Thomas More must have been relieved that his brother-in-law was not sufficiently close to the centre of things to cause any real harm or embarrassment through his idiosyncratic promotion of ideas that he, More, may have once entertained at a speculative level. Rastell was the kind of disciple he did not need.

There was one dramatist, however, who did fully understand the tenor of what More had written in Book 1 of Utopia about the indirect approach, and who, in seeking to follow More's advice, invented a brilliant new form of drama. This was John Heywood.

---

[52] Gentylnes and Nobylyte, in Three Rastell Plays: Four Elements, Calisto and Melebea, Gentleness and Nobility, ed. Richard Axton (Cambridge, 1979), p. 120. All references are to this edition.
[53] Ibid., ll. 1163–9.
[54] Ibid.

Unlike Rastell, his father-in-law, Heywood was close to the centre of things, enjoying a position as groom in the royal household between 1519 and 1528. Payments to Heywood recorded in Henry VIII's accounts describe him variously as a 'synger' and a 'player of the virginals'.[55] We can therefore suppose that he was closely associated with court entertainments during this period. The differing circumstances of Rastell and Heywood help to explain the salient difference in their respective dramatic methods. Rastell, through the Plowman, admits that he does not expect his play to have any real effect:

> . . . exortacyons, techyng, and prechyng,
> Gestyng, and raylyng, they mend no thyng.
> For the amendement of the world is not in me.
> Nor all the grete argumentes that we thre
> Have made syth we resonyd here togedyr
> Do not prevayle the weyght of a fether
> For the helpyng of any thyng that is amys.[56]

Consequently, both the Plowman and the Phylosopher, and Rastell along with them, see no other remedy than to wait

> . . . tyll God wyll send
> A tyme tyll our governours may intend
> Of all enormytees the reformacyon.[57]

In the meantime, a play like *Gentylnes and Nobylyte* was merely an exercise in academic speculation.

Heywood, on the other hand, *was* in a position to influence the 'governours', and sought consciously to do so. Rather than simply articulating a rationalistic viewpoint, Heywood devised his plays to induce the required response. Whereas Rastell used the dialogue in a monological way, Heywood used the dynamic processes of dialogue as a metaphor for a whole world view into which he hoped to lead his audience. As a result, Heywood's plays are far less static than Rastell's and generate a far more interactive relationship between players and onlookers.

The new method can be seen in Heywood's *The Foure PP.* (1520–22) and *The Play of the Wether* (1529–30), both written during times of crisis to illustrate the way that religious reformation and reform in general might be pursued. In 1520 and 1521 Luther's ideas had begun to filter into England, exacerbating the fervid anticlericalism that had afflicted England for many years. In particular, Luther's attacks on the sale of indulgences, pilgrimages, and the veneration of saints and

---

[55] See Reed, *Early Tudor Drama*, pp. 37–42.
[56] *Gentylnes and Nobylyte*, ll. 1002–8.
[57] Ibid., ll. 996–8; cf. ll. 1167–9.

relics opened the way for reform, which everyone agreed was necessary, to be hijacked by heterodoxy.

The members of the More circle seem to have been acutely aware of this danger. More himself discussed Luther with Erasmus in a letter (now lost) of 1521,[58] and in 1522 undertook to refute Luther's attack on the king with his *Responsio ad Lutherum*. Heywood's *The Foure PP.* seems to have been an attempt to address the same problem at the court itself, with the intent of defusing the potency of the Lutheran attack on ecclesiastical abuses.

Heywood's method is simple, yet at the same time subtle: he aims to remove the sting of the Lutheran attack through comic deflation. His main device is to introduce two characters who represent the religious practices the Lutherans and others were condemning. A Palmer who has just returned from the Holy Land represents the practice of seeking saints and going on pilgrimages to earn merit for salvation, while a Pardoner represents the sale of indulgences and the practice of making offerings to relics. Heywood then deprives these two characters of any sinister ambience by introducing two comic counterparts: the Potycary, whose bogus medicines mirror the Pardoner's fake relics, and the Pedler, whose trifling wares parody the objects of reverence of which the Palmer goes in search.

The contention that arises between these four characters similarly reflects the contemporary situation. The Palmer and the Pardoner deride the worth of each other's practices, highlighting not only current scepticism towards such matters, but also the divisiveness that was tearing the fabric of contemporary society. Once again, Heywood deflates the potential seriousness of this conflict by showing its causes in the form of two comic episodes: the first in the display by the Pardoner and the Potycary of their manifestly false wares, and the second in the contest to see which of the characters can tell the biggest lie. These episodes allow Heywood to present a comic symbolic representation of the worst abuses of religious practices that were causing grievance. The Pardoner, for example, opens his pack to reveal such 'relics' as 'the great-toe of the Trinite', 'a buttocke-bone of Pentecoste', 'a box full of humble-bees / That stonge Eue as she sat on her knees / Tastynge the frute to her forbydden', and the glass which Adam and Eve drank from at their wedding, inviting his audience to believe in their supernatural powers.[59] The real-life audience is thus presented with a comic exposure of the frauds that an unscrupulous Pardoner could perpetrate.

In the lying contest, when each of the rivals must try to tell a tale containing the greatest lie, to decide who has precedence, the Pardoner describes how he used his influence with Lucifer to gain the delivery of a shrewish woman from hell. The action of the tale depicts the effect claimed for indulgences by the church, but

---

[58] See Erasmus, *Opus epistolarum*, ed Allen, no. 1218, p. 541/46.

[59] *The Foure PP.*, in *Chief Pre-Shakespearean Dramas*, ed. Joseph Quincy Adams (Cambridge, Massachusetts, 1924), ll. 509–21, 546–8, 556–7. All references to *The Foure PP.* and *The Play of the Wether* are to this edition.

again the comic presentation removes any possibility that dealing with such a topic might aggravate the situation. When the Pardoner reaches hell, for instance, he takes proprietorial pleasure in how well decked-out the devils are:

> Thys deuyll and I walket arme in arme,
> So farre tyll he had brought me thyther
> Where all the deuylls of hell togyther
> Stode in a-ray in suche apparell
> As for that day there metely fell:
> Theyr hornes well gylt, theyr clowes full clene,
> Theyr taylles well kempt, and, as I wene,
> With sothery butter theyr bodyes anoynted, –
> I neuer sawe deuyls so well appoynted.[60]

The ironic implication – that the Pardoner is more familiar with hellish matters than he ought to be – makes him just as much a victim of, as a victor in, his own tale.

Heywood's decision to present a comic image of a situation which, in reality, was very ominous and threatening, was very astute, because of its likely psychological effect on his audience. By admitting the existence of the abuse, he could expect to gain at least the provisional forebearance of those whose own experience told them the same, and who would not, therefore, feel that they were being treated like fools. Then, having gained their attention, he could expect that the depiction of ecclesiastical abuse in such extreme terms would move them to recover a more balanced and moderate viewpoint, from which they would be able to distinguish the abuse of the practices from their possible good use. The real goal of the play, in fact, is to induce a deeper understanding of the mixed nature of the human condition. Heywood wants to persuade his audience of the need to allow legitimate diversity, and thus promote a tolerance that can pacify social divisiveness.

He achieves this by showing the characters themselves moving towards such an understanding. Under the influence of the comic spirit, the rivals give over their contention and become reconciled to each other in good will. Even though the Palmer wins the lying contest, with his claim that 'I neuer sawe, nor knewe, in my consyens, / Any one woman out of paciens',[61] he releases the others from their obligation to wait upon him, and they in turn agree to reform themselves. The Pedler, who had adjudicated the contest, sums up the lesson they have learnt. He points out to the Palmer and the Pardoner that, 'thoughe ye walke nat bothe one waye', nevertheless, 'bothe your walkes come to one ende', as does the path of anyone who seeks with the aid of God's grace to follow virtue. There is room for

---

[60] Ibid., ll. 872–80.
[61] Ibid., ll. 1003–4.

a great variety of diverse practices. Some people prefer to live an ascetic life, some an active life in the world, some to maintain priests to pray for departed souls:

> These, with all other vertues well marked,
> All-though they be of sondry kyndes,
> Yet be they nat vsed with sondry myndes.

Indeed, God moves men to different forms of virtuous practice through the influence of his Holy Spirit, so that it is foolish for anyone to maintain their own practice narrowly to the exclusion of other peoples'.[62] By showing the four characters reconciled in harmonious amity, the play thus dramatizes the positive effect of its own processes.

Heywood, furthermore, deliberately attempts to involve the members of the audience in those same processes. He primes them to feel shame by making the Pedler observe to the Potycary that he is 'well beloued of all thys sorte' – that is, the audience – 'By your raylynge here openly / At pardons and relyques so leudly.'[63] In this way, he implicates the audience in the narrow, bigoted attitude that the play has rejected. However, he immediately allays any offence, by declaring that the scepticism they may have been harbouring might have a beneficial purpose in God's providential scheme:

> But where ye dout the truthe, nat knowynge,
> Beleuynge the beste, good may be growynge.[64]

Heywood is here allowing for good to arise from wise doubting, just as King Utopus had done in More's *Utopia*. He quickly adds, nevertheless, that it remains safest to accept the judgement of the church in all doubtful matters.[65]

Readers familiar with the works of Thomas More will recognize in these doctrines the distinctive world view that More tried to assert in all his works from *Utopia* onwards. Like More, Heywood assumes that there is a teleological purposefulness underlying the diversity of things. Just as More believed that God reveals truth progressively and historically, using the Holy Spirit to lead men into truth through the exercise of their faculties,[66] so too did Heywood believe that doubt and disputation could be a means for attaining a good conclusion. His plays were designed to imitate and reproduce that providential process, with the moving effect of the comic spirit serving as a correlative for the action of the Holy Spirit. In the nature and workings of *The Foure PP.*, therefore, Heywood achieved everything that More would later seek to achieve in the abortive fiction

---

[62] Ibid., ll. 1154–86.
[63] Ibid., ll. 1200–2.
[64] Ibid., ll. 1209–10.
[65] Ibid., ll. 1213–15.
[66] See, for example, *A Dialogue Concerning Heresies, CW Thos. More*, 6, pp. 146/17–24.

of *A Dialogue Concerning Heresies*. Tragically for More, by 1529 the situation had deteriorated so badly that it was too late for this vision to carry much conviction.

The worsening of the reformation crisis had its destructive effect on Heywood, too. He attempted to use drama a second time to address an urgent political situation in *The Play of the Wether*, but it shows a marked falling-off from the achievement of *The Foure PP.* that can be ascribed to the change in circumstances in England between 1520 and 1529. Heywood no longer dared to address political issues as directly as he had in *The Foure PP.*, and was forced to invent a symbolic allegory that is too remote from the matter to which it refers to be really effective.

The play opens with Jupiter seated on his throne, reporting how

> Before our presens, in our hye parlyament,
> Both goddes and goddeses of all degrees
> Hath late assembled, by comen assent,
> For the redres of certayne enormytees,
> Bred amonge them thorow extremytees
> Abusyd in eche to other of them all.[67]

The gods, he continues, have fallen into defaming each other out of malice, with deleterious effects on the weather of the sublunar world. Now that the parliament has finished, Jupiter has descended to Earth,

> . . . onely to satysfye and content
> All maner people whyche have ben offendyd
> By any wether mete to be amendyd.[68]

Accordingly, he appoints a jester, Merry-reporte, to preside over the presentation of grievances, which done, Merry-report receives the petitions of the suitors in what constitutes the bulk of the play.

In these basic elements of the fable, one can detect a thinly disguised allusion to the first session of the Reformation Parliament, which assembled between November 3 and December 17 in 1529. This parliament was marked by extra-ordinary acrimony, as a flood of pent-up grievances was released following Wolsey's fall. Heywood devised his allegory to be performed at court in the hope that it would help calm things down, promoting sanity and moderation, as he had tried to do with *The Foure PP.*.

Compared with *The Foure PP.*, *The Play of the Wether* is very simple in its working. The fable serves simply to show the blind selfishness of each suitor's request, and how their desires are mutually incompatible. The gentleman wants

---

[67] *The Play of the Wether*, (in Adams) ll. 22–7.
[68] Ibid., ll. 86–9.

fine weather so that he can hunt; the merchant wants temperate weather so that he can travel safely; the forest ranger wants strong winds to blow down trees for timber he can sell; the windmiller wants more wind and no rain, while the watermiller wants rain and no wind, and so on. In conclusion, Jupiter decrees that they shall all get what they desire, but often, not always. It would be disastrous, he declares, if any of the interested orders got everything it desired, because this would destroy the foundation of men's collective existence:

> Myche better have we now devysed for ye all
> Then ye all can perceyve, or coude desyre.
> Eche of you sewd to have contynuall
> Suche wether as his crafte onely doth requyre.
> All wethers in all places yf men all tymes myght hyer,
> Who could lyve by other?[69]

Having realized that all crafts are interdependent, everyone applauds Jupiter's wise judgement.

The function Heywood intends for the play is the same as that of *The Foure PP.* – to laugh men out of folly, and persuade them of the need for tolerance, charity, and commitment to the common good. But compared with the earlier play, *The Play of the Wether* is a tame affair, because it is so generalized and lacking in the humour that enlivened its predecessor.

Heywood does, nevertheless, make striking use of the affective potential of dramatic form in several ways. Just before Jupiter pronounces judgement, Merry-reporte invites members of the real audience to add their requests to those of the suitors:

> Oyes! yf that any knave here
> Be wyllynge to appere,
> For wether fowle or clere,
> Come in before thys flocke;
> And be he hole or syckly,
> Come shew hys mynde quyckly;
> And yf hys tale be not lyckly
> Ye shall lycke my tayle in the nocke.[70]

Given that the fictional suitors have already demonstrated the folly of pursuing partisan interests, Heywood's device serves to trap the audience into a recognition that, if they are reluctant to imitate the selfish suitors, then they have no right to pursue their equally partisan, sectional interests in the Reformation Parliament. In this way he hoped that the dramatic representation might stimulate them into an awareness of their own perversity.

[69] Ibid., ll. 1183–8.
[70] Ibid., ll. 1057–64.

Heywood also used his actors to provide a metaphorical statement about how the members of the audience had been acting in real life. The final suitor to appear is a boy, who wants more frost and snow so that he can make plenty of snowballs and pitfalls. Marking his entrance is a significant stage direction: 'The Boy comyth in, the lest that can play.'[71] Heywood requires the smallest boy in the company to play this role, which implies that all the rest of the actors are boys also. This, combined with the topical references to the Reformation Parliament in the play, give us a clue as to the company and the auspices. Records show that the children of the Chapel Royal played at court during this period,[72] and Heywood, although no longer a permanent member of the household, must have been commissioned to write The Play of the Wether for them to perform before the king and his nobles.[73] The play thus presents its intended audience with a very ironic image of themselves. Jupiter sitting on his throne mirrors Henry VIII sitting in the hall watching the performance, and offers him instruction-by-praise, in depicting him as a wise arbitrator. The squabbling suitors represent the disaffected nobles and commons who are pursuing their own self-interest at the expense of the commonweal. The fact that these displaced images of the real-life spectators are acted by boys cunningly offers a symbolic visual suggestion of the immaturity they are manifesting. Heywood thus underscores the point he wishes to make in his handling of the dramatic form, as well as more explicitly in its argument.

The falling-off of dramatic vitality evident in The Play of the Wether foreshadowed worse. Drama, like every other form of fictive representation, suffered a general decline as the pressures unleashed by the reformation conflict grew. Anglo has traced the decline in court festivals and pageantry after 1533 as the pageanteer, court reveller, and scenic artist were succeeded by the political pamphleteer, preacher, and public executioner.[74] Ideological commitment, as shown in the previous chapter, was the villain of the piece, for it usually overpowered a dramatist's willingness to sustain the dramatic integrity of the fable he was presenting.

John Bale's sprawling King Johan, written about 1534 in an attempt to urge Henry VIII to proceed further with reformation after the establishment of the Royal Supremacy, marks a half-way point in this degeneration. Bale's basic conception held great promise. The historical episode he chose – King John's unsuccessful struggle to subdue the clergy in England and assert his royal sovereignty against the power of the pope – ideally suited his purpose. He could develop John's attempt to alleviate the suffering of Widow Englande into an

---

[71] Ibid., ll. 1001.
[72] See Lancashire, Dramatic Texts and Records of Britain, p. 198, no. 1012.
[73] See David Bevington, From 'Mankind' to Marlowe (Cambridge, Massachusetts, 1962), pp. 40–1.
[74] See Anglo, Spectacle, Pageantry, and Early Tudor Policy, p. 261.

image of what Henry had already accomplished with the Submission of the Clergy in 1532 and the Act in Restraint of Appeals and the Act of Supremacy in 1533–4. He could then use the humiliating submission forced upon John by the alliance between the nobles and the clergy to warn Henry of what could happen if he did not take further measures to forestall it. Bale also put the conventional personified abstractions of the morality play to good use, scoring palpable hits by his identification of Sedicyon with Stephen Langton, Usurpid Powre with the pope, and Privat Welth with Cardinal Pandulphus. His instructions for symbolic doubling by the actors – Civil Order, for example, dresses for Sedition – [75] likewise show him exploiting the potential of drama for polemical effect.

Much of the potential effectiveness of this design, however, is lost in the execution, for Bale's zeal overpowers his aesthetic discretion. He is entirely indifferent to dramatic consistency or verisimilitude. When, for instance, King Johan asks Sedicyon who he is, Sedicyon answers:

> As I sayd afore, I am Sedycyon playne:
> In every relygyon and munkysh secte I rayne,
> Havyng yow prynces in scorne, hate and dysdayne.

Were Sedicyon truly 'sedition', he would hardly tell the king this to his face, nor would the king reply with the friendly nonchalance he displays: 'I pray the, good frynd, tell me what ys thy facyon.'[76] Bale is more concerned to get his message across than to sustain any dramatic credibility.

Things get worse as the play proceeds. Bale revised the play extensively several times after 1538 to tailor it to new circumstances. In the process, he shattered any notion of chronology by introducing a new character, Imperyall Majestye (representing Henry VIII), who refers to King John as one of 'our predecessours',[77] apparently forgetting that John has taken part in an action that is supposed to be taking place in the present. Similarly, Clergy is suddenly transformed into a good character, which breaches the decorum of the historical fable as Bale first developed it. Bale, in fact, altered the conception of the play pragmatically as it suited him. The sudden transformation of Clergy can be explained as a measure to make the play more suitable for the performance before Cranmer, the Archbishop of Canterbury, that took place on 2 January 1539.[78] Bale was not concerned with the art of his drama, merely to use it as a rhetorical device. Hence, the dramatic form in his hands loses most of its representational integrity.

In 1538 and 1539, Bale briefly enjoyed the patronage of Thomas Cromwell, who sponsored the production of his surviving biblical plays, *God's Promises*,

---

[75] *King Johan*, in *The Complete Plays of John Bale*, ed. Peter Happé, 2 vols (Cambridge, 1985), 1, l. 556. All references to Bales's plays are to this edition.

[76] Ibid., ll. 186–9.

[77] Ibid., ll. 2322.

[78] See ibid., p. 5.

Johan Baptystes Preachynge, The Temptation of Our Lord, and *Three Laws*. These protestant polemics show early Tudor drama at rock bottom. They are barely dramatic in any representational sense at all, but are entirely homiletic. Bale had abandoned any attempt to sustain characterization. In *Three Laws*, for example, Naturae lex and Infidelitas sound exactly the same. Instead, he is content to exploit dramatic form for the schematization it allows him in expressing his reformist doctrines. In these plays the transformation of representational drama into assertive polemic is complete.

Even polemical drama was killed off after the execution of Thomas Cromwell in July 1540, with *Godly Queene Hester* being the notable exception. Bale had to flee to the continent, and remained in exile until the accession of Edward VI. Bonner, Bishop of London, issued an injunction against religious plays in April 1542, and measures to repress them were taken by parliament in January 1543 and October 1544.[79] Events had proved yet again that with drama, as with every other fictive form, there were certain conditions under which imaginative representation could not thrive.

---

[79] See Anglo, *Spectacle*, pp. 270–1.

14

The Unquiet Mind of Sir Thomas Wyatt

Early Tudor drama displays the public response to Henrician policy of various political factions. One particular group existed whose members were affected by Henry VIII's actions at a much more personal level: the courtiers attendant on the king whose function was to sustain the ethos of the court.

The role of such courtiers – drawn for the most part from the nobility – differed from those of career administrators like Cromwell or counsellors like More. In addition to any practical services they might perform as ambassadors or military leaders, these noble courtiers were required to proclaim the aesthetic style of the dynasty. From the outset, Tudor monarchs tried to foster an image of themselves as embodying the best qualities of medieval chivalry and romance. Henry VIII, in particular, not only took pains to display his own prowess and that of his knights in the martial arts, but also encouraged his courtiers to conduct their social relationships as if they were courtly lovers in a medieval romance. The 'game of love' had developed into an elaborate code of behaviour, requiring courtiers to engage in ritual flirtation with court ladies, in the form of seasonal revels, disguisings, dancing, the exchange of riddles and jokes, of gifts such as posies and love-hearts, and, of course, amorous verses.[1] Courtly manuscripts that have survived from the period, for example the 'Devonshire Manuscript' (owned by Mary Shelton, one of the ladies in the household of Anne Boleyn), illustrate the light-hearted banter that took place, as members of the two sexes teased each other with the possibility of erotic encounters that might be fulfilled, but more often were not. Next to an acrostic written to Mary Shelton by Sir Thomas Wyatt, for instance, in which the poet describes the 'suffryng' caused him by his unrequited love for his mistress, and begs Mary to 'aplye to ease me of my payne', Mary has written in the margin 'fforget thys'. Next to several other poems in which Wyatt declares his intention of leaving off loving out of despair,

---

[1] See John Stevens, *Music and Poetry in the Early Tudor Court* (London, 1961), pp. 156–91.

she also writes 'and thys', 'and thys', 'and thys chefly'.[2] Elsewhere in the manuscript someone has drawn in the picture of a heart in the middle of a poem to signify the word 'heart',[3] and at another point a riddle is proposed:

> am el men
> an em e
> as I haue dese
> I ama yowrs an.[4]

Some scholars have resolved this by transposing the second and fourth letters to read:

> a lemmen [i.e. sweetheart]
> amene
> ah I saue dese
> I ama yowrs an [i.e. Anne].[5]

Such trifles as these suggest the playful level at which the game of love was pursued. No doubt flirtation could deepen into a serious passion, as did indeed occur in the case of Wyatt when he made his suit to Anne Boleyn, but more often than not the flirtation remained relatively harmless.

The tenor of the whole game suddenly changed after about 1525, when Henry VIII finally despaired of having a son by Katherine of Aragon and, obsessed with providing for the succession, decided to look elsewhere. The king's entry into the marriage stakes fundamentally altered the rules by which the game was played. Not only was the king the chief player, but he was playing for real. No woman who attracted his attention, and wanted it, could afford to engage in flirtation in the old way, nor was it safe for her to have indulged in such flirtations in the past. This seems to have been a lesson that Anne Boleyn, for all her political skill, never

---

[2] British Library, Additional MS 17492, fos 6ᵛ, 9ᵛ, 13ᵛ, 14ᵛ, 17ʳ. The poems are respectively nos 165, 131, 39, 66, and 186 in *Collected Poems of Sir Thomas Wyatt*, ed. Kenneth Muir and Patricia Thomson (Liverpool, 1969), from which all quotations from Wyatt's verse are taken unless otherwise stated. Hereafter cited as Wyatt, *Collected Poems*.

[3] British Library, Additional MS 17492, fo. 19ʳ.

[4] Ibid., fo. 59ᵛ.

[5] See Raymond Southall, *The Courtly Maker: An Essay on the Poetry of Wyatt and His Contemporaries* (Oxford, 1964), p. 18. This riddle may be the inscription to which Wyatt refers in 'That tyme that myrthe dyd stere my shypp':

> Then in my boke wrote my mystresse:
> 'I am yowres you may be well sure,
> And shall be whyle my lyff dothe dure'.

(Wyatt, *Collected Poems*, no. 173, ll. 5–7). See also Kenneth Muir, *Life and Letters of Sir Thomas Wyatt* (Liverpool, 1963), pp. 16–17 and note. Hereafter cited as Muir, *Life and Letters*.

quite grasped – with fatal consequences for herself and others. Similarly, no other relationship could be allowed to flourish that might imperil the king's dynastic interests. Lady Margaret Douglas, the king's niece, and Lord Thomas Howard, for example, discovered this to their cost in July 1536 when they contracted a secret marriage. Since the execution of Anne Boleyn in May 1536 had put the succession in doubt, the King of Scotland, Margaret Douglas's brother, could be viewed as the nearest heir, and Thomas Howard himself had rather more royal blood in his veins than Henry could have wished. Such a marriage, therefore, could not be tolerated, and the two lovers were imprisoned. Thomas Howard died in the Tower from the rigours of his confinement on 31 October 1537.[6]

A further consequence of Henry VIII's anxiety over the succession was that the very magnificence that he had encouraged his courtiers to display became dangerous when practised by those whom the king might suspect of having an ulterior motive. Another Howard, Henry, the youthful and reckless Earl of Surrey, was brought to the block because he incorporated the arms of Edward the Confessor into his own and affected a style of living too princely for the king's comfort.

The whole atmosphere at court thus underwent a radical transformation during the last two decades of Henry VIII's reign, and courtiers found themselves having to tread a fine line between performing the decorous and decorative functions expected of them, and arousing the antagonism of an increasingly paranoid king. A vivid testimony to the acute psychological stresses experienced by courtiers who had to live through these years has been left by the two greatest poets of the court circle – Wyatt and Surrey.

Sir Thomas Wyatt (born 1503) was one of the first to suffer from the changed circumstances at court after the mid 1520s. One of the most handsome and precocious younger men at Henry's court, in his earlier career Wyatt served in a number of capacities in the royal household, being first a sewer extraordinary (an officer who superintended banqueting arrangements), then an esquire of the royal body, and finally Clerk of the King's Jewels in 1524. Recognized as an accomplished amatory verser – the man who introduced the Petrarchan sonnet to England – Wyatt appeared to contemporaries as the embodiment of the ideal courtier Castiglione had recently described in *Il libro del Cortegiano*.

There was one fatal deficiency in Wyatt's life, however, that was to be directly and indirectly responsible for all his future tribulations and political troubles: he was married to a woman he did not love. In 1520, at the age of 17, he married Elizabeth Brooke, the daughter of Thomas, Lord Cobham, but soon separated from her. The best comment on the unhappiness of this marriage is Wyatt's own.

[6] For the impassioned verses Margaret Douglas and Thomas Howard exchanged during this imprisonment, see Kenneth Muir, 'Unpublished Poems in the Devonshire MS', *Proceedings of the Leeds Philosophical and Literary Society*, 6: 4 (1947), pp. 253–82, esp. pp. 254–5.

While on his way to Spain in April 1537 to take up his appointment as ambassador to the Emperor, Wyatt wrote to his son, who had recently married, offering him advice on how to be a good husband. At the conclusion of this letter he observes that 'the blissing of god for good agrement between the wife and husband is fruyt of many children, which I for the like thinge doe lack, and the faulte is both in your mother and me, but chieflie in her.'[7] We need not suppose that Wyatt separated from his wife because she had been unfaithful; the truth of the matter is that the two of them were incompatible – in short, they could not abide one another.

Wyatt sought for the rest of his life to find substitutes for the lack of emotional and sexual satisfaction in his marriage, both in the form of liaisons with other women, and also in the intense friendship he shared with Thomas Cromwell. His marital dissatisfaction explains why, when Anne Boleyn returned to the English court in 1522 full of French accomplishments and graces, Wyatt was particularly susceptible to her charms, and why the ritual flirtation of the game of love quickly turned into a serious passion on his part.

Some scholars have rejected the idea that Wyatt's poems refer to a real love affair, let alone one with Anne Boleyn, but the evidence leaves no room for doubt that this was so. Wyatt makes it clear that the mistress 'wherof I plain, and have done many a daye', was one particular woman whom he identifies implicitly in a number of poems as Anne Boleyn.[8] In the riddle he proposes – 'What wourde is that that chaungeth not, / Though it be tourned and made in twain?' – the answer is 'Anna'.[9] Similarly, in a poem written in October 1532, when Wyatt was obliged to accompany Henry VIII and Anne Boleyn to Calais, he reflects bitterly upon his previous passion for her, and records his relief at finding the old flame of desire is extinguished:

> Some tyme I fled the fyre that me brent
> By see, by land, by water and by wynd;
> And now I folow the coles that be quent
> From Dovor to Calais against my mynde.
> Lo! how desire is boeth sprong and spent!
> And he may se that whilome was so blynde;
> And all his labor now he laugh to scorne.
> Mashed in the breers that erst was all to torne.[10]

Finally, having found a new mistress of his affections in Elizabeth Darrell, he alludes to how in the past he 'did refrayne / Her that did set our country in a rore', which, after Anne's execution, he discreetly changed to 'Brunet that set my

---

[7] Muir, *Life and Letters*, p. 41.
[8] Wyatt, *Collected Poems*, no. 54, l. 2.
[9] Ibid., no. 50.
[10] Ibid., no. 59.

welth in such a rore.'[11] In the light of such allusions there can be no doubt that Wyatt's passion was real, not just conventional, and that Anne Boleyn had been the object of his desire.

Anne and her faction, however, were angling for a bigger fish than Wyatt, and whatever encouragement she may initially have given him, she soon threw him over once she had begun to attract the attentions of the king. Wyatt found Anne's desertion traumatic, and he turned to writing poetry as a means of relief from his turbulent emotions. The first group of politically orientated poems Wyatt wrote, therefore, are those referring to this episode, for sex and politics had become inseparably confused in his life.

Wyatt had several compelling reasons for turning to poetry. In the first place, the king was his social superior, and both decorum and discretion rendered Wyatt powerless to resist him in this matter or complain of it directly. He therefore had to find some indirect mode of expression. For this purpose the stereotyped themes and conventions of courtly love poetry proved ideal. Wyatt found that the pose of an unrequited lover suffering his mistress's disdain approximated all too closely to his own situation. He was therefore able to project sincere emotions through the pretext of merely playing the game of love. This explains why, in Wyatt's lyrics, the conventions often seem loaded with a much greater weight of feeling than they customarily are required to bear. It is conventional, for example, for disappointed lovers from *Le Roman de la Rose* onwards to lament time misspent in the pursuit of love as they are in the process of renouncing it, but no previous poet had ever done it with quite the force of bitterness that Wyatt invests in lines like the following:

> Ffarewell, Love, and all thy lawes for ever;
> Thy bayted hookes shall tangill me no more;
>
> . . .
>
> For hetherto though I have lost all my tyme,
> Me lusteth no lenger rotten boughes to clyme,[12]

or

> Tanglid I was yn loves snare,
> Opprest with payne, tormente with care,
>
> . . .
>
> Was never birde tanglid yn lyme
> That brake awaye yn bettre tyme,
> Then I that rotten bowes ded clyme,

[11] Ibid., no. 97.
[12] Ibid., no. 13.

And had no hurte, but scaped fre.
Now ha, ha, ha, full well is me,
For I am nowe at libretye.[13]

The idea is conventional, but the sentiment that is woven into its expression is
not. Images of baited hooks, bird-lime snares, and entanglement evoke the
memory of a sexual desirability in Wyatt's lady which she flaunted provocatively,
but insincerely, and to which the poet succumbed. By laughing derisively at his
earlier gullibility in believing her to be sincere, and by likening her to a 'rotten
bough' which he no longer desires to climb, Wyatt diminishes both her and the
experience of loving in a way that shatters the ethos of courtly conventionality.
He does, however, manage to convey his wounded self-esteem, the transformation of his desire into an equally powerful but over-emphatic disgust, and his
wish to restore his ego by punishing her – by circulating around the court poems
as these.

Wyatt found a still more indirect means of expression in the form of translation, or creative imitation. Specifically, he found that the translation of Petrarch's
sonnets concerning Laura enabled him to give the fullest possible expression to
his own feelings, while remaining protected from the charge of malice at the
personal level, and treason at the political. If challenged, Wyatt could always
profess that he had merely been translating originals, and that any apparent
similarity between the contents of the poem and the situation at court was
coincidental.

Perhaps the most striking example of Wyatt's creative adaptation of a Petrarchan original is the sonnet 'Who so list to hounte'.[14] Petrarch's poem reads:

> Una candida cerva sopra l'erba
>   Verde m'apparve, con duo corna d'oro,
>   Fra due riviere, a l'ombra d'un alloro,
>   Levando 'l sole, a la stagione acerba.
> Era sua vista sí dolce superba,
>   Ch'i'lasciai per seguirla ogni lavoro;
>   Come l'avaro che'n cercar tesoro
>   Con diletto l'affano disacerba.
> 'Nessun mi tocchi,' al bel collo d'intorno
>   Scritto avea di diamanti e di topazi;
>   'Libera farmi al mio Cesare parve'.
> Et era 'l sol già vòlto al mezzo giorno;
>   Gli occhi miei di mirar, non sazi;
>   Quand'io caddi ne l'acqua, et ella sparve.[15]

---

[13] Ibid., no. 224.
[14] For an excellent reading of this poem, see Stephen Greenblatt, *Renaissance Self-*
fashioning, pp. 146–9.
[15] Petrarch, *Rime*, no. 190; reprinted in Wyatt, *Collected Poems*, p. 266.

[A white hind appeared to me on the green grass, with two horns of gold, between two rivers, in the shade of a laurel tree, as the sun was rising in the youthful season. Her look was so sweetly proud that I left all work to follow her, like the miser who, as he searches for treasure, sweetens his trouble with delight. 'Let no one touch me', was written in diamonds and topazes around her lovely neck, 'it has pleased my Caesar to make me free.' And the sun had already turned to midday, my eyes weary with looking, but not satiated, when I fell into the water, and she vanished.]

Here is what Wyatt did with it:

> Who so list to hounte I know where is an hynde;
>   But as for me, helas, I may no more:
>   The vayne travaill hath weried me so sore,
>   I ame of theim that farthest cometh behinde;
> Yet may I by no meanes my weried mynde
>   Drawe from the Diere: but as she fleeth afore
>   Faynting I folowe; I leve of therefore,
>   Sithens in a nett I seke to hold the wynde.
> Who list her hount I put him owte of dowbte,
>   As well as I may spend his tyme in vain:
>   And graven with Diamondes in letters plain
> There is written her faier neck rounde abowte:
>   'Noli me tangere for Cesars I ame,
>   And wylde for to hold though I seme tame'.[16]

Wyatt subtly alters the source so as to transmute Petrarch's mystical adoration for his mistress into an expression of embittered contempt for his own. Petrarch's 'candida cerva', or white hind, is an exalted neo-Platonic symbol suggesting the purity of Laura, his dead beloved, the white deer with golden horns signifying Diana, the goddess of chastity. All the other imagery of spring, the sun rising, the green grass, and the sparkling streams, serves to enhance this idea of her purity. Wyatt, on the other hand, by introducing the imagery of a hunt, transmutes 'hind' into traditional English sexual bawdy. In this way, Petrarch's idealism is transformed into cynicism. Whereas Petrarch's deer had been unattainable because she had been liberated by her lord (that is, by God, through death), Wyatt's hind is unattainable because she is literally Caesar's – the king's. This difference is emphasized by another subtle dislocation. The motto inscribed in diamonds and topazes on the collar of Petrarch's deer – 'Nessun mi tocchi; Libera farmi al mio Cesare parve' – is an Italian rendering of the words that used to be inscribed on the collars of Caesar's hinds in classical times: 'Noli me tangere quia Caesaris sum.' By reverting the motto from Italian to Latin, Wyatt invokes yet another significant text. Not only does the word 'graven' suggest 'graven images' and

---

[16] Wyatt, *Collected Poems*, no. 7.

materialistic greed, divesting Petrarch's diamonds and topazes of any exalted symbolism they may have had, but the Latin *Noli me tangere* evokes John 20:17, where Jesus tells Mary Magdalen not to touch his body: 'Noli me tangere, nondum enim ascendi ad Patrem meum' ('Do not touch me, for I have not yet ascended to my Father'). There is also an allusion in that line to Matthew 22:21, where Jesus tells the Pharisees to render to Caesar the things that are Caesar's. By invoking these biblical texts, Wyatt is emphasizing the grotesque contrast between his mistress and Petrarch's on one hand, and between his mistress and Christ on the other. Spirituality has been replaced by carnality, and devotion to God has become the worship of material things. With cynical pragmatism, Wyatt's mistress has allowed herself to be bought by the king, and Wyatt has to render to Caesar what belongs to him, not because of any spiritual duty, but because he is powerless to do otherwise. The adaptation thus turns the original into a very powerful personal and political protest.

Almost every other translation Wyatt made from Petrarch can be shown to provide a covert comment on his own personal predicament, and near the end of his life he returned to Petrarch to find a means of expressing his grief at the loss of his friend and protector, Thomas Cromwell.[17] Paradoxically, translation, the most indirect of all possible forms of literary expression, gave Wyatt the fullest scope for self-revelation that he ever attained.

Wyatt himself summed up the value of writing poetry as a relief for the emotional turbulence caused by Anne Boleyn's desertion. In one of his lyrics he declares:

> All hevy myndes
> Do seke to ese their charge
> And that that moost theim byndes
> To set at large.[18]

In another poem he confesses to being 'one off them whom plaint doth well content.'[19] Poetry, in other words, served as a form of psychic therapy for Wyatt.

One may deduce the sources of the therapeutic effectiveness Wyatt found in versifying by examining the poems themselves. The stereotyped attitudes and situations of courtly love poetry, and in particular the archetypal experience of erotic frustration depicted in Petrarch's *Rime*, furnished Wyatt with material for fictive dramatizations of his own emotional experience. He seems to have found it necessary to objectify the perturbations arising from his dilemma, as the precondition for responding to them. Once that objectification had begun to take place, he could confront the sources of his anxiety. This means that the poetry

---

[17] See 'The piller pearisht is whearto I lent' (ibid., no. 236), which translates Petrarch's 'Rotta è l'alta colonna' (*Rime*, no. 269); reprinted in Wyatt, *Collected Poems*, p. 429.

[18] Wyatt, *Collected Poems*, no. 84.

[19] Ibid., no. 98 ('So feble is the threde'), l. 57.

written on the Boleyn affair often shows several contradictory mental processes occurring simultaneously, sometimes within the one poem. Half the time Wyatt is concerned to confess the vulnerability to which his perturbations expose him, and the rest of the time he is trying out various forms of self-assertion to protect himself against them. Therapy, for Wyatt, seemed to consist of admitting his weakness in order to counter it by asserting his strength.

The main source of perturbation for Wyatt was a sense of betrayal, arising from the recognition that the moral values his society preached, and to which he believed himself to be committed, counted for nothing in the actual practice of the Henrician court:

> What vaileth truth? or, by it, to take payn?
> To stryve, by stedfastnes, for to attayne,
> To be iuste, and true: and fle from dowbleness:
> Sythens all alike, where rueleth craftines
> Rewarded is boeth fals, and plain.
> Sonest he spedeth, that moost can fain;
> True meanyng hert is had in disdayn.[20]

It is often notoriously difficult to discern whether a Wyatt poem has an erotic or a political signification, and this *rondeau* shows why. Anne Boleyn's behaviour had become symptomatic for Wyatt of the condition of the whole world he inhabited in the late 1520s – a world that was rotten to the core with hypocrisy, where men acted in a way that belied the values they professed. Wyatt had discovered the same reality that Skelton and More had identified earlier, except that he was more shocked and surprised than they at the discovery. He really seems to have believed that such sincere devotion and 'seruise' as he had shown would be deservedly rewarded with a reciprocal fidelity; instead, he found that

> . . . for reward of ouer great desire
> Disdaynfull dowbleness have I for my hiere.

As in 'Who so list to hounte', Wyatt attributes this unjust outcome to the lady's venality, finding that 'price hath priuilege trouth to prevent.'[21] His cynical perception of this motive leaves him not only with a sense of the contrast between his own previous 'stedfastnes' and her 'dowblenes', but also the humiliating naivety of that steadfastness.

The shattering of Wyatt's confidence in the worth of the moral values by which he had shaped his life prepared the way for an even greater anxiety: a sense of the disintegration of his own identity. This arose from his feeling that, in order to keep his head above water in the duplicitous world of Henry's court, he had to

---

[20] Ibid., no. 2, ll. 1–7.
[21] Ibid., no. 5 ('Alas the greiff'), ll. 5–6, 24.

act out a role like everyone else. He recognized the inconsistencies into which this
contrived outward behaviour led him:

> Eche man me telleth I chaunge moost my devise.
>   And on my faith me thinck it goode reason
>   To chaunge purpose like after the season,
>   Ffor in every cas to keep still oon gyse
> Ys mytt for theim that would be taken wyse,
>   And I ame not of suche maner condition,
>   But treted after a dyvers fasshion,
>   And therupon my dyvernes doeth rise.

Wyatt's answer to those who have criticized him for his variability is blunt:

> Chaunge you no more . . .
> And while with me doeth dwell this weried goost,
>   My word nor I shall not be variable,
>   But alwaies oon, your owne boeth ferme and stable.[22]

One gets the impression that Anne Boleyn's defection unleashed a metaphysical
panic in Wyatt. It destroyed his belief in conventional values, and filled him with
a sense of endless mutability in the world. Above all, it destroyed his confidence,
and this made him prey to an uncontrollable anxiety stronger than any specific
cause that could be identified to explain it. Wyatt conveys the paradox of this
state very powerfully in one of his best lyrics:

> It may be good, like it who list,
> But I do dowbt: who can me blame?
> For oft assured yet have I myst,
> And now again I fere the same:
> The wyndy wordes, the Ies quaynt game,
> Of soden chaunge maketh me agast:
> For dred to fall I stond not fast.
>
>   . . .
>
> Assured, I dowbt I be not sure;
> And should I trust to suche suretie
> That oft hath put the prouff in vre
> And never hath founde it trusty?[23]

This is far more than simply the 'contrarious state' of the conventional Petrarchan lover. Fear of change and doubleness deprives the poet of any ability to trust

---

[22] Ibid., no. 10, ll. 1–8, 10–14. I have adopted the Devonshire Manuscript's reading 'purpose' in
preference to the Egerton Manuscript's 'propose', printed by Muir.

[23] Ibid., no. 21, ll. 1–7, 15–18.

in, or accept, the thing he most desires, even when, as here, it seems to be offered to him. Ostensibly, Wyatt is talking about love in this poem, and his unwillingness to trust in the permanence of a new relationship, but the expression is so generalized that it suggests a far wider application than love alone. Wyatt did not just long for a stable love relationship, he longed for a stable self, a stable set of values, and a stable world that he felt he did not possess. In the absence of those things, all he could do was to 'plain', or give expression to his perturbation, to punish the woman he believed was responsible for his misery by exposing her to the court circle in his poems, and to assert various 'selves' in an attempt to bolster his shattered ego.[24]

If Wyatt's equilibrium was shaken by the failure of his love affair with Anne Boleyn, it received a body blow from the events surrounding her fall. In May 1536, Anne and half a dozen of her suitors and intimates were beheaded, having been convicted of adultery, and hence treason against the king. Wyatt, too, was imprisoned as a suspected adulterer. Most people thought that he would be executed with the rest, and he probably would have been, had he not been protected by Thomas Cromwell.[25] It is highly unlikely that Wyatt was guilty of physical intimacy with the queen after her marriage, for on his own admission he had 'refrained' her, and was not so stupid as to risk compromising himself in such a foolhardy way. More probably, as a known former suitor of Anne Boleyn, he was simply a convenient pawn in the plot by which the anti-Boleyn faction brought her to destruction. Charles Brandon, the Duke of Suffolk, seems to have used the occasion to settle some score with Wyatt. Certainly, Wyatt later declared that he imputed his imprisonment to Suffolk alone, and had held a grudge against him for it ever after.[26]

During Wyatt's imprisonment he witnessed the beheading of Anne within the Tower, and the horrific spectacle shocked him profoundly:

> The bell towre showed me suche syght
> That in my hed stekys day and nyght;
>   Ther dyd I lerne out of a grate
> Ffor all vauoure, glory or myght,
>   That yet *circa Regna tonat*.

The effect on him can be gauged from his own words:

> These blodye dayes haue brokyn my hart;
> My lust, my youth dyd then departe.[27]

---

[24] See Greenblatt's very pertinent comments in *Renaissance Self-fashioning*, pp. 137–44.
[25] See Muir, *Life and Letters*, pp. 28–31.
[26] Ibid., p. 201.
[27] Wyatt, *Collected Poems*, no. 176, ll. 16–20, 11–12.

For Wyatt, the violent and sudden death of Anne and her 'lovers', and his own narrow escape from the same fate, served to deepen his sense of the world's mutability, and prompted him more urgently to seek protection against the metaphysical nightmare that had come to haunt him.

In June 1536 Wyatt was released from the Tower into his father's custody, to undergo voluntary correction according to the king's pleasure. Here was yet another circumstance to abase Wyatt's self-esteem. Not only was he being punished for an offence of which he knew himself innocent, but he also had to suffer the humiliation of being treated like a schoolboy. As his father reported to Cromwell in a letter of 14 June 1536, Sir Henry had 'not only commandyd hym his obediens in all pointes to the kynges pleasure, but also the leving of such slaunderus ffacion, as hath engendered vnto hym both the displeasure of god and of his maister.'[28] Understandably, quite apart from his shock and grief at the death of his friends,[29] Wyatt chafed with resentment at this treatment, which must have seemed to him yet another token of the world's hypocrisy.

He responded to these accumulating tribulations by seeking to construct a new sense of identity, and to find it he explored the opposite pose to the one he had adopted earlier. Instead of depicting himself as a fragmented, inconstant, de-centred personality, he swung to the opposite extreme of projecting himself as the most constant and balanced of all possible personalities – a man of Stoic fortitude and inflexible virtue, who would rather live in seclusion than compromise his integrity. In order to adopt this persona, Wyatt necessarily had to switch literary models. Instead of imitating Petrarch and the poets of *amour courtois*, he now imitated Seneca, Horace, and a contemporary Italian neo-Stoic, Luigi Alamanni; and instead of writing courtly lyrics, he now wrote moral satires in the classical vein.

We can see him beginning to formulate this new pose in two closely related poems referring to the executions of 1536: 'Who lyst his welthe and eas Retayne', and 'Stond who so list', both drawing upon Seneca, and both preaching the desirability of the 'mean estate'. The theme of the poems is the same: beware of aspiring too high at court, because such ambition exposes one to the caprice of tyrants and Fortune, and often leads to sudden catastrophe:

---

[28] *LP*, X, no. 1131, p. 474.

[29] In Wyatt's elegy on Rochford, Norris, Weston, Brereton, and Smeaton, he recorded his grief thus:

> The Axe ys home, your hedys be in the stret;
> The trykklyngge tearys dothe ffall so from my yes,
> I skarse may wryt, my paper ys so wet.
> But what can he[l]pe when dethe hath played his part,
> Thoughe naturs cours wyll thus lament and mone?
> Leve sobes therffor, and euery crestyn hart
> Pray ffor the sowlis of thos be dead and goone.

(Wyatt, *Collected Poems*, no. 146, ll. 58–64).

Who lyst his welthe and eas Retayne,
Hym selffe let hym vnknowne contayne;
  Presse not to ffast in at that gatte
Wher the Retorne standes by desdayne:
  For sure, *circa Regna tonat.*

The hye montaynis ar blastyd oft,
When the lowe vaylye ys myld and soft;
  Ffortune with helthe stondis at debate;
The ffall ys grevous ffrome Aloffte:
  And sure, *circa Regna tonat.*[30]

Wyatt's later reference in the poem to the terrible sight he witnessed from the Bell Tower makes it quite clear that his new interest in this classical theme was stimulated by his shock at the death of Anne Boleyn and his friends.

In the second poem, his translation of a passage from a chorus in Seneca's *Thyestes,* his rephrasing of the original suggests the same associative link:

Stond who so list vpon the Slipper toppe
Of courtes estates, and lett me heare reioyce;
And vse me quyet without lett or stoppe,
Vnknowen in courte, that hath suche brackish ioyes.
In hidden place, so lett my dayes forthe passe,
That when my yeares be done, withouten noyse,
I may dye aged after the common trace.
For hym death greep'the right hard by the croppe
That is moche knowen of other, and of him self, alas,
Doth dye vnknowen, dazed with dreadfull face.[31]

For the last three lines of this poem, Seneca had written:

Illi mors grauis incubat
Qui notus nimis omnibus
Ignotus moritur sibi.[32]

[Death falls heavily on the man who, too well known to the world, dies unknown to himself].

Here, the description of death is generalized. Wyatt, however, added several specific details that conjure up the image of beheading as the actual means of death:

---

[30] Ibid., no. 176, ll. 1–10. The refrain echoes Seneca's *Phaedra;* see Wyatt, *Collected Poems,* p. 415.

[31] Ibid., no. 240.

[32] *Thyestes,* ll. 391–403. The original passage from Seneca's play is reprinted in Wyatt, *Collected Poems,* p. 431.

> . . . hym death greep'the right hard *by the croppe*
> That is moche knowen of other, and of him self alas,
> Doth dye vnknowen, *dazed with dreadfull face.*[33]

A further detail located the poem as having been written soon after the executions, when Wyatt was at Allington Castle. Whereas in Thyestes the character speaking wishes to be allowed to enjoy sweet quiet in an obscure spot ('me dulcis saturet quies, / obscuro positus loco'), Wyatt in enjoying it 'heare', that is, in Kent. We can therefore assume that Wyatt started to develop the *beatus ille* theme not merely as a generalized moral reflection, but partly because it expressed the revulsion he felt after the bloody events of May 1536.

The matter is not, however, that simple. Wyatt's withdrawal from court was as much enforced as voluntary, as his rapid return to it in late 1536, once things had quietened down, confirms. In proclaiming the virtues of the mean estate, he was making a virtue of necessity, which makes one suspect that he may have adopted this theme as much to bolster his bruised ego as from genuine conviction. Indeed, that Wyatt was protesting too much becomes abundantly clear in the first of his formal verse satires, 'Myne owne John Poyntz'.

Wyatt found an exemplar of exactly the new Stoic identity he felt moved to adopt in the satiric verse epistle Luigi Alamanni had addressed to his friend, Thommaso Sertini, in 1532.[34] In this satire, Alamanni explains why he prefers to live in poverty in Provence rather than follow the progresses of princes and kings. After enumerating the dishonest things required of a courtier that he could never bring himself to do, Alamanni extols the superior freedom and peace of mind he enjoys in Provence, dwelling in solitude with the Muses. In order to turn the poem into an indirect depiction of his own situation, and a statement of the defiantly Stoical attitude towards it he wanted to project, Wyatt had to do little more than substitute English details for the original Italian ones. Hence his translation, for the most part, remains fairly literal.

The changes and additions he makes, however, give him away by betraying what was uppermost in his mind. Whereas Alamanni prefers to live alone in Provence 'Piu tosto chel sequir signori & Regi' ('rather than follow lords and kings'), Wyatt has withdrawn 'homeward',

> Rather then to lyve thrall vnder the awe
> Of lordly lookes, wrappid within my cloke,
> To will and lust lerning to set a lawe.[35]

---

[33] My italics. For a similar opinion of these lines, see H. A. Mason, *Sir Thomas Wyatt: A Literary Portrait* (Bristol, 1986), p. 236.

[34] Alamanni's Italian text and an English translation can conveniently be found in Mason, *Sir Thomas Wyatt: A Literary Portrait*, pp. 260–6.

[35] Mason, *Sir Thomas Wyatt: A Literary Portrait*, p. 261; Wyatt, *Collected Poems*, no. 105, ll. 4–6.

His phrasing is far more explicit, and conjures up the recent events at court in which he had, indeed, had to learn to set a law to his will and desire, in awe of lordly looks, and to dissemble ('cloak') his real feelings, when he had to give Anne Boleyn up to Henry VIII. Similarly, Wyatt declares that he cannot 'wrest the law to fill the coffer, / With innocent blode to fede my sellff ffat' – a detail missing from Alamanni – whereas Henry VIII had done exactly that, in Wyatt's estimation, first in his specious divorce from Katherine of Aragon, and then in his execution of Anne and her courtiers.[36] Nor can Wyatt, he avers,

> . . . alow the state
> Off highe Cesar and dam Cato to dye,
> That with his dethe dyd skape owt off the gate
> From Cesares handes, if Lyvye do not lye,
> And wolld not lyve whar lyberty was lost.

By omitting Alamanni's 'Sulla' and substituting 'Cato' for Alamanni's 'Brutus', Wyatt thus turns the original into a covert reference to Henry VIII's judicial murder of Sir Thomas More for opposing the divorce.[37] Finally, Wyatt cannot allow

> The letcher a lover, and tirannye
> To be the right of a prynces reigne,

which more explicitly identifies Henry VIII as the particular lecher and tyrant meant.[38] From these and other alterations to the source, one can see that uppermost in Wyatt's mind was the absolutist and wilful tyranny of Henry VIII, to which he had been forced to submit. This makes his climactic protestation (in a line which is not in Alamanni) that he would find it impossible to consent to these pretences, all the more ironic:

> I cannot, I; no, no, it will not be.[39]

Sadly, it could be, and Wyatt had done so – which the accumulation of reiterated negatives merely serves to underline. Wyatt desperately wanted to be like the Stoic stereotype of his choice, but knew, in reality, that he was very far from matching up to it. So, in spite of all his bravado, he was affecting a pose of unmovable constancy because he knew he was beaten and that there was nothing he could do about it. He pulls the rug out from under his whole argument by admitting that he is not in Kent entirely by his own choice:

[36] Ibid., ll. 34–5.
[37] Ibid., ll. 37–41.
[38] Ibid., ll. 74–5.
[39] Ibid., l. 76.

> No man doeth marke where so I ride or goo;
> In lusty lees at libertie I walke,
> And of these newes I fele nor wele nor woo,
> *Sauf that a clogg doeth hang yet at my hele*:
> No force for that for it is ordered so,
> That I may lepe boeth hedge and dike full well.[40]

Wyatt, in other words, is under house arrest, even though this does not prevent him from going hunting. The admission makes a mockery of his assertion of unbending Stoic integrity, since it is his lack of it that has landed him in the ignominious rural banishment that now makes such a pose necessary.

Unsurprisingly, the two other formal verse satires Wyatt wrote similarly betray a moral uncertainty they seek to deny. In 'My mothers maydes', Wyatt uses the fable of the country mouse who, sick of her privations in the country, went to live with her cousin, a town mouse, and discovered to her cost that the presence of a cat blighted the apparent felicity she believed her cousin enjoyed. This satire reflects Wyatt's acknowledgement that 'eche kynd of lyff hath with him his disease', in spite of what he had pretended about the delights of rural domesticity in translating Alamanni's epistle. His response marks a further retreat from his earlier court experience, this time not merely into the country, but into the deeper recesses of the mind:

> Then seke no more owte of thy self to fynde
> The thing that thou haist sought so long before,
> For thou shalt fele it sitting in thy mynde.[41]

All that Wyatt can wish upon his former associates at court is that they might 'frete inward' for losing the chance to experience the contentment that he wants us to believe he now enjoys.

In the last satire, 'A spending hand that alway powreth owte', Wyatt simply reasserts the tenor of the first in the form of blame by praise, satirically urging another friend, Sir Francis Bryan, to practice every form of court vice if he wants to purchase friends and seek to please. When Bryan demurs, Wyatt pretends to dismiss him contemptuously:

> Nay, then, farewell, and if you care for shame
> Content the then with honest pouertie
> With fre tong what the myslikes to blame
> And for thy trouth sumtyme aduersitie.[42]

---

[40] Ibid., ll. 83–97. My italics.
[41] Ibid., no. 106, ll. 80, 97–9.
[42] Ibid., no. 107, ll. 85–8.

Wyatt has turned Bryan into a displaced projection of himself in order to attribute to him the naive virtues that, he would like to believe, have been responsible for his own disgrace. It is a pleasant fantasy, but far from the truth for both Wyatt and Bryan (especially given the latter's nickname of 'the Vicar of Hell'). In spite of Wyatt's satiric bravado, he cannot quite conceal the insubstantial nature of his new Stoical persona. The forcefulness of these satires, therefore, can be seen as Wyatt's attempt to disguise the fact that, in spite of his desire for it to be otherwise, he desperately lacked the stable centre of being that he sought.

Because it was contrived, Wyatt's pose as the just man who preferred to stand alone rather than compromise his integrity, did not last. Previous experience should have taught him that he could only find the calm he sought within the security of a stable sexual relationship. It is not surprising, therefore, to discover that within months of his release from the Tower he had formed a new liaison, this time with Elizabeth Darrell, one of Katherine of Aragon's former maids of honour, who had entered the service of the Marchioness of Exeter in 1536.[43]

On the evidence of a string of poems that trace the development of this affair, one can infer that Wyatt must have begun his suit to Elizabeth Darrell soon after his return to court in late 1536. In the first of these poems, 'If waker care if sodayne pale Coulour', Wyatt muses upon the symptoms he is experiencing that show he is in love once again. He even invites the reader to guess who his new mistress is:

> If thow aske whome, sure sins I did refrayne
> [Her that did set our country in a rore],
> Th'unfayned chere of Phillis hath the place
> That Brunet had: she hath and ever shal.[44]

The counterpoising of Phillis against Brunet in these lines emphasizes how, in pursuing Elizabeth Darrell, Wyatt was seeking a substitute for Anne Boleyn, just as he had pursued Anne in search of the erotic and emotional satisfaction lacking in his marriage to Elizabeth Brooke.

The affair cannot have advanced very far by February 1537 when Wyatt, now fully restored to favour with the king, was appointed ambassador to the Emperor's court. His departure for Spain interfered at a crucial stage with his suit, just when he was most eager to press it. To express his frustration, Wyatt turned once again to the translation of Petrarch:

[43] See Muir, *Life and Letters*, pp. 84–5.

[44] Wyatt, *Collected Poems*, no. 97, ll. 7–10. I have quoted the earlier version of l. 8, which Wyatt later cancelled, as it makes the topical identification of Brunet as Anne Boleyn much more explicit. For the identification of Phillis as Elizabeth Darrell, see also E. K. Chambers, *Sir Thomas Wyatt and Some Collected Studies* (London, 1933), pp. 140–5.

Off Cartage he that worthie warrier
Could ouercome, but cowld not vse his chaunce,
And I like wise off all my long indeuor
The sherpe conquest tho fortune did avaunce
Cowld not it vse: the hold that is gyvin ouer
I vnpossest. So hangith in balaunce
Off warr, my pees, reward of all my payne;
At Mountzon thus I restles rest in Spayne.[45]

Just as Wyatt had earlier used the translation of Petrarchan love poetry for political protest, here he uses one of Petrarch's political poems for amorous complaint. Each of the two modes could be used to signify the other, because the conditions imposed by erotic and political experience during these years were much the same. Petrarch's original poem ('Vinse Anibal, e non seppe usar poi / Ben la vittoriosa sua ventura') is unambiguously a poem of advice to Stefano Colonna on the need to follow up his victory over the Orsini.[46] Wyatt picks up the imagery evoking an indecisive military victory as a metaphor to suggest the insecure state of his love affair.

A similar kind of displacement, which Wyatt seems to have found almost a precondition for the expression of his deepest personal feelings, can be seen operating in the poem he wrote on the eve of one of his two returns to England from Spain, either that of June 1538, or that of April 1539:

Tagus, fare well, that westward with thy stremes
Torns vp the grayns off gold alredy tryd:
With spurr and sayle for I go seke the Tems
Gaynward the sonne, that shewth her welthi pryd
And to the town which Brutus sowght by drems
Like bendyd mone doth lend her lusty syd.
My kyng, my Contry, alone for whome I lyve,
Of myghty love the winges for this me gyve.[47]

It has been rightly observed that this remarkable poem is charged with an emotion far in excess of that for which its ostensible subject matter calls.[48] One can see why this is so by comparing it to another poem written to Elizabeth Darrell at about the same time. Addressing the verses he is writing, Wyatt says:

My song, thou shalt ataine to fynd that plesant place
Where she doth lyve by whome I lyve; may chaunce the have this grace:
When she hath red and seene the dred wherein I sterve

[45] Wyatt, Collected Poems, no. 81. Wyatt was at Monçon on 16 October 1537.
[46] Petrarch, Rime, no. 103; reprinted in Wyatt, Collected Poems, p. 320.
[47] Wyatt, Collected Poems, no. 99.
[48] See Mason, Sir Thomas Wyatt: A Literary Portrait, pp. 220–2.

By twene her brestes she shall the put there shall she the reserve.
Then tell her that I come she shall me shortly se;
Yff that for whayte the body fayle, this sowle shall to her fle.[49]

It was to more than king and country that Wyatt hoped to fly. In 'Tagus, fare well', the displacement of erotic desirability onto the Thames, with her 'lusty side' curved like a bended moon, foreshadows the erotic fulfilment that Wyatt anticipated on his return, as does his wish that the poem might prepare his way by nestling between her breasts. In 'Tagus, fare well', the highly charged emotion springs from the fact that Wyatt was simply transferring to his king and country much of the erotic passion he felt for Elizabeth Darrell.

One final poem serves to show the comfort and peace that Wyatt did indeed find in this relationship. He expresses it in one of the few poems he wrote that declare unmitigated happiness:

> After great stormes the cawme retornis
> And pleasanter it is thereby;
> Fortune likewise that often tornis
> Hath made me now the moost happy.
>
> Thevin that pited my distres,
> My iust desire and my cry,
> Hath made my languor to cesse
> And me also the most happy.
>
> Whereto dispaired ye, my frendes?
> My trust always in [her did] ly.
> That knoweth what my thought intends
> Whereby I lyve the most happy.
>
> Lo! what can take hope from that hert
> That is assured stedfastly?
> Hope therefore ye that lyve in smert,
> Whereby I ame the most happy.
>
> And I that have felt of your paine
> Shall pray to god continuelly
> To make your hope, your helth retayne,
> And make me also the most happy.[50]

Perhaps more than any other poem, this one reveals how dependent Wyatt was on the love of one woman he could trust. He could only gain the calm and

---

[49] Wyatt, *Collected Poems*, no. 98 ('So feble is the threde'), ll. 95–100.

[50] Ibid., no. 83. I have adopted Nott's emendation for the Egerton MS's reading 'hid' in l. 10, rather than Muir's 'hevin did', as 'hid' seems a more probable unintended elision of 'her did' than of 'hevin did'.

stability for which he longed, from feeling that his heart was 'assured stedfastly'. That is why his relationship with Elizabeth Darrell was so important to him, and why, after his return from Spain, he installed her at Allington Castle and had an illegitimate son by her. She was, *de facto*, the wife he needed to take the place of the wife from whom he felt irrevocably alienated; she was also the steadfast lover who could compensate him for the loss of Anne Boleyn. I have dealt with the formation of this relationship at such length because some sense of its force is necessary if one is to understand the psychology of Wyatt's reaction to the forcible destruction of his liaison in 1541. Through an incredible stroke of bad luck, Wyatt was constrained for a second time by political circumstances and the will of the king to give up the woman he loved, and the effect on him was soul-destroying.

Sex and politics seemed doomed to be entangled in Wyatt's life, for his affair with Elizabeth Darrell brought him, directly and indirectly, into a second political crisis even more dangerous than the first. The foundations for this crisis were laid on his embassy to Spain in 1537–8. As poems written during this period suggest, Wyatt was highly distracted by the unresolved nature of his love affair, and his distraction made him negligent. Cromwell wrote to him in June 1537 complaining that 'ye have ben hitherto somwhat slak and negligent to write vnto me', and in October he advised Wyatt: 'It is moche mervailed that you haue not yet delyuered my Lady Maries grace letteres.'[51] In April 1538, Cromwell again upbraided Wyatt for his carelessness, and warned him of the king's growing displeasure at his performance.[52] Consequently, in April 1538, Edmund Bonner and Simon Heynes were sent to assist Wyatt and expedite matters. They were to be the architects of his downfall.

Bonner was dissatisfied with the behaviour he witnessed in Wyatt, probably for the most part out of his wounded *amour propre* at not being consulted over actions taken by his colleague, and in September 1538 he sent a long letter to Cromwell denouncing Wyatt on a number of grounds: he had been slack in the king's cause with the Emperor, he had conducted secret meetings with Granvelle, the Emperor's chancellor, he was over familiar with one Mason, a notorious papist, and consorted with 'nunnes' and lived a life of dissoluteness.[53] Most damaging of all, in a further letter of 15 October 1538, Bonner reported that Wyatt had instructed Mason to get in touch with Reginald Pole, the English traitor who had a claim to the throne through his descent from the Plantagenet line.[54] For the time being Wyatt was safe, because Cromwell, having remon-

[51] Roger Bigelow Merriman, *Life and Letters of Thomas Cromwell*, 2 vols (London, 1902), II, no. 189, p. 58; no. 222, p. 92.
[52] Ibid., no. 250, p. 133; cf. no. 257 (4 March 1538), p. 137.
[53] Muir, *Life and Letters*, pp. 64–9.
[54] Ibid., p. 70; *LP*, XIII (ii), no. 615.

strated with him about the charges, suppressed the evidence. When Cromwell was attainted of treason and executed in July 1540, however, the original charges were discovered in his papers, which had been seized.

The discovery of Bonner's letter put Wyatt, retrospectively, in a very bad light once again, because of actions into which his passion for Elizabeth Darrell had led him. In December 1538, two other Plantagenet pretenders, Henry Courtenay, Marquis of Exeter, and Henry Pole, Lord Montague (Reginald Pole's elder brother), had been beheaded for treasonous conspiracy against the crown. Elizabeth Darrell was a member of the Marchioness of Exeter's household, and on his brief return to England in June 1538, for reasons that have been explained, Wyatt visited her.[55] The timing could not have been worse. Together with Bonner's allegation of September 1538 that Wyatt had instructed Mason to contact Reginald Pole, this visit made it look as if Wyatt had been deeply implicated in the Exeter conspiracy. Accordingly, Wyatt was arrested at Hampton Court in January 1541 and taken, as Marillac, the French ambassador reported, 'so bound and handcuffed that everyone could only suppose ill . . . since he has earned the malevolence of all those who leagued against Cromwell.'[56] The charge of treason thus exposed Wyatt to the enmity of three powerful parties: the king, determined to eliminate all threats to the Tudor succession; Cromwell's enemies, seeking to purge the court of all those who had been in league with him; and the relatives of Wyatt's estranged wife, who, Marillac reports, were seeking to exact revenge for his treatment of Elizabeth Brooke. For Wyatt, the situation was very dangerous indeed.

Wyatt recorded his growing distress at this turn of events, once again, in a string of poems. He adapted yet another sonnet by Petrarch to express indirectly his grief at the death of Cromwell (he had been made to witness his beheading on the scaffold), and eloquently attested to the support he had received from his mentor:

> The piller pearisht is whearto I Lent
>   The strongest staye of myne vnquyet mynde;
>   The lyke of it no man agayne can fynde
>   From East to west still seking though he went.[57]

At some time before his imprisonment, he reflected upon the desertion of his friends once they realized that he had become *persona non grata*:

> Luckes, my faire falcon, and your fellowes all,
>   How well pleasaunt yt were your libertie!
>   Ye not forsake me that faire might ye befall.

[55] See Muir, *Life and Letters*, p. 85; *LP*, XIII (ii), no. 702.
[56] Muir, *Life and Letters*, p. 176.
[57] Wyatt, *Collected Poems*, no. 236, ll. 1–4.

> But they that somtyme lykt my companye
> Like lyse awaye from ded bodies thei crall:
> Loe what a profe in light adversytie!
> But ye my birdes, I swear by all your belles,
> Ye be my fryndes, and so be but few elles.[58]

And in one of the most melancholy poems he wrote, Wyatt expressed the oppressive effects on him of his imprisonment, and the way that he felt it eroding his soul:

> Syghes ar my foode, drynke are my teares;
> Clynkinge of fetters suche musycke wolde crave;
> Stynke and close ayer away my lyf wears;
> Innocencie is all the hope I have.
> Rayne, wynde, or wether I iudge by myne eares.
> Mallice assaulted that rightiousnes should have.
> Sure I am, Brian, this wounde shall heale agayne,
> But yet, alas, the scarre shall styll remayne.[59]

Wyatt's worst tribulation was still to come, however, and in order to understand fully the final masterpiece he wrote in response to it, we must examine what brought it about.

Wyatt knew that he was innocent of treason, and when he was ordered by the Privy Council to make a written statement in answer to the charges, he did so, asserting his innocence.[60] To reinforce this, Wyatt also prepared a long, detailed defence to be delivered before his judges after his indictment and the presentation of the evidence. The text of his defence survives, and it shows Wyatt to have been indignant and scathing in his customary manner.[61] It also betrays Wyatt's fear that his judges would be too intimidated by Henry VIII's wrath to acquit him, even if they were persuaded of his innocence:

> The confidens put in my affares is for you to acquyte me. And yt is an nawghtie fere yf any man have any suche, to thynke a queste dare not acquyte a man of treason when theie thynke hym clere; for yt were a fowle sclaundere to the kynges maieste. God be thanked, he is no tyrant. He woll no suche thynges agaynst mens consciens. He will but his lawes and his lawes with mercie. What dyspleasure bare he to the lordes for the acquy-

---

[58] Ibid., no. 241.

[59] Ibid., no. 244. The echo of the final line of this poem in Wyatt's 1541 defence (see Muir, *Life and Letters*, p. 193) confirms that this poem dates to his later imprisonment rather than his earlier one of 1536.

[60] Muir, *Life and Letters*, pp. 178–84.

[61] The defence is reprinted in Muir, *Life and Letters*, pp. 187–209.

tinge of the Lorde Dacres: neuer none, nor woll not vnto you yf you do as your consciens leades you.[62]

It is pitiful to see Wyatt here struggling to deny what his intuition tells him is the case, trying to fortify his judges against condemning him out of fear – yet knowing they would not dare to acquit him against the king's wishes.

In spite of the fire and bravado of his defence, in the event Wyatt crumbled. The Spanish ambassador records that on 19 March 1541, Queen Catherine (Howard) entreated Henry to release Wyatt. After lengthy supplications the king agreed, but only on two harsh conditions: first, that Wyatt should confess his guilt, and second, that he should resume conjugal relations with his estranged wife and forbear the adulterous relationships he had led with other women – under pain of death and the confiscation of his property.[63] Nothing could have been more astutely calculated to break Wyatt's spirit, and a letter of the Privy Council to Lord William Howard reports Wyatt's abject submission to the king's will:

> Nowe to Wyat; he confessed uppon his examymnation all the thinges objected unto him, in a like lamentable and pitifull sorte as Wallop did . . . delyvering his submission in writing, declaring thole history of his offences, but with a like protestation, that the same proceeded from him in his rage and folishe vaynglorios fantazie, without the spott of malice; yelding himself only to His Majesties marcy, without the whiche he sawe he might and must nedes be justcly condempned.[64]

Some scholars have doubted that Wyatt did suppress his original defence and submit in the way described here, but one poem that I believe Wyatt wrote at this time reveals that he knew precisely what his options were:

> Lyke as the byrde in the cage enclosed,
> The dore vnsparred and the hawke without,
> Twixte deth and prison piteously oppressed
> Whether for to chose standith in dowt.
> Certes so do I, wyche do syeke to bring about
> Wyche shuld be best by determination,
> By losse off liefe libertye or liefe by preson.[65]

Wyatt knew that to maintain his integrity by protesting his innocence would provoke Henry (the 'hawke') to kill him; yet he also knew that to submit,

[62] Ibid., p. 208.

[63] Ibid., p. 209; Cal. SP Spanish, VI, 1, no. 155.

[64] State Papers Published under the Authority of His Majesty's Commission, 9 vols (London, 1830–49), VIII, p. 546; Muir, Life and Letters, p. 210.

[65] Wyatt, Collected Poems, no. 246, ll. 1–8.

although it might save his life, would imprison him for the rest of his life in a state of self-disgust. In the remainder of this poem he toys with the solution to this dilemma that Thomas More chose: to die rather than compromise his conscience:

> Oh myscheffe by myschieffe to be redressed,
> Wher payne is the best their lieth litell pleasure,
> By schort deth out off daunger yet to be delyuered
> Rather then with paynfull lieffe thraldome and doloure,
> Ffor small plesure moche payne to suffer
> Soner therfore to chuse me thincketh it wysdome
> By losse off life lybertye then liefe by preson.[66]

This is not a love affair Wyatt is talking about – it is his very spiritual survival – but Wyatt was not made of More's stuff, and the solution he proposes here was a remedy desired, rather than one he could bring himself to accept. Wyatt capitulated and saved his neck, but in so doing he lost the last vestiges of his self-respect.

It is absolutely essential to understand this context before one can grasp the essential motive and function for Wyatt of his last great work, his translation of the *Penitential Psalms*. Hitherto, even though they have received many fine critical expositions,[67] half their meaning has lain concealed because of the erroneous assumption that they were written in 1536, to hold a mirror up to Henry VIII in which he could view his lust for Anne Boleyn and the need to repent of it. In fact, they were composed to assist Wyatt in accepting the injunctions to which, broken, he was forced to submit.

Both the date and the function of the *Penitential Psalms* are suggested by the additions and expansions Wyatt made to the main sources he was adapting, specifically Pietro Aretino's *I setti salmi*, which had appeared in 1534, and the Latin text of the Vulgate bible. As Wyatt insisted in his suppressed 1541 defence, he imputed his imprisonment in 1536 to the Duke of Suffolk, and to him alone.[68] Throughout the *Penitential Psalms*, he refers to his enemies as a *group* who are determined to destroy him:

> Thus drye I vpp among my foes in woe,
> That with my fall do rise and grow with all.[69]

---

[66] Ibid., ll. 8–14.
[67] See Mason, *Humanism and Poetry in the Early Tudor Period*, (London, 1959), pp. 206ff; Greenblatt, *Renaissance Self-fashioning*, pp. 115–27.
[68] Muir, *Life and Letters*, p. 201.
[69] Wyatt, *Collected Poems*, Psalm 6, p. 103, ll. 152–3.

> This while my foes conspird continually,
> And did provoke the harme off my dises.[70]

> Rydd me, o lord, from that that do entend
> My foos to me . . .[71]

None of these lines occurs in either the Vulgate or Aretino, and the sentiment in them does not apply to 1536, when Wyatt believed that Suffolk alone had caused him to be imprisoned. They do, however, apply to the unholy alliance of Bonner and Heynes, Wyatt's wife's relations, and the anti-Cromwell faction at court who were conspiring in 1541 to procure his downfall.

Another major reason for assigning the *Penitential Psalms* to 1541 rather than 1536 is their repeated emphasis on the sexual pleasure to which David/Wyatt had become habituated, and must now forgo. In Psalm 6 Wyatt adds the following lines that do not appear in the sources:

> By nightlye playntes in stede of pleasures olde
> I wasshe my bed with teares contynuall,
> To dull my sight that it be never bolde
> To stirr mye hart agayne to suche a fall.[72]

Other passages similarly express his wish to be 'voydyd from fylthye lust', and confess the difficulty he is experiencing in this, because of 'secrete lust' which has 'ranklyd vnder skyn, / Not duly Curyd by my penitens.'[73] These and other such passages are unlikely to refer to 1536, for there is no sound evidence that Wyatt ever had sexual intercourse with Anne Boleyn, and he certainly had had no physical intimacy with her after she had attracted the attentions of the king.[74] There was no reason, therefore, for Wyatt to lay such emphasis on sexual intimacy as a habit from which he is trying to detach himself with reference to Anne Boleyn. Far less did he dare in 1536 to write anything that could be remotely construed as a mirror for Henry VIII, in which he was supposed to see the error of his lustful ways. This sexual emphasis does bear closely, however, on Wyatt's obligation to forego intimacy with Elizabeth Darrell.

---

[70] Ibid., Psalm 102, p. 117, ll. 567–8.
[71] Ibid., Psalm 143, p. 124, ll. 762–3.
[72] Ibid., Psalm 6, p. 103, ll. 148–51.
[73] Ibid., Psalm 51, p. 114, l. 480; Psalm 38, p. 110, ll. 347–8.
[74] Wyatt's grandson effectively exposed reports that Wyatt had admitted to the Council his carnal knowledge of Anne Boleyn before her marriage as the malicious fabrications of Catholic propagandists (see 'A Defence of Sir Thomas Wyatt the Elder . . . against the Accusations of Nicholas Sanders', in *The Papers of George Wyatt Esquire of Boxley Abbey in the County of Kent, Son and Heir of Sir Thomas Wyatt the Younger*, ed. D. M. Loades, Camden Series, vol. 5 (London, 1968), pp. 183–4). See also E. W. Ives, *Anne Boleyn* (Oxford, 1986), pp. 89–99.

In many other instances one can see Wyatt expanding and rephrasing his source, so as to make it reflect his situation in 1541. For example, he observes that

> . . . when myn enmys did me most assayle,
> My frendes most sure, wherein I sett most trust,
> Myn own vertus, sonest then did ffaile.[75]

At the figurative level, these lines refer to the failure of his own rational faculties to control the desire of his senses, but the phrasing also recalls the desertion of his former friends of which he complained in 'Luckes, my faire falcon', suggesting that the lines express a complex conflation of related associations, and are to be read on two levels of reference. Likewise, Wyatt freely expands the Vulgate to make it refer to the suppression of his 1541 defence. When his enemies 'sowght my deth by nowghty word and dede', he declares,

> . . . I like deffh and domme forth my way yede,
> Lyke one that heris not, nor hath to replye
> One worde agayne, knowyng that from thi hand
> Thes thinges procede . . . o lord . . .[76]

Again, these lines work on two levels. At a moral level, they express Wyatt's acceptance of tribulation as part of God's providence; at a political level, they express his awareness that the measures against him proceed from the king, and that he dare not say a word in his defence because of it. There is nothing in Aretino or the Vulgate's Latin to suggest this slant:

> Et factus sum sicut homo non audiens: et non habens in ore suo redargutiones. Quoniam in te Domine speraui: tu exaudies me Domine Deus meus. [Thus I was as a man that heareth not, and in whose mouth are no reproofs. For in thee, O Lord, do I hope: thou wilt hear, O Lord my God][77]

The tone in these alterations is very different from the defiant self-assertiveness of the satires written after Wyatt's 1536 crisis, and generally their matter fits his situation in 1541 far better than 1536.

One final piece of evidence clinches 1541 as the date of the *Penitential Psalms*: the unmistakable Lutheran bias they display. It has been persuasively argued that Wyatt's version of Psalm 51 shows the influence of Luther's argument concerning justification in his *Enarratio Psalmi LI*.[78] A comment in Wyatt's 1541 defence

---

[75] Wyatt, *Collected Poems*, Psalm 38, p. 110, ll. 364–6.
[76] Ibid., p. 111, ll. 370–5.
[77] Vulgate, Psalm 37; Authorized Version, Psalm 38: 14–15.
[78] See Mason, *Sir Thomas Wyatt: A Literary Portrait*, pp. 160–3; also 211–14.

confirms that by this time he was suspected as a Lutheran sympathizer. Dismissing the idea that he is a papist, Wyatt declares: 'I thynke I shulde have more adoe with a great sorte in Inglande to purge my selffe of suspecte of a Lutherane then of a Papyst.'[79] Given that Luther's exposition did not appear until 1538, together with the fact that there is not the slightest trace of any Lutheran influence in Wyatt's work before this date, the Lutheran doctrine of the *Penitential Psalms* reinforces the other evidence that they were written in 1541.

In the context of these later circumstances, the function of the *Penitential Psalms* emerges in an entirely new light. For centuries the seven Psalms had provided a pattern which could serve to stimulate and guide the penitence of Christian believers, but in Aretino's contextualization of them, Wyatt found far more than that. Aretino's rather lubricious prologues had turned the psalms into dramatized utterances in a novelistic narrative in which David repents of his love for Bathsheba, she 'whom more then god or hymsellff he myndyth'.[80] They trace the psychological process whereby David, having had his adultery denounced to him, tries to free himself from the 'creping fyre' of lust that had caused him to forget wisdom and God's majesty, in order to replace it 'with farr more hote affect / Of god'.[81] Wyatt thus found in Aretino's paraphrase a perfect displaced correlative for his own situation and the action required of him. In the experience of David, he saw an image of what, for the sake of attaining peace of mind, he should strive for were he to be able to give up Elizabeth Darrell. Moreover, David's withdrawal

> ... into a dark Cave
> Within the grownd wherin he myght hym hyde,
> Fleing the lyght, as in pryson or grave,[82]

must have struck him as remarkably evocative of his own incarceration in the filth and obscurity of the Tower, just as David's emotional turmoil mirrored his own.

In the light of this connection between the work and Wyatt's own circumstances, one can see that the *Penitential Psalms* had several important functions for him. At the deepest and most personal level, they were an instrument to help him conform his will to what he had, under pain of death, been ordered to do. Wyatt sums up this function when he shows David begging God to fortify him: 'My will conferme with spryte off stedfastnesse.'[83] Further on, another striking addition again stresses this purpose when he entreats God to observe in him 'my

---

[79] Muir, *Life and Letters*, pp. 195–6.
[80] Wyatt, *Collected Poems*, Prologue to Psalm 6, p. 99, l. 26.
[81] Ibid., Prologue to Psalm 38, p. 109, ll. 317–18.
[82] Ibid., p. 100, ll. 60–2.
[83] Ibid., p. 115, l. 484.

will to ryse'.[84] Manifestly, Wyatt was having to struggle with himself because of 'gruging off the worme within / That neuer dyth':[85] the only way he could bring himself to give up his mistress was to persuade himself that God, morality, and his own conscience required him to do it as much as the king, but this he found very hard to accept with total conviction. Part of the purpose of the *Penitential Psalms* was to help make him believe it.

An equally powerful function of the work, one suspects, was to purge Wyatt of the guilt he felt over his own surrender of integrity. The Psalms enabled him to transfer this guilt onto the fact of his adultery, but the weight of emotion in his phrasing recurrently evokes the other cause:

> ... my enmy hath pursuyd my lyff,
> And in the dust hath foyld my lustynes;
> Ffor that in heins to fle his rage so ryff,
> He hath me forst as ded to hyd my hed;
> And for by cawse within my sellff at stryffe
> My hert and spryte with all my force were fled.[86]

Thus, there were deeper feelings motivating Wyatt's plea for divine forgiveness than those arising from an adultery he felt reluctant to renounce. This underlying perturbation obtrudes in the hypnotic alliterating repetitions of his powerful rendering of Psalm 130:

> Ffrom depth off sinn and from a diepe dispaire,
> Ffrom depth off deth, from depth off hertes sorow,
> From this diepe Cave off darknes diepe repayre,
> The have I cald o lord to be my borow.[87]

Wyatt had lost his spiritual identity, and was desperately trying to recover it.

If one traces the pattern of Wyatt's life, one sees in it a perpetual search for some kind of emotional stability capable of withstanding the repeated shocks that eroded his confidence. The final, and perhaps the most important, function of the *Penitential Psalms*, was to procure for Wyatt a replacement for the stability he had briefly enjoyed in his relationship with Elizabeth Darrell. Wyatt's emotional and political tribulations had kept him on the run, spiritually. A lover's betrayal had shattered his youthful ego, and political intimidation had destroyed his self respect. After his first crisis he had retreated literally into the country, and metaphorically into Stoicism. His affair with Elizabeth Darrell had given him a brief respite, but that too had now been destroyed. He had nowhere else to retreat to, except the transcendental sanctuary of religious faith.

[84] Ibid., p. 121, l. 670.
[85] Ibid., p. 110, l. 351–2. This is another of Wyatt's own additions to the source.
[86] Ibid., pp. 123–4, ll. 740–5.
[87] Ibid., p. 121, ll. 664–7.

Psychologically, by projecting himself through the Psalms and Aretino's para-phrase, Wyatt was intuitively seeking the only stable identity that now remained for him. To make himself submit to the king's will, he used the Psalms to persuade himself that it was also God's will, and by adopting Luther's conception of justification through faith alone, Wyatt was able to transform his abject submission to the king into a complete submission to God. In this way, the stigma of the former could be cancelled out in the merit of the latter. Wyatt's *Penitential Psalms* had not been written primarily for others, but were his final, desperate bid to attain the quiet of mind that had always eluded him.

It is impossible to tell whether Wyatt found the peace he sought. Having 'confessed' and thrown himself upon the king's mercy, he was quickly restored to favour and was soon performing as a royal servant once more. One suspects, however, that Wyatt's heart and spirit were broken, and his concern to set his house in order by making his will on 12 June 1541 (in which he made provision for Elizabeth Darrell and her son) suggests that he probably neither desired nor expected to live much longer. He died, just over a year later, in September 1542, to the grief of many. In him, Henrician England had lost the poet who, more powerfully than any other, could reveal the shocks and heartaches to which his countrymen had become heirs.

15

Memento mori: The Biblical Paraphrases of the Earl of Surrey

Wyatt's younger contemporary, Henry Howard, Earl of Surrey, was altogether less complicated a personality, and, in spite of his genuine lyric gift, ultimately a far less considerable poet. Nevertheless, the final group of poems he wrote – his paraphrases of a number of chapters from Ecclesiastes, and three of the Psalms – provide a fitting postscript for this book. Both the circumstances that led Surrey to write them and also the intrinsic nature of the paraphrases themselves help to explain why the fictive impulse was practically arrested during these years, and why, when it re-emerged in the reign of Henry VIII's daughter, Elizabeth I, it had been fundamentally transformed. Originating in rivalry between opposing factions, each of which sought to control the course of reform by influencing the succession, Surrey's paraphrases show the breakdown of the old codes by which early Tudor society had been accustomed to conduct itself. Largely through his own fault, Surrey was the victim of converging political forces that were to smother the ability of writers to depict experience symbolically in the old ways. It has been claimed that Henry VIII killed the poets during the final years of his reign;[1] it is truer to say that the conditions he needed to ensure the survival of England in its new incarnation necessarily destroyed the fictions by which the poets had previously sustained their imaginative response to life. Surrey's tragic fate and the poetry that accompanied it are therefore symbolic: they manifest in an extreme form the cost exacted from contemporaries by the new order that was coming into being, and they record the passing of the old. And because the forces that brought Surrey to the block were also those that irreversibly transformed the old order, his death-song serves as a fitting elegy for the early Tudor era as a whole.

In retrospect, Surrey seems to have been doomed from the outset, imprisoned as he was in a world constructed of outworn fantasies from the past. Significantly, his best poetry is almost all memorial, whether he is remembering his own happy

---

[1] See R. W. Chambers, *Thomas More* (London, 1935), p. 379.

youth, the Tuscan ancestry of his lady's 'worthi race', the virtues of Wyatt, his dead preceptor, or the deeds of Aeneas and his Trojan followers as he found them in Virgil's *Aeneid*, two books of which he translated.[2] Even when he is recalling his own recent past, he does so in terms that evoke the vanished world of medieval chivalry and romance:

> The graveld ground, with sleves tyed on the helme,
> On fomynge horse, with swordes and frendlye hertes,
> With chere as thoughe the one should overwhelme,
> Where we have fought and chased oft with dartes.[3]

Characteristically, when he was arrested and faced with the charge of treason that was to end his life, Surrey offered to fight his accuser in single combat – a brave flourish, but one that betrayed a naive lack of comprehension as to the brutal realities of his predicament.

Surrey was temperamentally inclined to inhabit this anachronistic world because of his overweening pride of blood. Quite simply, Surrey was too well connected for his own good. Not only was he the son of the Duke of Norfolk, one of England's two great warlords, but through his ancestors he also claimed descent from Edward III, and his mother was Elizabeth Stafford, daughter of the Duke of Buckingham, who until his execution in 1521 had been the foremost nobleman in the land.[4] The natural superiority Surrey felt from his birth was reinforced by a privileged upbringing, the young man being raised as the companion and confidant of Henry Fitzroy, Duke of Richmond, the king's bastard son.[5] Surrey's aristocratic pride left him with the feeling that he was above the law and immune from its penalties, as a constitutional rashness and arrogance of action proved. More seriously, he believed that he could put back the clock to the time before the Tudors when the great nobles had ruled with a fairly free hand. None of this might have proved fatal to him had not the revolution achieved under Henry VIII led to the promotion of a new breed of men at court – men of relatively humble origins, such as Cromwell, Paget, and the Seymours, who acquired rank through their services, rather than vice versa. By the mid 1540s the court had become sharply divided between a reactionary faction led by the Howards, and a more radical one led by the Seymours.

---

[2] For the poems referred to, see, respectively, *Henry Howard, Earl of Surrey: Poems*, ed. Emrys Jones (Oxford, 1964), nos 26, 27, 9, 28, 41, and 42. All references to Surrey's poetry are taken from this edition except for those to several poems not printed by Jones. Hereafter cited as *Howard Poems*, ed. Jones.

[3] Ibid., no., 27, ll. 17–20.

[4] For the facts of Surrey's life, see Edwin Casady, *Henry Howard, Earl of Surrey*, Modern Languages Association Revolving Fund Series, no. 8 (New York, 1938); and Hester W. Chapman, *Two Tudor Portraits: Henry Howard, Earl of Surrey and Lady Katherine Grey* (London, 1960).

[5] Surrey recalls the happiness of these years in several of his finest lyric poems; see, in particular, 'So crewell prison howe could betyde, alas', *Howard Poems*, ed. Jones, no. 27.

Having risen to prominence through the marriage of Jane Seymour to Henry VIII after the execution of Anne Boleyn, the Seymours seemed assured of extending their power into the next reign when Edward, the king's son and heir, was born in October 1537. Given his pride and personal ambitions, Surrey could not stomach the presence of these rivals, especially as the Howard bid for hegemony had been dashed to pieces by the adultery of Queen Catherine (Howard) and her execution. Even before this catastrophe, Surrey had developed an almost pathological hatred for his rival at court, Edward Seymour, Earl of Hertford and brother to the late Queen Jane, and his younger brother, Sir Thomas Seymour, whom he had prevented his sister Mary from marrying, to her lasting bitterness.[6]

Surrey's downfall came in 1546 when ambition, pride, and his hatred of the new upstarts provoked him to contemplate a plot that is stunning in its stupidity. By late 1546 it had become obvious that Henry VIII's health was failing, and that the king would not live much longer. Surrey was so indiscreet as to reveal to a friend, Sir George Blage, his determination that his father, Norfolk, and not the Seymours or anyone else, should preside over any regency to guide the young Edward VI in the event of the king's death. Not content with that idea, he also hatched a scheme, according to another friend, Richard Southwell, whereby Hertford and his followers would be swiftly attainted of treason and executed, thus clearing the way for a Howard hegemony.[7] As if to tempt fate, Surrey went so far as to threaten Thomas Seymour with the revenge he plotted, in a letter that was duly presented as evidence against him.[8]

What probably sealed Surrey's fate was the charge of usurping the arms of St Edward the Confessor. As early as the spring of 1544, Surrey had designed for himself a new coat of arms that combined the quarterings of the Earls of Mowbray and Brotherton, of Edward the Confessor, and of the Dukes of Anjou.[9] Richard II had indeed granted Surrey's ancestors the right to bear the arms of Edward the Confessor, but Surrey chose to ignore the fact that since the death of the last Plantagenet king, Richard III, the bearing of the arms had been the sole prerogative of the heir to the throne. Although technically guilty of no fault other than insulting the crown, Surrey was almost certainly guilty of the most heinous form of treason he could have contemplated: that of aspiring to usurp the throne. His accusers produced plenty of evidence to support this suspicion, and

---

[6] Surrey's animus is displayed in the churlish poem 'Eache beeste can chuse his feere', occasioned by the refusal of Lady Hertford to dance with him (see *The Poems of Henry Howard Earl of Surrey*, ed. Frederick Morgan Padelford (Seattle, 1928), no. 34, pp. 88–90).

[7] Van der Delft reported to Charles V on 24 December 1546 that two gentlemen (presumably Southwell and Blage), had come forward and charged Surrey and Norfolk with conspiring to kill all the Council and take complete control over the prince (see *LP*, XXII, ii, no. 605; also no. 568).

[8] See Chapman, pp. 118–20.

[9] Ibid., p. 84.

Surrey's own verses written after his arrest confirm it. The alterations made to his new escutcheon are transparent in their implications. Not only did he incorporate the arms of Edward the Confessor in the fifth quarter, but he also transferred the three Brotherton points, or 'labels' of silver, from the Brotherton quartering to that of Edward the Confessor, thus implying that his Brotherton ancestors were directly descended from Edward, and that he was directly in the line of succession.[10] Typically, Surrey had this new escutcheon blazoned on the windows and the silver of the new palace he was building for himself at Mount Surrey, in Norfolk.

His folly extended still further. In 1546 he commissioned a painting of himself dressed in a doublet and hose of the purple silk and gold tissue reserved for members of the royal family, and had the painter include two mottoes in the portrait. The first, still visible on the base of the column against which Surrey is leaning, reads 'Sat Superest' ('It is enough to prevail'). The other, originally inscribed on his Garter, read 'Tel Dandus' (which Surrey himself translated as 'Till then, thus').[11] Understandably horrified when he saw this, Norfolk ordered Surrey to have both mottoes removed, but although Surrey complied with regard to the second, more incriminating one, he could not bring himself to expunge the other, 'Sat Superest', by which he nurtured his hopes of avenging himself on the Seymours.

It is difficult to see, given the fraught circumstances of late 1546, how Surrey's actions could have been construed as signifying anything other than the treasonous intent imputed to him by those who denounced him: his erstwhile friends Southwell and Blage, and his own sister Mary, whom he had irrevocably alienated by preventing the marriage to Thomas Seymour both she and Norfolk desired. Henry VIII's own annotations on the text of Surrey's indictment show how astutely he registered the real implications of Surrey's behaviour. The words printed in capitals below were interlined by the dying king in a tremulous hand. Surrey's examiners are to consider

If a man cummyng OF THE COLATERALL LYNE TO THE HEYRE OFF the Crown, who ought not to beare thArmes of England BUT ON the seconde quarter, with the difference of THEYRE auncestre, doo PRESUME to chaunge his right place, and beare them in the first quarter, leaving out the true difference of thauncestre, and, in the lieu therof, use THE VERY PLASE only of the Heire Masle Apparant; HOW THYS MANS INTENT IS TO BE JUGGYD; AND WHETHER THYS importe any daunger, peril, or slaundre to the title of the Prince, or very Heire apparant.[12]

[10] Ibid., p. 116.
[11] Ibid., pp. 85, 116–17.
[12] See *State Papers Published Under the Authority of His Majesty's Commission*, I, Part 2, p. 891.

The series of questions that were to be put to Surrey at his interrogation also clearly imply the suspicion in the king's mind. Among these questions are the following:

(4) Whether you are next heir or akin to St Edward, and if so, how?

(6) Whether William the Conqueror did your said ancestor that at the time of the Conquest was then alive any wrong by his Conquest, or no?

(7) To what intent you put the arms of St Edward in your coat?

(8) Why you bear them at this time more than you or your father at other times before?[13]

Henry was seriously worried that Surrey aimed to usurp not merely control of the prince in the event of his death, but the succession itself. From the moment he conceived this suspicion, in spite of the fact that Surrey had earlier been one of his personal favourites, the earl was as good as dead. For the sake of his dynasty, Henry was compelled to kill him.

Surrey was arrested on 1 December 1546. After being examined before the Council, he was given five weeks to prepare for his trial, which was set for 13 January. We can suppose that he wrote his verse paraphrases on the five chapters of Ecclesiastes, and also the first two of his three translations from the Psalms, during his imprisonment while awaiting trial.

Although he knew that his plight was extremely serious, Surrey did not expect to die – that much is clear from the hysterical outburst, after he had been condemned, in his adaptation of Psalm 55. Surrey refers to

> . . . those false wolves, with cootes which doo their ravin hyde,
> That sweare to me by heaven, the fotestole of the Lord,
> Who though force had hurt my fame, they did not touche my lyfe.[14]

Surrey had been in serious scrapes before: once when he was condemned to have his right hand amputated for striking Hertford within the precincts of Hampton Court Palace in June 1537; again when, three years later, he challenged another courtier, John à Leigh to a duel within the precincts of the court; and for a third time, in January 1543, when he led a band of rowdies through the streets of London, breaking the windows of the city merchants and neighbouring churches with stones fired from catapults.[15] Always, the king had exercised special

[13] *LP*, XXI, ii, no. 555 (8).
[14] *Howard Poems*, ed. Jones, no. 50, ll. 43–5.
[15] See 'London, hast thow accused me', *Howard Poems*, ed. Jones, no. 33, and Jones's note, p. 127.

forebearance towards the bosom friend of Fitzroy, his son. One suspects that Surrey, unconscionably immature even at the age of 29, still expected that to happen in his latest predicament.

His paraphrases of Ecclesiastes are therefore written as a kind of emotional contingency. Somewhere in Surrey's mind there dawned a dim realization that things might be different this time – that he needed to be prepared for the worst. Having been deeply influenced by Wyatt, and having before him the *Penitential Psalms* Wyatt had written in response to a similarly threatening situation, Surrey went through the mental exercise of preparing himself for death.

Surrey's attempts to comport his mind sprang, once again, from his sense of what *noblesse* obliged him to do. He knew the commonplaces that his religion taught him should be applied in such circumstances, and found a perfect expression of them, as Wyatt had done, in the Latin paraphrases of the Psalms and Ecclesiastes by Joannes Campensis.[16] His translation of these paraphrases exposes a mind in the process of trying to order itself according to beliefs towards which it does not naturally incline. Surrey's real tragedy was that, at the end, he could not make himself believe in his protective fiction. As with the code of courtly chivalry, he found that the gap between the imaginative constructions of his religious code and his experience of immediate realities had become too great to be bridged.

The paraphrases of the first five chapters of Ecclesiastes seem to have been composed earlier than the three Psalms. Surrey had over a month to prepare himself for his trial, and the adaptation of Campensis's *Paraphrasis* was a natural way of occupying the time. His purpose was similar to that of Wyatt: to purge himself spiritually by confessing and repenting of past faults, accepting the vanity of human wishes, and striving for a pious contempt for the world that could make him content to leave it. The effect he aimed at is summed up in the opening lines of *Ecclesiastes 5*:

> When that repentant teares hathe clensyd clere from ill
> The charged brest, and grace hathe wrought therin amending will,
>   With bold demands then may his mercy well assaile
> The speche man sayth, with owt the which request may not preuaile.[17]

Surrey was treating God as he had treated Henry VIII during his past crises: as someone who would let him off if he only showed that he was sufficiently sorry for what he had done. It had always worked in the past. When, for example, Surrey was imprisoned in 1542 for challenging John à Leigh to a duel in the court precincts, he sent a long letter of apology to the Privy Council acknowledging his

---

[16] Joannes Campensis, *Psalmorum omnium iuxta Hebraicam veritatem paraphrastica interpretatio. . . . Paraphrasis in concionem Salomonis Ecclesiastae* (1532).
[17] *Howard Poems*, ed. Padelford, no. 52, ll. 1–4.

fault, and putting it down to 'the fury of reckless youth', promising to make up for his misdemeanours if the king would pardon him.[18] In the paraphrases of Ecclesiastes and the first two of the three Psalms he is, metaphorically speaking, trying to do exactly the same thing by working himself into a state of penitence in the hope that God will remit the capital punishment he knows he could face.

Surrey's intention to turn his sources into an instrument of penitent confession is revealed by the changes he makes to the Vulgate original and Campensis's Latin paraphrase of it. In *Ecclesiastes* 2, especially, he confesses his princely aspirations with remarkable candour. For the Vulgate's 'Magnificaui opera mea. Edificaui mihi domos et plantaui vineas' ('I made me great works; I builded me houses; I planted me vineyards'), Surrey substitutes the following:

> To buylde my howses faier then sett I all my cure:
> By princely acts thus strave I still to make my fame indure.[19]

Nothing corresponds to this in either the Vulgate or Campensis, which underlines how Surrey is using his source as a way of admitting the pretensions that lay behind the building of his opulent palace at Mount Surrey.

Time and again, Surrey's phrasing betrays the desire to appear as a prince, which tempts one to credit the charge levelled against him, that he was aiming to usurp the succession. For Ecclesiastes 2:12 Campensis had written:

> Deprehendi in vino insaniam multam, & in reliquis manifestam stultitiam: Quid enim est homo, ut imitatione regis Dei, aliquid magni conetur . . .?

> [Wine filled me with much madness, and led me to commit manifest folly; for what is man that he strives to equal the works of God, the almighty king?]

In Surrey's version this becomes:

> What fancis in my hed had wrought the licor of the grape.
> The erroure then I sawe that their fraile harts dothe move,
> Which strive in vaine for to compare with him that sitts above.[20]

Surrey's substitution of 'fancies' for Campensis's 'insaniam', and 'error' for 'stultitiam' somewhat changes the sense, and implies that he entertained fantasies of a specific worldly ambition, not just a generalized spiritual ambition. The last line of this passage also gives him away. Surrey no longer retains Campensis's explicit identification of the Vulgate's 'regem' with God, but allows for the line to

---

[18] See Chapman, p. 75.
[19] *Howard Poems*, ed. Jones, no. 44, ll. 11–12; Ecclesiastes 2: 4.
[20] Ibid., ll. 38–40.

refer ambiguously to the king in an earthly sense. Again, whether consciously or unconsciously, Surrey is revealing the real goal of his ambitions.

Further instances of self-revelation occur in *Ecclesiastes 3* and *Ecclesiastes 4*. Whereas Campensis changed the Vulgate's 'tempus plantandi et tempus evellendi quod plantatum est' ('a time to plant and a time to pluck up that which is planted') in Ecclesiastes 3:2 to 'quae nunc plantantur, alio tempore evellentur' ('that which is planted now will be plucked up at another time'), Surrey altered it to read:

> The grafted plants with payn, wherof wee hoped frute,
> To roote them upp, with blossomes sprede, then is our chief porsute.[21]

The change of tense from the present to the past implies an actual outcome for which Surrey hoped, while the more specific image of '*grafted* plants' may reflect his consciousness of having tried to graft himself into the succession. An astonishing expansion of the Vulgate's 'tempus tacendi; et tempus loquendi' ('a time to keep silence, and a time to speak') in Ecclesiastes 3:7 even alludes to the actual encounter during which Surrey revealed his ambition to Richard Southwell:

> In sober sylence now our quiet lipps we closse,
> And with unbrydled toungs furth with our secret herts disclosse.[22]

The evidence of precisely what passed between Surrey and Southwell has not survived, but given that Southwell was the one who affirmed that Surrey's alteration to his escutcheon signified his belief that he had a direct right to the crown of England,[23] it is altogether possible that Surrey revealed his mind on that score. Certainly, it was to Southwell that Surrey alludes in his translation of Psalm 55:

> It was a frendly foo, by shadow of good will,
> Myne old fere and dere frende, my guyde, that trapped me;
> Where I was wont to fetche the cure of all my care,
> And in his bosome hyde my secreat zeale to God.[24]

In spite of the fact that Surrey was trying to 'amend his will', to attain a spiritual calm that would enable him to face the worst should it come, one receives no impression of any real repentance on his part. It was of political indiscretion and errors of judgement that Surrey was repenting, not sin. Hence, it is not surprising to find turbulent emotions recurrently erupting in the para-

[21] Ibid., no. 45, ll. 5–6; p. 156.
[22] Ibid., ll. 17–18.
[23] See Casady, p. 191.
[24] *Howard Poems*, ed. Jones, no. 50, ll. 22–5.

phrases that run counter to the professed intent. Surrey cannot, for example, restrain his loathing of Henry VIII. In *Ecclesiastes 3* he describes how

> I saw a roiall throne wheras that Justice should have sitt;
> In stede of whom I saw, with fyerce and crwell mode,
> Wher Wrong was set, that blody beast, that drounke the giltles blode.[25]

Similarly, in *Ecclesiastes 4* he refers to 'aged kyngs wedded to will that worke with out advice.'[26] Surrey could not forgive Henry VIII for having executed Catherine Howard, nor could he forgive the exclusion from power of his own faction that it betokened. Henry was well advised to be wary of Surrey for, as these lines show, the younger man believed his monarch possessed the throne unjustly, and regarded him with the mixture of malice and contempt already expressed in an earlier poem, depicting Henry as the effeminate and degenerate Assyrian king, Sardanapalus.[27] Surrey expresses no real regrets at the treasons he may have meditated, only that he had been foiled from accomplishing them and been placed in mortal danger because of them. His vindictive outbursts show that he still considered himself to have been justified, which makes the penitence he is trying to fashion in these poems ultimately hollow and insincere.

The three Psalms Surrey translated show a distinctly different cast of mind, and one can presume that they were written much closer to the time of his actual trial than the paraphrases of Ecclesiastes. The first two have prefatory poems attached that show Surrey trying to influence those who would be involved with his trial, in the hope that they might procure his pardon. Before his translation of Psalm 88 he affixes a poem addressed to Sir Anthony Denny, chief gentleman of the Privy Chamber and Henry VIII's most intimate confidant, in which, as always, he pleads the excuse of his 'recheles youth' and then, having confessed his error, implicitly expresses his hope for a pardon:

> My Deny, then myne errour, depe imprest,
> Began to worke dispaire of libertye,
>   Had not David, the perfyt warriour, tought
>   That of my fault thus pardon shold be sought.[28]

It is not spiritual liberty Surrey seeks, but real liberty, and the prefatory poem turns the translation of the Psalm that follows into a piece of persuasive pleading. If only he shows himself sufficiently contrite, Surrey thinks, his judges will let him off.

---

[25] Ibid., no. 45, ll. 44–6.
[26] Ibid., no. 46, l. 36.
[27] See 'Th'Assyryan king, in peas with fowle desyre', ibid., no. 32.
[28] *Howard Poems*, ed. Jones, no. 36.

The Psalms themselves reveal a mixture of conflicting emotions: terror at the prospect of death, resentment at the pride and gloating of the enemies who have put him in this situation, and the hope that God will still intervene to rescue him. His distress is imaged as a boat 'fraughted full with greif of follies past', and surrounded by 'roring waves', beset by 'sundrye stormes . . . of terrour and distresse.'[29] Surrey comforts himself by remembering that 'when I stode in drede to drenche, thy hands still did me stay': God saved him from drowning in previous shipwrecks, and he expects him to do it again now.[30] As in the paraphrases of Ecclesiastes, one sees Surrey trying to blackmail God into helping him escape his fate:

> My duraunce doth perswade of fredom such dispaire
> That, by the teares that bayne my brest, myne eye sight doth appaire.
> Yet did I never cease thyne ayde for to desyre,
> With humble hart and stretched hands for to appease thy yre.
> Wherfore dost thow forbeare, in the defence of thyne,
> To shewe such tokens of thy power, in sight of Adams lyne?[31]

Surrey has expanded the thought of Psalm 88: 9–10 so that it emphasizes much more explicitly his hope of some miraculous intervention on God's part. He had good cause to believe it necessary, for his own attempt to help providence along had failed. Surrey's suite in the Tower overlooked the river, into which its privy dropped directly. To compound his folly, Surrey attempted to escape from his captivity by lowering himself through this privy to a boat waiting below, but was discovered in the attempt.[32] His escape attempt, itself a capital offence, was of course alleged at his trial as further evidence of his guilt. Surrey had every need of God's assistance: he had made it impossible for anyone else to help him.

His expressions of fear are offset by vindictive utterances against the enemies whom he imagines to be gloating in triumph. He admits to Blage, in the prefatory poem to Psalm 73, that he is 'constrayned . . . to beare my sayles ful loo',[33] but that does not stop him from denouncing the 'lothsom pryde' of those 'that glorey in ther golde', that is, the Seymour faction, and the 'skornfull pryde' of them 'whose glutten cheks slouth feads so fatt as scant their eyes be sene', by whom he means Henry VIII himself. Surrey still could not bring himself to concede that Henry had any right to exercise power over him. He regards the king as one of those

---

[29] Ibid., no. 48, ll. 5, 41, 12.
[30] Ibid., no. 49, l. 54.
[31] Ibid., no. 48, ll. 15–20.
[32] See Chapman, pp. 133–5.
[33] *Howard Poems*, ed. Jones, no. 37, l. 5.

> Unto whose crewell power most men for dred ar fayne
> To bend and bow with loftye looks, whiles they vawnt in their rayne
>   And in their bloody hands, whose creweltye doth frame
> The wailfull works that skourge the poore with out regard of blame.[34]

Inwardly, Surrey had not repented, nor could he make himself repent, of his belief that Henry had no right to occupy the throne.

He consoles himself for the triumph of his enemies by contemplating the prospect of their fall. He appropriates God, in fact, to be the instrument by which he can still exact revenge upon them:

> Oh, how their ground is false and all their buylding vayne!
> And they shall fall, their power shall faile that did their pryde mayntayne.
>   As charged harts with care, that dreme some pleasaunt tourne,
> After their sleape fynd their abuse, and to their plaint retourne,
>   So shall their glorye faade; thy sword of vengeaunce shall
> Unto their dronken eyes, in blood disclose their errours all.[35]

It is amazing to think that Surrey could believe he could procure pardon by threatening his enemies with God's vengence in this way, or that he was truly sincere in professing to Blage, in the poem that prefaces this paraphrase, that he now saw his error. In trying to fashion for himself the persona of a humble and contrite penitent, Surrey was trying to hold sand in a seive.

That much is proven by the outburst of emotion in his final paraphrase, the translation of Psalm 55, which was obviously written in the days intervening between his condemnation on 13 January 1547 and his execution on 19 January. It is distressing to see how completely the composure Surrey had tried to knit up for himself comes unravelled. Surrey rails against his foes that 'bray so lowde'; he admits the fear that grips him, and longs for a means of escape:

> Care perceth my entrayles and traveyleth my sprite;
> The greslye feare of death envyroneth my brest;
> A tremblynge cold of dred clene overwhelmeth my hert.
> 'O,' thinke I, 'hadd I wings like to the symple dove,
> This peryll myght I flye, and seke some place of rest
> In wylder woods, where I might dwell farr from these cares.'
> What speady way of wing my playnts shold thei lay on,
> To skape the stormye blast that treatned is to me![36]

He then, following his text, launches into recrimination against those who he believes have tricked him:

[34] Ibid., no. 49, ll. 5–6, 11, 14–18.
[35] Ibid., ll. 41–6.
[36] Ibid., no. 50, ll. 3–12.

> Ne my declared foo wrought me all this reproche;
> By harme so loked for, yt wayeth halfe the lesse.
> For though myne ennemyes happ had byn for to prevaile,
> I cold have hidd my face from venym of his eye.[37]

Surrey had been caught with his guard down. He had known how to dissemble his innermost thoughts from enemies like Hertford, but revealed them to the 'frendly foo', Southwell, who betrayed him. Changing the sense of the scriptural version of verse 18 ('He hath delivered my soul in peace from the battle that was against me'), Surrey reworks it to express a fervent hope that God might still rescue him as he has in the past:

> With words of hott effect, that moveth from hert contryte,
> Such humble sute, O Lord, doth perce thy pacyent eare.
> It was the Lord that brake the bloody compackts of those
> That preloked on with yre to slaughter me and myne.[38]

Here, one detects a specific allusion to the destruction of Cromwell, who Surrey believed had been conspiring the deaths of Norfolk and himself before he was hoist with his own petard.[39] Surrey is still hoping that it can happen again, that, as he declares, he could believe in the injunction 'Iacta curam tuam super dominum et ipse te enutriet' ('Cast thy burden upon the Lord, and he shall sustain thee').[40] In the final lines of the poem, however, he gives up all pretext at translating his original as he declares yet again his sense of betrayal on the part of 'those false wolves' that had sworn to him that, however dire his predicament seemed, 'they did not touche my lyfe.'[41] However he might try to sustain the hope that it might be otherwise, Surrey now knew he was doomed.

According to his son Surrey wrote his last poem on the eve of his execution and this shows him attempting to restore the pose he had tried to construct for himself:

> The stormes are past, these cloudes are overblowne,
> And humble chere great rygour hath represt;
> For the defaute is set a paine foreknowne,
> And pacience graft in a determed brest.

But even before the poem has ended, one sees the pose coming apart as Surrey contemplates 'the curelesse wound that bledeth day and night', which his imagination paints for him literally as the image of his decapitated trunk, and

---

[37] Ibid., ll. 18–21.
[38] Ibid., ll. 30–3.
[39] See the deposition of Sir Edmond Knyvet, *LP*, XXI, ii, no. 555(i).
[40] *Howard Poems*, ed. Jones, no. 50, l. 48.
[41] Ibid., ll. 43–5.

figuratively as his dishonour. His conscience was also troubled because he felt responsible for his father's death as well as his own. Soon after he and Norfolk had been arrested, Surrey had written to the Council declaring himself to be sorely enfeebled by sorrow to see 'the long approved truth of mine old father brought in question by any stir between Sowthwell and me.'[42] A month later, on 12 January 1547, the Duke of Norfolk had pleaded guilty to concealing his son's treason in using the arms of St Edward the Confessor, and had been condemned to death also. As it turned out he was reprieved at the last moment, for Henry VIII died in the early hours of the morning on which he was to be executed, but Surrey was not to know this, and in this poem already considers him to be a dead man:

> To think, alas, such hap should graunted be
> Unto a wretch that hath no hart to fight,
>   To spill that blood that hath so oft bene shed
>   For Britannes sake, alas, and now is ded.[43]

The condemnation of his father brought it home to Surrey – perhaps for the first time in his life – that his actions affected others apart from himself, and the realization must have weighed heavy on his conscience.

In the poems written in the Tower, Surrey had been striving for a religious conviction that he had difficulty in making himself feel. His lack of secure resolve displayed itself on the morning of his execution, when his composure once again vanished. According to eyewitnesses, he made so many vociferous protests that he had to be forcibly silenced.[44]

His paraphrases from the bible thus provide further evidence of a breakdown in the efficacy of fiction as a device capable of allowing men to cope with their experience in the later years of Henry VIII's reign. If they are compared with Wyatt's adaptation of The Penitential Psalms, an instructive difference emerges. Wyatt was able to sustain the integrity of his fiction, using the image of David undergoing penitence to relinquish Bathsheba as a means of interpreting himself and ordering his will to what he must. Surrey tries for the same effect – to resign himself to relinquishing worldly ambitions by projecting himself through the personae of the preacher in Ecclesiastes and David in the Psalms, respectively. He is unable, however, to sustain the integrity of his fiction – that he considers the world a vanity and is happy to leave it, as conventional religious beliefs taught he should. Surrey had found that his poses could no longer protect him against the reality of his times. Fictive invention, whether in the form of poetry or literary self-projection, had lost its efficacy for him, as for so many others, because the

---

[42] LP, XXI, ii, no. 541 (Letter of 13 December 1546).
[43] Howard Poems, ed. Jones, no. 38, ll. 1–4, 13–17.
[44] See Chapman, pp. 141–2.

pressure of immediate events had overpowered it with a literal and metaphorical violence.

His tragic career suggests a paradigm for what happened generally in literature once the main crises of Henry's reign began to develop after 1525. The issues to be resolved had become too pressing and urgent to allow imaginative latitude for fictive representation to play a crucial part in them. The contemporary world was resolving itself into one of immediate actions, with immediate consequences, and the axe and the fires of Smithfield had become the chief means of signifying this fact to everyone. The poets would have to wait until the political and social identity of England was again much more secure before they would recover the impulse to explore their experience with greater imaginative freedom. For the time being, fiction was a luxury that few felt they could afford.

Conclusion

Surrey's death and the destruction of the Howard faction marks the completion of the process started with Henry Tudor's victory over the last Yorkist king on Bosworth Field. Power had now been consolidated, Henry VIII had ensured that a Tudor heir would succeed him, and the Tudor dynasty was leading England in a new direction with which national aspirations could be identified. When Mary I succeeded to the throne after the premature death of her younger brother, she found that the direction of change had already become irreversible.

These radical changes meant that by the second half of the sixteenth century, the world experienced by Englishmen was fundamentally different from that which their predecessors had known. Early Tudor writers had needed to respond to a world that was inchoate, where the social and political policies that would determine its destiny were in process of formation. Their writings were conditioned by the tensions and irresolution they experienced. For mid Tudor writers, on the other hand, the choices had grown stark, while by the reign of Elizabeth there was no longer any doubt as to the direction in which England had confidently committed itself to travel. There is a clear link between socio-political, emotional, and intellectual conditions and the nature of the literary strategies through which people expressed themselves in each of the three phrases of the sixteenth century. As this study has shown, fictive representation, which had been so important in the first two decades, began to recede in importance as political pressures became more desperate in the third and fourth. During the 1530s and 1540s, the developing crisis forced most people to commit themselves to ideological positions that allowed no latitude for imaginative exploration, and fictive literature was replaced by propaganda and polemic. Creative literary minds had to wait until a new national ethos and sense of identity emerged in the latter part of the century, before they felt once more the impulse to explore their experience through inventing fictions on a large scale.

Because the literary output of each period was conditioned by radically different circumstances, it is fruitless to judge the literature of any one phase in terms that fail to take into consideration either the circumstances or the function of the works that are contrived to address them. The accomplishment of early Tudor literature does not depend, for the most part, on verbal or formal beauty –

precisely those things that the Elizabethans, under the influence of a new ethos, strove after. Instead, its accomplishment derives from the writers' ingenuity in finding ways of encompassing the situations they had to face. Because political discretion and social decorum restricted the freedom with which they could express themselves directly, the need for indirect expression was a stimulus to literary invention. Writers constantly manipulated the conventions and stereotypes available to them so as to mean other than what they appeared to say, and placed their nearest concerns at a safe distance from themselves by dramatizing them. As a result, early Tudor literature is endemically ironic and ambiguous. Not until the twentieth century would there again be a literary period in which literature would be so generally dialogical and thematically 'open'. In writers such as Skelton, Erasmus, and More, these representational techniques combined with intellectual sharpness and imaginative power to produce works as skilful and subtle as the best in any language, and even the lesser writers such as Barclay and Hawes, are interesting in their own terms.

The final point I want to make is therefore this: critics and historians should cease lamenting the absence in early Tudor literature of qualities it never set out to achieve. Read sympathetically, it will be found at its best to be as accomplished as any other literature, even when it appears unattractive. It is not as a rule a happy literature – the times were too grim for that – but rather a literature of anxiety. It gives powerful expression to the human experience of change and uncertainty, and given developments in the late twentieth century, these are ever more relevant to the modern mind and condition.

Bibliography

Adams, Joseph Quincy, ed. *Chief Pre-Shakespearean Dramas* (Cambridge, Massachusetts, 1924)

Altman, Joel B. *The Tudor Play of Mind: Rhetorical Inquiry and the Development of Elizabethan Drama* (Berkeley, 1978)

Anderson, Judith H. *Biographical Truth: The Representation of Historical Persons in Tudor-Stuart Writing* (New Haven and London, 1984)

Anglo, Sydney. *Spectacle, Pageantry, and Early Tudor Policy* (Oxford, 1969)

Anon. *A New Enterlude of Godly Queene Hester.* Ed. W. W. Greg, in *Materialien zur Kunde des älteren Englischen Dramas.* Ed. W. Bang, vol. 5 (Louvain, 1904)

Anon. *Merie Tales newly imprinted & made by Master Skelton Poet Laureat* (London, n.d. [1567]), reprinted in *Poetical Works of John Skelton.* Ed. Alexander Dyce (London, 1843)

Anon. *Pamphilus de amore cum commento familiari: recenter ac vigilanter impressus* (Rouen: Raulinus Gautier), 1508

Anon. *The Divorce Tracts of Henry VIII.* Ed. Edward Surtz and Virginia Murphy (Angers, 1988)

Bale, John. *Index Britanniae scriptorum.* Ed. Reginald Lane Poole, Anecdota Oxoniensia (Oxford, 1902)

—— *The Complete Plays of John Bale.* Ed. Peter Happé, 2 vols (Cambridge, 1985)

—— *Scriptorum illustrium maioris Brytanniae* (Basel, 1557–9)

Bang, W, ed. *Materialien zur Kunde des älteren Englischen Dramas,* vol. 5 (Louvain, 1904)

Barclay, Alexander, trans. *The Ship of Fools.* Ed. T. H. Jamieson (Edinburgh, 1874)

—— *The Ship of Fooles.* See under Brandt

—— *The Eclogues of Alexander Barclay from the Original Edition by John Cawood.* Ed. Beatrice White, Early English Text Society, Original Series, 175 (London, 1928)

—— *The Introductory to Wryte and to Pronounce Frenche* (London, 1521?)

—— *The Life of Saint George.* Ed. William Nelson, Early English Text Society, Original Series, no. 230 (London 1955)

Barker, Arthur E. '*Clavis Moreana*: The Yale Edition of Thomas More', *Journal of English and Germanic Philology*, 65 (1966), pp. 318–30

Barlowe, John and William Roye. *Rede Me and Be Nott Wrothe, For I Saye Nothinge but Trothe.* Ed. Edward Arber, English Reprints (London, 1871)

Berdan, John M. *Early Tudor Poetry, 1485–1547* (New York, 1920)

Bevington, David. *From 'Mankind' to Marlowe* (Cambridge, Massachusetts, 1962)

—— *Tudor Drama and Politics: A Critical Approach to Topical Meaning* (Cambridge, Massachusetts, 1968)

Bietenholz, B, and others. *Contemporaries of Erasmus: A Biographical Register of the Renaissance and Reformation*, 3 vols (Toronto, 1985–7)

Boccaccio, Giovanni. *Genealogiae Ionnis Boccatii* (Venice, 1494)

Bouck, C. 'On the Identity of Papyrius. Germinus Eleates', *Transactions of the Cambridge Bibliographical Society*, 2, Part IV (1958), pp. 352–8

Brandt, Sebastian. *Stultifera nauis, qua omnium mortalium narratur stultitia . . . The Ship of Fooles, Wherein is Shewed the Folly of all States. . . . . Translated out of Latin into Englishe by Alexander Barclay Priest* (London 1570) (see under Barclay)

Brownlow, F. W. '*Speke Parrot*: Skelton's Allegorical Denunciation of Cardinal Wolsey', *Studies in Philology*, 65 (1968), pp. 124–39.

Calendar of Letters, Dispatches and State Papers, Relating to the Negotiations between England and Spain, Preserved in the Archives at Vienna, Brussels, Simancas and Elsewhere. Ed. G. A. Bergenroth, Don Pascual de Gayangos, and others, 13 vols (London, 1862–1954)

Cameron, K. W. *Authorship and Sources of 'Gentylnes and Nobylyte'* (Raleigh, North Carolina, 1941)

Campensis, Joannes. *Psalmorum omnium iuxta Hebraicam veritatem paraphrastica interpretatio. . . . Paraphrasis in concionem Salomonis Ecclesiastae* (1532)

Casady, Edwin. *Henry Howard, Earl of Surrey*, Modern Languages Association Revolving Fund Series, no. 8 (New York, 1938)

Cavendish, George. *The Life and Death of Cardinal Wolsey*. Ed. Richard S. Sylvester, Early English Text Society, no. 243 (London, 1959)

Chambers, E. K. *Sir Thomas Wyatt and Some Collected Studies* (London, 1933)

Chambers, R. W. *Thomas More* (London, 1935)

Chapman, Hester W. *Two Tudor Portraits: Henry Howard, Earl of Surrey and Lady Katherine Grey* (London, 1960)

Chatterjee, Kalyan K. *In Praise of Learning: John Colet and Literary Humanism in England* (New Delhi, 1974)

Colie, Rosalie, *Paradoxia epidemica* (Princeton, 1966)

Cromwell, Thomas. *Life and Letters of Thomas Cromwell*. Ed. Roger Bigelow Merriman, 2 vols (London, 1902)

Davis, J. C. 'More, Morton, and the Politics of Accommodation', *Journal of British Studies*, 9: 2 (1970), pp. 27–49

The Dictionary of National Biography from the Earliest Times to 1900. Ed. Sir Leslie Stephen and Sir Sidney Lee, 22 vols (London, 1921–2)

Dollimore, Jonathan. *Radical Tragedy: Ideology and Power in the Drama of Shakespeare and His Contemporaries* (Chicago, 1984)

Dorsch, T. S. 'Sir Thomas More and Lucian: An Interpretation of *Utopia*', *Archiv für das Studium der neueren Sprachen und Literaturen*, 203 (1966–9), pp. 345–63

Dowling, Maria. *Humanism in the Age of Henry VIII* (London, 1986)

Edwards, A. S. G. *Stephen Hawes* (Boston, 1983)

Edwards, H. L. R. 'The Dating of Skelton's Later Poems', *Publications of the Modern Language Association*, 53 (1938), pp. 601–11

—— *Skelton: The Life and Times of an Early Tudor Poet* (London, 1949)

Elton, G. R. *Reform and Reformation: England 1509–1558* (London, 1977)

—— 'Thomas More, Councillor', in *Studies in Tudor and Stuart Politics and Government*, Vol. 2 (Cambridge, 1974), pp. 129–33

Elyot, Thomas. *Four Political Treatises by Sir Thomas Elyot*. Ed. Lillian Gottesman (Florida, 1967)

—— *The Dictionary of Syr Thomas Eliot Knyght* (London, 1538)

—— 'The Letters of Sir Thomas Elyot'. Ed. K. J. Wilson, *Studies in Philology*, 73:5 (1976), pp. 33–7

—— *Of the Knowledge which Maketh a Wise Man*. Ed. Edwin Johnston (Oxford, Ohio, 1946)

Erasmus, Desiderius. *Christian Humanism and the Reformation: Selected Writings of Erasmus with the Life of Erasmus by Beatus Rhenanus*. Ed. John C. Olin, revised edition (New York, 1975)

—— *Collected Works of Erasmus*, 78 vols, various editors (Toronto, 1974–)

—— *Enchiridion Militis Christiani: An English Version*. Ed. Anne M. O'Donnell, Early English Text Society, no. 282 (London, 1981)

—— *The Essential Erasmus*. Trans. and ed. John P. Dolan (New York, 1964)

—— *Moriae encomion / Stultitiae laus* (Basel, 1676)

—— *Opus Epistolarum Des. Erasmi Roterodami*, ed. P. S. Allen and others (Oxford, 1906–47)

—— *The Praise of Folly*. Trans. and ed. Clarence H. Miller (New Haven and London, 1979)

Ferguson, Arthur B. *The Indian Summer of Chivalry* (Durham, North Carolina, 1960)

Fish, Simon. *A Supplicacyon for the Beggers Wrytten about the Year 1529 by Simon Fish*. Ed. Frederick J. Furnivall, Early English Text Society, Extra Series, no. 13 (London, 1871)

Fish, Stanley. *John Skelton's Poetry* (Hamden, Connecticut, 1965)

Fox, Alistair. 'Stephen Hawes and the Political Allegory of *The Comfort of Lovers*', *English Literary Renaissance*, 17 (1987), pp. 3–21

—— *Thomas More: History and Providence* (Oxford, 1982)

—— and John Guy. *Reassessing the Henrician Age: Humanism, Politics, and Reform 1500–1550* (Oxford, 1986)

Fox, Richard. *Letters of Richard Fox 1486–1527*. Ed. P. S. and H. M. Allen (Oxford, 1929)

Foxe, John. *The Acts and Monuments of John Foxe*. Ed. Josiah Pratt, 4th edn, 8 vols (London, n. d.)

Frith, John. *The Workes of the Excellent Martyr of Christ, John Frith*, in *The Whole Workes of W. Tyndall* . . . See under Tyndale

Furnivall, Frederick J., ed. *Ballads from Manuscripts*, Vol. 1: *Ballads on the condition of England in Henry VIII's and Edward VI's Reigns, on Wolsey, Anne Boleyn, Somerset, and Lady Jane Grey; with Wynkyn de Worde's Treatise of a Galaunt* (London, 1868–72)

Gairdner, James, ed. *Memorials of King Henry the Seventh*, Rolls Series, (London, 1858)

Gingerich, Owen. 'The Astronomical Dating of Skelton's *Garland of Laurel*', *Huntington Library Quarterly*, 32 (1969), pp. 207–20.

Godfray Thomas. *The Plouuman's Tale Compylled by Syr Geffray Chaucer Knyght* (London, [?1545])

Gordon, Ian A. 'A Skelton Query', *Times Literary Supplement*, 15 November 1934, p. 795

—— *John Skelton, Poet Laureate* (Melbourne, 1943)

Grant, Patrick. 'Thomas More's *Richard III*: Moral Narration and Humanist Method', *Renaissance and Reformation / Renaissance et Réforme*, New Series, 7 (1983), pp. 157–72.

Greenblatt, Stephen. *Renaissance Self-fashioning from More to Shakespeare* (Chicago and London, 1980)

Guy, John. *The Cardinal's Court: The Impact of Thomas Wolsey in Star Chamber* (Hassocks, 1977)

—— *The Public Career of Sir Thomas More*, (Brighton, 1980)

—— *Tudor England* (Oxford and New York, 1988)

Hall, Edward. *The Union of the Two Noble and Illustre Famelies of Lancastre & Yorke* (London, 1548)

Hanham, Alison. *Richard III and his Early Historians 1483–1535* (Oxford, 1975)

Hardison, O. B. *The Enduring Monument: A Study of the Idea of Praise in Renaissance Literary Theory and Practice* (Westport, Connecticut, 1973)

Hawes, Stephen. *The Pastime of Pleasure*. Ed. William Edward Mead, Early English Text Society, Original Series, no. 173 (London, 1928)

—— *Stephen Hawes: The Minor Poems*. Ed. Florence W. Gluck and Alice B. Morgan, Early English Text Society, no. 271 (London, 1974)

Hay, Denys. *Polydore Vergil: Renaissance Historian and Man of Letters* (Oxford, 1952)

Heiserman, A. R. *Skelton and Satire* (Chicago, 1961)

Hogrefe, Pearl. *The Sir Thomas More Circle: A Programme of Ideas and their Impact on Secular Drama* (Urbana, Illinois, 1959)

Howard, Henry. *Henry Howard, Earl of Surrey: Poems*. Ed. Emrys Jones (Oxford, 1964)

—— *The Poems of Henry Howard Earl of Surrey*. Ed. Frederick Morgan Padelford (Seattle, 1928)

Howard, Jean. E. 'The New Historicism in Renaissance Studies', *English Literary Renaissance*, 16 (1986), pp. 13–43

Hume, Anthea. 'English Protestant Books Printed Abroad, 1525–1535: An Annotated Bibliography', in More, *CW Thos. More, 8: The Confutation of Tyndale's Answer*, Part 2, Appendix B, pp. 1065–91

Ives, E. W. *Anne Boleyn* (Oxford, 1986)

Jones, Judith P. *Thomas More*, Twayne's English Author Series, no. 247 (Boston, 1979)

King, John N. *English Reformation Literature: The Tudor Origins of the Protestant Tradition* (Princeton, 1982)

Kingsford, C. L. *English Historical Literature in the Fifteenth Century* (Oxford, 1913)

Kinney, Arthur F. *John Skelton, Priest as Poet: Seasons of Discovery* (Chapel Hill and London, 1987)

Kinney, Daniel. 'King's Tragicomedies: Generic Misrule in More's *History of Richard III*', *Moreana*, 86 (1985), pp. 128–50

Kinsman, Robert S. 'The Voices of Dissonance: Pattern in Skelton's *Colyn Cloute*,' *Huntingdon Library Quarterly*, 26 (1963), pp. 99–125

Kipling, Gordon. 'Henry VII and the Origins of Tudor Patronage', in *Patronage in the Renaissance*. Ed. Guy Fitch Lytle and Stephen Orgel (Princeton, 1981), pp. 117–64

—— *The Triumph of Honour: Burgundian Origins of the Elizabethan Renaissance* (The Hague, 1977)

Lancashire, Ian. *Dramatic Texts and Records of Britain: A Chronological Topography to 1558* (Toronto, 1986)

——, ed. *Two Tudor Interludes: The Interlude of Youth; Hick Scorner* (Manchester, 1980)

Lanham, Richard A. *The Motives of Eloquence: Literary Rhetoric in the Renaissance* (New Haven, 1976)

Letters and Papers, Foreign and Domestic, of the Reign of Henry VIII. 21 vols. Ed. J. S. Brewer and others (London, 1862–1932)

Letters and Papers Illustrative of the Reigns of Richard III and Henry VII. Ed. James Gairdner (London, 1861)

Levy, F. J. *Tudor Historical Thought* (San Marino, California, 1967)

Lewis, C. S. *English Literature in the Sixteenth Century Excluding Drama* (Oxford, 1954)

Martines, Lauro. *Society and History in English Renaissance Verse* (Oxford, 1985)

Mason, H. A. *Humanism and Poetry in the Early Tudor Period* (London, 1959)

—— *Sir Thomas Wyatt: A Literary Portrait* (Bristol, 1986)

Mayer, Thomas F. 'Faction and Ideology: Thomas Starkey's *Dialogue*', *Historical Journal*, 28: 1 (1985), pp. 1–25

—— *Thomas Starkey and the Commonweal: Humanist Politics and Religion in the Reign of Henry VIII* (Cambridge, forthcoming)

McConica, James Kelsey. *English Humanists and Reformation Politics under Henry VIII and Edward VI* (Oxford, 1965)

McCutcheon, Elizabeth. 'Denying the Contrary: More's Use of Litotes in the *Utopia*', *Moreana*, 31–31 (1971), pp. 107–21; reprinted in *Essential Articles for the Study of Thomas More*. See under Sylvester

Meale, Carol M. 'The Compiler at Work: John Colyns and BL MS Harley 2252', in *Manuscripts and Readers in Fifteenth-Century England: The Literary Implications of Manuscript Study*. Ed. Derek Pearsall (Cambridge, 1983)

Merriman, Roger Bigelow, ed. *Life and Letters of Thomas Cromwell*. 2 vols (London, 1902)

Milton, John. *Complete Prose Works of John Milton*. Ed. Donald M. Wolfe and others (New Haven, 1953–82)

More, Thomas. *The Correspondence of Sir Thomas More*. Ed. Elizabeth Frances Rogers (Princeton, 1947)

—— *St Thomas More: Selected Letters*. Ed. E. F. Rogers (New Haven and London, 1961)

—— *The Workes of Sir Thomas More Knyght, Sometyme Lorde Chauncellor of England, Wrytten by Him in the Englysh Tonge*. Ed. William Rastell (London, 1557)

—— *The Yale Edition of the Complete Works of St Thomas More*, 15 vols Various editors (New Haven and London, 1963–)

MS British Library Additional 17492

MS British Library Additional 26787

MS British Library Additional 33736

MS British Library Harleian 336

MS British Library Harley 2252

MS British Library Lansdowne 762

MS British Library 16 E. xi

MS Public Record Office E 101/414–16

MS Public Record Office LC2/1

MS Public Record Office SP 1/63

MS Public Record Office E. 36/228, fos 7–8

Muir, Kenneth. *Life and Letters of Sir Thomas Wyatt* (Liverpool, 1963)

—— 'Unpublished Poems in the Devonshire MS', *Proceedings of the Leeds Philosophical and Literary Society*, 6: 4 (1947), pp. 253–82

Nelson, William. *John Skelton, Laureate* (New York, 1939)

Ovide [P. Ovidius Naso]. *Les métamorphoses.* Ed. and trans. J. Chamonard. 2 vols (Paris, n.d.)

Pace, Richard. *De fructu qui ex doctrina percipitur (On the Benefit of a Liberal Education).* Trans. and ed. Frank Manley and Richard S. Sylvester (New York, 1967)

Padelford, F. M. and A. R. Benham, eds. 'The Songs in Manuscript Rawlinson C. 813', *Anglia*, 31 (1908), pp. 309–97.

Peter, John. *Complaint and Satire in Early English Literature* (Oxford, 1956)

Phillips, Margaret Mann. *The Adages of Erasmus: A Study with Translations* (Cambridge, 1964)

—— *Erasmus and the Northern Renaissance* (London, 1949)

Piccolomini, Aeneas Sylvius. *Aeneae Sylvii Piccolominei ... opera quae extant omnia* (Basel, 1557)

Pineas, Rainer. *Thomas More and Tudor Polemics* (Bloomington and London, 1968)

Plautus, M. Accius. *Plauti comoediae.* Ed. Fridericus Leo. 2 vols (Berlin, 1958)

Pollard, A. F. *Wolsey* (London, 1929)

Puttenham, George. *The Arte of English Poesie.* Ed. Edward Arber, English Reprints (London, 1869)

Rastell, John. *A New Boke of Purgatory, whiche is a Dyaloge betwene Comyngo & Gyngemyn* (London, 1530)

—— *Three Rastell Plays: Four Elements, Calisto and Melebea, Gentleness and Nobility.* Ed. Richard Axton (Cambridge, 1979)

Reed, A. W. *Early Tudor Drama: Medwall, the Rastells, Heywood, and the More Circle* (London, 1926)

Roper, William. *The Lyfe of Sir Thomas Moore, Knighte.* Ed. Elsie Vaughan Hitchcock, Early English Text Society, Original Series, no. 197 (London, 1935)

Rous, John. *Joannis Rossi[js] Antiquarii Warwicensis historia regum Angliae.* Ed. Thomas Hearne, 2nd edn. (Oxford, 1745)

Sabbadini, R. *Il metodo degli umanisti* (Florence, [1922])

Sale, Helen Stearns. 'John Skelton and Christopher Garnesche', *Modern Language Notes*, 43 (1928), pp. 518–23

—— 'The Date of Skelton's *Bowge of Court*', *Modern Language Notes*, 52 (1937), pp. 572–4

Salter, F. M., ed. 'Skelton's *Speculum Principis*', *Speculum*, 9 (1934), pp. 25–37

Scarisbrick, J. J. *Henry VIII* (London, 1968)

Screech, M. A. *Ecstasy and the Praise of Folly* (London, 1980)

Skelton, John. *John Skelton: The Complete English Poems.* Ed. John Scattergood (Harmondsworth and New Haven, 1983)

—— *Magnyfycence.* Ed. R. L. Ramsay, Early English Text Society, Extra Series, no. 98 (London, 1908)

—— *Magnyfycence.* Ed. Paula Neuss (Manchester, 1980)

—— *The Poetical Works of John Skelton.* Ed. Alexander Dyce, 2 vols (London, 1843–4)

Southall, Raymond. *The Courtly Maker: An Essay on the Poetry of Wyatt and His Contemporaries* (Oxford, 1964)

Stapleton, Thomas. *The Life and Illustrious Martyrdom of Sir Thomas More.* Trans. P.

Hallett (London, 1929)

Starkey, David. 'Intimacy and Innovation: The Rise of the Privy Chamber, 1485–1547', in *The English Court from the Wars of the Roses to the Civil War*. Ed. David Starkey (London and New York, 1987), pp. 71–118

—— *The Reign of Henry VIII: Personalities and Politics* (London, 1985)

Starkey, Thomas. *A Dialogue between Thomas Lupset and Reginald Pole, in England in the Reign of King Henry the Eighth*. Ed. Sidney J. Herrtage, Early English Text Society, Extra Series, nos 12, 32 (London, 1871, 1878)

State Papers Published Under the Authority of His Majesty's Commission. 9 vols (London, 1830–49)

Stevens, John. *Music and Poetry in the Early Tudor Court* (London, 1961)

Strype, John. *Ecclesiastical Memorials; Relating Chiefly to Religion and the Reformation of It, and the Emergencies of the Church of England, under King Henry VIII, King Edward VI, and Queen Mary I*. 6 vols (Oxford, 1822)

Surtz, Edward L. *The Praise of Pleasure: Philosophy, Education and Communism in More's Utopia* (Chicago, 1957)

Sylvester R. S. and G. P. Marc'hadour, eds. *Essential Articles for the Study of Thomas More* (Hamden, Connecticut, 1977)

Thompson, Sister Geraldine. *Under Pretext of Praise: Satire Mode in Erasmus' Fiction* (Toronto, 1973)

Thynne, Francis. *Animaduersions uppon the Annotacions and Corrections of some Imperfections of Impressiones of Chaucers Workes*, ed. G. H. Kingsley, Early English Text Society, Original Series, no. 9 (London, 1865)

Tucker, Melvin J. 'The Ladies in Skelton's Garland of Laurel', *Renaissance Quarterly*, 22 (1969), pp. 333–45

—— 'Setting in Skelton's *Bowge of Courte*: A Speculation', *English Language Notes*, 7 (1970), pp. 168–75

—— 'Skelton and Sheriff Hutton', *English Language Notes*, 4 (1967), pp. 254–9

Turner, William. *The Huntyng & Fyndyng out of the Romishe Fox* (Basel, 1543)

Tyndale, William. *An Aunswere vnto Syr Thomas Mores Dialogue*, in *The Whole Workes of W. Tyndall, Iohn Frith and Doct. Barnes* (London, 1573)

Vergil, Polydore. *Anglica historia* (Basel, 1546)

—— *The Anglica historia of Polydore Vergil, A.D. 1485–1537*. Ed. and trans. Denys Hay. Camden Series, vol. 74 (London, 1950)

—— *Polydore Vergil's English History*. Ed. Henry Ellis, Camden Society (London, 1846)

—— *Three Books of Polydore Vergil's English History, Comprising the Reigns of Henry VI, Edward IV, and Richard III*. Ed. Henry Ellis. Camden Series, no. 29 (London, 1844)

Walker, Greg. *John Skelton and the Politics of the 1520s* (Cambridge, 1988)

Waller, Gary. *English Poetry of the Sixteenth Century* (London, 1986)

Wegg, Jervis. *Richard Pace: A Tudor Diplomatist* (London, 1932)

Williams, Franklin B. *Index of Dedications and Commendatory Verses in English Books before 1641* (London, 1962)

Wilson, K. J. *Incomplete Fictions: The Formation of English Renaissance Dialogue* (Washington, 1985)

—— ed. 'The Letters of Sir Thomas Elyot', *Studies in Philology*, 73:5 (1976), pp. 33–7

Wilson, Thomas. *The Rule of Reason; Conteining the Art of Logike* (London, 1567)

Wyatt, George. *The Papers of George Wyatt Esquire of Boxley Abbey in the County of Kent, Son and Heir of Sir Thomas Wyatt the Younger*. Ed. D. M. Loades, Camden Series, vol. 5 (London, 1968)

Wyatt, Thomas. *Collected Poems of Sir Thomas Wyatt*. Ed. Kenneth Muir and Patricia Thomson (Liverpool, 1969)

Zeeveld, W. Gordon. *Foundations of Tudor Policy* (Cambridge, Mass., 1948)

Index

21899